CORE
PHP Programming
Using PHP to Build
Dynamic Web Sites

LEON ATKINSON

PH
PTR

Prentice Hall PTR, Upper Saddle River, NJ 07458
www.phptr.com

Library of Congress Cataloging-in-Publication Date
Atkinson, Leon.
    Core PHP programming : using PHP to build dynamic Web sites / Leon Atkinson.--
    2nd ed.
        p.   cm.
    Includes bibliographical references and index.
    ISBN 0-13-089398-6
    1. PHP (Computer program language) 2. Web sites--Design. I. Title.

QA76.73.P22A85   2000
005.2'762--dc21

                                                         00-034019

Editorial/Production Supervision: Jan H. Schwartz
Acquisitions Editor: Mark Taub
Editorial Assistant: Sarah Hand
Marketing Manager: Kate Hargett
Manufacturing Manager: Alexis Heydt
Cover Design: Talar Agasyan
Cover Design Director: Jerry Votta
Art Director: Gail Cocker-Bogusz
Series Interior Design: Meg VanArsdale

© 2001 Prentice Hall PTR
Prentice-Hall, Inc.
Upper Saddle River, NJ 07458

The publisher offers discounts on this book when ordered in bulk quantities.
For more information, contact
Corporate Sales Department,
Prentice Hall PTR
One Lake Street
Upper Saddle River, NJ 07458
Phone: 800-382-3419; FAX: 201-236-7141
E-mail: corpsales@prenhall.com

Printed in the United States of America
10 9 8 7 6 5 4 3 2 1

ISBN 0-13-089398-6

Prentice-Hall International (UK) Limited, London
Prentice-Hall of Australia Pty. Limited, Sydney
Prentice-Hall Canada Inc., Toronto
Prentice-Hall Hispanoamericana, S.A., Mexico
Prentice-Hall of India Private Limited, New Delhi
Prentice-Hall of Japan, Inc., Tokyo
Pearson Education Asia Pte. Ltd.
Editora Prentice-Hall do Brasil, Ltda., Rio de Janeiro

Contents

PART ONE:

PART TWO:

PART THREE:

Foreword

For those of you new to PHP, let me begin with a brief recap. PHP started in late 1994 as a quick Perl hack written by Rasmus Lerdorf. Over the next two to three years it evolved into what we know today as PHP/FI 2.0. Zeev Suraski and I introduced a new parser in the summer of 1997 that led to PHP 3. At that time PHP syntax and semantics were formalized, thereby establishing a foundation for growth.

Today, PHP3 has established itself as one of the most popular Web scripting languages available. At the time of this Foreword, PHP has been installed on some 2 million Web servers. Its salient features include:

- Very short development times
- Platform independence
- Multiple database support

PHP has risen to an even higher level. Featuring the use of the "Zend Engine," PHP 4 is much faster and more powerful in every respect. The new version supports multithreaded Web server environments including an ISAPI module (Microsoft's IIS). Other features include a new Web server abstraction layer, Java connectivity, and a much-improved build process for better PHP configuration.

Where do we go from here? Today the major concern of entrants into the PHP community is application support. People know PHP functionality is good, but can it be backed up? The answer is yes. Zend Technologies has arisen to give commercial backing for PHP, thereby enabling undecided companies to take the plunge and benefit from superior open-source software.

Leon's second edition of *Core PHP Programming* is also serving in a supportive role. The second edition features:

- Coverage of PHP 4's language changes and features, such as the improved `include` function and the new NULL and Boolean types.
- Coverage of most of PHP 4's extensions.
- Tighter typesetting for readers looking for a functional reference.
- Added screenshots and comments for new users interested in quickly learning PHP functionality.

Commercial backing and reference materials will continue to drive PHP's gradual acceptance as *the* standard in Web scripting.

Let me take this opportunity to thank everybody for bringing PHP to where it is today. May we keep on working together to make it even better!

I hope this book will give novices a quick start to PHP and more experienced users a handy reference manual.

Andi Gutmans

Preface

My first inkling that I might like to write a book about PHP was born out of the frustration I felt with the original PHP manual. It was a single, large HTML file with all the functions in alphabetical order. It was also on a Web server thousands of miles away from me in Canada, so it was slow to show up in my browser, even across a T1 connection. It wasn't long before it was saved on my desktop. After struggling for several months, it started to dawn on me that I could probably organize the information into a more usable format. Around that time the next version of PHP began to take shape, and with it a new manual was developed. It was organized around PHP's source code but was less complete than the old PHP manual. I contributed descriptions for some of the missing functions, but I still had the idea to write my own manual. In the spring of 1998 Prentice Hall gave me the opportunity to do so. It is an honor for my book to be among Prentice Hall classics such as *The C Programming Language* by Brian Kernighan and Dennis Ritchie.

This book assumes a certain familiarity with the Internet, the Web, and HTML programming, but it starts with the most basic ideas of programming. It will introduce you to concepts common to all programming languages and how they work in PHP. You can expect this book to teach you how to create rich, dynamic Web sites. You can also expect it to remain on your desk as a reference for how PHP works, or even as a recipe book for solving common design problems.

This book is not for dummies, nor is it for complete idiots. That you are considering PHP is a great indication of your intelligence, and I'd hate to insult it. Some of the ideas in this book are hard to understand. If you don't quite get them the first time, I encourage you to reread and experiment with the examples.

If you are uncomfortable writing HTML files, you may wish to develop this skill first. Marty Hall's *Core Web Programming* provides an excellent introduction. Beyond HTML, numerous other topics I touch on fall out of scope. Whenever I can, I suggest books and Web sites that provide more information. There are even some aspects of PHP that range too far from the focus on writing PHP scripts. An example is writing extensions for PHP in C. This involves a healthy knowledge of C programming that I cannot provide here. Related to this is compiling and installing PHP. I attempt to describe the process of installing PHP, which can involve compiling the source code, but I can't attempt to pursue all the different combinations of operating system, Web server, and extensions. If you are comfortable running `make` files, you will find the information that comes with the PHP source code more than adequate.

Along with the explanation text I've provided real-world examples. Nothing is more frustrating than trying to adapt some contrived academic problem to the Web site you must have working by the end of the week. Some of the examples are based on code from live Web sites I have worked on since discovering PHP in 1997. Others are distilled from the continual discussion being conducted on the PHP mailing lists.

This book is organized into four main sections: an introduction to programming; a reference for all the functions in PHP; a survey of common programming problems; and finally a guide for applying this knowledge to Web site development. The first section deals with the issues involved with any programming language: what a PHP script looks like; how to control execution; how to deal with data. The second section organizes the functions by what they do and gives examples of their use. PHP offers many functions, so this section is larger than the rest. The third section deals with solving common programming problems such as sorting and generating graphics. The last section offers advice about how to create a whole Web site with PHP.

I've chosen a few conventions for highlighting certain information, and I'm sure you will find them obvious, but for the sake of clarity I'll spell them out. Whenever I use a keyword such as the name of a script or a function, I place it in a monospace font. For example, I may speak about the `print` function. Another convention I've used is to place email addresses and Web addresses inside angle brackets. Examples are the email address by which you can contact me, `<corephp@leonatkinson.com>`, and my Web site, `<http://www.leonatkinson.com/>`.

Acknowledgments

Writing a book requires dedication and sacrifice—mostly from one's family and friends. There were many weekends when I had to stay home writing, and I'm grateful for the patience everyone has shown me. This includes my wife, Vicky, my parents, Rhonda and Leonard, and my grandmother, Afton. It also includes all my buddies who wanted me to come out and play—especially the ones who wanted me to help out with engineering gigs.

Once again, I've had a couple of phenomenal technical editors. Vicky read through every word of the book, including the functional reference. The story gets fairly predictable in those middle chapters, so I really appreciate her effort. Shannon "JJ" Behrens provided valuable feedback, including catching some of my "hand-waving".

No PHP book is complete without thanks going out to the PHP developers. It might seem like a cliché, but Rasmus Lerdorf really is a nice guy. Take the opportunity to hear him speak if you have it. The contributions of Zeev Suraski and Andi Gutmans are tremendous. I would like to thank Andi in particular for providing the foreword to this book. There are too many people to thank individually, but one other person deserves mention: Egon Schmid. Aside from improving PHP's online manual, he never fails to answer every query about books on the mailing list with the URL to the books page on the php.net site.

Working with Prentice Hall has been a pleasure. I've enjoyed the wisdom and guidance of Mark Taub. The rest of the team were always professional.

Finally, let me thank all the people who bought the first edition of *Core PHP Programming*, especially those who took the time to send me email. The response has been overwhelmingly positive. I'm delighted to have introduced so many people to PHP.

TABLE OF LISTINGS

Part 1

PROGRAMMING
WITH PHP

The first part of this book is a thorough discussion of PHP as a programming language. You will be introduced to common concepts of computer science and how they are implemented in PHP. No prior programming experience beyond the use of simple mark-up languages is necessary. That is, you must be familiar with HTML. These chapters focus on building a foundation of understanding rather than on how to solve specific problems. If you have experience programming in a similar language, such as C or Perl, you may choose to read Chapter 1 and skim the rest, saving it as a reference. In most situations, PHP treats syntax much as these two languages do.

Chapter 1 is an introduction to PHP—how it began and what it looks like. It may be sufficient for experienced programmers, since it moves quickly through PHP's key features. If you are less experienced, I encourage you to treat this chapter as a first look. Don't worry too much about exactly how the examples work. I explain the concepts in depth in later chapters.

Chapter 2 introduces the concepts of variables, operators, and expressions. These are the building blocks of a PHP script. Essentially, a computer stores and manipulates data. Variables let you name values; operators and expressions let you manipulate them.

Chapter 3 examines the ways PHP allows you to control program execution. This includes conditional branches and loops.

Chapter 4 deals with functions, how they are called, and how to define them. Functions are packages of code that you can call upon repeatedly.

Chapter 5 is about arrays—collections of values that are identified by either numbers or names. Arrays are a very powerful way to store information and retrieve it efficiently.

Chapter 6 is about classes, presenting an object-oriented approach to grouping functions and data. Although not strictly an object-oriented language, PHP supports many features found in OO languages like Java.

Chapter 7 deals with how PHP sends and receives data. Files, network connections, and other means of communication are covered.

AN INTRODUCTION TO PHP

Chapter 1

This chapter will introduce you to PHP. You will learn how it came about, what it looks like, and why it is the best server-side technology. You will also be exposed to the most important features of the language.

PHP began as a simple macro replacement tool. Like a nice pair of shoes, it got you where you needed to go, but you could go only so far. On the hyperspeed development track of the Internet, PHP has become the equivalent of a 1960s muscle car. It's cheap, it's fast, and there's plenty of room under the hood for you and your virtual wrench.

You probably don't need convincing that whether it's Internet, intranet, or extranet, the Web is no longer about plain HTML files. Web pages are being replaced with Web applications. The issue many Web engineers face is choosing among hundreds of technologies.

This chapter will let you poke around the PHP engine, get your hands a little dirty, and take it for a spin. There are lots of small examples you can try immediately. Like all the examples in this book, you can easily adapt them to provide real solutions. Don't be intimidated if you don't fully understand the PHP code at first. Later chapters will deal with all the issues in detail.

This chapter talks about some things that you already know, like what a computer is, just to make sure we're all on the same page. You may be a wizard with HTML, but not fully appreciate the alien way computers are put together. Or you may find you learned all these things in a high school computer class. If you get too bored with the basics, skip to Chapter 2, "Variables, Operators, and Expressions."

The Origins of PHP

Wonderful things come from singular inspiration. PHP began life as a simple way to track visitors to Rasmus Lerdorf's online resume. It also could embed SQL queries in Web pages. But as often happens on the Web, admirers quickly asked for their own copies. As a proponent of the Internet's ethic of sharing, as well as a generally agreeable person, Rasmus unleashed upon an unsuspecting Web his Personal Home Page Tools version 1.0.

"Unleashed upon himself" may be more accurate. PHP became very popular. A consequence was a flood of suggestions. PHP 1.0 filtered input, replacing simple commands for HTML. As its popularity grew, people wondered if it couldn't do more. Loops, conditionals, rich data structures—all the conveniences of modern structured programming seemed like a next logical step. Rasmus studied language parsers, read about YACC and GNU Bison, and created PHP 2.0.

PHP 2.0 allowed developers to embed structured code inside HTML tags. PHP scripts could parse data submitted by HTML forms, communicate with databases, and make complex calculations on the fly. And it was very fast, because the freely available source code compiled into the Apache Web server. A PHP script executed as part of the Web server process and required no forking, often a criticism of Common Gateway Interface (CGI) scripts.

PHP was a legitimate development solution and began to be used for commercial Web sites. In 1996 Clear Ink created the SuperCuts site (www. supercuts.com) and used PHP to created a custom experience for the Web surfer. In January of 1999 the PHP Web site reported almost 100,000 Web servers were using PHP. By November that figure had climbed higher than 350,000!

A community of developers grew up around PHP. Feature requests were balanced by bug fixes and enhancements. Zeev Suraski and Andi Gutmans made a significant contribution by writing a new parser. They observed that the parser in PHP 2.0 was the source of many problems. Rasmus decided to begin work on PHP 3.0 and called for developers to commit to its creation. Along with Zeev and Andi, three others lent their support: Stig Bakken, Shane Caraveo, and Jim Winstead.

After seven months of developments, PHP version 3.0 was released on June 6, 1998. Work began immediately on the next version. Originally a 3.1 version was planned, but thanks to more revolutionary work by Zeev and Andi, work shifted to PHP 4.0, which used the new Zend library.

On January 4, 1999, Zeev and Andi announced a new framework that promised to increase dramatically the performance of PHP scripts. They named the new framework Zend, cleverly combining letters from their names. Early tests showed script execution times dropping by a factor of one hundred. In addition, new features for compiling scripts into binary, optimization, and profiling were planned.

Work on Zend and PHP 4.0 continued in parallel with bug fixes and enhancement to PHP 3.0. During 1999, eight incremental versions were released, and on December 29, 1999, PHP version 3.0.13 was announced. During the same year, Open Source projects written in PHP flourished. Projects like Phorum tackled long-time Internet tasks such as hosting online discussion. The PHPLib project provided a framework for handling user sessions that inspired new code in PHP. FreeTrade, a project I lead, offered a toolkit for building e-commerce sites.

Writing about PHP increased as well. More than twenty articles appeared on high-traffic sites such as webmonkey.com and techweb.com. Sites dedicated to supporting PHP developers were launched. The first two books about PHP were published in May 1999. Egon Schmid, Christian Cartus, and Richard Blume wrote a book in German called *PHP: Dynamische Webauftritte professionell realisieren.* Prentice Hall published the first edition of my book, *Core PHP Programming.* Since then several other books have been published and others planned.

PHP is not a shrink-wrapped product made by faceless drones or wizards in an ivory tower. PHP started as a simple tool brought into the bazaar described by Eric Raymond in his essay *The Cathedral and the Bazaar* `<http://www.tuxedo.org/~esr/writings/cathedral-bazaar/>`.

Once it was there, anyone could make improvements, and many did. Their aim seems to be to achieve solutions of direct, personal interest. If a client comes along that requires a project use a database not supported by PHP, you simply write an extension. Then you give it to the PHP project. Soon other people are fixing your bugs.

Yet, the vast majority of PHP users never write an extension. They happily find everything they need in the contributed works of others. Those who've contributed thousands of lines of code to PHP perhaps never consider themselves heroes. They don't trumpet their accomplishments. But because each part of PHP came from a real person, I would like to point them out. When appropriate, I'll note who added a particular extension.

You can find an up-to-date list of credits on the PHP site <http:// www.php.net/version4/credits.php>.

What Makes PHP Better than Its Alternatives

The skeptics are asking themselves, "Why should I learn PHP?" The days of static Web sites built with HTML files and a few CGI scripts are over: Today's sites must be dynamic. All the stale company brochures littering the streets of the Internet will transform into 24-hour virtual storefronts or be swept away. The toughest decision facing the creator of a Web application is choosing from hundreds of technologies.

Perl has adapted well to being a CGI solution and it has been used to drive complex Web technology like CyberCash and Excite's EWS search engine. Microsoft provides its Active Server Pages with Internet Information Server. Middleware like Allaire's Cold Fusion is yet another solution. ServerWatch.com lists hundreds of Web technologies, some costing tens of thousands of dollars. Why should you choose PHP over any of these alternatives?

The short answer is that PHP is better. It is faster to code and faster to execute. The same PHP code runs unaltered on different Web servers and different operation systems. Additionally, functionality that is standard with PHP is an add-on in other environments. A more detailed argument follows.

PHP is free. Anyone may visit the PHP Web site <http://www.php.net/> and download the complete source code. Binaries are also available for Windows. The result is easy entry into the experience. There is very little risk in trying PHP, and its license allows the code to be used to develop works with no royalties. This is unlike products such as Allaire's Cold Fusion or Everyware's Tango Enterprise that charge thousands of dollars for the software to interpret and serve scripts. Even commercial giants like Netscape and IBM now recognize the advantages of making source code available.

PHP runs on UNIX, Windows 98, Windows NT, and the Macintosh. PHP is designed to integrate with the Apache Web Server. Apache, another free technology, is the most popular Web server on the Internet and comes with source code for UNIX and Windows. Commercial flavors of Apache like WebTen and Stronghold support PHP, too. But PHP works with other Web servers, including Microsoft's Internet Information Server. Scripts may be moved between server platforms without alteration. PHP supports ISAPI to allow for the performance benefits of tightly coupling with Microsoft Web servers.

PHP is modifiable. PHP has been designed to allow for future extension of functionality. PHP is coded in C and provides a well-defined Application Programming Interface (API). Capable programmers may add new functionality easily. The rich set of functions available in PHP are evidence that they often do. Even if you aren't interested in changing the source code, it's comforting to know you can inspect it. Doing so may give you greater confidence in PHP's robustness.

PHP was written for Web page creation. Perl, C, and Java are very good general languages and are certainly capable of driving Web applications. The unfortunate sacrifice these alternatives make is the ease of communication with the Web experience. PHP applications may be rapidly and easily developed because the code is encapsulated in the Web pages themselves.

Support for PHP is free and readily available. Queries to the PHP mailing list are often answered within hours. A custom bug-tracking system on the PHP site shows each problem along with its resolution. Numerous sites, such as phpbuilder.com and zend.com, offer original content to PHP developers.

PHP is popular. Internet service providers find PHP to be an attractive way to allow their customers to code Web applications without the risks exposed by CGIs. Developers worldwide offer PHP programming. Sites coded in PHP will have the option of moving from one host to another as well as a choice of developers to add functionality.

Programming skills developed in other structured languages can be applied to PHP. PHP takes inspiration from both Perl and C. Experienced Perl and C programmers learn PHP very quickly. Likewise, programmers who learn PHP as a first language may apply their knowledge toward not only Perl and C, but other C-like languages such as Java. This is very different from learning to code in a visual editor such as Microsoft Visual InterDev.

Interfaces to External Systems

PHP is somewhat famous for interfacing with many different database systems, but it also has support for other external systems. Support comes in the form of modules called extensions. They either compile directly into PHP or are loaded dynamically. New extensions are added to the PHP project regularly. The extensions expose groups of functions for using these external systems. As I've said, some of these are databases. PHP offers functions for talking natively with most popular database systems, as well as providing access to ODBC drivers. Other extensions give you the ability to send messages using a particular network protocol, such as LDAP or IMAP. These functions are described in detail in Section Two, but you might find the highlights listed here interesting. Because PHP developers are enthusiastic and industrious, you will undoubtedly find more extensions have been added since I wrote this.

Aspell is a system for checking spelling. An extension provides support for numbers of arbitrary precision. There is an extension for dealing with various calendar systems. An extension provides support for DBM-style databases. You can read from filePro databases. You can interact with Hyperwave. You can use the ICAP, IMAP, and LDAP protocols. The Interbase and Informix databases are supported natively, as are mSQL, Mysql, MS SQL, Sybase, Oracle, and Postgres. You can also parse XML or create WDDX packets.

How PHP Works with the Web Server

The normal process a Web server goes through to deliver a page to a browser is as follows. It all begins when a browser makes a request for a Web page. Based on the URL, the browser resolves the address of the Web server, identifies the page it would like, and gives any other information the Web server may need. Some of this information is about the browser itself, like its name (Mozilla), its version (4.08), or the operating system (Linux). Other information given the Web server could include text the user typed into form fields.

If the request is for an HTML file, the Web server will simply find the file, tell the browser to expect some HTML text, and then send the contents of the file. The browser gets the contents and begins rendering the page based on the HTML code. If you have been programming HTML for any length of time, this will be clear to you.

Hopefully you have also had some experience with CGI scripts. When a Web server gets a request for a CGI, it can't just send the contents of the file. It must execute the script first. The script will generate some HTML code, which then gets sent to the browser. As far as the browser is concerned, it's just getting HTML. The Web server does a bunch of work that it gets very little recognition for, but Web servers rarely get the respect they deserve. The medium is definitely not the message.

When a PHP page is requested, it is processed exactly like a CGI, at least to the extent that the script is not simply sent to the browser. It is first passed through the PHP engine, which gives the Web server HTML text.

What happens when the user clicks the stop button before the page finishes downloading? The Web server detects this situation and usually terminates the PHP script. It is possible to force a script to finish despite an aborted connection. You may also allow the script to terminate but execute special code first. The functions to allow this functionality are listed in Chapter 8, "I/O Functions," and Chapter 11, "Time Date, and Configuration Functions."

Hardware and Software Requirements

One great advantage of Open Source software is that it provides the opportunity for adaptation to new environments. This is true of PHP. Although originally intended as a module for the Apache Web server, PHP has since embraced the ISAPI standard, which allows it to work equally well with Microsoft's Internet Information Server. With regard to hardware requirements, I have personally witnessed PHP running on 100-MHz Pentium machines running Slackware Linux and Windows NT, respectively. Performance was fine for use as a personal development environment. A site expected to receive thousands of requests a day would need faster hardware, of course. Although more resources are needed when comparing a PHP-powered site to a flat HTML site, the requirements are not dramatically different. Despite my example, you are not limited to Intel hardware. PHP works equally well on PowerPC and Sparc CPUs.

When choosing an operating system, you have the general choice between Windows and a UNIX-like OS. PHP will run on Windows 95 and 98, although these operating systems aren't suited for high-traffic Web servers. It will also run on Windows NT and its successor, Windows 2000. For UNIX operating systems, PHP works well with Linux and Solaris, as well as others. If you have chosen a PPC-based system, such as a Macintosh, you may choose LinuxPPC, a version of Linux. You may pursue the commercial WebTen Web server that runs in the Macintosh OS. Chad Cunningham has contributed patches for compiling PHP in Apple's OS X. In 1999 Brian Havard added support for IBM's OS/2.

PHP still works best with the Apache Web server. But it now works very well with IIS. It also compiles as a module for the fhttpd Web server. You can make PHP work with almost any Web server using the CGI version, but I don't recommend this setup for production Web sites. If you are using UNIX, I recommend compiling PHP as an Apache module. If you are using Windows NT, pursue IIS.

Installation on Apache for UNIX

If you are using Linux, you can easily find an RPM for Apache and PHP, but this installation may not include every PHP feature you want. I recommend this route as a very quick start. You can always pursue compiling Apache and PHP from scratch later. PHP will compile on most versions of UNIX-like operating systems, including Solaris and Linux. If you have ever compiled software you've found on the Net, you will have little trouble with this installation. If you don't have experience extracting files from a tar archive and executing make files, you may wish to rely on your sysadmin or someone else more experienced. You will need to have root privileges to completely install PHP.

The first step is to download the tar files and unpack them. The CDROM that accompanies this book has recent versions of both PHP and Apache, but you may wish to check online for the newest versions, `<http://www.php.net/>` and `<http://www.apache.org/>`, respectively.

After unpacking the tar file, the first step is to configure Apache. This is done by running the configure script inside the Apache directory:

```
./configure —prefix=/www
```

The script will examine your system and prepare a make file for Apache. The `prefix` directive will cause a directory to be created in the root of your file system.

Next, configure and compile PHP:

```
./configure —with-apache=/usr/local/src/apache_1.3.9 —enable-track-vars
make
make install
```

This is done within the PHP directory. The —with-apache and —enable-track-vars options are minimal. You might add —with-mysql if you have the MySQL database installed. PHP can usually find the MySQL libraries on its own. Appendix E, "Compile-Time Configuration" lists the compile-time configuration directives. Running make will create the PHP library, and make install will prepare Apache for including the PHP module. Notice that the call to configure includes a path to your Apache source code directory. This can be a relative path, as you may have put the Apache source code parallel to the PHP source code. However, do not make the mistake of using relative paths for any of the other directives.

Next, you will need to reconfigure Apache and run make. Return to the Apache source code directory and run configure again, this time with an option that tells Apache to include the PHP module:

```
./configure —prefix=/www —activate-module=src/modules/php4/libphp4.a
make
make install
```

This will create a new make file and then run it. The new httpd binary will be installed in the /www/bin directory, or wherever you specified the files should be installed.

To supply additional configuration options PHP uses a file called php.ini. This file should reside in /usr/local/lib, so copy it from the PHP source directory:

```
cp php.ini-dist /usr/local/lib/php.ini
```

It is not likely you will need to edit this file, but if you do, there are instructive comments inside.

The last step is to associate a file extension with PHP. This is done by editing the httpd.conf file. It can be found in Apache's conf directory, /www/conf/httpd.conf, for example. Add the following line:

```
AddType application/x-httpd-php .php
```

This causes all files with the extension .php to be executed as PHP scripts. You may choose another, such as phtml. You may also wish to insert index.php as a default document. When the Apache server is started, it will process PHP scripts. The documentation for Apache has hints for starting Apache automatically. If you have been running Apache previously, you will need to restart it, not just use a kill -HUP command.

Installation on IIS for Windows NT

The first step is to install PHP. You do not need to compile PHP for Windows. A binary distribution is available on the Web site. Download the zip file and expand it wherever you wish. I put mine in `c:\php4`. Next, copy the file `php.ini-dist` into your system root directory, which is probably `c:\winnt`. Rename it `php.ini`. When PHP is invoked, it looks first for `php.ini` in this directory. Although you don't need to, you may wish to edit it to change configuration parameters, including automatically loading extensions. Comments in the file explain the purpose of each configuration directive.

The next step is to make sure the required DLL files are in your path. One way is to copy the two required files to your system directory, such as `c:\winnt\system32`. Alternatively, you can click on the `system` icon in the control panel and add your PHP directory to the system path.

You need to tell IIS that files ending with a particular extension, such as `.php`, should be processed with PHP. IIS calls this process an ISAPI filter. Open the Management Console that allows you to configure all aspects of IIS. One of the tabs for editing a Web server allows you to edit ISAPI filters. Add one. You should call it PHP, and point to the `php4isapi.dll` file, which should be with the rest of the files you installed with PHP. This file is really small, but it loads the PHP core from another library, `php4ts.dll`.

Now that you've added the filter, you need to associate it with an extension. Look for the home directory configuration button in the properties dialog. Add a new entry to the list of application mappings. Choose .php for the extension, and find your `php4isapi.dll` file again. Leave the text box labeled "method exclusions" blank, and check the script engine checkbox.

The last step is to restart the Web server. Stopping it from the management console is not sufficient. You must stop the service itself either from the command line with `net stop w3svc`, or by using the services control panel. After stopping it, restart it.

Editing Scripts

PHP scripts are just text files, and you can edit and create them just as you would HTML files. Certainly, you can telnet into your Web server and start creating files with `vi`. Or you can create files with notepad and use `ftp` to upload them one by one. But these aren't ideal experiences. One handy feature of newer editors is built-in FTP. These editors can open files on a remote Web server as if they were on a local drive. A single click saves them back to the remote Web server. Another feature you may enjoy is syntax highlighting. This causes PHP keywords to be colored in order to help you read the code faster.

Everyone has a favorite editor for PHP scripts. I use UltraEdit `<http://www.ultraedit.com/>`. I know many Windows users prefer Macromedia's Dreamweaver

`<http://www.macromedia.com/software/dreamweaver/>`

and Allaire's HomeSite

`<http://www.allaire.com/products/homesite/>`

to edit PHP scripts. Quad Systems offers a free package called phpWeave that allows Dreamweaver to build some PHP scripts automatically `<http://phpweave.quad-sys.com/>`. The Macintosh users I know prefer BBedit `<http://www.barebones.com/products/bbedit/bbedit.html>`.

On a UNIX operating system, you may prefer emacs or vi, of course. You might also consider nEdit `<ftp://ftp.fnal.gov/pub/nedit/>`. A module for PHP is available in the `contrib` directory. The topic of which editor is best appears frequently on the PHP mailing list. Reading the archives can be amusing and informative

`<http://www.progressive-comp.com/Lists/?l=php3-general>`.

Algorithms

Whenever we interact with a computer, we are instructing it to perform some action. When you drag an icon into the waste basket on your desktop, you are asking the computer to remove the file from your hard disk. When you write an HTML file, you are instructing the computer in the proper way to display some information. There are usually many incremental steps to any process the computer performs. It may first clear the screen with the color you specified in the `body` tag. Then it may begin writing some text in a particular color and typeface. As you use a computer, you may not be entirely aware of each tiny step it takes, but you are giving it a list of ordered instructions that you expect it to follow.

Instructions for baking a cake are called a recipe. Instructions for making a movie are called a screenplay. Instructions for a computer are called a program. Each of these is written in its own language, a concrete realization of an abstract set of instructions. Borrowing from mathematics, computer science calls the abstract instructions an algorithm.

You may at this moment have in mind an algorithm that you'd like to implement. Perhaps you wish to display information in a Web browser that changes frequently. Imagine something simple, such as displaying today's date. You could edit a plain HTML file once a day. You could even write out a set of instructions to help remind you of each step. But you cannot perform the task with HTML alone. There's no tag that stands for the current date.

PHP is a language that allows you to express algorithms for creating HTML files. With PHP, you can write instructions for displaying the current date inside an HTML document. You write your instructions in a file called a script. The language of the script is PHP, a language that both you and the computer can understand.

What a PHP Script Looks Like

PHP exists as a tag inside an HTML file. Like all HTML tags, it begins with a less-than symbol, or opening angle bracket (<) and ends with a greater than symbol, or closing angle bracket (>). To distinguish it from other tags, the PHP tag has a question mark (?) following the opening angle bracket and preceding the closing angle bracket. All text outside the PHP tag is simply passed through to the browser. Text inside the tag is expected to be PHP code and is parsed.

To accommodate XML and some picky editors such as Microsoft's Front Page, PHP offers three other ways to mark code. Putting php after the opening question mark makes PHP code friendly to XML parsers. Alternatively, you may use a script tag as if you were writing JavaScript. Lastly, you can use tags that appear like ASP, using <% to start blocks of code. Appendix D explains how these alternatives work. I use the simple <? and ?> method for all my examples.

Listing 1.1 shows an ordinary HTML page with one remarkable difference: the PHP code between the <? and the ?>. When this page is passed through the PHP module, it will replace the PHP code with today's date. It might read something like, Friday May 1, 1999.

Listing 1.1   Printing Today's Date

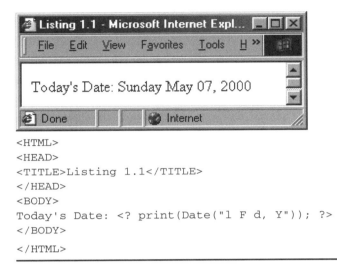

```
<HTML>
<HEAD>
<TITLE>Listing 1.1</TITLE>
</HEAD>
<BODY>
Today's Date: <? print(Date("l F d, Y")); ?>
</BODY>
</HTML>
```

Whitespace, that is spaces, tabs, and carriage returns, is ignored by PHP. Used judiciously, it can enhance the readability of your code. Listing 1.2 is functionally the same as the previous example, though you may notice more easily that it contains PHP code.

Listing 1.2   Reformatting for Readability

```
<HTML>
<HEAD>
<TITLE>Listing 1-2</TITLE>
</HEAD>
<BODY>
Today's Date:
<?
        /*
        ** print today's date
        */
        print(Date("l F d, Y"));
?>
</BODY>
</HTML>
```

You may also notice that in Listing 1.2 there is a line of code that begins with a slash followed by an asterisk. This is a comment. Everything between the /* and the */ is equivalent to whitespace. It is ignored. Comments can be used to document how your code works. Even if you maintain your own code you will find comments necessary for all but simple scripts.

In addition to the opening and closing comment statements, PHP provides two ways to build a single-line comment. Double-slashes or a pound sign will cause everything after them to the end of the line to be ignored by the parser.

After skipping over the whitespace and the comment in Listing 1.2, the PHP parser encounters the first word: print. This is one of PHP's functions. A function collects code into a unit you may invoke with its name. The print function sends text to the browser. The contents of the parentheses will be evaluated, and if it produces output, print will pass it along to the browser.

Where does the line end? Unlike BASIC and JavaScript, which use a line break to denote the end of a line, PHP uses a semicolon. On this issue PHP takes inspiration from C.

The contents of the line between print and ; is a call to a function named date. The text between the opening and closing parentheses is the parameter passed to date. The parameter tells date in what form you want the date to appear. In this case we've used the codes for the weekday name, the full month name, the day of the month, and the four-digit year. The current date is formatted and passed back to the print function.

The string of characters beginning and ending with double quotes is called a string constant or string literal. PHP knows that when quotes surround characters you intend them to be treated as text. Without the quotes, PHP will assume you are naming a function or some other part of the language itself. In other words, the first quote is telling PHP to keep hands off until it finds another quote.

Notice that print is typed completely in lowercase letters, yet date has a leading uppercase letter. I did this to illustrate that PHP takes a very lenient attitude toward the names of its built-in functions. Print, PRINT, and PrInT are all valid calls to the same function. However, for the sake of readability, it is customary to write PHP's built-in functions using lowercase letters only.

Saving Data for Later

Often it is necessary to save information for later use. PHP, like most programming languages, offers the concept of variables. Variables give a name to the information you want to save and manipulate. Listing 1.3 expands on our example by using variables.

Listing 1.3   Assigning Values to Variables

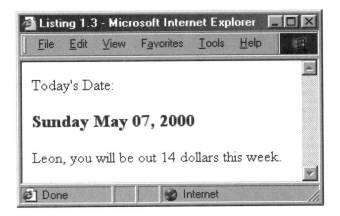

```
<?
        $YourName = "Leon";
        $Today = date("l F d, Y");
        $CostOfLunch = 3.50;
        $DaysBuyingLunch = 4;
?>
<HTML>
<HEAD>
<TITLE>Listing 1-3</TITLE>
</HEAD>
<BODY>
Today's Date:
<?
        /*
        ** print today's date
        */
        print("<H3>$Today</H3>\n");

        /*
        ** print message about lunch cost
        */
        print("$YourName, you will be out ");
        print($CostOfLunch * $DaysBuyingLunch);
        print(" dollars this week.<BR>\n");
?>
</BODY>
</HTML>
```

The first block of PHP code puts values into some variables. The four variables are `YourName`, `Today`, `CostOfLunch`, and `DaysBuyingLunch`. PHP knows they are variables because they are preceded by a dollar sign (`$`). The first time you use a variable in a PHP script, some memory is set aside to store the information you wish to save. You don't need to tell PHP what kind of information you expect to be saved in the variable; PHP can figure this out on its own.

The script first puts a character string into the variable `YourName`. As I noted earlier, PHP knows it's textual data because I put quotes around it. Likewise I put today's date into a variable named `Today`. In this case PHP knows to put text into the variable because the `date` function returns text. This type of data is referred to as a string, which is shorthand for character string. A character is a single letter, number, or any other mark you make by typing a single key on your keyboard.

Notice that there is an equal sign (`=`) separating the variable and the value you put into it. This is the assignment operator. Everything to its right is put into a variable named to its left.

The third and fourth assignments are putting numerical data into variables. The value 3.5 is a floating-point, or fractional, number. PHP calls this type a double, showing some of its C heritage. The value 4 in the next assignment is an integer, or whole number.

After printing some HTML code, another PHP code block is opened. First the script prints today's date as a level-three header. Notice that the script passes some new types of information to the `print` function. You can give string literals or string variables to `print` and they will be sent to the browser.

When it comes to variables, PHP is not so lenient with case. `Today` and `today` are two different variables. Since PHP doesn't require you to declare variables before you use them, you can accidentally type `today` when you mean `Today` and no error will be generated. If variables are unexpectedly empty, check your case.

The script next prints `Leon, you will be out 14.00 dollars this week`. The line that prints the total has to calculate it with multiplication using the `*` operator.

Receiving User Input

Manipulating variables that you set within your script is somewhat interesting, but hardly anything to rave about. Scripts become much more useful when they use input from the user. When you call PHP from an HTML

> **Listing 1.4   HTML Form for Lunch Information**

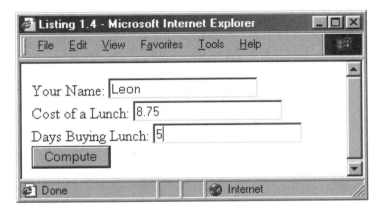

```
<HTML>
<HEAD>
<TITLE>Listing 1-4</TITLE>
</HEAD>
<BODY>
<FORM ACTION="1-5.php" METHOD="post">
Your Name:
<INPUT TYPE="text" NAME="YourName"><BR>
Cost of a Lunch:
<INPUT TYPE="text" NAME="CostOfLunch"><BR>
Days Buying Lunch:
<INPUT TYPE="text" NAME="DaysBuyingLunch"><BR>
<INPUT TYPE="submit" NAME="x" VALUE="Compute">
</FORM>
</BODY>
</HTML>
```

form, the form fields are turned into variables. Listing 1.4 is a form that calls Listing 1.5, a further modification of our example script.

Listing 1.4 is a standard HTML form. If you have dealt at all with CGIs, it will look familiar. There are three form fields that match up with the variables from our previous example. Instead of simply putting data into the variables, we will provide a form and use the information the user types. When the user presses the submit button, the script named in the ACTION attribute will receive the three form fields and PHP will convert them into variables.

Listing 1.5   Computing the Cost of Lunch from a Form

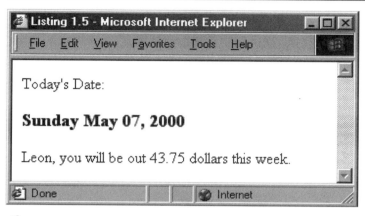

```
<?
        $Today = date("l F d, Y");
?>
<HTML>
<HEAD>
<TITLE>Listing 1-5</TITLE>
</HEAD>
<BODY>
Today's Date:
<?
        /*
        ** print today's date
        */
        print("<H3>$Today</H3>\n");

        /*
        ** print message about lunch cost
        */
        print("$YourName, you will be out ");
        print($CostOfLunch * $DaysBuyingLunch);
        print(" dollars this week.<BR>\n");
?>
</BODY>
</HTML>
```

Notice that in the first segment of the PHP script, I have eliminated the lines setting the variables, except for today's date. The rest of the script is unchanged. The script assumes there will be data in the variables. Try experimenting with the scripts by entering nonsense in the form fields.

One thing you should notice is that if you put words where the script expects numbers, PHP seems to just assign them values of zero. The variables are set with a text string, and when the script tries to treat it as a number, PHP does its best to convert the information. Entering 10 Little Indians for the cost of lunch will be interpreted as 10.

Listing 1.6   Conditional Daily Message

```
<HTML>
<HEAD>
<TITLE>Listing 1-6</TITLE>
</HEAD>
<BODY>
<H1>
<?
        /*
        ** get today's day of the week
        */
        $Today = date("l");

        if($Today == "Friday")
        {
          print("Thank Goodness It's Friday!");
        }
        else
        {
          print("Today is $Today.");
        }
?>
</H1>
</BODY>
</HTML>
```

Choosing between Alternatives

PHP allows you to test conditions and execute certain code based on the result of the test. The simplest form of this is the `if` statement. Listing 1.6 shows how you can customize the content of a page based on the value of a variable.

The `Today` variable is set with the name of today's weekday. The `if` statement evaluates the expression inside the parentheses as either true or false. The `==` operator compares the left side to the right side. If `Today` contains the word `Friday`, the block of code surrounded by curly braces (`{` and `}`) is executed. In all other cases the block of code associated with the `else` statement is executed.

Repeating Code

The last type of functionality in this brief introduction is looping. Looping allows you to repeat the execution of code. Listing 1.7 is an example of a `for` loop. The `for` statement expects three parameters separated by semicolons. The first parameter is executed once before the loop begins. It usually initializes a variable. The second parameter makes a test. This is usually a test against the variable named in the first parameter. The third parameter is executed every time the end of the loop is reached.

The `for` loop in Listing 1.7 will execute three times. The initialization code sets the variable `count` to be one. Then the testing code compares the value of count to three. Since one is less than or equal to three, the code inside the loop executes. Notice that the script prints the value of `count`. When you run this script you will find that `count` will progress from one to three. The reason is that the third part of the `for` statement is adding one to `count` each time through the loop. The `++` operator increments the variable immediately to its left.

The first time through the loop `count` is one, not two. This is because the increment of `count` doesn't occur until we reach the closing curly brace. After the third time through the loop, `count` will be incremented to four, but at that point four will not be less than or equal to three, so the loop will end. Execution continues at the command following the loop code block.

Listing 1.7   Today's Daily Affirmation

```
<HTML>
<HEAD>
<TITLE>Listing 1-7</TITLE>
</HEAD>
<BODY>
<H1>Today's Daily Affirmation</H1>
Repeat three times:<BR>
<?
      for($count = 1; $count <= 3; $count++)
      {
        print("<B>$count</B> I'm good enough, ;");
        print("I'm smart enough, ");
        print("and, doggone it, people like me!<BR>\n");
      }
?>
</BODY>
</HTML>
```

Conclusion

Hopefully this chapter has convinced you of the power of PHP. You have seen some of the major features of the language and read arguments why PHP is better than its many competitors. The rest of the book will look at PHP in more detail.

VARIABLES, OPERATORS, AND EXPRESSIONS

Topics in This Chapter

- Identifiers
- Data Types
- Variable Creation and Scope
- Assigning Values to Variables
- Retrieving Values
- Freeing Memory
- Constants
- Operators
- Logical and Relational Operators
- Bitwise Operators
- Miscellaneous Operators
- Assignment Operators
- Expressions

Chapter 2

Everything in PHP is either an identifier or an operator. An identifier can be a function or variable. An operator is usually one or two symbols that stand for some sort of data manipulation like addition or multiplication. When identifiers and operators are combined, they become an expression. This chapter introduces the concepts that form the basis of all PHP code.

Identifiers

Identifiers give names to the abstract parts of PHP: functions, variables, and classes. Some of them are created by PHP in the form of built-in functions or environment variables. Others you create. Identifiers may be of any length and can consists of letters, numbers, or underscores. The first character of an identifier must be either a letter or an underscore. Table 2.1 contrasts acceptable identifiers with unacceptable ones.

Upper- and lowercase letters are recognized as different. That is, the variables `UserName` and `username` are two distinct identifiers. The exception is built-in functions. As stated in Chapter 1, "An Introduction to PHP," functions like `print` can be called as `Print` if you prefer.

Table 2.1 Acceptable and Unacceptable Identifiers	
Acceptable	*Unacceptable*
LastVisit	Last!Visit
_password	~password
compute_Mean	compute-Mean
Lucky7	7Lucky

Variables, discussed in detail below, are always preceded by $. The side effect of this is that a function and a variable can share a name. You may also create a variable with the same name as a built-in function. Consider that this can be very confusing to anyone reading your code, including you. You may never create a function with the same name as a built-in function.

Data Types

PHP has three elemental types of data: integers, floating-point numbers, and strings of text. Integers are sometimes referred to as whole or natural numbers; they contain no decimal point. Floating-point numbers are sometimes called real numbers. They always contain a decimal point, even when only a zero follows it. PHP refers to these as doubles, which is short for double-precision floating-point numbers. Strings are collections of textual data. String constants are always surrounded by double quotes (") or single quotes (').

In addition to these, PHP has four aggregate data types that use the other three: arrays, objects and booleans, and resources. An array is a collection of values associated with indexes. Arrays are discussed in full in Chapter 5, "Arrays." Objects are similar to arrays, but may also contain functions. They are discussed in Chapter 6, "Classes and Objects." Boolean values are either true or false. Historically, PHP did not support a separate type for booleans; instead zero and an empty string were understood to be false, while any other value was considered to be a true value. With PHP 4, this changed. Now data may be cast or set to be of boolean type. Resources are integers used to identify system resources, such as open files or database connections.

As you write PHP code, you will usually be unaware of the distinction between types because variables are multitype. You do not declare a variable to be a particular type. You just assign it a value. PHP will remember what type of data you put into the variable. When you retrieve data from the variable, they are returned with that same type.

There are two ways to override this behavior. The first way is to use the `settype` function. This tells PHP that you want to start considering a variable to be a certain type. The data associated with the variable will be converted to the new type. The alternative is to use one of the type conversion functions or a cast. Consider Listing 2.1, which contrasts `settype`, the type conversion functions, and casts.

Listing 2.1   Experimenting with Type Conversion

```
Listing 2.1 - Microsoft Internet ...

 File   Edit   View   Favorites   Tools  »

Using settype
String: 60.5 degrees
Double: 60.5
Integer: 60
String: 60
Using strval, intval, and doubleval
String: 60.5 degrees
Double: 60.5
Integer: 60
Original: 60.5 degrees
Using casts
String: 60.5 degrees
Double: 60.5
Integer: 60
Original: 60.5 degrees

Done              Internet
```

```php
<?
        print("<B>Using settype</B><BR>\n");
        $AverageTemperature = "60.5 degrees";
        print("String: $AverageTemperature <BR>\n");
```

```
settype($AverageTemperature, "double");
print("Double: $AverageTemperature <BR>\n");

settype($AverageTemperature, "integer");
print("Integer: $AverageTemperature <BR>\n");

settype($AverageTemperature, "string");
print("String: $AverageTemperature <BR>\n");


print("<B>Using strval, intval, ");

print("and doubleval</B><BR>\n");
$AverageTemperature = "60.5 degrees";

print("String: ");
print(strval($AverageTemperature));
print("<BR>\n");

print("Double: ");
print(doubleval($AverageTemperature));
print("<BR>\n");

print("Integer: ");
print(intval($AverageTemperature));
print("<BR>\n");

print("Original: ");
print($AverageTemperature);
print("<BR>\n");


print("<B>Using casts</B><BR>\n");
$AverageTemperature = "60.5 degrees";

print("String: ");
print((string)$AverageTemperature);
print("<BR>\n");

print("Double: ");
print((double)$AverageTemperature);
print("<BR>\n");

print("Integer: ");
print((integer)$AverageTemperature);
```

```
        print("<BR>\n");

        print("Original: ");
        print($AverageTemperature);
        print("<BR>\n");
?>
```

When `AverageTemperature` is first used, PHP marks it internally as a string because it is assigned the value of a string literal. Setting the type to be double causes the value to be reevaluated. If you check the output, you will notice that some information is lost as a result. The text following the number is dropped off because it has no meaning in the context of a floating-point number. Likewise, when the script sets the type to be integer, the fractional part of the number is dropped. Even when we change the type back to string, the previous information is gone.

In contrast to this, the use of the type conversion commands preserves the value of the variable because it does the conversion on the fly. The data inside the variable are not changed.

The `settype` function is described in full in Chapter 9, "Data Functions," as are the type conversion functions `intval`, `strval`, and `doubleval`. Casts, identical in operation to type conversion functions, take the form of preceding an expression with a datatype in parentheses. Valid casts are `(boolean)`, `(integer)`, `(string)`, `(double)`, `(array)`, and `(object)`. Arrays and objects are discussed in Chapters 5 and 6.

Another type of data sometimes discussed in this text is the bitfield. Rather than a data type exactly, it is a way of viewing an integer. Instead of a single value, it is viewed as a sequence of ones and zeroes. Bitfields are discussed later in this chapter in relation to bitwise operators.

Variable Creation and Scope

Although you've seen variables in the previous pages, you may wonder what they are exactly. Part of a computer is called RAM, or random access memory. This is a volatile medium for storing information. That is, it all disappears when you shut off the machine. The computer sees this memory as a long string of single characters, or bytes, each numbered. In PHP, however, you cannot

Listing 2.2   Experimenting with Scope

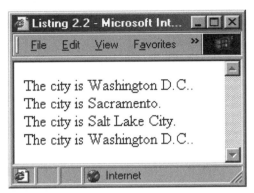

```
<?
    function printCity($NameOfCity)
    {
        print("The city is $NameOfCity.<BR>\n");
    }

    function California()
    {
        $capital = "Sacramento";
        printCity($capital);
    }

    function Utah()
    {
        $capital = "Salt Lake City";
        printCity($capital);
    }

    function Nation()
    {
        global $capital;
        printCity($capital);
    }

    $capital = "Washington DC";

    Nation();
    California();
    Utah();
    Nation();
?>
```

actually get to memory at this level. You must use a variable. You provide a name, and PHP takes care of matching the name to physical memory.

You do not need to let PHP know about a variable before you use it. Some languages like C require you to declare every variable along with its type. This is because a specific amount of memory needs to be set aside. But this is generally a problem associated with compiled languages, not interpreted ones. The first time you use a variable in PHP, the engine adds it to the list of variables it knows about and makes a best guess at what type of data the variable holds.

The first place you use a variable establishes the scope—the range within the code in which the variable may be seen. Every function you define has its own variable space. That is, there are variables that exist just for that function, and they are invisible to all other parts of your script. In addition there is a global scope for variables created outside any function. In some programming languages global variables are visible inside functions. This is not the case with PHP. When you create a function in PHP, you must explicitly tell PHP you want a global variable to be present in the function. Listing 2.2 uses the metaphor of the United States to demonstrate.

The script sets up a function, `printCity`, that prints out the name of a city. It will be used to show the contents of the variables named `capital`. Variables is plural because there are actually three variables in the script named `capital`. One is global and the other two are local to the `California` and `Utah` functions.

When you run this script you will find that the cities are printed in the order Washington DC, Sacramento, Salt Lake City, and Washington DC. Notice that even though we have given `capital` a new value inside `California`, it is not the same variable we set to Washington DC. The variables inside `California` and `Utah` exist within their own space and are created and destroyed each time the functions are called.

It is important to remember that when you create a variable inside a function, it exists only while that function is executing. Once execution finishes and control is passed back the calling process, all the variable space for that function is cleaned up. Sometimes this is not desirable; sometimes you want the function to remember the values of the variables between calls. You could implement this by using global variables, but a more elegant solution is to use the `static` command.

At the beginning of a function, before any other commands, you may declare a static variable. The variable will then retain any value it holds, even after leaving the function. You might wonder why you would ever need to do this. Suppose you'd like to build a table where the rows alternate in background color. Listing 2.3 does just this.

Listing 2.3 will print out a table with 10 rows. Each row will alternate background colors between an intense green and a lighter green. I have used

Listing 2.3   Demonstrations of Static Variables

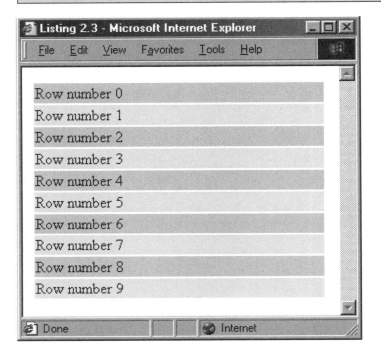

```
<?
    function useColor()
    {
        /*
        ** remember the last color we used
        */
        static $ColorValue;

        /* choose the next color */
        if($ColorValue == "#00FF00")
        {
            $ColorValue = "#CCFFCC";
        }
        else
        {
            $ColorValue = "#00FF00";
        }

        return($ColorValue);
    }
```

```
print("<TABLE WIDTH=\"300\">\n");
for($count=0; $count < 10; $count++)
{
        /*
        ** get color for this row
        */
        $RowColor = useColor();

        /*
        ** print out HTML for row
        ** set background color
        */
        print("<TR><TD BGCOLOR=\"$RowColor\">");
        print("Row number $count</TD></TR>\n");
}
print("</TABLE>\n");
?>
```

this technique in a project where I pulled data from a database and separated rows with alternating blue and green lines. Instead of using background colors, I chose between single-pixel images that I stretched to span the browser window.

There is another way a variable can appear in a function's variable space: as an argument. Functions are described in detail in Chapter 4, "Functions," but by now you have noticed functions with variables inside their parentheses. Take another look at Listing 2.2. The printCity function takes an argument called NameOfCity. When the function is called, the variable is set with the value passed in the function call. In all other respects the variable is the same as other local variables.

Assigning Values to Variables

The equal sign (=) is used to set the value of a variable. This is called the assignment operator. On the left side of the assignment operator is a variable that will receive a value. On the right side is an expression, which could be a simple string constant or a complex combination of operators, variables, and constants.

When you assign a value to a variable, its type will change to fit the type of data you put into it. This is in contrast to C, which tries to convert values to

Table 2.2	Examples of Variables Assignments	
String Constants	*Integer Constants*	*Double Constants*
$myString = "leon";	$myInteger = 1;	$myDouble = 123.456;
$myString = "\n";	$myInteger = -256;	$myDouble = -98.76e5;

fit the type of the variable. Assigning an integer to a variable that previously held a string converts the variable to an integer.

The simplest form of assignment is from a constant expression. This could be a number or a string surrounded by quotes. Table 2.2 lists some examples.

By now you have probably noticed \n showing up in most of the examples. When a \ appears inside a string constant surrounded by double quotes, it has special meaning: Do not print the next character. Instead the code stands for another character. This is so you can override the special meaning of certain characters, or make certain characters more visible. Strings surrounded by single quotes are treated literally. Any backslash codes are ignored, except for escaping single quotes within the string. Table 2.3 lists some backslash codes. The \n code stands for an end-of-line character.

Though it isn't strictly necessary, I use \n frequently. PHP allows you to create an entire HTML page on a single line. This is acceptable to browsers, but it's very hard to debug your PHP script. Put a linefeed where a linefeed would appear if you were coding the page without PHP. You will spend less time picking through your output.

Related to backslash codes are embedded variables. You may write a variable inside a string surrounded by double quotes, and its value will appear in

Table 2.3	Backslash Codes
Code	*Description*
\"	Double Quotes
\\	Backslash Character
\n	New Line
\r	Carriage Return
\t	Horizontal Tab
\x00 - \xFF	Hex Characters

its place. This even works with arrays and objects. Listing 2.3 is an example of this technique. Notice that the `RowColor` variable appears within a `print` statement between double quotes.

Borrowing from Perl, PHP also allows what are sometimes called "here docs". A special operator allows you to specify your own string of characters that mean the end of a string. This is helpful when you have large blocks of text that span multiple lines and contain quotes. Backslash codes and variables are recognized inside the text block, just as they are with string surrounded by double quotes. To mark an area of text, begin by using the `<<<` operator. Follow it by the identifier you'll use to end the string. When that identifier is found alone on a line, PHP will consider it equivalent to a closing quote character. The identifier you choose must follow the same rules governing the naming of any other identifier, as described above. It's customary to use HERE or EOD (end of data). See Listing 2.4 for an example.

Retrieving Values

To use the value stored in a variable, use it anywhere where a value is required, such as the argument to a function or in an expression. For example, if you wish to print the value to the browser, you can type `print($s)` to print the value of a variable named s. You can even set a variable with the value of another, such as `$s = $t`.

If a variable contains a string, you may refer to each character using square brackets. Each character is numbered starting with zero. To refer to the seventh character in the s variable, you would type `$s[6]`. This notation works both ways, in fact. You can set a single character of a string with an expression like `$s[6] = 'x'`. Only the first character of the value on the right-hand side will be used to replace the specified character. If the variable on the left-hand side is not a string, it will be unchanged. Listing 2.5 demonstrates the use of square brackets to reference single characters.

Freeing Memory

Each time you create a variable, system memory is set aside for it. Although there is a limit to the memory available to any computer, you will rarely need to consider conserving its use when programming in PHP. Your scripts are

Listing 2.4   HERE docs

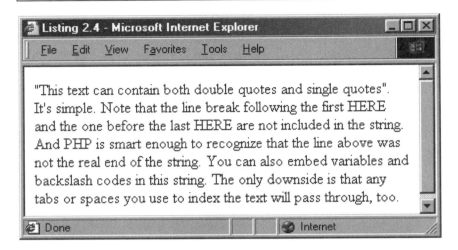

```
<?
        $text = <<< HERE
"This text can contain both double quotes
and single quotes". It's simple.

Note that the line break following the
first HERE and the one before the last
HERE are not included in the string. And
PHP is smart enough to recognize that the
line above was not the real end of the string.

You can also embed variables and backslash
codes in this string.

                The only downside is that any tabs or
                spaces you use to index the text will
                pass through, too.
HERE;

        print("$text\n");
?>
```

Listing 2.5   Referencing a Single Character

```
<?
        //replace space with underscore
        $s = "a string";
        $s[1] = "_";
        print($s);
?>
```

---

likely to use very small amounts of data. And when your script finishes, the memory needed for variables is freed for use by other processes.

I am simplifying the process somewhat. There are some ways in PHP to create memory that persists longer than a single page load, and in modern operating systems physical memory does not match one-for-one with a program's view of available memory. In most cases you will be doing fine to consider that memory is a finite but abundant resource.

If you do run into memory shortages, or have some other reason for destroying a variable, you use the unset statement. This statement completely removes a variable or an array element from memory. The variable name itself will no longer be recognized. Paired with this statement is the isset function discussed in Chapter 9. This function returns TRUE when a variable exists.

Constants

Constants are similar to variables, but they may be set only once. Some of them are created automatically by PHP; others you will create with the define function discussed in Chapter 9. You do not use the dollar-sign operator to get the value of a constant, and a constant may never be used on

---
Listing 2.6   Using a Constant

```
<?
        define("STANDARD_GREETING", "Hello, World!");
        print(STANDARD_GREETING);
?>
```

---

the left side of an assignment operator. Constants ignore scope and are therefore visible inside functions without the use of the `global` statement.

Although it is not necessary, it is customary to name constants exclusively with capital letters. This helps make them stand out in your script, as in Listing 2.6.

PHP creates several constants upon startup. `PHP_VERSION` contains the version of PHP running the script. `TRUE` is set to 1. `FALSE` is set to 0. `PHP_OS` describes the operating system. `E_ERROR`, `E_WARNING`, `E_NOTICE`, `E_PARSE`, `E_ALL` are for use with the `error_reporting` function. You can also use `__FILE__` and `__LINE__` to get the name of the executing script and the line number, respectively. The value of `pi` is stored in the constant `M_PI`. Some extensions create constants, too.

Operators

An operator is a symbol that tells PHP to perform a mathematical or logical operation. Some operators expect two arguments, some only one. Most operators fall into three categories: arithmetic, logical, and bitwise. There are some exceptions, however. Table 2.4 lists the arithmetic operators.

Addition, subtraction, multiplication, and division are familiar concepts. They may be applied to integers or doubles. Using a string with an arithmetic operator causes the string to be converted to a number first. Modulo division

Table 2.4	Arithmetic Operators

Operator	*Operation It Performs*
+	Addition
–	Subtraction and Negation
*	Multiplication
/	Division
%	Modulo Division
++	Increment
– –	Decrement

returns the integer remainder of a division. The – operator may also be used to swap the sign on a number or variable.

The increment and decrement operators are shorthand for adding or subtracting 1 from a variable. You might remember that we used it in Listing 2.3 inside the `for` loop. You may put an increment or decrement operator before or after a variable. If the variable is within an expression, you will get one of two behaviors. If an increment operator precedes the variable, the variable will be incremented prior to evaluation of the expression; otherwise the variable isn't operated on until after the value of the expression is computed. Listing 2.7 demonstrates this concept.

Listing 2.7	Comparing Preincrement to Postincrement

```
<?
    $VisitorsToday = 1;

    // prints 1
    print($VisitorsToday++);

    // VisitorsToday is now 2
    print("<BR>\n");

    // prints 3
    print(++$VisitorsToday);

    print("<BR>\n");
?>
```

In this first `print` statement `VisitorsToday` still contains the value 1 when it is printed, because the increment operator isn't applied until after the expression is evaluated. In the third `print` statement `VisitorsToday` is incremented before the expression is evaluated; therefore 3 is sent to the browser.

Logical and Relational Operators

Relational operators compare values and return either TRUE or FALSE. Logical operators perform logical operations on TRUE and FALSE. Values used with a logical operator are converted into booleans prior to being evaluated. For numerical values, zero will be interpreted as FALSE, and other values will be TRUE. Empty strings are considered be FALSE, and any nonempty string is TRUE. Table 2.5 lists the logical and relational operators.

Notice that the equality operator is very similar to the assignment operator. That's reasonable. One performs the action of making both sides equal; the right-side value is copied to the variable on the left side. The other asks the question, "Are both sides equal?" The inherent danger is that the two can be confused, and it is difficult to discover. PHP will allow you to put an assignment inside the parentheses of an `if` statement. If you have an `if`

Table 2.5   Logical and Relational Operators

Operator	Operation Performed
<	Is Less Than
>	Is Greater Than
<=	Is Less Than or Equal To
>=	Is Greater Than or Equal To
==	Is Equal To
!=	Is Not Equal To
AND &&	And
OR ||	Or
XOR	Exclusive Or
!	Not

Table 2.6		Truth Table for Logical Operators			
p	*q*	*p AND q*	*p OR q*	*p XOR q*	*!p*
false	false	false	false	false	true
false	true	false	true	true	true
true	false	false	true	true	false
true	true	true	true	false	false

statement that always seems to evaluate one way, check to make sure you haven't typed = when you meant ==.

If you are unfamiliar with logical operations, refer to Table 2.6. The first two columns enumerate all the possible combined values of p and q, which stand for relational expressions. The other four columns show the results of performing a logical operation on p and q.

You might have noticed in Table 2.5 two versions of the logical operators. For instance, there is both && and AND. Operationally, they are the same, but they differ in precedence—a topic discussed at the end of this chapter. Aside from precedence, you are free to use them interchangeably.

Bitwise Operators

A binary digit, which may be 1 or 0, is called a bit. Bitwise operators are similar to logical operators, but where logical operators work on TRUE and FALSE, bitwise operators view numbers from a binary perspective. When using logical operators, 1 and 10 are both TRUE, but to a bitwise operator 1 looks like 0001 and 10 looks like 1010. A logical AND of 1 and 10 results in TRUE. A bitwise AND of 1 and 10 results in 0. This is because each bit of the two numbers is compared by a bitwise AND. Table 2.7 lists PHP's bitwise operators.

See Table 2.8 for an example of a bitwise operation, which shows that (12 & 10) == 8. Matching bits are operated on. In the rightmost position 0 and 0 are operated on with a bitwise AND. The result is 0, so a 0 is put in this position of the result.

Bitwise operators are very useful in C, from which PHP takes inspiration, but you rarely will need to use them in a PHP script. You will find some functions in the reference chapters (8 through 14) that use bitfields.

Table 2.7	Bitwise Operators
Operator	*Operation Performed*
&	And
|	Or
^	Exclusive Or
~	One's Complement or NOT
>>	Shift all bits to the right
<<	Shift all bits to the left

Miscellaneous Operators

There are operators that don't fit into any of the previous categories: the concatenation operator, the variable marker, the reference operator, and others. Table 2.9 lists them.

The concatenation operator is similar to the addition operator except that it joins two strings. I find this operator indispensable. When issuing a `print`, it is convenient to concatenate several strings. I also use the concatenation operator to build database queries. Listing 2.8 is an example of doing this.

When variables were discussed earlier, it was shown that a dollar sign always precedes the name of a variable. This is true whether the variable is global, local, or a function argument. The operator can be taken to mean, "Use the value stored in the named variable." If an ampersand precedes the dollar sign, it changes the meaning of the operation to be, "Use the memory set aside to store the data for the variable." This is similar to the `new` operator in C++ and other languages. This subtle difference is useful in declaring and calling functions.

Table 2.8	Bitwise AND of 12 and 10				
	1	1	0	0	(12)
&	1	0	1	0	(10)
	1	0	0	0	(8)

Table 2.9	Miscellaneous Operators

Operator	*Operation Performed*
.	Concatenate
$	Reference a Variable
&	Reference Variable Storage
->	Reference a Class Method or Property
=>	Set Argument Default or Assign Array Element Index
@	Suppress Error Messages
?	Tertiary Conditional Expression
{}	Variable Embedded in a String

When a function is called with an argument, the value of the argument is passed to the function and put into the special argument variable in the function declaration. If a variable is used inside a function call, only the value of the variable is sent to the function. If you choose to change the value of an argument, the original variable will be unchanged.

However, if you put an ampersand before the dollar sign in a function declaration, the function will expect a reference to a variable. Inside the function the argument acts like an alias to the supplied variable; any change to the argument changes the variable named in the function call. This behavior is discussed and demonstrated in Chapter 4.

Outside of functions, the ampersand allows you to make more than one variable point to the same area of memory. This is like making an alias. Operations on either variable will change the underlying memory, as demonstrated in Listing 2.9.

Listing 2.8	The Concatenation Operator

```
<?
      $Query = "SELECT LastName, FirstName " .
          "FROM Clients " .
          "WHERE Disposition = 'Pleasant' " .
          "ORDER BY LastName ";


      print($Query);
?>
```

Listing 2.9   The Reference Operator

```
<?
        $s = "Leon";
        $t = &$s;
        $t .= " Atkinson";

        print("$s<BR>\n");
        print("$t<BR>\n");
?>
```

The dollar-sign operator may operate on the result of another dollar-sign operator. In the simplest case a variable holds the name of another variable. This is shown in Listing 2.10.

Note that { and } is used for grouping as the parentheses are used for numbers. This eliminates the ambiguity that can arise when referencing arrays. It also allows you to specify elements of multidimensional arrays inside strings. But even when not strictly necessary, it's a good idea to use curly braces as I have in Listing 2.10. It's clear that I mean to use a variable to name another variable here.

The dollar-sign operator is unique because it is executed when placed inside double quotes. This allows you to avoid the extra code needed to break from a string to insert the value of a variable. But dollar signs inside double quotes do not behave exactly like dollar signs outside double quotes. When two or more dollar signs appear together, all but the last will be treated as any other character with no meaning. To use one variable to name another, use curly braces. Listing 2.10 demonstrates the subtleties of this functionality.

The -> operator is used strictly to reference either methods or properties of classes, which are discussed in Chapter 6. The left-hand side of the

Listing 2.10	Using Variables to Name Variables

```
<?
        //set variables
        $var_name = "myValue";
        $myValue = 123.456;
        $array_name = "myArray";
        $myArray = array(1,2,3);

        //prints "123.456"
        print($$var_name . "<BR>\n");

        //prints "$myValue"
        //perhaps not what you expect
        print("$$var_name<BR>\n");

        //prints "123.456"
        print("${$var_name}<BR>\n");

        //prints "3"
        print(${$array_name}[2] . "<BR>\n");
?>
```

operator is the name of an instantiated class; the right-hand side is the name of a function or variable inside the class.

The => operator is used in declaring arrays, discussed in Chapter 5. When creating an array with the array statement, you may specify the index for an element with the => operator. The left-hand side of the operator is the index and the right-hand side is the value. This operator is also used by the foreach statement in much the same way.

The ? operator is equivalent to an if statement. It is called a tertiary operator, because it takes three parameters: an expression that is evaluated to be TRUE or FALSE, an expression that's evaluated if the first is true, and an expression that's evaluated if the first is false. A complete discussion of the ? operator appears in Chapter 3, "Control Statements."

The @ operator suppresses any error messages when it precedes an expression. Normally when a built-in function encounters an error, text is sent directly to the browser. Sometimes this is just warning text. If you want to suppress any error or warning messages, place @ directly before the name of the function. You may also place @ before an expression if you anticipate an error condition, such as division by zero. Error messages may also be suppressed for all functions in a script with the `error_reporting` function.

Assignment Operators

There really is only one assignment operator, but PHP offers a handful of shortcut operators for combining assignment with another operator. Table 2.10 lists all the assignment operators.

All the assignment operators put a value into a variable. Specifically, they put a value on the right side into a variable on the left side. You may not reverse the order. The operators that combine another operator with an assignment operator operate on both the right and left sides and then put the result in the variable on the left. Listing 2.11 demonstrates equivalent statements.

Expressions

Expressions are combinations of identifiers and operators. In most cases, they are the familiar formulas you learned about in high school algebra. They are executed from left to right; some operators are processed before others,

Table 2.10	Assignment Operators
Operator	*Operation Performed*
=	Assign right side to left side
+=	Add right side to left side
-=	Subtract right side from left side
*=	Multiply left side by right side
/=	Divide left side by right side
%=	Set left side to left side modulo right side
&=	Set left side to bitwise AND of left side and right side
|=	Set left side to bitwise OR of left side and right side
^=	Set left side to bitwise XOR of left side and right side
.=	Set left side to concatenation of left side and right side

Listing 2.11   Using Assignment Operators

```
<?
     // this assignment
     $Count = $Count + 1;

     // is the same as this assignment
     $Count += 1;
?>
```

and you can use parentheses to force an operation to occur before the rest of the expression. But since the expression may be a mix of different data types, you must be aware of how types are converted.

Two general rules are at work when an expression is evaluated. First, some operators work only on certain data types. Second, if the operation is on a mix of an integer and a double, the integer will be converted to a double.

Most operators work on numbers. If you attempt to add a string, the string will be converted to a number. The contents of the string will determine whether it becomes an integer or a double. PHP will make a good attempt at converting your string to a number. It will strip leading whitespace and it will strip off all characters after a string of digits. It will even read doubles with

Listing 2.12   String/Number Conversion

```
<?
     //1 + 1 == 2
     print((1 + "1") . "<BR>\n");

     //1 + 2 == 3
     print((1 + " 2") . "<BR>\n");

     //1 + 3 == 4
     print((1 + "3extra stuff") . "<BR>\n");

     //1 + 4500000 == 4500001
     print((1 + "4.5e6") . "<BR>\n");

     //1 + 0 == 1
     print((1 + "a7") . "<BR>\n");
?>
```

an exponent. But if PHP can't decide on a reasonable numerical value, it will treat your string as zero.

Listing 2.12 is a good test of how PHP will convert strings to numbers. All the commands will produce a number from the string, except the last. Since the string in the last line begins with a letter, PHP gives up and treats it as zero. Notice that after the addition the script uses a concatenation operator. This causes the integer created inside the parentheses to be converted to a string for the purposes of printing. The concatenation operator forces both sides to be treated as strings.

Listing 2.13 demonstrates the use of parentheses to force the order in which the expression is evaluated. The first line evaluates to 17, the second to 35. In addition to evaluation from left to right, operators execute in a specific precedence. For example, multiplication is resolved before addition.

A programming language must order all its operators, but in practice it is difficult for the programmer to keep it all straight. The best policy is to use parentheses to explicitly force the precedence you want on complex expressions. Table 2.11 lists the operators in order of precedence. Operators on the same line are of equal precedence, therefore falling back to left-to-right precedence.

Listing 2.13   Using Parentheses

```
<?
     print ((3 + 2 * 7) . "<BR>\n");
     print (((3 + 2) * 7) . "<BR>\n");
?>
```

Table 2.11	Precedence of Operators

Highest	[ ]
	( ) { }
	~ ! ++ − − $ & @
	(double) (integer) (string) (array) (object)
	* / %
	+ − .
	<< >>
	< > <= >=
	== !=
	&
	^
	&&
	? :
	= += −= *= /= &= |= ^= .= <<= >>=
	AND
	XOR
	OR
Lowest	'

CONTROL STATEMENTS

Chapter 3

C ontrol statements allow you to execute blocks of code depending on conditions. They also allow you to repeat a block of code, which leads to simpler, more efficient scripts. This chapter will introduce you to the decision-making statements `if` and `switch`. You will also learn about loops using `for` and `while`.

True and False

As you remember from Chapter 2, PHP has the concepts of true and false. Zero and an empty string are considered to be false. Any other numerical value or string is true. These concepts were discussed in regard to relational operators, but they are also used in control statements. Control statements like `if` expect a boolean value, so any value they are given will be converted to a boolean.

The `if` Statement

Figure 3–1 lays out the form of an `if` statement.

```
if(expression1)
{
    This block gets executed if expression1 is true.
}
elseif(expression2)
{
    This block gets executed if expression1
    is false and expression 2 is true.
}
else
{
    This block gets executed if both expression1
    and expression2 are false.
}
```

Figure 3–1 The form of an `if` statement.

The `if` statement executes a statement if the expression inside the parentheses evaluates to true; otherwise the code is skipped. It may be a single statement followed by a semicolon. Usually it's a compound statement surrounded by curly braces. An `else` statement may appear immediately after the statement and has a statement of its own. It, too, may be either single or compound. It is executed only when the previous expression is false. In between an `if` statement and an `else` statement you may put as many `elseif` statements as you'd like. Each `elseif` expression is evaluated in turn, and control skips past those that are `false`. If an `elseif` statement evaluates to true, then the rest of the code in the greater `if` statement is skipped. That is to say, only one match will be made. Listing 3.1 demonstrates an `if-elseif-else` statement.

Of course, you are not obligated to have an `elseif` or an `else`. Sometimes you might want to build a very simple `if` statement as in Listing 3.2.

You can use `if` to build a series of checks that covers all possible cases. Just start by checking for the first condition with an `if`; then check for each following condition with an `elseif`. If you put an `else` at the end, you will have accounted for all possible cases. Listing 3.3 uses this method to print the day of the week in German. The script gets today's name and then com-

---

Listing 3.1   An `if-elseif-else` Statement

```
<?
    if($name == "")
    {
        print("You have no name.");
    }
    elseif(($name == "leon") OR ($name == "Leon"))
    {
        print("Hello, Leon!");
    }
    else
    {
        print("Your name is '$name'.");
    }
?>
```

pares it to the days Monday through Saturday. If none of these match, it is assumed to be Sunday.

Listing 3.2   A Simple `if` Statement

```
<?
    if(date("D") == "Mon")
    {
        print("Remember to put the trash out.");
    }
?>
```

The **?** Operator

PHP offers an abbreviated version of the `if` statement which borrows syntax from C. It uses the question mark as a tertiary operator. Figure 3–2 outlines the format.

```
conditional expression ? true expression : false expression;
```

Figure 3–2   The **?** operator.

Listing 3.3   Covering All Cases with `if-elseif-else`

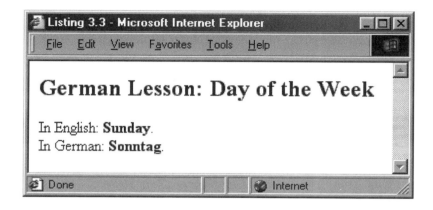

```
<?
    /*
    ** Get today's weekday name
    */
    $english_Day = date("l");
    /*
    ** Find the today's German name
    */
    if($english_Day == "Monday")
    {
        $deutsch_Day = "Montag";
    }
    elseif($english_Day == "Tuesday")
    {
        $deutsch_Day = "Dienstag";
    }
    elseif($english_Day == "Wednesday")
    {
        $deutsch_Day = "Mittwoch";
    }
    elseif($english_Day == "Thursday")
    {
        $deutsch_Day = "Donnerstag";
    }
    elseif($english_Day == "Friday")
    {
        $deutsch_Day = "Freitag";
    }
```

```
        elseif($english_Day == "Saturday")
        {
                $deutsch_Day = "Samstag";
        }
        else
        {
                // It must be Sunday
                $deutsch_Day = "Sonntag";
        }

        /*
        ** Print today's English and German names
        */
        print("<H2>German Lesson: Day of the Week</H2>\n");
        print("In English: <B>$english_Day</B>.<BR>\n");
        print("In German: <B>$deutsch_Day</B>.<BR>\n");
?>
```

The conditional expression is evaluated to be either true or false. If true, the expression between the question mark and the colon is executed. Otherwise, the expression after the colon is executed. The following code fragment

```
($clientQueue > 0) ? serveClients() : cleanUp();
```

does the same thing as

```
if($clientQueue > 0)
        serveClients();
else
        cleanUp();
```

The similarity is deceiving. Although the abbreviated form seems to be equivalent to using if-else, at a deeper level it is not. As I said, ? is an operator, not a statement. This means that the expression as a whole will be evaluated. The value of the matched expression takes the place of the ? expression. In other words, something like

```
print(true ? "it's true" : "it's false");
```

is a valid statement. Since the conditional expression is true, the line will be transformed into

```
print("it's true");
```

which is something you can't do with an `if` statement.

The `?` operator can be confusing to read and is never necessary. It wouldn't be bad if you never used it. On the other hand it allows you to write very compact code.

The `switch` Statement

An alternative to `if-elseif-else` structures is the `switch` statement, which works on the assumption that you compare a single expression to a set of possible values. Figure 3–3 demonstrates the structure of a `switch` statement.

```
switch(root-expression)
{
      case case-expression:
      default:
}
```

Figure 3–3   The `switch` statement.

The root expression inside a switch statement is evaluated and then compared to each expression following a `case` statement. At the end of the list of cases you can put a `default` statement that works exactly like an `else` statement; it matches if no other case matches.

Notice that cases don't have curly braces after them. This reveals an important difference between `if` and `switch`. When an `if` block matches and is executed, control skips to the end of the entire `if` statement. In Listing 3.3, if today is Tuesday, `deutsch_Day` is set to `Dienstag`, and control jumps down to after the closing curly brace closing the `else` block.

A `case` statement serves as a starting point for execution. The root expression is compared to each case expression until one matches. Each line of code after that is executed. If another `case` statement is reached, it is ignored. Sometimes this is useful, but most often a `break` statement is used to escape from the `switch` statement.

Take a look at Listing 3.4. I've recoded Listing 3.3 using a `switch` statement. The best argument for using `switch` is that it can be much easier to understand. Since PHP allows you to compare strings, the `switch` statement

Listing 3.4   Covering All Cases with `switch`

```php
<?
    /*
    ** Get today's weekday name
    */
    $english_Day = date("l");
    /*
    ** Find the today's German name
    */
    switch($english_Day)
    {
        case "Monday":
            $deutsch_Day = "Montag";
            break;
        case "Tuesday":
            $deutsch_Day = "Dienstag";
            break;
        case "Wednesday":
            $deutsch_Day = "Mittwoch";
            break;
        case "Thursday":
            $deutsch_Day = "Donnerstag";
            break;
        case "Friday":
            $deutsch_Day = "Freitag";
            break;
        case "Saturday":
            $deutsch_Day = "Samstag";
            break;
        default:
            // It must be Sunday
            $deutsch_Day = "Sonntag";
    }
    /*
    ** Print today's English and German names
    */
    print("<H2>German Lesson: Day of the Week</H2>\n");
    print("In English: <B>$english_Day</B>.<BR>\n");
    print("In German: <B>$deutsch_Day.</B><BR>\n");
?>
```

is much more useful than in other languages. If you have experience with BASIC, you might wonder if PHP's `switch` statement allows cases to contain ranges. It doesn't. It's probably best to code this situation with an `if-elseif-else` statement.

Loops

Loops allow you to repeat lines of code based on some condition. You might want to read lines from a file until the end is reached. You might want to print a section of HTML code exactly ten times. You may even wish to attempt to connect to a database three times before giving up. You can do all of these things with loops.

The `while` Statement

The simplest of loops is the `while` statement. When first reached, the expression is evaluated. If false, the code block is skipped. If true, the block is executed and then control returns to the top where, again, the expression is evaluated. Figure 3–4 shows the structure of a `while` statement.

```
while(expression)
{
      Zero or more statements
}
```

Figure 3–4   The `while` statement.

A `while` loop is useful when you aren't sure exactly how many times you will need to iterate through the code—for example, when reading lines from a file or fetching rows from a database query. For the sake of a simple demonstration, let's examine some code that prints the days of the week between now and Friday.

The `while` loop in Listing 3.5 tests that the date stored in `currentDate` is not a Friday. If it is, then the loop will be finished, and execution will continue after the closing curly brace. But if the current date is not a Friday,

Listing 3.5   Using **while** to Print Day Names

```
<?
     /*
     ** get the current date in number of seconds
     */
     $currentDate = time();
     /*
     ** print some text explaining the output
     */
     print("Days left before Friday:\n");
     print("<OL>\n");
     while(date("l", $currentDate) != "Friday")
     {
          /*
          ** print day name
          */
          print("<LI>" . date("l", $currentDate) . "\n");
          /*
          ** add 24 hours to currentDate
          */
          $currentDate += (60 * 60 * 24);
     }
     print("</OL>\n");
?>
```

then a list item with the name of the day is printed and `currentDate` is advanced 24 hours. At that point, the end of the code block is reached, so control jumps back to the beginning of the loop.

Again the current date is tested for being a Friday. Eventually, `current-Date` will be a Friday and the loop will end. But what if I had done something silly such as comparing the current date to `"Workday"`? There is no weekday with that name, so the expression will always be true. That is, `date("l", $currentDate) != "Workday"` must always be true. The result is a loop that goes on forever. I might as well write it as `while(true)` and make it very clear.

When a loop continues with no end, it's called an infinite loop. If you find your page loading forever and ever, you may have accidentally written an infinite loop. At times, you may intentionally create an infinite loop but stop execution somewhere in the middle of the code block. This is accomplished with the `break` statement.

The break Statement

When a `break` statement is encountered, execution jumps outside the innermost loop or `switch` statement. You've seen that this is essential to the usefulness of `switch` statements. It also has some application for loops. There are cases when you need to leave a loop block somewhere in the middle. Listing 3.6 shows this in action.

Listing 3.6   Leaving a Loop Using `break`

```
<?
    while(true)
    {
        print("This line is printed.");
        break;
        print("This line will never be printed.");
    }
?>
```

The continue Statement

The continue statement is similar to the break statement except that instead of stopping the loop entirely, only the current execution of the loop is stopped. Control is returned to the closing curly brace and the loop continues. Inside for loops, described below, increments will occur just as if control had reached the end of the loop otherwise.

As you might imagine, this function is used to skip parts of a loop when a condition is met. Listing 3.7 demonstrates this idea. Random numbers are

Listing 3.7   The continue Statement

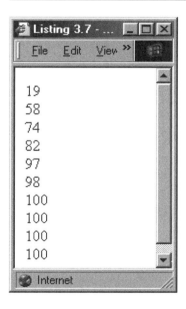

```
<?
    /*
    ** get ten random numbers,
    ** each greater than the next
    */
    //seed random number generator
    srand(time());

    //init variables
```

```
$count = 0;
$max = 0;

//get ten random numbers
while($count < 10)
{
        $value = rand(1,100);

        //try again if $value is too small
        if($value < $max)
        {
                continue;
        }

        $count++;
        $max = $value;

        print("$value <BR>\n");
}
?>
```

generated inside a loop until ten numbers, each greater than the previous, are produced. Most of the time the body of the loop is skipped due to the `if` statement that triggers a `continue` statement.

The do...while Statement

You can delay the decision to continue executing a loop until the end by using a do...while statement. Listing 3.8 retools Listing 3.7. You won't notice a difference unless you run the script on a Friday. On Fridays the original will print nothing in its list of days. The new version will put Friday in the list because the body of the loop is executed before `currentDate` is tested. By switching to a do...while loop, the loop now lists the days until next Friday.

Listing 3.8   Using do...while to Print Day Names

```
<?
    /*
    ** get the current date in number of seconds
```

```
*/
$currentDate = time();
/*
** print some text explaining the output
*/
print("Days left before next Friday:\n");
print("<OL>\n");
do
{
        /*
        ** print day name
        */
        print("<LI>" . date("l", $currentDate) . "\n");
        /*
        ** add 24 hours to currentDate
        */
        $currentDate += (60 * 60 * 24);
}
while(date("l", $currentDate) != "Friday");
print("</OL>\n");
?>
```

The for Statement

Strictly speaking, the for loop is unnecessary. Any for loop can be implemented as easily as a while loop. What for offers is not new functionality, but a better structure for building the most common loops. Many loops involve incrementing a counter variable every time through the loop, iterating until some maximum is reached.

Imagine that you wanted to step through the numbers 1 through 10. Using while, you would first set a variable to be 1. Then you would make a while loop that tests if your counter is less than or equal to 10. Inside the code block you would increment your counter, making sure you do this as the last statement in the block.

The problem is that it is very easy to forget to put the increment in. The result is an infinite loop. The for loop puts all this functionality in one place. Inside the for statement you give it three things: an initialization statement, a boolean expression, and an increment statement. Figure 3–5 defines a for loop.

```
for(initialization; continue; increment)
{
    Zero or more statements
}
```

Figure 3–5   The **for** statement.

When first encountered, the initialization statement is executed. This traditionally takes the form of assigning a variable to be 0 or 1. Then, as with a while statement, the boolean expression is evaluated. If FALSE, control jumps to just after the code block. Otherwise, the code block is executed. Before the boolean expression is evaluated again, the increment statement is executed. This puts all the information needed for running the loop in one place and forces you to think about all the steps. Listing 3.9 is a very simple for loop but is typical in form.

Listing 3.9   A Typical for Loop

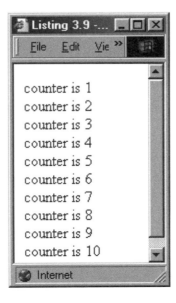

```
<?
        for($counter = 1; $counter <= 10; $counter++)
        {
                print("counter is $counter<BR>\n");
        }
?>
```

Most `for` loops look like Listing 3.9. They use a counter that increments by one each time through the loop. However, the `for` statement is not particular about what you put in the three slots. You can use more complex expressions if you wish. The initialization slot allows a comma-separated list of assignments. This can be used to assign values to two or more variables. You may also leave a slot blank. Listing 3.10 converts the code in Listing 3.6 into a `for` loop. I've added line breaks to the `for` statement to keep the code from wrapping. It also makes it easier to see the three parts. Although the `for` statement is longer and looks more complicated, it really is no different from the simple example in Listing 3.9. A variable, in this case `currentDate`, is set to some initial value. That value is used to test for an end condition. And the value is incremented by the number of seconds in a day instead of just one.

Listing 3.10   Using `for` to Print Day Names

```
<?
        /*
        ** print some text explaining the output
        */
        print("Days left before Friday:\n");
        print("<OL>\n");
        for($currentDate = date("U");
                date("l", $currentDate) != "Friday";
                $currentDate += (60 * 60 * 24))
        {
                /*
                ** print day name
                */
                print("<LI>" . date("l", $currentDate) . "\n");
        }
        print("</OL>\n");
?>
```

The foreach Statement

I must discuss the foreach statement here, although it is used with arrays, which are discussed in Chapter 5. An array is a collection of values referenced by keys. The foreach statement retrieves values from an array, one at a time. Like other looping structures, the foreach statement may have a simple or compound statement that's executed each time through the loop. Figure 3–6 shows the structure of a foreach statement.

```
foreach(array as key=>value)
{
      Zero or more statements
}
```

Figure 3–6   The **foreach** statement.

The foreach statement expects an array, the keyword as, and a definition of the variables to receive each element. If a single value follows as, such as foreach($array as $value), then with each turn of the loop, the variable named value will be set with the value of the next array element. You may capture the index of the array element if you form the foreach statement like foreach($array as $key=>$value). Keep this statement in mind and I will revisit it in Chapter 5.

exit, die, and return

Like break, the exit statement offers a way to escape from execution, but the exit statement stops all execution. Not even text outside of PHP tags is sent to the browser. This is useful when an error occurs and it would be more harmful to continue executing code than to just abort. This is often the case when preparing database queries. If the SQL statement cannot be parsed, it makes no sense to try to execute it.

The die statement is similar to exit, except that it may be followed by an expression that will be sent to the browser just before aborting the script. Using the fact that subexpressions in an if statement are evaluated left to right and only as necessary, the idiom in Listing 3.11 is allowed. Notice the parentheses around the string to be printed when the open fails. They are required.

Listing 3.11   Idiom for Using the `die` Statement

```
$fp = fopen("somefile.txt", "r") OR die("Unable to open file");
```

You will learn about the more traditional use of the `return` statement in Chapter 4, but there is an unusual use of `return` offered by PHP when a script uses the `include` function, described in Chapter 7. If called outside of a function, the `return` statement stops execution of the current script and returns control to the script that made a call to `include`. That is, when a script uses the `include` function, the included script may return prematurely. If you use `return` in a script that was not invoked by `include`, the script will simply terminate as if `exit` were used.

I admit this is a strange concept, and it probably deserves to have its own name instead of sharing one with the statement for returning from functions. On the other hand, in certain special cases, it allows for tidy code. One example is to avoid including a file twice, as described in Chapter 20.

Evaluation of Boolean Expressions

The conditional statements in this chapter may be compound expressions, of course. PHP will evaluate an expression only to the point of determining its ultimate value. The classic situation is an expression that uses the `or` operator. PHP first evaluates the left side of the `or` operator. If this subexpression is true, then there is no need to proceed. The entire expression will be true. This can lead to unexpected functionality if you are embedding function calls or assignment statements in your boolean expressions, but this isn't a good idea anyway. However, there are ways to take advantage of this behavior. An example is testing for something that should be true and calling an error-handling routine on the right side of an `or` statement.

FUNCTIONS

Topics in This Chapter

Chapter 4

You probably have noticed the use of several functions in the preceding chapters. `Date` and `print` are built-in functions that are always available for you. PHP also allows you to declare your own functions.

Functions expand the idea of repeating a block of code. They allow you to execute a block of code arbitrarily throughout your script. You declare a block of code as a function and then you are able to call the function anywhere. When calling a function, you pass any number of arguments, and the function, returns a value.

Declaring a Function

When you declare a function, you start with the `function` statement. Next comes a name for your function. Inside the parentheses is a list of arguments separated by commas. You may choose to have no arguments. Figure 4–1 shows you the form of a function declaration.

```
function function_name(arguments)
{
 code block
}
```

Figure 4–1   Declaring a function.

In other languages, including older versions of PHP, you must declare a function above any call to it. This is not true of PHP 4. You may put a function declaration after calls made to it. When you call a function, you write its name followed by parentheses, even if there are no arguments to pass.

Functions allow you to put together a block of code that you will repeat several times throughout your script. Your motivation may be to avoid typing identical code in two or more places, or it could be to make your code easier to understand. Consider Listing 4.1. It declares a function called printBold that prints any text with bold tags around it.

Listing 4.1   A Simple Function

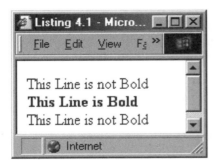

```
<?
        function printBold($inputText)
        {
                print("<B>" . $inputText . "</B>");
        }

        print("This Line is not Bold<BR>\n");
        printBold("This Line is Bold");
        print("<BR>\n");
        print("This Line is not Bold<BR>\n");
?>
```

The return Statement

At some point a function will be finished, ready to return control to its caller. This happens, for example, when execution reaches the end of the function's block of code. Execution then picks up directly after the point where the function was called. Another way to stop execution of the function is to use the return statement.

You may have multiple return statements in your function, though you have to consider how this reduces the readability of your code. Multiple return statements can be a barrier to understanding the flow of execution. Ideally functions should have one way in and one way out. In practice there are cases when multiple return statements are acceptable.

If you follow return with an expression, the value of the expression will be passed back. Listing 4.2 demonstrates this idea by taking a string and returning it wrapped in bold tags.

Listing 4.2   A Simple Function Using return

```
<?
    function makeBold($inputText)
    {
        $boldedText = "<B>";
        $boldedText .= $inputText;
        $boldedText .= "</B>";

        return($boldedText);
    }

    print("This Line is not Bold<BR>\n");
    print(makeBold("This Line is Bold") . "<BR>\n");
    print("This Line is not Bold<BR>\n");
?>
```

Scope and the global Statement

As discussed in Chapter 2, variables inside a function exist inside a name space separate from the global name space. Variables inside a function are private property and may never be seen or manipulated outside the function.

However, there are two ways a function may access variables in the global scope: the `global` statement and the `GLOBALS` array.

The `global` statement brings a variable into a function's name space. Thereafter the variable may be used as if it were outside the function. Any changes to the variable will persist after execution of the function ceases. In the same way, it is possible to refer to global variables through the array `GLOBALS`. The array is indexed by variable names, so if you create a variable named `userName` you can manipulate it inside a function by writing `$GLOBALS["userName"]`.

Also noted in Chapter 2 is the idea of static variables. If a variable is declared to be static, it retains its value between function calls. Listing 2.3 demonstrates the use of static variables.

Arguments

When declaring a function, you may declare arguments inside the parentheses, each separated by a comma. The arguments must be preceded by a dollar sign. They become variables inside the function. When the function is called, it expects values to be passed that will fill the arguments in the order declared.

Arguments, by default, copy the passed value into the local variable. If the variable is preceded by the `&` operator, the variable instead becomes an alias for the passed variable. This is commonly referred to as a variable reference. Changes made to referenced variables change the original.

To demonstrate this idea, imagine we wanted a function that stripped commas from numbers. That way if we got something like "10,000" from an input field we would know it was ten thousand, not ten. We could build the function by passing a string and returning it with the commas removed. But in this case we want to just pass the variable and have it be changed. Listing 4.3 demonstrates this functionality.

It is also possible to make an argument optional. Many built-in functions provide this functionality. The `date` function is one you should be familiar with by now. You can pass one or two arguments to `date`. The first argument is the format of the return value. The second argument is the timestamp, a date expressed in seconds since January 1, 1970. If the second argument is omitted, the current time is used.

You do this in your own functions by providing a default value using the `=` operator immediately after the argument. The right side of `=` is a literal value

Listing 4.3   Passing Arguments by Reference

```
<?
        function stripCommas(&$inputString)
        {
                $inputString = ereg_replace(",", "", $inputString);
        }

        $myNumber = "10,000";

        stripCommas($myNumber);
        print($myNumber);
?>
```

that the variable will be assigned. See Listing 4.4. Since arguments are matched up left to right, you must provide a default value for every argument after the first with a default value.

You may set an argument to be unset by default by making it equal to NULL, a special constant. Listing 4.5 demonstrates this functionality.

Other than named arguments, you may also access arguments by their position using three functions, func_get_arg, func_get_args, func_num_args. These functions are described in Chapter 8. You may either fetch one argument at a time using func_get_arg, or fetch them all as an array using func_get_args. To find out how many arguments were passed, use func_num_args. There is an implication lurking here. Calling a function

Listing 4.4   Arguments with Default Values

```
<?
        function printColored($Text, $Color="black")
        {
                print("<FONT COLOR=\"$Color\">$Text</FONT>");
        }

        printColored("This is black text");
        print("<BR>\n");

        printColored("This is blue text", "blue");
        print("<BR>\n");
?>
```

Listing 4.5   Using **unset** with a Default Argument

```
<?
        function myPrint($text, $size=NULL)
        {
                if(isset($size))
                {
                        print("<FONT SIZE=\"$size\">$text</FONT>")
                }
                else
                {
                        print($text);
                }
        }

        myPrint("Test");
        print("<BR>\n");

        myPrint("Test", 5);
        print("<BR>\n");
?>
```

with a number of arguments different from the prototype is not an error unless you write your function that way.

You might wonder why you'd ever want to pull arguments out using the functions mentioned above instead of naming them in the declaration. It's possible that you do not know how many arguments you will be given. Consider a function that creates a list, given any number of items. You could first place those items in an array, then pass the array to the function, which in turn would pull the items out of the array. Alternatively, you could write a function that accepted a variable number of arguments, as I have in Listing 4.6.

Listing 4.6   Function with Variable Number of Arguments

```
<?
    function makeList()
    {
        print("<OL>\n");

        for($i=0; $i < func_num_args(); $i++)
        {
            print("<LI>" . func_get_arg($i) . "\n");
        }

        print("</OL>\n");
    }

    makeList("PHP", "MySQL", "Apache");
?>
```

Recursion

Your functions may make calls to other functions, and they may also make calls to themselves. The process of a function calling itself is recursion. This circular definition usually leads to elegant algorithms. The problem is broken down into a small task that's repeated many times.

Recursive definitions are common in mathematics. Consider this definition of an integer: the sum or difference between one and any other integer, with one being an integer. Is three an integer? Yes, because one plus one must be an integer, which is two. And the sum of one and two must also be an integer.

Recursion is a difficult concept to understand, but it usually leads to clear code. Take a look at Listing 4.7. The function checkInteger takes a number as input. We know that the difference between an integer and one is an integer. So if the function gets a number bigger than one, it simply checks the number minus one. If we start out with a number less than zero, we multiply it by negative one and check it. Eventually we will reach one or a number between zero and one, unless we are passed zero, which is an integer.

Listing 4.7 Using Recursion

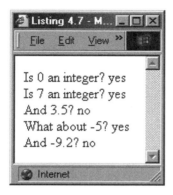

Is 0 an integer? yes
Is 7 an integer? yes
And 3.5? no
What about -5? yes
And -9.2? no

```
<?
        function checkInteger($Number)
        {
                if($Number > 1)
                {
                        // integer minus one is still an integer
                        return(checkInteger($Number-1));
                }
                elseif($Number < 0)
                {
                        /*
                        ** numbers are symmetrical, so
                        ** check positive version
                        */
                        return(checkInteger((-1)*$Number-1));
                }
                else
                {
                        if(($Number > 0) AND ($Number < 1))
                        {
                                return("no");
                        }
                        else
                        {
                                /*
                                ** zero and one are
                                ** integers by definition
                                */
                                return("yes");
                        }
                }
```

```
}
print("Is 0 an integer? " .
        checkInteger(0) . "<BR>\n");
print("Is 7 an integer? " .
        checkInteger(7) . "<BR>\n");
print("And 3.5? " . checkInteger(3.5) . "<BR>\n");
print("What about -5? " . checkInteger(-5) . "<BR>\n");
print("And -9.2? " . checkInteger(-9.2) . "<BR>\n");
?>
```

Dynamic Function Calls

You might find yourself in the position of not knowing which function should be called when you are writing a script. You want to decide based on data you have during execution. One way to accomplish this is to set a variable with the name of a function and then use the variable as if it were a function.

If you follow a variable with parentheses, the value of the variable will be treated as the name of a function. Listing 4.8 demonstrates this. Keep in mind that you can't refer to built-in functions in this way. Setting myFunction to be print will cause an error.

| Listing 4.8   Dynamically Calling a Function |

```
<?
    function write($text)
    {
        print($text);
    }

    function writeBold($text)
    {
        print("<B>$text</B>");
    }

    $myFunction = "write";
    $myFunction("Hello!");
    print("<BR>\n");

    $myFunction = "writeBold";
    $myFunction("Goodbye!");
    print("<BR>\n");
?>
```

ARRAYS

Topics in This Chapter

Chapter 5

rrays collect values into lists. You refer to an element in an array using an index, which is often an integer but can also be a string. And the value of the element can be text, a number, or even another array. When you build arrays of arrays, you get multidimensional arrays. Arrays are used extensively by PHP's built-in functions, and coding would be nearly impossible without them. There are many functions designed simply for manipulating arrays. They are discussed in detail in Chapter 9.

Single-Dimensional Arrays

To refer to an element of an array, you use square brackets. Inside the brackets you put the index of the element, as in Listing 5.1. This construct may be treated exactly like a variable. You may assign a value or pass its value to a function. You do not have to declare anything about the array before you use it. Like variables, any element of an array will be created on the fly. If you refer to an array element that does not exist, it will evaluate to be zero or an empty string depending on the context.

Single-dimensional arrays are lists of values under a common name. But you might wonder, "Why bother?" You could just as easily create variables

---

Listing 5.1   Referencing Array Elements

```
<?
        $Cities[0] = "San Francisco";
        $Cities[1] = "Los Angeles";
        $Cities[2] = "New York";
        $Cities[3] = "Martinez";

        print("I live in $Cities[3].<BR>\n");
?>
```

---

like "$Cities1, $Cities2, $Cities3" and not worry about square brackets. One reason is that it's easy to loop through all values of an array. If you know that all the elements of an array have been added using consecutive numbers, you can use a for loop to get each element. PHP makes it easy to create arrays that work this way; if you leave out an index when assigning an array element, PHP will start at zero and use consecutive integers thereafter. If you run the code in Listing 5.2, you will discover that the four cities have indexes of 0, 1, 2, and 3.

Indexing Arrays

So far we've only seen arrays indexed by integers, but it is also permissible to use strings. Sometimes these are called associative arrays, or hashes. They are helpful in situations where you are collecting different types of information into one array. You could build into your code a system where element zero is a name, element one is a location, and element two is an occupation. Listing 5.3 is a more elegant way to accomplish this.

Listing 5.2   Adding to an Array

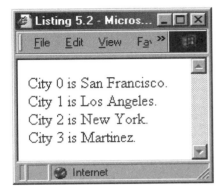

```
<?
        $Cities[] = "San Francisco";
        $Cities[] = "Los Angeles";
        $Cities[] = "New York";
        $Cities[] = "Martinez";

        /*
        ** count number of elements
        */
        $indexLimit = count($Cities);

        /*
        ** print out every element
        */
        for($index=0; $index < $indexLimit; $index++)
        {
                print("City $index is $Cities[$index]. <BR>\n");
        }
?>
```

Since we aren't indexing the array with integers, we can't just pull out each value starting at zero. If you've turned ahead briefly to skim the array functions in Chapter 9, you may have noticed functions like reset, next, and current. These functions offer one way to step through an array, and they are the best way if you need to do more than simply step through the array in order. You can also use the each function. However, PHP 4 added a new statement called

Listing 5.3   Indexing Arrays with Strings

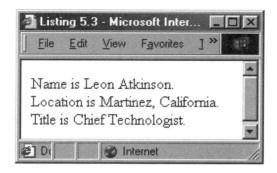

```
<?
        /*
        ** fill in some information
        */
        $UserInfo["Name"] = "Leon Atkinson";
        $UserInfo["Location"] = "Martinez, California";
        $UserInfo["Title"] = "Chief Technologist";

        foreach($UserInfo as $key=>$value)
        {
                print("$key is $value.<BR>\n");
        }
?>
```

foreach specifically for stepping through an array. The foreach statement is discussed in Chapter 3. It is like a for loop, but designed to pull elements from an array. You may wish to turn back and review it.

Initializing Arrays

In the situations where you want to fill an array with several values before you use it, it can become cumbersome to write an assignment for each element. PHP offers the array function to help in this matter. It takes a list of

---

Listing 5.4 Initializing an Array

```
<?
       $monthName = array(1=>"January", "February", "March",
             "April", "May", "June", "July", "August",
             "September", "October", "November", "December");

       print("Month 5 is $monthName[5] <BR>\n");
?>
```

---

values and returns an array. Listing 5.4 uses `array` to build an array of the months of the year.

Each value is just as it would be if it were on the right side of the assignment operator. Commas separate the values. By default, as with using empty brackets, elements will be numbered starting at zero. You can override this by using the `=>` operator. In Listing 5.4 I have set January to have the index 1. Each subsequent element is indexed by the next integer.

You aren't limited to setting the index for the first element, of course. You can assign the index for every element. And you aren't limited to assigning integers as indexes. Listing 5.5 builds an array for translating various ways to write a month into a single form.

Multidimensional Arrays

An array element can be any type of data. You've seen numbers and strings, but you can even put an array inside an array. An array of arrays is also called a multidimensional array. Imagine a ten-by-ten grid. You've got 100 different squares, each of which can have its own value. One way to represent this in code is a two-dimensional array: a ten-element array of ten-number arrays, ten rows of ten columns.

To reference a single element, you first use square brackets to pick the first dimension (row), then use a second pair of brackets to pick the second dimension (column). Row 3, column 7, would be written as `$someArray[3][7]`.

Listing 5.6 initializes a multidimensional array using the `array` function. This shows that multidimensional arrays are just arrays of arrays.

Listing 5.5   Using an Array to Translate Values

```
<?
    $monthName = array(
        1=>"January", "February", "March",
        "April", "May", "June",
        "July", "August", "September",
        "October", "November", "December",

        "Jan"=>"January", "Feb"=>"February",
        "Mar"=>"March", "Apr"=>"April",
        "May"=>"May", "Jun"=>"June",
        "Jul"=>"July", "Aug"=>"August",
        "Sep"=>"September", "Oct"=>"October",
        "Nov"=>"November", "Dec"=>"December",

        "January"=>"January", "February"=>"February",
        "March"=>"March", "April"=>"April",
        "May"=>"May", "June"=>"June",
        "July"=>"July", "August"=>"August",
        "September"=>"September", "October"=>"October",
        "November"=>"November", "December"=>"December"
        );

    print("Month 5 is " . $monthName[5] . "<BR>\n");
    print("Month Aug is " . $monthName["Aug"] . "<BR>\n");
    print("Month June is " .
    $monthName["June"] . "<BR>\n");
?>
```

Casting Arrays

You can cast an array as another data type to get results of various usefulness. When you cast an array as an integer, double or boolean, you will get a value of 1. When you cast an array as a string, you will get the word Array. This is useful as an indicator of when you have mistakenly used an array as a string. An array will be promoted to a string containing Array if you use it in a context that demands a string, such as in a print statement. You can't use an array in a con-

Listing 5.6   Creating and Referencing a Multidimensional Array

```
<?
    $Cities = array(
         "California"=>array(
                "Martinez",
                "San Francisco",
                "Los Angeles"
                ),
         "New York"=>array(
                "New York",
                "Buffalo"
                )
         );

    print($Cities["California"][1]);
?>
```

text that expects a number, such as with the addition operator. This will cause an error. Listing 5.7 explores casting an array as other data types.

The most useful cast of an array you can perform is to an object. The elements of the array will become properties of the object. However, elements indexed by values illegal as property names will remain inaccessible. These values are not lost, and if you recast the variable as an array, they will become available again. Objects are discussed in Chapter 6.

Referencing Arrays Inside Strings

As you know from Chapter 2, you may place a variable inside a string using double quotes. The variable's value will replace it. A single-dimensional array indexed by integers will be interpreted correctly inside double quotes, but other uses of arrays are problematic. To force the use of multidimensional arrays, use curly braces. These suspend the normal parsing that occurs within a double-quoted string. Of course, you may always concatenate strings. Listing 5.8 explores some different ways to use arrays inside strings.

Listing 5.7   Casting Arrays as Other Data Types

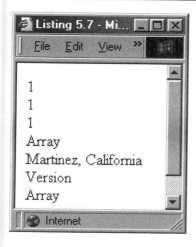

```
<?
    $userInfo = array("Name"=>"Leon Atkinson",
            "Location"=>"Martinez, California",
            "Occupation"=>"Web Engineer",
            "PHP Version"=>4.0);

    //Whether a boolean, integer or double,
    //PHP converts the array to 1
    $asBool = (boolean)$userInfo;
    print("$asBool <BR>\n");

    $asInt = (integer)$userInfo;
    print("$asInt <BR>\n");

    $asDouble = (double)$userInfo;
    print("$asDouble <BR>\n");

    //When converting to a string, PHP
    //returns the string "Array"
    $asString = (string)$userInfo;
    print("$asString <BR>\n");

    //When converting the array to an object,
    //PHP tries to convert all elements to properties.
```

```
        //Elements with spaces in their keys are not lost,
        //but are inaccessible.
        $asObject = (object)$userInfo;
        print("$asObject->Location <BR>\n");
        print("$asObject->PHP Version <BR>\n"); //doesn't work!

        //this causes a parse error
        //print($userInfo + 1);

        //PHP knows how to promote an array to a string, though
        //not with useful results.
        print($userInfo . "<BR>\n");

        //PHP won't promote an array to an object, but it
        //also won't complain if you do this.
        print($userInfo->Name . "<BR>\n");
?>
```

Listing 5.8	Referencing Strings

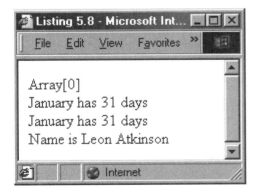

```
<?
        $monthInfo = array(1=>array("January", 31),
                array("February", 28),
                array("March", 31),
                array("April", 30),
```

```
        array("May", 31),
        array("June", 30),
        array("July", 31),
        array("August", 31),
        array("September", 30),
        array("October", 31),
        array("November", 30),
        array("December", 31));

$userInfo = array("Name"=>"Leon Atkinson",
        "Location"=>"Martinez, California",
        "Occupation"=>"Web Engineer");


//This does not parse as expected. It prints
//Array[0] because [0] isn't considered part of
//the expression.
print("$monthInfo[1][0] <BR>\n");

//Here the curly braces alert the parser to
//consider the entire array expression,
//including the second dimension.
print("{$monthInfo[1][0]} has {$monthInfo[1][1]} days <BR>\n");

//Here we've avoided the confusion by keeping
//the array values outside of the strings, perhaps
//at the expense of some readability.
print($monthInfo[1][0] . " has " . $monthInfo[1][1] . " days <BR>\n");

//This line would cause a parse error.
//print("Name is $userInfo["Name"] <BR>\n");

//Once again, curly braces are used to clear up
//confusion for the parser.
print("Name is {$userInfo["Name"]} <BR>\n");
?>
```

CLASSES
AND OBJECTS

Topics in This Chapter

- Defining a Class
- Creating an Object
- Accessing Properties and Methods

Chapter 6

Object-oriented programming was devised as a solution to problems associated with large software projects where many programmers work on a single system. When source code grows to be tens of thousands of lines of code or more, each change can cause unexpected side effects. This happens when modules form secret alliances like nations in pre-WWI Europe. Imagine a module for handling logins that allows a credit card processing module to share its database connection. Surely it was done with the best intentions, probably to save the overhead of acquiring another connection. Some time later, the login module severs the agreement by changing the variable name. The credit card processing code breaks; then the module that handles invoices breaks. Soon totally unrelated modules are dragged into the fray.

So, I'm being a bit dramatic. Most programmers pick up an appreciation for coupling and encapsulation. Coupling is the measure of how dependent two modules are. Less coupling is better. We'd like to take modules from existing projects and reuse them in new projects. We'd like to make wholesale changes to the internals of modules without worrying about how they affect other modules. The solution is to follow the principle of encapsulation. Modules are treated as independent states, and exchanges between modules are done through narrow, structured interfaces. Modules do not spy on each other by reaching into each other's variables. They ask politely through functions.

Encapsulation is a principle you can apply in any programming language, if you have discipline. In PHP, and many procedural languages, it's easy to be tempted to be lazy. Nothing prevents you from building a web of conceit between your modules. Object-oriented programming is a way of making it nearly impossible to violate encapsulation.

In object-oriented programming, modules are organized into objects. These objects have methods and properties. From an abstract perspective, methods are things an object does, and properties are the characteristics of the object. From a programming perspective, methods are functions and properties are variables. In an ideal object-oriented system, each part is an object. And the running of the system consists of objects exchanging objects with other objects using methods.

Each language takes a different approach to objects. PHP borrows from C++ and offers a data type that may contain functions and variables under a single identifier. When PHP was first conceived, even when version 3 was created, PHP wasn't intended as capable of powering projects of 100,000 lines or more of code. Due to recent advances built into PHP and Zend, this is a reality. But no matter the size of your project, building your scripts with classes will certainly aid you in writing code that can be reused. This is a good idea, especially if you wish to share your code.

The idea of objects is one of those mind-blowing concepts in computer science. It's hard to grasp at first, but I can attest that once you get it, it becomes quite natural to think in its terms. Never the less, you can ignore objects if you wish and return to this chapter later. Some built-in functions return objects. You can find alternatives that don't, or you can cast the objects as arrays, as described at the end of this chapter.

Defining a Class

When you declare a class, you are really making a template for the creation of objects. You list all the variables the object should have and all the functions it will need. Sometimes these are called properties and methods, respectively. Figure 6–1 displays the form of a class declaration. Note that inside the curly braces you can only declare variables with the `var` statement or declare functions. Listing 6.1 shows the definition of a class with three properties and two methods.

```
class name extends another class
{
    var Variable Declaration
    Function Declaration
}
```

Figure 6-1   Defining a class.

When you declare a property, you don't specify a data type. It is a variable like any other, and it may contain an integer, a string, or even another object. Depending on the situation, it might be a good idea to add a comment near the declaration of the property that states its intended use and data type. When you declare a method, you do so just as you would a function outside a class definition. Both methods and properties exist within their own scope, or name space. That means you can safely create methods that have the same name as functions declared outside of class definitions without conflicts. An exception to this are built-in functions. For example, you cannot have a print method.

Aside from the variables passed as arguments, methods contain a special variable called this. It stands for the particular instance of the class. You must use this to refer to properties and other methods of the object. Some object-oriented languages assume an unqualified variable that refers to a local property, but in PHP any variables referred to within a method are simply variables local to that scope. Note the use of the this variable in the constructor for the user class in Listing 6.1.

If you choose to declare a function within a class that has the same name as the class itself, the function will be considered a constructor and will be executed immediately upon creating an object from that class. Typically the constructor is used to initialize the object's properties. Like any other function, the constructor may have parameters and even default values. You can set up classes that allow you to create an object and set all its properties in one statement. Unlike other languages, PHP does not allow for destructors—functions that execute when the instance is deleted. However, if you choose to use unset on an object, all the memory associated with that object will be freed. In situations where you must execute some code when you finish using an object, create your own shutdown function and remember to call it.

One powerful aspect of classes is inheritance, the idea that a class can extend the functionality of another class. The new class will contain all the

Listing 6.1   Using Classes

```
<?
    /*
    ** define class for tracking users
    */
    class user
    {
        /*
        ** properties
        */
        var $name;
        var $password;
        var $last_login;

        /*
        ** methods
        */
        function user($inputName, $inputPassword)
        {
            $this->name = $inputName;
            $this->password = $inputPassword;
            $this->last_login = time();
        }

        // get the date of the last login
        function getLastLogin()
        {
            return(Date("M d Y", $this->last_login));
        }
    }

    //create an instance
    $currentUser = new user("Leon", "sdf123");
```

```
        //get the last login date
        print($currentUser->getLastLogin());
        print("<BR>\n");

        //print the user's name
        print($currentUser->name);
        print("<BR>\n");
?>
```

methods and properties of the class it extends, plus any others it lists within its body. You may also override methods and properties from the extended class. As shown in Figure 6–1, you extend a class using the `extends` keyword.

One issue you might wonder about is whether and how constructors are inherited. While they are inherited along with all other methods, they cease to have the property of being called when an object is created from the class. If you require this functionality, you must write it explicitly by calling the parent class's constructor within the child class's constructor.

Creating an Object

Once you have defined a class, you use the `new` statement to create an instance of the class, an object. If the definition of the class is the blueprint, the instance is the widget rolling off the assembly line. The `new` statement expects the name of a class and returns a new instance of that class. If a constructor with parameters has been declared, you may also follow the class name with parameters inside parentheses. Look for the line in Listing 6.1 that uses the `new` statement.

When you create an instance, memory is set aside for all the properties. Each instance has its own set of properties. However, the methods are shared by all instances of that class.

As you recall, PHP allows you to create variables without explicitly declaring the type. Objects are no different. You can create an object simply by using it in the proper context. That is, using the `->` operator on a variable will make it an object. You can create as many properties as you wish on this new object just by referring to them. Unfortunately, you will not be able to attach methods to an object this way.

Another way to create an object is to change the type of an array. When an array becomes an object, all the elements indexed by strings become properties. Elements indexed by numbers will remain with the variable but will be inaccessible. If the variable later returns to being an array, the numbered elements will be accessible again. This is similar to what happens when an object is cast as an array. All properties will be available as array elements, but methods are not. When an object is created through casting or inference, it is of type stdClass.

Accessing Properties and Methods

The properties of an instance are variables, just like any other PHP variable. To refer to them, however, you must use the -> operator. You do not use a dollar sign in front of the property name. For an example, refer to the line in Listing 6.1 that prints the name property of the currentUser object.

Use of -> can be chained. If an object's property contains an object itself, you can use two -> operators to get to a property on the inner object. The parser in PHP 3 was unable to deal with complex expressions like this. In PHP 4 you are not limited this way. You may even place these expressions within double-quoted strings. See Listing 6.2 for an example of an object that contains an array of objects.

Unlike object-oriented languages, such as C++, PHP does not allow properties of classes to be private. Any code may reach into the instance and change or read the values of properties.

Accessing methods is similar to accessing properties. The -> operator is used to point to the instance's method. This is shown in Listing 6.1 in the call to getLastLogin. Methods behave exactly as functions defined outside classes.

If a class extends another, the properties and methods of all ancestor classes are available in the child class, despite not being declared explicitly. As mentioned previously, inheritance is very powerful. If you wish to access an inherited property, simply refer to it as you would any other local property.

Three functions allow you to get information about a class as your script runs: get_class, get_parent_class, and method_exists. These functions are described in Chapter 8.

Listing 6.2   Objects Containing Other Objects

```
<?
    class room
    {
        var $name;

        function room($name="unnamed")
        {
            $this->name = $name;
        }
    }

    class house
    {
        //array of rooms
        var $room;
    }

    //create empty house
    $home = new house;

    //add some rooms
    $home->room[] = new room("bedroom");
    $home->room[] = new room("kitchen");
    $home->room[] = new room("bathroom");

    //show the first room of the house
    print($home->room[0]->name);
?>
```

I/O AND DISK ACCESS

Topics in This Chapter

- HTTP Connections
- Writing to the Browser
- Output Buffering
- Environment Variables
- Getting Input from Forms
- Cookies
- File Uploads
- PUT Method Requests
- Reading and Writing to Files
- Sessions
- The `include` and `require` Functions

Chapter 7

Ultimately, in order to be useful, a script must communicate with the outside world. We've seen PHP scripts that send text to the browser and get some information from functions like date. In this chapter we will examine all the ways a PHP script can exchange data without using special interfaces. This includes reading from local disk drives, connecting to remote machines on the Internet, and receiving form input.

PHP is similar to other programming environments—with one notable exception: User input generally comes from HTML forms. The fields in forms are turned into variables. You can't stop your script in the middle and ask the user a question. This situation provides unique challenges. Each time a script runs, it is devoid of context. It is not aware of what has gone on before unless you make it so.

HTTP Connections

It will be helpful to review how data travels between a browser and a Web server. I will review it simply for purposes of illustration, but you may wish to refer to detailed descriptions, such as those found on the W3C Web site `<http://www.w3.org/Protocols/>`.

When you type a URL into the location box on your browser, the first task of the browser is to break it up into important parts, the first of which is the protocol, HTTP. Next is the name of the Web server, to which the browser makes a connection. The browser must tell the Web server which document it wants, and it does so using the HTTP protocol. Before completing the request, the browser may provide lines of extra information called headers. These headers let the server know the brand of the browser, the type of documents the browser can accept, perhaps even the URL of a referring page.

The Web server places these headers into environment variables to conform with the Common Gateway Interface (CGI). When a PHP script begins, the environment variables are converted into PHP variables. One of the most useful headers describes the brand and version of the Web browser. This header is sent by the browser as `User-agent`. The Web server creates an environment variable called `HTTP_USER_AGENT` that holds the value of the header. PHP in turn creates a variable with this same name. You can refer to it using $, just as for any other variable. If you are using Apache, you also have the option of using the `getallheaders` function. It returns an array of all headers exchanged between the browser and the server.

As a PHP script begins to execute, the HTTP exchange is in the stage where some headers have been sent to the browser, but no content has. This is a window of opportunity to send additional headers. You can send headers that cause the browser to ask for authentication, headers that request that the browser cache a page, or headers that redirect the browser to another URL. These are just some of the many HTTP headers you can send using the `header` function. The most common tasks are described in the last section of this book.

Headers are placed on a stack, which is a data structure that resembles a literal stack of dinner plates. Imagine that each plate is a header. Each new plate is placed atop the previous plate. When it's time to send the headers, they are removed from the top, one at a time. This has the effect of sending the headers to the browser in the reverse of the order in which they were added. Usually this has no effect. HTTP doesn't define any special meaning to the order of headers. However, if you send the same header twice, the later header may overwrite the value of the earlier. This means that if you try resending a header, the browser most likely will ignore it. My advice is to write your scripts so they send headers only when they are certain of the value.

Once any content is sent, the opportunity to send headers is lost. This includes any text outside of PHP tags, even if it's just a linefeed. If you try to send a header after content is sent, an error message is generated. You can use the `headers_sent` function to test whether it's safe to add more headers to the stack, or too late. Cookies, described below, use headers, and therefore are limited in the same way.

As a script runs and sends content, the output is buffered. There is a bit of overhead to every network action, so a small amount of memory temporarily stores the information to be sent out in batches. This buffer is owned by the Web server, so PHP does not have control of it. However, you may request that the buffer be flushed—immediately sent to the browser—by using the `flush` function. This is most useful in long scripts. Both browsers and people have limits to how long they wait for a response, so you can let them know you're making progress by flushing the output. I've written scripts that print a single period and then flush the buffer each time through a long loop.

There are two ways a script may halt unexpectedly: when the script runs too long, and when the user clicks the stop button. By default, scripts are limited to a number of seconds specified in `php.ini`. This is usually 30 seconds, but you can change it. Look for the `max_execution_time` directive. But 30 seconds is a good setting. In case you write a script that could run forever, you want PHP to stop it. Otherwise a few errant scripts could slow your server to a crawl. For the same reason, you usually want to allow users to be able to abort a page request.

There are times when you do want a script to run to completion, and you can instruct PHP to ignore time limits and user aborts. The `set_time_limit` function resets PHP's timer. See Chapter 11 for a complete description and example. I've written some scripts that run on their own once a night, perhaps doing a lot of work. These scripts I allow to run for an hour or more. Likewise, `ignore_user_abort` tells PHP to continue even when the user has clicked the stop button.

Instead of just letting a script run, you may wish it to halt, but deal with the reason it halted with special code. To do this, you must first tell PHP to execute a special function whenever a script ends. This is done with `register_shutdown_function`. This function will execute regardless of why a script ended. It even executes when the script ends normally. You can test for the reason with two functions: `connection_aborted` and `connection_timeout`. These are described in Chapter 8.

Writing to the Browser

Three functions in PHP will send text to the browser: `echo`, `print`, and `printf`. Each does the same thing: They take values and print them to the browser. The `printf` function allows you to specify the format of the output rather than sending values as-is. I've used `print` so far in my examples, mostly out of personal preference. I don't usually need the formatting that `printf` provides. Many older PHP examples you will find on the Web use `echo` because it existed in PHP2. I avoid it, because it behaves more like an operator than a function. All three functions are discussed in Chapter 8.

It is important to remember everything you write is in the context of a Web browser. Unless you take measures to make it otherwise, your output will be treated as HTML text. If you send text that is HTML code, it will be decoded by the browser into its intended form. I've been sending `<BR>` via `print` throughout the book so far, but Listing 7.1 is a more dramatic example of this concept.

Listing 7.1   Sending HTML with `print`

```
<?
    print("You're using ");
    print($HTTP_USER_AGENT);
    print(" to see this page.<BR>\n");
?>
```

Of course, anything outside PHP tags is sent directly to the browser. This is undoubtedly the fastest and least flexible way to send content. You might wonder at this point when it's appropriate to use `print` and when you should place text outside PHP tags. There are issues of efficiency and readability to worry about, but put them aside for now. The final section of the book deals with this issue at length.

Output Buffering

As stated above, the Web server buffers content sent to the browser, and you can request that the buffer be flushed. PHP4 introduced a new mechanism for buffering output you can control completely. Four functions control PHP's output buffer: `ob_start`, `ob_end_flush`, `ob_end_clean`, and `ob_get_contents`. These are described in detail in Chapter 8, complete with examples, but I would like to give an overview here.

When you call the `ob_start` function, anything you send to the browser is placed into a buffer. This includes text outside of PHP tags. The Web server will not receive this content until the `ob_end_flush` function is called.

There are several powerful applications of these functions. One is to avoid the problem associated with sending headers. Because all headers are sent at once, before any content, you have to take care when using the `header` function. This results in a script design where early parts of a script are declared a "no output" zone, which can be annoying. If you use output buffering, you can safely add headers to the stack where you wish, and delay sending content until the last line of your script.

Another application of these functions is in building HTML tables. Imagine creating a table filled with data from a database. You first print the opening tags for the table. You execute a query and loop over the results being returned. If everything executes without error, you print a closing table tag. If an error occurs within the loop, you may have to abort, and the code that closes the table is never reached. This is bad because of the behavior of Netscape Navigator: It won't display information inside an unclosed table. The solution is to turn on output buffering before assembling the table. If assembly completes successfully, you can flush the buffer. Otherwise you can use `ob_end_clean`, which throws away anything in the buffer.

Environment Variables

PHP also makes environment variables available. These are the variables that are created when you start a new shell. Some are the standard variables like `PATH`. Others are variables defined by the CGI. Examples are `REMOTE_ADDR` and `HTTP_USER_AGENT`. These are turned into PHP variables for your convenience. Listing 7.2 tells you which browser someone is using to surf your page.

Similar to environment variables are the variables the PHP itself creates for you. The first is `GLOBALS`, which is an associative array of every variable available to the script. Exploring this array will reveal all the environment variables as well as a few other variables. Similar to `GLOBALS` are `HTTP_GET_VARS`, `HTTP_POST_VARS`, and `HTTP_COOKIE_VARS`. As their names suggest, these are associative arrays of the variables created by the three methods the browser may use to send information to the server.

The combination of Web server and operating system will define the set of environment variables. You can always write a script to dump the `GLOBALS` array to see which are available to you. Alternatively, you can simply view the output of the `phpinfo` function.

Listing 7.2   Viewing Environment Variables

```
<?
    /*
    ** make a multiplication table
    */

    // start table
    print("<TABLE BORDER=\"1\">\n");

    for($Row=1; $Row<=12; $Row++)
    {
        //start row
        print("<TR>\n");

        //do each column
        for($Column=1; $Column <= 12; $Column++)
        {
            print("<TD>");
            print($Row * $Column);
            print("</TD>");
        }

        //end row
        print("</TR>\n");
    }

    //end table
    print("</TABLE>\n");
?>
```

Getting Input from Forms

Sending text to the browser is easy to understand. Getting input from forms is a little tricky. HTML offers several ways to get information from the user via forms. There are text fields, text areas, selection lists, and radio buttons among others. Each of these becomes a string of text offered to the Web server when the user clicks the submit button.

When a form is submitted, PHP turns each form field into a variable. The variables created this way are like any other variable. You may even change their values. They are created as if you had written the PHP code to put values into the variables. This means that if you put two form variables on a page with the same name, the second one may overwrite the value of the first. Other CGI solutions might create an array in this situation. If you wish to pass arrays through form fields, you can define form fields with square brackets. This issue is dealt with in more detail in later chapters.

Listing 7.3 is an example of using variables created from form fields. The script expects a variable named inputColor. The first time this page is viewed, inputColor will be empty, so the script sets it to be six Fs, the RGB code for pure white. On subsequent calls to the page, the value of the text box will be used to set the background color of the page. Notice that input-Color is also used in the INPUT field to prepopulate it. This way, each time you submit the form, you remember what you entered. As an aside, you should also take note of the technique used here, in which a page calls itself.

Listing 7.3   Getting Form Input

```
<?
        print("<HTML>\n");
        print("<HEAD>\n");
        print("<TITLE>Listing 7.3</TITLE>\n");
        print("</HEAD>\n");

        /*
        ** if here for the first time
        ** use white for bgcolor
        */
        if($inputColor == "")
        {
                $inputColor = "FFFFFF";
        }

        /*
        ** open body with background color
        */
        print("<BODY BGCOLOR=\"#$inputColor\">\n");

        /*
        ** start form, action is this page itself
        */
        print("<FORM ACTION=\"$PHP_SELF\" METHOD=\"post\">\n");

        /*
        ** get color
```

```
        */
        print("<B>Enter HTML color:</B> ");
        print("<INPUT ");
        print("TYPE=\"text\" ");
        print("NAME=\"inputColor\" ");
        print("VALUE=\"$inputColor\">\n");

        /*
        ** show submit button
        */
        print("<INPUT ");
        print("TYPE=\"submit\" ");
        print("NAME=\"Submit_Button\" ");
        print("VALUE=\"Try It\">\n");

        print("</FORM>\n");

        print("</BODY>\n");
        print("</HTML>\n");
?>
```

Cookies

Cookies are small strings of data created by a Web server but stored on the client. In addition to having names and values, cookies have an expiration time. Some are set to last for only a matter of minutes. Others persist for months. This allows sites to recognize you without requiring a password when you return. To learn more about cookies, you may wish to visit Netscape's site <http://developer.netscape.com/docs/manuals/communicator/jsguide4/cookies.htm>.

Using cookies with PHP is almost as easy as using form fields. Any cookies passed from the browser to the server are converted automatically into variables. In addition, cookies are stored in the HTTP_COOKIE_VARS array.

If you wish to send a cookie, you use the setcookie function, described in Chapter 8. A cookie is sent to the browser as a header. Just like other headers, you must set cookies before sending any content. When you do set a cookie, the browser may refuse to accept it. Many people turn off cookies. So, you cannot count on the cookie being present the next time a user requests a page.

Setting a cookie does not create a variable—not immediately. When setting a cookie, you are asking the browser to store information that it will return when it next requests a page. Subsequent page requests will cause the cookie to be created as a variable for your use. If you write a script that requires the cookie variable always be set, set it immediately after sending the cookie.

Cookies are a sensitive topic. Some people view them as intrusive. You are asking someone to store information on their computer, although each cookie is limited in size. My advice with cookies is to keep them minimal. In most cases it is practical to use a single cookie for your entire site. If you can identify that user with a unique ID, you can use that ID to look up information you know about them, such as preferences. Keep in mind that each page load causes the browser to send the cookie. Imagine an extreme case where you have created ten 1K cookies. That's 10K of data the browser must send with each page request.

File Uploads

A file upload is a special case of getting form input. Half of the story is putting together the correct HTML. File uploads are specified in RFC 1867. They are supported by Netscape Navigator 2 and above, as well as Internet Explorer 4 and above. Placing an input tag inside an HTML form with the type attribute set to `file` causes a text box and a button for browsing the local file system to appear on the Web page. Browsers that do not support uploads will likely render this as a text box, so it's best to present uploading forms only to capable browsers. The forms must use the post method to allow for uploads, and they must also contain the `enctype` attribute with a value of `multipart/form-data`. A hidden form variable, `MAX_FILE_SIZE`, must precede the file input tag. Its value is the maximum file size in bytes to be accepted.

When the form is submitted, PHP will detect the file upload. The file will be placed in a temporary directory on the server, such as `/var/tmp`. Several variables will be created based on the name of the file field. A variable with the same name as the file field will contain the complete path to the file in the local file system. A variable with `_name` appended to the file field name will contain the original file name as provided by the browser. A variable with `_size` appended to the file field name will contain the size of the file in bytes. Finally, a variable with `_type` appended to the file field name will contain the MIME type of the file, if it was offered by the browser.

Listing 7.4   File Upload

```
<?
    //check for file upload
    if(isset($UploadedFile))
    {
        unlink($UploadedFile);
        print("Local File: $UploadedFile <BR>\n");
        print("Name: $UploadedFile_name <BR>\n");
        print("Size: $UploadedFile_size <BR>\n");
        print("Type: $UploadedFile_type <BR>\n");
        print("<HR>\n");
    }
?>
<FORM ENCTYPE="multipart/form-data"
    ACTION="<? $PHP_SELF ?>" METHOD="post">
<INPUT TYPE="hidden" name="MAX_FILE_SIZE" value="4096">
<INPUT NAME="UploadedFile" TYPE="file">
<INPUT TYPE="submit" VALUE="Upload">
```

If you plan on using the file later, move the new file into a permanent spot. If you do not, PHP will delete the file when it finishes executing the current page request. Listing 7.4 is an example script that accepts uploads and immediately deletes them.

File uploads are limited in size by a directive in php.ini, upload_max_filesize. It defaults to two megabytes. If a file exceeds this limit, your script will execute as if no file were uploaded. A warning will be generated, as well.

Like other form fields, the upload form field is treated like setting the value of a variable. If you place square brackets at the end of the field name, an array will be created. As you would expect, the size and type values will be placed in similarly named arrays. You can take advantage of this to allow for multiple file upload fields.

PUT Method Requests

The PUT method is an HTTP request for a file to be placed on the remote server. It's like a file upload that doesn't come from a form and tells you where to place the file in your document tree. You might guess that this is a very dangerous thing to allow for anonymous users. It's especially dangerous when users could be uploading PHP scripts.

Not all browsers support PUT requests, and neither do all servers. Netscape Composer and the W3C's Amaya browsers reportedly allow PUT requests. Apache for UNIX will accept them if configured to do so. To configure Apache to allow PUT requests, you use the `Script` directive inside a configuration file. See the Apache site for more information `<http://www.apache.org/docs/mod/mod_actions.html#script>`. You could tell Apache to run all PUT requests through a PHP script with a line like `Script PUT /handle_put.php` in `httpd.conf`.

The `PHP_UPLOADED_FILE_NAME` variable will be set with the path to the uploaded file, which will be in a temporary directory. Just as with file uploads using the POST method, this file will be automatically deleted when your script ends if you don't move it. If you need to know the requested URI, look in the `REQUEST_URI` variable.

Reading and Writing to Files

Communication with files follows the pattern of opening a stream to a file, reading from or writing to it, and then closing the stream. When you open a stream, you get an integer that refers to the open stream. Each time you want to read from or write to the file, you use this stream identifier. Internally PHP uses this integer to refer to all the necessary information for communicating with the file.

To open a file on the local file system, you use the `fopen` function. It takes a name of a file and a string that defines the mode of communication. This may be `r` for read-only or `w` for write-only, among other modes. It is also possible to specify an Internet address by starting the file name with `http://` or `ftp://` and following it with a full path including a host name. The file functions are fully defined in Chapter 8.

Two other functions create file streams. You may open a pipe with the `popen` function or you may open a socket connection with the `fsockopen` function. If you have much experience with UNIX, you will recognize pipes as temporary streams of data between executing programs. A common Perl method for sending mail is to open a pipe to `sendmail`, the program for sending mail across the Internet. Because PHP has so many built-in functions, it is rarely necessary to open pipes, but it's nice to know it's an option.

You can open a file stream that communicates through TCP/IP with
fsockopen. This function takes a hostname and a port and attempts to establish
a connection. It is described in Chapter 8, along with the rest of the I/O functions.

Once you have opened a file stream, you can read or write to it using commands like fgets, and fputs. Listing 7.5 demonstrates this. Notice that a
while loop is used to get each line from the example file. It tests for the end
of the file with the feof function. When you are finished with a file, end of
file or not, you call the fclose function. PHP will clean up the temporary
memory it sets aside for tracking an open file.

Keep in mind that PHP scripts execute as a separate user. Frequently this is
the "nobody" user. This user probably won't have permission to create files in
your Web directories. Take care with allowing your scripts to write in any directory able to be served to remote users. In the simple case where you are saving something like guest book information, you will be allowing anyone to view
the entire file. A more serious case occurs when those data files are executed by
PHP, which allows remote users to write PHP that could harm your system or
steal data. The solution is to place these files outside the Web document tree.

Listing 7.5   Writing and Reading from a File

```php
<?
    /*
    ** open file for writing
    */
    $filename = "data.txt";
    if(!($myFile = fopen($filename, "w")))
    {
        print("Error: ");
        print("'$filename' could not be created\n");
        exit;
    }

    //write some lines to the file
    fputs($myFile, "Save this line for later\n");
    fputs($myFile, "Save this line too\n");

    //close the file
    fclose($myFile);


    /*
    ** open file for reading
```

```
        */
        if(!($myFile = fopen($filename, "r")))
        {
                print("Error:");
                print("'$filename' could not be read\n");
                exit;
        }

        while(!feof($myFile))
        {
                //read a line from the file
                $myLine = fgets($myFile, 255);

                print("$myLine <BR>\n");
        }

        //close the file
        fclose($myFile);
?>
```

Sessions

If you build a Web application, it's likely you will have information to associate with each user. You may wish to remember the user's name from page to page. You may be collecting information on successive forms. You could attempt to pass the growing body of information from page to page inside hidden form fields, but this is impractical. An elegant solution is to use the idea of a session. Each visitor is assigned a unique identifier with which you reference stored information, perhaps in a file or in a database.

In the past, PHP developers were required to create their own code for handling sessions, but Sascha Schumann and Andrei Zmievski added new functions for session handling to PHP 4. The concept is as follows. You register global variables with the session handler. The values of these variables are saved in files on the server. When the user requests another page, these variables are restored to the global scope.

The session identifier is a long series of numbers and letters and is sent to the user as a cookie. It is possible that the user will reject the cookie, so a constant is created that allows you to send the session identifier in a URL. The constant is SID and contains a full GET method declaration, suitable for attaching to the end of a URL.

Consider Listing 7.6, a simple script that tracks a user's name and the number of times they've visited the page. The first step is to call the `session_start` function. This sends the cookie to the browser, and therefore it must be called before sending any content. Next, two variables are registered with the session, `Name` and `Count`. The former will be used to track the user's name, and the latter to count the number of times the user redisplays the page. Once registered, the values of these variables will be preserved in the session. Before starting the HTML document, the example script sets `Name` with input from a form submission if present, and then it increments the page counter.

The first bit of content the page provides is diagnostic information about the session. The session name is set inside `php.ini`, along with several other session parameters. It is used to name the cookie holding the session identifier. The identifier itself is a long string of letters and numbers, randomly generated. By default, PHP stores sessions in `/tmp` using a built-in handler called `files`. This directory isn't standard on Windows, and if it is not present, sessions will not work correctly.

It's likely that other handlers will be added for storing sessions in relational databases, but you do have the option of creating your own handler in PHP code using the `session_set_save_handler` function. You can read about how you'd do that in Chapter 17. Sessions are encoded using serializa-

Listing 7.6   Using Sessions

```php
<?
    //Start the session.
    //This must be called before
    //sending any content.
    session_start();

    //Register a couple of variables
    session_register("Name");
    session_register("Count");

    //Set variable based on form input
    if($inputName != "")
    {
        $Name = $inputName;
    }

    //Increment counter with each page load
    $Count++;
```

```
?>
<HTML>
<HEAD>
<TITLE>Listing 7.6</TITLE>
</HEAD>
<BODY>
<?
       //print diagnostic info
       print("<B>Diagnostic Information</B><BR>\n");
       print("Session Name: " . session_name() . "<BR>\n");
       print("Session ID: " . session_id() . "<BR>\n");
       print("Session Module Name: " . session_module_name() . "<BR>\n");
       print("Session Save Path: " . session_save_path() . "<BR>\n");
       print("Encoded Session:" . session_encode() . "<BR>\n");

       print("<HR>\n");

       if($Name != "")
       {
              print("Hello, $Name!<BR>\n");
       }

       print("You have viewed this page $Count times!<BR>\n");


       //show form for getting name
       print("<FORM ACTION=\"$SCRIPT_NAME?".SID."\" METHOD=\"POST\">");
       print("<INPUT TYPE=\"text\" NAME=\"inputName\" VALUE=\"$Name\"><BR>\n");
       print("<INPUT TYPE=\"submit\" VALUE=\"Change Name\"><BR>\n");
       print("</FORM>");

       //use a link to reload this page
       print("<A HREF=\"$SCRIPT_NAME?".SID."\">Reload</A><BR>\n");
?>
</BODY>
</HTML>
```

tion, a method for compacting variables into a form suitable for storing as text strings. If you examine the files saved in /tmp, you will find they match the strings returned by session_encode.

As stated earlier, session identifiers are sent by cookies, but a browser may refuse them. As a backup, you may use the SID constant. It will contain a string consisting of the session name, an equal sign, and the session identifier. This is suitable for placing in a URL, as I have done in both the form action and the anchor tag below it. If the browser returns a session cookie to the script, the SID constant will be empty.

All the session functions are described in Chapter 8.

The include and require Functions

The include and require functions take the path to a file. The file is parsed as if it were a stand-alone PHP script. This is similar to the include directive in C and the require directive in Perl. There is a subtle difference between the two functions. When the require function is processed, it is replaced with the file it points to. The include function acts more like a function call.

The difference is most dramatic inside a loop. Imagine having three files you wanted to execute one after the other. You could put an include inside a for loop, and if the files were named something like include1.php, include2.php, and include3.php, you would have no problem. You could just build the name based on a counter variable.

If you used require, however, you would execute the first file three times. That's because on the first time through the loop, the call to require would be replaced with the contents of the file. As I said, the difference is subtle but can be very dramatic.

Listings 7.7 and 7.8 show one possible use of the include function. Here we revisit an example from the chapter on arrays. I've taken the definition of the array from the main file and put it into its own file. All the code that matches ways to refer to months with a preferred output form is not necessarily interesting to the main script. It is enough to know that we've included the translation array. This makes the script in Listing 7.8 a lot easier to understand.

This strategy of modularization will enhance the readability of your code. It gives the reader a high-level view. If more detail is needed, it takes a few clicks to open the included file. But more than enhancing readability, coding in this way tends to help you write reusable code. Today you may use the translation array for a catalog request form, but in a week you may need it for displaying data from a legacy database. Instead of cutting out the array definition, you can simply copy the file.

Listing 7.7   Included File

```
<?
        /*
        ** Build array for referencing months
        */
        $monthName = array(
                1=>"January", "February", "March",
                "April", "May", "June",
                "July", "August", "September",
                "October", "November", "December",

                "Jan"=>"January", "Feb"=>"February",
                "Mar"=>"March", "Apr"=>"April",
                "May"=>"May", "Jun"=>"June",
                "Jul"=>"July", "Aug"=>"August",
                "Sep"=>"September", "Oct"=>"October",
                "Nov"=>"November", "Dec"=>"December",

                "January"=>"January", "February"=>"February",
                "March"=>"March", "April"=>"April",
                "May"=>"May", "June"=>"June",
                "July"=>"July", "August"=>"August",
                "September"=>"September", "October"=>"October",
                "November"=>"November", "December"=>"December"
        );
?>
```

Listing 7.8   Including a File

```
<?
        /*
        ** Get monthName array
        */
        include("7-7.php");

        print("Month 5 is " . $monthName[5] . "<BR>\n");
        print("Month Aug is " . $monthName["Aug"] . "<BR>\n");
        print("Month June is " . $monthName["June"] . "<BR>\");
?>
```

Part 2

FUNCTIONAL REFERENCE

The chapters in this section of the book, Chapters 8 through 14, are a functional reference. They describe how each PHP function works: what arguments are expected, what value is returned, and how they ought to be used. The functions are grouped generally by what they do.

Chapter 8 is concerned with I/O—input and output. Input functions send and receive information to the browser, and output functions read and write to the file system or to the network. Chapter 9 is all about manipulating data. There are functions for handling arrays, functions for searching for information inside strings, and functions for encoding and decoding information. Chapter 10 is concerned with mathematics. Aside from the standard mathematical functions you expect, PHP offers some unique features for handling arbitrarily large or small numbers. Chapter 11 is a bit of a catch-all chapter that deals with time-related functions and functions that affect the configuration of PHP. There are functions for normal dates and times, but there are also functions for working with obscure calendars. In addition, there are plenty of functions for changing the operation of PHP itself. Chapter 12 is a short but important chapter on graphics functions. The GD library allows you to create and manipulate images on the fly. Chapter 13 is a long chapter about all the different database functions. If PHP can boast of one great achievement, it is certainly support for many databases. In this chapter, you will find native support for popular commercial databases such as Oracle and Sybase, as well as support for free technologies like MySQL. Chapter 14 contains miscellaneous functions, most of which interface with specialized libraries, such as functions for communicating with LDAP and IMAP servers.

Throughout this section I've used a standard format for showing how a function works. The form I've chosen is compact yet clear. Each description begins with a prototype for the function. This tells you what type of data the function returns and what type of data is expected to be passed. When a function returns nothing, it will not be preceded with a datatype. Likewise, if a function takes no arguments, the parentheses following the function's name will be empty.

Some functions are part of PHP's basic functions and are always available. Others are part of an extension which must be loaded through special files, or added when you compile PHP. Without doing either of these things, you will get an error reporting an unrecognized function. There are more extensions than I cover here. Some may have been written after this text went to press. Others are very specialized.

A lot of effort went into checking for bugs in the functional reference, but it's possible some will slip through. As I did with the first edition, I will make an errata page available on my Web site <http://www.leonatkinson. com/>. If an example doesn't work as you expect, check there first.

I/O FUNCTIONS

Topics in This Chapter

- Sending Text to the Browser
- Output Buffering
- Files
- Compressed Files
- POSIX
- Debugging
- Session Handling
- Shell Commands
- HTTP Headers
- Network I/O
- FTP

Chapter 8

No useful program can be useful in a vacuum. The functions described in this chapter are concerned with I/O (Input and Output), whether it's to the browser, files, or across a network. Some of them perform very specialized duties such as manipulating files. Others are simply for debugging or reporting information about the environment.

If you are experienced in traditional application development, you may be challenged by the unique characteristics of a stateless operating environment. Your script can't sit in a loop and get input from the user until the quit button is clicked. Although there are ways to force the preservation of state—that is, a collection of variables for each user—I encourage you to work within PHP's world. You may come to find what at first were limitations are refreshing opportunities.

Sending Text to the Browser

Any text outside PHP tags is automatically sent to the browser. This is as you would expect. Chapter 18, "Network" deals with the decision to send text via a PHP function. PHP offers three functions that simply send text to the browser: `echo`, `print`, and `printf`.

echo string first, string second, ..., string last

The echo function sends any number of parameters, separated by commas, to the browser. Each will be converted to a string and printed with no space between them. Unlike most other PHP functions, the echo function does not require parentheses. In fact, echo is more of a statement than a function.

```
<?
    echo "First string", 2, 3.4, "last string";
?>
```

flush()

As text is sent to the browser via functions like print and echo, it may be stored in a memory buffer and written out only when the buffer fills. The flush function attempts to force the buffer to be dumped to the browser immediately. Since the Web server ultimately controls communication with the browser, the flush may not be effective.

If your script takes a long time to execute, it's a good idea to output a status message and flush the buffer. This keeps the user from clicking away.

```
<?
    //simulate long calculation
    //flush output buffer with each step
    for($n=0; $n<5; $n++)
    {
        print("Calculating...<BR>\n");
        flush();
        sleep(3);
    }
    print("Finished!<BR>\n");
?>
```

print(string output)

The output argument of print is sent to the browser.

```
<?
    print("hello world!<BR>\n");
?>
```

printf(string format, ...)

The `printf` function converts and outputs arguments to the browser based on a format string. The format string contains codes, listed in Table 8.1, for different data types. These codes begin with a percentage sign, %, and end with a letter that determines the type of data. The codes match up with a list of values that follow the format string in the argument list. Any text outside these codes will be sent unchanged to the browser.

You also have the option of placing characters between the % and the type specifier that control how the data is formatted. Immediately following the % you may place any number of flags. These flags control padding and alignment. They are listed in Table 8.2.

After any flags, you may specify a minimum field length . The converted output will be printed in a field at least this wide, longer if necessary. If the output is shorter than the minimum width, it will be padded with a padding character, a space by default. The padding will normally be placed to the left but, if the – flag is used, it will be placed to the right.

Next, you may specify a precision. It must start with a period to separate it from the minimum field length. For strings, the precision is taken to mean a

Table 8.1 `printf` Type Specifiers

Type Specifier	Description
d	Integer, decimal notation.
o	Integer, octal notation.
x, X	Integer, hexadecimal notation. 'x' will use lowercase letters; "X" will use uppercase letters.
b	Integer, binary notation.
c	Character specified by integer ASCII code. See Appendix B for a complete list of ASCII codes.
s	String.
f	Double.
e	Double, using scientific notation such as 1.2e3.
%	Print a percentage sign. This does not require a matching argument.

Table 8.2	`printf` Flags

Flag	Description
–	Align text to the left.
space	Pad output with spaces. This is the default padding character.
0	Pad output with zeros.
' plus any character	Pad output with the character.

maximum field length. For doubles, the precision is the number of digits that appear after the decimal point. Precision has no meaning for integers.

```
<?
    printf("%-10s %5d %05.5f <BR>\n", "a string", 10, 3.14);
?>
```

Output Buffering

The output buffering commands add a layer of buffering controlled by PHP in addition to whatever buffering the Web server uses. Some performance penalty may be incurred by adding another layer of buffering, but you may decide the greater control you have is worth the price.

When `ob_start` is called, all output by functions such as `print` and `echo` are held back in a buffer, a large area of memory. The contents of the buffer may be sent to the browser using `ob_end_flush`, or it may be thrown away using `ob_end_clean`. As you recall from Chapter 7, "I/O and Disk Access," headers cannot be sent after the first content is sent. Therefore, these functions allow you to avoid errors created by sending headers after content.

ob_start()

The `ob_start` function begins output buffering. All text sent by `print` and similar functions is saved in a buffer. It will not be sent to the browser until `ob_end_flush` is called. The buffer will also be flushed when the script ends.

```
<?
      //begin output buffering
      ob_start();
?>
<HTML>
<HEAD>
<TITLE>ob_start</TITLE>
</HEAD>
<BODY>
<?
      print("At this point ");
      print(strlen(ob_get_contents()));
      print(" characters are in the buffer.<BR>\n");
?>
</BODY>
</HTML>
<?
      //add a test header
      header("X-note: COREPHP");

      //dump the contents
      ob_end_flush();
?>
```

ob_end_flush()

The ob_end_flush function halts output buffering and sends the contents of the buffer to the browser.

ob_end_clean()

The ob_end_clean function halts output buffering and eliminates the contents of the buffer. Nothing is sent to the browser.

string ob_get_contents()

The ob_get_contents function returns the contents of the output buffer.

Files

These functions manipulate or return information about files. Many of them are wrappers for the commands you execute in a UNIX or Windows command shell.

When the functions in this section call for a filename or a directory, you may name a file in the same directory as the script itself. You may also use a full or relative path. The . and .. directories are valid in both UNIX and Windows. You may also specify drive letters on a Windows machine. Back-slashes can delimit directories and filenames when running under Windows, but forward slashes are interpreted correctly, so you stick with them.

boolean chdir(string directory)

When a PHP script begins to execute, its default path is the path to the script itself. That is, if the fully qualified path to the script were /users/leon/public_html/somescript.php, then all relative paths would work off /users/leon/public_html/. You may change this default path with the chdir function. It returns TRUE if the change was made, FALSE if the script was unable to change directories.

```
<?
    if(chdir("/tmp"))
    {
        print("current directory is /tmp");
    }
    else
    {
        print("unable to change to /tmp");
    }
?>
```

boolean chgrp(string filename, string group)

The chgrp function invokes the UNIX idea of changing the group to which a file belongs. If successful, TRUE is returned. If the group cannot be changed, FALSE is returned. Under Windows this function always returns TRUE and leaves the file unchanged. Two similar functions are chmod and chown. If you want to find the group to which a file is currently assigned, use the `filegroup` function.

You may wish to refer to the UNIX man page for the shell command of the same name.

```
<?
    if(chgrp("log.txt", "editors"))
    {
        print("log.txt changed to editors group");
    }
    else
    {
        print("log.txt not changed to editors group");
    }
?>
```

boolean chmod(string filename, integer mode)

The `chmod` function sets the UNIX permissions for the given file based on the mode supplied. The mode is interpreted like the UNIX shell command, except that it is not converted to octal. Unless prefixed with a 0, `mode` is treated as a decimal number.

Under UNIX, three octal numbers specify access privileges for owner, group, and others, respectively. The modes may be added in order to combine privileges. For example, to make a file readable and executable, use mode 5. Refer to Table 8.3. You also may wish to refer to the man page for `chmod` on your UNIX system.

Under Windows, `chmod` has limited use. The modes described in Table 8.4 are defined by Microsoft. They may be combined with the bitwise-or (|), but in practice only write permission has any meaning. All files in Windows are readable and the file extension determines whether the file will execute.

Table 8.3   File Modes

Mode	Description
0	No access
1	Execute
2	Write
4	Read

Table 8.4	Windows File Modes
Mode	Description
0000400	read permission, owner
0000200	write permission, owner
0000100	execute/search permission, owner

This function is part of a group of three functions that change similar information about files. The other two are `chgrp` and `chown`. The `fileperms` function will tell you the file's current modes.

```
<?
    /*
    ** allow everyone to read and write to file
    ** when running PHP under UNIX
    */
    if(chmod("data.txt", 0666))
    {
        print("mode change successful");
    }
    else
    {
        print("mode change unsuccessful");
    }
?>
```

boolean chown(string filename, string user)

The owner of the named file is changed by the `chown` function. If successful, TRUE is returned. Otherwise the function returns FALSE. Under Windows this function does nothing and always returns TRUE. This function is similar to `chgrp` and `chmod`. If you need to know the current owner of a file, use the `fileowner` function.

```
<?
    /*
    ** change owner to leon
    */
    if(chown("data.txt","leon"))
    {
```

```
        print("owner changed");
    }
    else
    {
        print("couldn't change owner");
    }
?>
```

closedir(integer directory_handle)

The `closedir` function closes a directory after it has been opened with the `opendir` function. PHP will close a directory connection for you when the script ends, so use of this function is not strictly necessary.

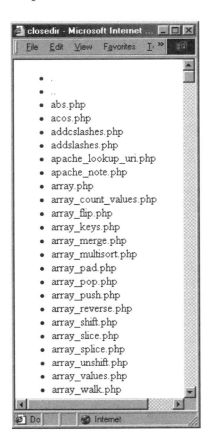

Figure 8-1 `closedir`.

```
<?
        // print the current directory in unordered list
        print("<UL>\n");

        // open directory
        $myDirectory = opendir(".");

        // get each entry
        while($entryName = readdir($myDirectory))
        {
                        print("<LI>$entryName \n");
        }

        // close directory
        closedir($myDirectory);

        print("</UL>\n");
?>
```

Figure 8-1   Continued

boolean copy(string source, string destination)

The copy function copies a file specified by the source argument into the file specified by the destination argument. This results in two separate and identical files. A similar function is link, which is described below.

```
<?
    if(copy("data.txt", "/tmp/data.txt"))
    {
        print("data.txt copied to /tmp");
    }
    else
    {
        print("data.txt could not be copied");
    }
?>
```

float diskfreespace(string path)

The diskfreespace function returns the number of free bytes for the given path.

```
<?
    print(diskfreespace("/"));
    print(" bytes free");
?>
```

object dir(string directory)

The `dir` function creates a directory object to be used as an alternative to the group of functions that includes `opendir` and `closedir`. The returned object has two properties: `handle` and `path`. The `handle` property can be used with other directory functions such as `readdir` as if it were created with `opendir`. The `path` property is the string used to create the directory object. The object has three methods: `read`, `rewind`, and `close`. These behave exactly like `readdir`, `rewinddir`, and `closedir`.

boolean fclose(integer file_handle)

The `fclose` function closes an open file. When a file is opened, you are given an integer that represents a file handle. This file handle is used to close the file when you are finished using it. The functions used to open files are: `fopen` and `fsockopen`. To close a pipe, use `pclose`.

```
<?
    // open file for reading
    $myFile = fopen("data.txt","r");

    // make sure the open was successful
    if(!($myFile))
    {
        print("file could not be opened");
        exit;
    }

    while(!feof($myFile))
    {
        // read a line from the file
        $myLine = fgets($myFile, 255);
        print("$myLine <BR>\n");
    }

    // close the file
    fclose($myFile);
?>
```

boolean feof(integer file_handle)

As you read from a file, PHP keeps a pointer to the last place in the file you read. The feof function returns TRUE if you are at the end of the file. It is most often used in the conditional part of a while loop where a file is being read from start to finish. See the description of fclose, above, for an example of use. If you need to know the exact position you are reading from, use the ftell function.

string fgetc(integer file_handle)

The fgetc function returns a single character from a file. It expects a file handle as returned by fopen, fsockopen, or popen. Some other functions for reading from a file are: fgetcsv, fgets, fgetss, fread, gzgetc.

```
<?
    // open file and print each character
    if($myFile = fopen("data.txt", "r"))
    {
        while(!feof($myFile))
        {
            $myCharacter = fgetc($myFile);
            print($myCharacter);
        }

        fclose($myFile);
    }
?>
```

array fgetcsv(integer file_handle, integer length, string separator)

The fgetcsv function is used for reading comma-separated data from a file. It requires a valid file handle as returned by fopen, fsockopen, or popen. It also requires a maximum line length. The optional separator argument specifies the character to separate fields. If left out, a comma is used. Fields may be surrounded by double quotes, which allows embedding of commas and line breaks in fields.

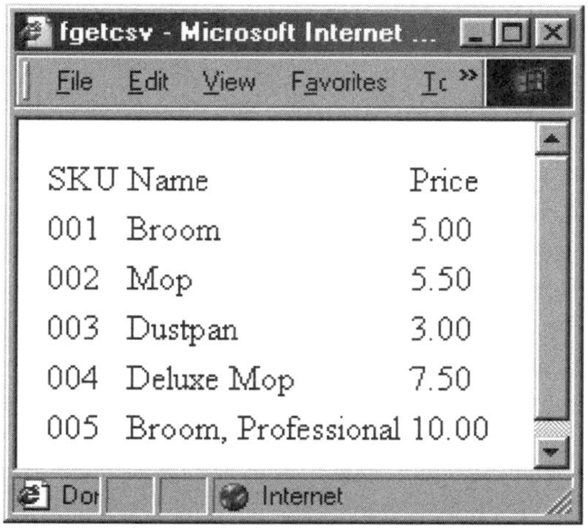

```php
<?
    // open file
    if($myFile = fopen("data.csv", "r"))
    {
        print("<TABLE>\n");

        while(!feof($myFile))
        {
            print("<TR>\n");

            $myField = fgetcsv($myFile, 1024);

            for($n=0; $n<count($myField); $n++)
            {
                print("\t<TD>");
                print($myField[$n]);
                print("</TD>\n");
            }

            print("</TR>\n");
        }

        fclose($myFile);

        print("</TABLE>\n");
    }
?>
```

Figure 8–2   `fgetcsv`.

string fgets(integer file_handle, integer length)

The `fgets` function returns a string it reads from a file specified by the file handle, which must have been created with `fopen`, `fsockopen`, or `popen`. It will attempt to read as many characters as specified by the length argument less one. A linebreak character is treated as a stopping point as is the end of the file. It will be included in the returned string.

Some other functions for reading from a file are: `fgetc`, `fgetcsv`, `fgetss`, `fread`, `gzgets`.

```
<?
    // open file and print each line
    if($myFile = fopen("data.txt", "r"))
    {
       while(!feof($myFile))
       {
          $myLine = fgets($myFile, 255);
          print($myLine);
       }
       fclose($myFile);
    }
?>
```

string fgetss(integer file_handle, integer length, string ignore)

The `fgetss` function is in all respects identical to `fgets` except that it attempts to strip any HTML or PHP code before returning a string. The optional ignore argument specifies tags that are allowed to pass through unchanged. Note that if you wish to ignore a tag, you need only specify the opening form. Some other functions for reading from a file are: `fgetc`, `fgetcsv`, `fgetss`, `fread`, `gzgets`. If you wish to preserve HTML but prevent it from being interpreted, you can use the `htmlentities` function.

```
<?
       // open file and print each line,
       //stripping HTML except for anchor tags
       if($myFile = fopen("index.html", "r"))
       {
          while(!feof($myFile))
          {
             $myLine = fgetss($myFile, 1024, "<A>");
             print($myLine);
```

```
            }
            fclose($myFile);
    }
?>
```

array file(string filename)

The file function returns an entire file as an array. Each line of the file is a separate element of the array, starting at zero. If it would be more convenient to work with the file as one string, use the implode function, as I have in the following example. If you are planning on sending a file directly to the browser, use readfile instead.

```
<?
    // open file
    $myFile = file("data.txt");

    //fold array elements into one string
    $myFile = implode($myFile, "");

    //print entire file
    print($myFile);
?>
```

boolean file_exists(string filename)

The file_exists function returns TRUE if the specified file exists and FALSE if it does not. This function is a nice way to avoid errors with the other file functions. The example below tests that a file exists before trying to send it to the browser.

```
<?
    $filename = "data.txt";

    //if the file exists, print it
    if(file_exists($filename))
    {
            readfile($filename);
    }
    else
    {
            print("'$filename' does not exist");
    }
?>
```

integer fileatime(string filename)

The `fileatime` function returns the last access time for a file in standard timestamp format, the number of seconds since January 1, 1970. FALSE is returned if there is an error. A file is considered accessed if it is created, written, or read. Unlike some other file-related functions, `fileatime` operates identically on Windows and UNIX.

Two other functions for getting timestamps associated with files are `filectime` and `filemtime`.

```
<?
    $LastAccess = fileatime("data.txt");
    print("Last access was ");
    print(date("l F d, Y", $LastAccess));
?>
```

integer filectime(string filename)

When running on UNIX, the `filectime` function returns the last time a file was changed in standard timestamp format, the number of seconds since January 1, 1970. A file is considered changed if it is created or written to or its permissions have been changed. When running on Windows, `filectime` returns the time the file was created. If an error occurs, FALSE is returned.

Two other functions for getting timestamps associated with files are `fileatime` and `filemtime`.

```
<?
    $LastChange = filectime("data.txt");
    print("Last change was ");
    print(date("l F d, Y", $LastChange));
?>
```

integer filegroup(string filename)

The `filegroup` function returns the group identifier for the given file, or FALSE when there is an error. This function always returns FALSE under Windows. Other functions that return information about a file are `fileinode`, `fileowner`, and `fileperms`. To change a file's group, use `chgrp`.

```
<?
    print(filegroup("data.txt"));
?>
```

integer fileinode(string filename)

The `fileinode` function returns the inode of the given file, or FALSE on error. This function always returns FALSE under Windows. Similar functions are `filegroup`, `fileowner`, and `fileperms`.

```
<?
    print(fileinode("data.txt"));
?>
```

integer filemtime(string filename)

The `filemtime` function returns the last time a file was modified in standard timestamp format, the number of seconds since January 1, 1970. FALSE is returned if there is an error. A file is considered modified when it is created or its contents change. Operation of this function is identical under any operating system. There are two other functions related to timestamps on files: `fileatime` and `filectime`.

```
<?
    $LastMod = filemtime("data.txt");
    print("Last modification was ");
    print(date("l F d, Y", $LastMod));
?>
```

integer fileowner(string filename)

The `fileowner` function returns the user identifier of the owner, or false if there is an error. This function always returns FALSE under Windows. If you need to change the owner of a file, use the `chown` function. Similar functions for getting information about a file are `filegroup`, `fileinode` and `fileperms`.

```
<?
    print(fileowner("data.txt"));
?>
```

integer fileperms(string filename)

The `fileperms` function returns the permission number for the given file, or false when there is an error. If you are using UNIX, you may wish to refer to the man page for the stat system function. You may be surprised to find that printing this number in octal, as is customary, produces six digits. The first three give you information about the file that don't actually refer to read/write/execute permissions. You may wish to filter that information out, as I have in the example, by performing a logical AND operation. If you need to change the mode of a file, use the chmod function.

```
<?
    printf("%o", (fileperms("data.txt") & 0777));
?>
```

integer filesize(string filename)

The filesize function returns the size of the given file in bytes.

```
<?
    print(filesize("data.txt"));
?>
```

string filetype(string filename)

The filetype function returns the type of the given file as a descriptive string. Possible values are block, char, dir, fifo, file, link, and unknown. This function is an interface to C's stat function, whose man page may be helpful in understanding the different file types.

```
<?
    print(filetype("data.txt"));
?>
```

boolean flock(integer file_handle, integer mode)

Use the flock function to temporarily restrict access to a file. PHP uses its own system for locking, which works across multiple platforms. However, all processes must be using the same locking system, so the file will be locked for PHP scripts, but likely not locked for other processes.

The file_handle argument must be an integer returned by fopen. The mode argument determines whether you obtain a lock that allows others to read the file (1), you obtain a lock that doesn't allow others to read the file (2), or you release a lock (3). When obtaining a lock, the process may block. That is, if the file is already locked, it will wait until it gets the lock to continue execution. If you prefer, you may turn off blocking using modes 5 and 6. Table 8.5 lists the modes in a table.

Table 8.5	`flock` Modes

Mode	Operations Allowed
1	Allow reads
2	Disallow reads
3	Release lock
5	Allow reads, do not block
6	Disallow reads, do not block

```
<?
    $fp = fopen("log.txt", "a");

    //get lock
    flock($fp, 2);

    //add a line to the log
    fputs($fp, date("h:i A l F dS, Y\n"));

    //release lock
    flock($fp, 3);

    fclose($fp);

    //dump log
    print("<PRE>");
    readfile("log.txt");
    print("</PRE>\n");
?>
```

integer fopen(string filename, string mode)

The `fopen` function opens a file for reading or writing. The function expects the name of a file and a mode. It returns an integer, which is called a file handle. Internally, PHP uses this integer to reference a block of information about the open file. The file handle is used by other file-related functions, such as `fputs` and `fgets`.

Ordinarily, the `filename` argument is a path to a file. It can be fully qualified, or relative to the path of the script. If the filename begins with `http://` or `ftp://`, the file will be opened using HTTP or FTP protocol over the Internet.

Table 8.6	File Read/Write Modes
Mode	*Operations Allowed*
r[b]	reading only [binary]
w[b]	writing only, create if necessary, discard previous contents if any [binary]
a[b]	append to file, create if necessary, start writing at end of file [binary]
r+[b]	reading and writing [binary]
w+[b]	reading and writing, create if necessary, discard previous contents if any [binary]
a+[b]	reading and writing, create if necessary, start writing at end of file [binary]

The mode argument determines whether the file is to be read from, written to, or added to. Modes with a plus sign (+) are update modes that allow both reading and writing. If the letter b appears as the last part of the mode, the file is assumed to be a binary file, which means no special meaning will be given to end-of-line characters. Table 8.6 lists all the modes.

While it is an error to open a file for writing when an HTTP URL is specified, this is not the case with FTP. You may upload an FTP file by using write mode. However, this functionality is limited. You can create remote files, but you may not overwrite existing files. With either HTTP or FTP connections, you may only read from start to finish from a file. You may not use fseek or similar functions.

Sometimes files on HTTP and FTP servers are protected by usernames and passwords. You can specify a username and a password exactly as popular Web browsers allow you to do. After the network protocol and before the server name you may insert a username, a colon, a password, and an at-symbol (@).

Three other ways to open a file are the fsockopen, gzopen, popen functions.

```
<?

print("<H1>HTTP</H1>\n");

//open a file using http protocol
//Use username and password
```

```
if(!($myFile = fopen("http://leon:password@www.clearink.com/", "r")))
{
      print("file could not be opened");
      exit;
}

while(!feof($myFile))
{
      // read a line from the file
      $myLine = fgetss($myFile, 255);
      print("$myLine <BR>\n");
}

// close the file
fclose($myFile);

print("<H1>FTP</H1>\n");
print("<HR>\n");

// open a file using ftp protocol
if(!($myFile = fopen("ftp://ftp.php.net/welcome.msg", "r")))
{
      print("file could not be opened");
      exit;
}

while(!feof($myFile))
{
      // read a line from the file
      $myLine = fgetss($myFile, 255);
      print("$myLine <BR>\n");
}

// close the file
fclose($myFile);

print("<H1>Local</H1>\n");
print("<HR>\n");

// open a local file
if(!($myFile = fopen("data.txt", "r")))
{
      print("file could not be opened");
      exit;
}
```

```
while(!feof($myFile))
{
        // read a line from the file
        $myLine = fgetss($myFile, 255);
        print("$myLine <BR>\n");
}

// close the file
fclose($myFile);
?>
```

boolean fpassthru(integer file_handle)

The fpassthru function prints the contents of the file to the browser. Data from the current file position to the end are sent, so you can read a few lines and output the rest. The file is closed after being sent. If an error occurs, fpassthru returns FALSE. The gzpassthru function offers the same functionality for compressed files.

```
<?

/*
** Get a Web page, change the title tag
*/

// open a file using http protocol
if(!($myFile = fopen("http://www.clearink.com/", "r")))
{
        print("file could not be opened");
        exit;
}

$KeepSearching = TRUE;

while(!feof($myFile) AND $KeepSearching)
{
        // read a line from the file
        $myLine = fgets($myFile, 1024);

        //watch for body tag
        if(eregi("<body", $myLine))
        {
                //no chance to find a title tag
                //after a body tag
                $KeepSearching = FALSE;
```

```
        }

        //try adding some text after the title tag
        $myLine = eregi_replace("<title>",
                "<title>(fpassthru example)", $myLine);

        //send line to browser
        print("$myLine");
    }

    // send the rest of file to browser
    fpassthru($myFile);
?>
```

integer fputs(int file_handle, string output)

The `fputs` function writes data to an open file. It expects a file handle as returned by `fopen`, `fsockopen`, or `popen`. The number of bytes written is returned, or –1 when an error occurs. The `gzputs` function performs the same task on compressed files.

```
<?
    // open file for writing
    $myFile = fopen("data.txt","w");

    // make sure the open was successful
    if(!($myFile))
    {
        print("file could not be opened");
        exit;
    }

    for($index=0; $index<10; $index++)
    {
        // write a line to the file
        fputs($myFile, "line $index\n");
    }

    // close the file
    fclose($myFile);
?>
```

string fread(integer file_handle, integer length)

The fread function is a binary-safe version of the fgets function. That means it does not pay attention to end-of-line characters. It will always return the number of bytes specified by the length argument, unless it reaches the end of the file. This function is necessary if you wish to read from binary files, such as JPEG image files.

```
<?
        /*
        ** Check that a file is a GIF89
        */

        $filename = "php.gif";

        $fp = fopen($filename, "r");

        //get first 128 bytes
        $data = fread($fp, 128);

        //close file
        fclose($fp);

        //check for GIF89
        if(substr($data, 0, 5) == "GIF89")
        {
                print("$filename is a GIF89 file.\n");
        }
        else
        {
                print("$filename isn't a GIF89 file.\n");
        }
?>
```

integer fseek(integer file_handle, integer offset)

To change PHP's internal file pointer, use fseek. It expects a valid file handle as created by fopen. It also expects an offset, the number of bytes past the beginning of the file. If an error occurs, fseek returns negative one (–1); otherwise it returns zero (0). Take note that this is different from most other PHP functions.

Seeking past the end of the file is not an error; however, using `fseek` on a file opened by `fopen` if it was used with `http://` or `ftp://` is forbidden.

If you need to know where the file pointer points, use the `ftell` function.

```
<?
    // open a file
    if($myFile = fopen("data.txt", "r"))
    {
        // jump 32 bytes into the file
        fseek($myFile, 32);

        // dump the rest of the file
        fpassthru($myFile);
    }
    else
    {
        print("file could not be opened");
    }
?>
```

array fstat(integer file_handle)

The `fstat` function gets information from C's `stat` function about an open file and returns it in an associative array. The elements of the array are `atime`, `blksize`, `blocks`, `ctime`, `dev`, `gid`, `ino`, `mode`, `mtime`, `nlink`, `rdev`, `size`, `uid`. This function returns the same information returned by `stat` and `lstat`.

integer ftell(integer file_handle)

Given a valid file handle, `ftell` returns the offset of PHP's internal file pointer. If you wish to move the file pointer, use the `fseek` function.

```
<?
    // open a file
    if($myFile = fopen("data.txt", "r"))
    {
        //read characters until we find a space
        $c = "";
        while(!(feof($myFile)) AND ($c != " "))
        {
```

```
            $c = fgetc($myFile);
    }

    print("File pointer at " . ftell($myFile) . " bytes");
}
else
{
    print("file could not be opened");
}
?>
```

integer ftruncate(integer file_handle, integer size)

The `ftruncate` function truncates a file to a specified size, expressed in number of bytes.

integer fwrite(integer file_handle, string data, integer length)

The `fwrite` function writes a string to a file. It is similar to `fputs`, except that it is binary-safe. The `file_handle` argument must be an integer returned by `fopen`, `fsockopen`, or `popen`. The `length` argument is optional, but if present will cause the magic quotes functionality to be suspended. This means backslashes inserted into the string by PHP to escape quotes will not be stripped before writing.

```
<?
    // open file for writing
    $myFile = fopen("data.txt","w");

    // make sure the open was successful
    if(!($myFile))
    {
        print("file could not be opened");
        exit;
    }

    for($index=0; $index<10; $index++)
    {
        // write a line to the file
        fwrite($myFile, "line $index\n");
```

```
    }

    // close the file
    fclose($myFile);
?>
```

array get_meta_tags(string filename, boolean use_include_path)

The `get_meta_tags` function opens a file and scans for HTML meta tags. The function assumes it is a well-formed HTML file that uses native line breaks. An array indexed by the `name` attribute of the `meta` tag is returned. If the name contains any characters illegal in identifiers, they will be replaced with underscores. This helps if you wish to make all the elements of the array into variables using `extract`, a function discussed in Chapter 9, "Data Functions."

The optional `use_include_path` will cause `get_meta_tags` to look for the file in the include path instead of the current directory. The include path is set in `php.ini` and normally is used by the `include` function.

Like many of the file functions, `get_meta_tags` allows specifying a URL instead of a path on the local filesystem.

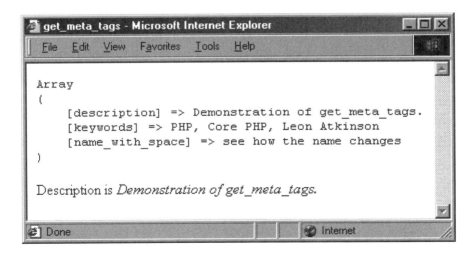

Figure 8-3 `get_meta_tags`.

```
<HTML>
<HEAD>
<TITLE>get_meta_tags</TITLE>
<META NAME="description" CONTENT="Demonstration of
get_meta_tags.">
<META NAME="keywords" CONTENT="PHP, Core PHP, Leon Atkin-
son">
<META NAME="Name With Space" CONTENT="see how the name
changes">
</HEAD>
<BODY>
<?
    $tag = get_meta_tags("get_meta_tags.php");

    //dump all elements of returned array
    print("<PRE>");
    print_r($tag);
    print("</PRE>\n");

    //get all tags as variables
    extract($tag, EXTR_PREFIX_ALL, "meta");

    print("Description is <I>$meta_description</I><BR>\n");
?>
</BODY>
</HTML>
```

Figure 8-3   Continued

include(string filename)

The `include` function causes the PHP parser to open the given file and execute it. The file is treated as a normal PHP script. That is, text is sent directly
to the browser unless PHP tags are used. You may use a variable to specify
the file, and if the call to include is inside a loop, it will be reevaluated each
time.

You may also specify files by URL by starting them with `http://` or
`ftp://`. PHP will fetch the file via the stated protocol and execute it as if it
were in the local filesystem.

Use of this function is discussed in detail in Chapter 7. Compare this function to `require`.

boolean is_dir(string filename)

The `is_dir` function returns TRUE if the given filename is a directory; otherwise it returns FALSE. Similar functions are `is_file` and `is_link`.

```
<?
        $filename = "data.txt";

        if(is_dir($filename))
        {
                print("$filename is a directory");
        }
        else
        {
                print("$filename is not a directory");
        }
?>
```

boolean is_executable(string filename)

The `is_executable` function returns TRUE if a file exists and is executable; otherwise it returns FALSE. On UNIX this is determined by the file's permissions. On Windows this is determined by the file extension. Two related functions are `is_readable` and `is_writeable`.

```
<?
        $filename = "data.txt";

        if(is_executable($filename))
        {
                print("$filename is executable");
        }
        else
        {
                print("$filename is not executable");
        }
?>
```

boolean is_file(string filename)

The `is_file` function returns TRUE if the given filename is neither a directory nor a symbolic link; otherwise it returns FALSE. Similar functions are `is_dir` and `is_link`.

```
<?
        $filename = "data.txt";

        if(is_file($filename))
        {
                print("$filename is a file");
        }
        else
        {
                print("$filename is not a file");
        }
?>
```

boolean is_link(string filename)

The is_link function returns TRUE if the given filename is a symbolic link; otherwise it returns FALSE. Similar functions are is_dir and is_file.

```
<?
        $filename = "data.txt";

        if(is_link($filename))
        {
                print("$filename is a link");
        }
        else
        {
                print("$filename is not a link");
        }
?>
```

boolean is_readable(string filename)

The is_readable function returns TRUE if a file exists and is readable; otherwise it returns false. On UNIX this is determined by the file's permissions. On Windows, TRUE is always returned if the file exists. This function is similar to is_executable and is_writeable.

```
<?
        $filename = "data.txt";

        if(is_readable($filename))
        {
```

```
                print("$filename is readable");
        }
        else
        {
                print("$filename is not readable");
        }
?>
```

boolean is_writeable(string filename)

The `is_writeable` function returns TRUE if a file exists and is writeable; otherwise it returns `false`. Similar functions are `is_executable` and `is_readable`.

```
<?
        $filename = "data.txt";

        if(is_writeable($filename))
        {
                print("$filename is writeable");
        }
        else
        {
                print("$filename is not writeable");
        }
?>
```

boolean link(string source, string destination)

The `link` function creates a hard link. A hard link may not point to a directory, may not point outside its own filesystem, and is indistinguishable from the file to which it links. See the man page for `link` or `ln` for a full description. The `link` function expects a source file and a destination file. On Windows this function does nothing and returns nothing. You can create a symbolic link with the `symlink` function.

```
<?
        link("/www/htdocs/index.php", "/www/htdocs/index2.php");
?>
```

integer linkinfo(string filename)

The linkinfo function calls the C function lstat for the given filename
and returns the st_dev field lstat generates. This may be used to verify the
existence of a link. It returns false on error. You can read more about
lstat on the man page, or in the help file for Microsoft Visual C++.

```
<?
        print(linkinfo("data.txt"));
?>
```

array lstat(string filename)

The lstat function executes C's stat function and returns an array. The
array contains 13 elements, numbered starting with zero. If the filename argument points to a symbolic link, the array will reflect the link, not the file to
which the link points. To get information about the files to which the link
points, use the stat function. Table 8.7 lists the contents of the array.

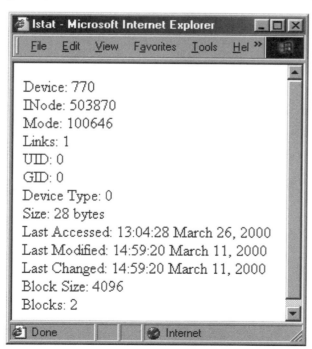

Figure 8–4   lstat.

```php
<?
      /*
      ** print stat information based on OS
      */

      // get stat information
      $statInfo = lstat("data.txt");

      if(eregi("windows", $OS))
      {
            // print useful information for Windows
            printf("Drive: %c <BR>\n", ($statInfo[0]+65));
            printf("Mode: %o <BR>\n", $statInfo[2]);
            print("Links: $statInfo[3] <BR>\n");
            print("Size: $statInfo[7] bytes<BR>\n");
            printf("Last Accessed: %s <BR>\n",
                    date("H:i:s F d, Y", $statInfo[8]));
            printf("Last Modified: %s <BR>\n",
                    date("H:i:s F d, Y", $statInfo[9]));
            printf("Created: %s <BR>\n",
                    date("H:i:s F d, Y", $statInfo[10]));
      }
      else
      {
            // print UNIX version
            print("Device: $statInfo[0] <BR>\n");
            print("INode: $statInfo[1] <BR>\n");
            printf("Mode: %o <BR>\n", $statInfo[2]);
            print("Links: $statInfo[3] <BR>\n");
            print("UID: $statInfo[4] <BR>\n");
            print("GID: $statInfo[5] <BR>\n");
            print("Device Type: $statInfo[6] <BR>\n");
            print("Size: $statInfo[7] bytes<BR>\n");
            printf("Last Accessed: %s <BR>\n",
                    date("H:i:s F d, Y", $statInfo[8]));
            printf("Last Modified: %s <BR>\n",
                    date("H:i:s F d, Y", $statInfo[9]));
            printf("Last Changed: %s <BR>\n",
                    date("H:i:s F d, Y", $statInfo[10]));
            print("Block Size: $statInfo[11] <BR>\n");
            print("Blocks: $statInfo[12] <BR>\n");
      }
?>
```

Figure 8–4   Continued

boolean mkdir(string directory, integer mode)

The `mkdir` function creates a new directory with the supplied name. Permissions will be set based on the `mode` argument, which follows the same rules as `chmod`. On Windows the `mode` argument is ignored. You can use the `rmdir` function to remove a directory.

```
<?
    if(mkdir("myDir", 0777))
    {
        print("directory created");
    }
    else
    {
        print("directory cannot be created");
    }
?>
```

integer opendir(string directory)

The `opendir` function requires a directory name and returns a directory handle. This handle may be used by `readdir`, `rewinddir`, and `closedir`. The `dir` function described above provides an alternative to this group of functions.

```
<?
    // print the current directory in a table
    print("<TABLE BORDER=\"1\">\n");

    // create header row
    print("<TR>\n");
    print("<TH>Filename</TH>\n");
    print("<TH>File Size</TH>\n");
    print("</TR>\n");

    // open directory
    $myDirectory = opendir(".");

    // get each entry
    while($entryName = readdir($myDirectory))
    {
        print("<TR>");
```

```
            print("<TD>$entryName</TD>");
            print("<TD ALIGN=\"right\">");
            print(filesize($entryName));
            print("</TD>");
            print("</TR>\n");
    }

    // close directory
    closedir($myDirectory);

    print("</TABLE>\n");
?>
```

integer pclose(integer file_handle)

The `pclose` function closes a file stream opened by `popen`. The return value of the process called in the call to `popen` is returned.

integer popen(string command, string mode)

The `popen` function opens a pipe to an executing command that may be read from or written to as if it were a file. A file handle is returned that is appropriate for use with functions such as `fgets`. Pipes work in one direction only, which means you can't use update modes with `popen`.

When you open a pipe, you are executing a program in the local filesystem. As with the other functions that execute a command (`exec`, `passthru`, and `system`), you should consider both the high cost of starting a new process and the security risk if user input is included in the `command` argument. If you must pass user-supplied data to a command, pass the information through the `escapeshellcmd` function first.

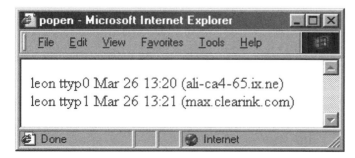

Figure 8–5 popen.

```
<?
    /*
    ** see who's logged in
    */
    $myPipe = popen("who", "r");

    while(!feof($myPipe))
    {
            print(nl2br(fgets($myPipe, 255)));
    }

    pclose($myPipe);
?>
```

Figure 8-5   Continued

string readdir(integer directory_handle)

The `readdir` function returns the name of the next file from a directory handle created by `opendir`, or `FALSE` when no entries remain. You can place `readdir` in the conditional expression of a `while` loop to get every entry in a directory. Keep in mind that `.` and `..` are always present and will be returned. See `closedir` for an example of use.

integer readfile(string filename)

The file given is read and sent directly to the browser by the `readfile` function, and the number of bytes read is returned. If an error occurs, `FALSE` is returned. If the filename begins with `http://` or `ftp://`, the file will be fetched using HTTP or FTP, respectively. Otherwise the file is opened in the local filesystem. If you need to send a compressed file to the browser, use `readgzfile`. If you'd rather read a file into a variable, use the `file` function.

```
<?
    print("Here is some data <BR>\n");

    readfile("data.txt");
?>
```

string readlink(string filename)

The `readlink` function returns the path to which a symbolic link points. It returns `FALSE` on error. Another function that gets information about a link is `linkinfo`.

```
<?
    print(readlink("data.txt"));
?>
```

boolean rename(string old_name, string new_name)

The `rename` function changes the name of a file specified by the `old_name` argument to the name specified in the `new_name` argument. The new and old names may contain complete paths, which allows you to use `rename` to move files.

```
<?
    //move data.txt from local directory
    //to the temp directory
    rename("./data.txt", "/tmp/data.dat");
?>
```

boolean rewind(integer file_handle)

The `rewind` function moves PHP's internal file pointer back to the beginning of the file. This is the same as using `fseek` to move to position zero.

```
<?
    /*
    ** print a file, then print the first line again
    */

    // open a local file
    $myFile = fopen("data.txt", "r");

    while(!feof($myFile))
    {
        // read a line from the file
        $myLine = fgetss($myFile, 255);
```

```
        print("$myLine <BR>\n");
    }
    rewind($myFile);
    $myLine = fgetss($myFile, 255);
    print("$myLine <BR>\n");

    // close the file
    fclose($myFile);
?>
```

boolean rewinddir(integer handle)

The rewinddir function resets PHP's internal pointer to the beginning of a directory listing. It returns TRUE unless an error occurs, in which case it returns FALSE. The handle is an integer returned by opendir.

```
<?
    /*
    ** print the current directory in a table
    */
    print("<TABLE BORDER=\"1\">\n");

    // open directory
    $myDirectory = opendir(".");

    print("<TR>\n");
    print("<TH>Filename</TH>\n");

    // get each entry
    while($entryName = readdir($myDirectory))
    {
        print("<TD>$entryName</TD>\n");
    }

    print("</TR>\n");

    // Go back to beginning
    rewinddir($myDirectory);

    print("<TR>\n");
    print("<TH>Size</TH>\n");

    // get each entry
    while($entryName = readdir($myDirectory))
    {
```

```
            print("<TD ALIGN=\"right\">");
            print(filesize($entryName));
            print("</TD>\n");
        }
        print("</TR>\n");

        // close directory
        closedir($myDirectory);

        print("</TABLE>\n");
?>
```

boolean rmdir(string directory)

Use the rmdir function to remove a directory. The directory must be empty.
To remove a file, use unlink.

```
<?
    if(rmdir("/tmp/leon"))
    {
        print("Directory removed");
    }
    else
    {
        print("Directory not removed"):
    }
?>
```

set_file_buffer(integer file_handle, integer size)

Use set_file_buffer to set the size of the write buffer on a file stream. It
requires a valid file handle as created by fopen, fsockopen, or popen. The
size argument is a number of bytes, and if you set a buffer size of zero, no
buffering will be used. You must call set_file_buffer before making any
reads or writes to the file stream. By default, file streams start with 8K
buffers.

```
<?
    // open file for writing
    $myFile = fopen("data.txt","w");

    // make sure the open was successful
```

```
        if(!($myFile))
        {
                print("file could not be opened");
                exit;
        }

        //use 1K buffer
        print(set_file_buffer($myFile, 1024));


        for($index=0; $index<10; $index++)
        {
                // write a line to the file
                fwrite($myFile, "line $index\n");
        }

        // close the file
        fclose($myFile);
?>
```

array stat(string filename)

The stat function executes C's stat function and returns an array. The array contains 13 elements, numbered starting at zero. If the filename argument points to a symbolic link, the array will reflect the file to which the link points. To get information about the link itself, use the lstat function. Table 8.7 lists the contents of the array.

```
<?
        /*
        ** print stat information based on OS
        */

        // get stat information
        $statInfo = stat("data.txt");

        if(eregi("windows", $OS))
        {
                // print useful information for Windows
                printf("Drive: %c <BR>\n", ($statInfo[0]+65));
                printf("Mode: %o <BR>\n", $statInfo[2]);
                print("Links: $statInfo[3] <BR>\n");
                print("Size: $statInfo[7] bytes<BR>\n");
```

```
        printf("Last Accessed: %s <BR>\n",
                date("H:i:s F d, Y", $statInfo[8]));
        printf("Last Modified: %s <BR>\n",
                date("H:i:s F d, Y", $statInfo[9]));
        printf("Created: %s <BR>\n",
                date("H:i:s F d, Y", $statInfo[10]));
    }
    else
    {
        // print UNIX version
        print("Device: $statInfo[0] <BR>\n");
        print("INode: $statInfo[1] <BR>\n");
        printf("Mode: %o <BR>\n", $statInfo[2]);
        print("Links: $statInfo[3] <BR>\n");
        print("UID: $statInfo[4] <BR>\n");
        print("GID: $statInfo[5] <BR>\n");
        print("Device Type: $statInfo[6] <BR>\n");
        print("Size: $statInfo[7] bytes<BR>\n");
        printf("Last Accessed: %s <BR>\n",
                date("H:i:s F d, Y", $statInfo[8]));
        printf("Last Modified: %s <BR>\n",
                date("H:i:s F d, Y", $statInfo[9]));
        printf("Last Changed: %s <BR>\n",
                date("H:i:s F d, Y", $statInfo[10]));
        print("Block Size: $statInfo[11] <BR>\n");
        print("Blocks: $statInfo[12] <BR>\n");
    }
?>
```

Table 8.7   Array Elements Returned by the `stat` `Function`

Element	Name	Description
0	Device or Drive Letter	This is a number identifying the device of the `filesystem`.On Windows this number denotes the drive letter the file is on, with the A drive being zero.
1	Inode	A unique identifier for the file, always zero on Windows. This is the same value you will get from the `fileinode` function.
2	Mode	This is the same value you will get from `fileperms`, the read/write/execute permissions.

(continued)

3	Number of Links	Number of links to file. On Windows, this will always be 1 if the file is not on an NTFS partition.
4	User	User ID of the owner, Always zero on Windows. This is the same value you will get from the `fileowner` function.
5	Group	Group ID, always zero on Windows. This is the same value you will get from the `filegroup` function.
6	Device Type	This is the type of the device. On Windows it repeats the device number.
7	Size	Size of the file in bytes, which is the same as reported by `filesize`.
8	Last Accessed	Last time the file was accessed, as defined in the description of `fileatime`.
9	Last Modified	Last time the file was modified, as defined in the description of `filemtime`.
10	Last Changed	Last time the file was changed, as defined in the description of `filectime`.\ On Windows this is the time the file was created.
11	Block Size	Suggested block size for I/O to file, −1 under Windows.
12	Number of Blocks	Number of blocks used by file, −1 under Windows.

boolean symlink(string source, string destination)

The `symlink` function creates a symbolic link to the source argument with the name in the destination argument. To create a hard link, use the `link` function.

```
<?
    //link moredata.txt to existing file data.txt
    if(symlink("data.txt", "moredata.txt"))
    {
        print("Symbolic link created");
    }
    else
```

```
        {
                print("Symbolic link not created");
        }
?>
```

integer tmpfile()

The tmpfile function opens a new temporary file and returns its file handle. This handle may be used in the same way as one returned by fopen using an update mode. When you close the file, or your script ends, the file will be removed. This function is a wrapper for the C function of the same name. If for some reason a temporary file cannot be created, FALSE is returned.

```
<?
        //open a temporary file
        $fp = tmpfile();

        //write 10K of random data
        //to simulate some process
        for($i=0; $i<10240; $i++)
        {
                //randomly choose a letter
                //from a range of printables
                fputs($fp, chr(rand(ord(' '), ord('z'))));
        }

        //return to start of file
        rewind($fp);

        //dump and close file,
        //therefore deleting it
        fpassthru($fp);
?>
```

boolean touch(string filename, integer time)

The touch function attempts to set the time the file was last modified to the given time, expressed in seconds since January 1, 1970. If the time argument is omitted, the current time is used. If the file does not exist, it will be created with zero length. This function is often used to create empty files.

To find out when a file was last modified, use `filemtime`.

```
<?
    touch("data.txt");
?>
```

integer umask(integer umask)

The `umask` function returns the default permissions given files when they are created. If the optional `umask` argument is given, it sets the `umask` to a logical-and (&) performed on the given integer and 0777. Under Windows this function does nothing and returns `false`. To find out the permissions set on a particular file, use `fileperms`.

```
<?
    printf("umask is %o", umask(0444));
?>
```

boolean unlink(string filename)

The `unlink` function removes a file permanently. To remove a directory, use `rmdir`.

```
<?
    if(unlink("data2.txt"))
    {
        print("data2.txt deleted");
    }
    else
    {
        print("data2.txt could not be deleted");
    }
?>
```

Compressed File Functions

The functions in this section use the zlib library to work with files compressed with GNU compression tools, such as `gzip`. The library was written by Jean-loup Gaill and Mark Adler. The two are authors of the `gzip` tool, in fact. You can obtain more information and the library itself from the zlib home page <http://www.cdrom.com/pub/infozip/zlib/>.

In order to activate these functions, you must include the zlib extension. On a UNIX operating system, you configure PHP to use zlib as you compile it. On Windows you may activate the `php_zlib.dll` extension either in `php.ini` or using the `dl` function.

Most of the functions for reading and writing files are duplicated here and they operate similarly. One difference is the lack of support for specifying files using HTTP or FTP protocol.

boolean gzclose(integer file_handle)

The `gzclose` function closes a file opened with `gzopen`. TRUE is returned if the file closed successfully. FALSE is returned if the file cannot be closed. See `gzgets` for an example of use.

boolean gzeof(integer file_handle)

As you read from a compressed file, PHP keeps a pointer to the last place in the file you read. The `gzeof` function returns TRUE if you are at the end of the file. See `gzgets` for an example of use.

array gzfile(string filename, boolean use_include_path)

The `gzfile` function reads an entire file into an array. The file is first un-compressed. Each line of the file is a separate element of the array, starting at zero. The optional `use_include_path` argument causes `gzfile` to search for the file within the include path specified in `php.ini`.

```
<?
    // open file and print each line
    $myFile = gzfile( "data.gz");
    for($index = 0; $index < count($myFile); $index++)
    {
        print($myFile[$index]);
    }
?>
```

string gzgetc(integer file_handle)

The `gzgetc` function returns a single character from a compressed file. It expects a file handle as returned by `gzopen`.

```
<?
    // open compressed file and print each character
    if($myFile = gzopen("data.gz", "r"))
    {
        while(!gzeof($myFile))
        {
            $myCharacter = gzgetc($myFile);
            print($myCharacter);
        }

        gzclose($myFile);
    }
?>
```

string gzgets(integer file_handle, integer length)

The `gzgets` function returns a string it reads from a compressed file specified by the file handle, which must have been created with `gzopen`. It will attempt to read as many characters as specified by the `length` argument less one (presumably this is PHP showing its C heritage). A linebreak is treated as a stopping point, as is the end of the file. Linebreaks are included in the return string.

```
<?
    // open file and print each line
    if($myFile = gzopen("data.gz", "r"))
    {
        while(!gzeof($myFile))
        {
            $myLine = gzgets($myFile, 255);
            print($myLine);
        }

        gzclose($myFile);
    }
?>
```

string gzgetss(integer file_handle, integer length, string ignore)

The gzgetss function is in all respects identical to gzgets except that it attempts to strip any HTML or PHP code before returning a string. The optional ignore argument may contain tags to be ignored.

```
<?
    // open compressed file and print each line
    if($myFile = gzopen("data.gz", "r"))
    {
        while(!gzeof($myFile))
        {
            $myLine = gzgetss($myFile, 255);
            print($myLine);
        }

        gzclose($myFile);
    }
?>
```

integer gzopen(string filename, string mode, boolean use_include_path)

The gzopen function is similar in operation to the fopen function, except that it operates on compressed files. If the use_include_path argument is TRUE, the include path specified in php.ini will be searched. See gzgets and gzputs for examples of use.

The mode argument accepts a few extra parameters compared to fopen. In addition to the modes listed in Table 8.6, you may specify a compression level and a compression strategy if you are creating a new file. Immediately following the write mode, you may place an integer between zero and nine that specifies the level of compression. Zero means no compression, and nine is maximum compression. After the compression level, you may use h to force Huffman encoding only, or f to optimize for filtered input. Filtered data is defined by the zlib source code as being small values of somewhat random distribution. In almost all cases the default settings are a good choice and the extra mode settings are unnecessary.

It is possible to open an uncompressed file with gzopen. Reads from the file will operate as expected. This can be convenient if you do not know ahead of time whether a file is compressed.

boolean gzpassthru(integer file_handle)

The gzpassthru function prints the contents of the compressed file to the browser, exactly like the fpassthru function.

```
<?
    // open a compressed file
    if(!($myFile = gzopen("data.html.gz", "r")))
    {
            print("file could not be opened");
            exit;
    }

    // send the entire file to browser
    gzpassthru($myFile);
?>
```

boolean gzputs(int file_handle, string output, integer length)

The gzputs function writes data to a compressed file. It expects a file handle as returned by gzopen. It returns TRUE if the write was successful, FALSE if it failed. The optional length argument specifies a maximum number of input bytes to accept. A side effect of specifying length is that the magic_quotes_runtime configuration setting will be ignored.

```
<?
    // open file for writing
    // use maximum compress and force
    // Huffman encoding only
    $myFile = gzopen("data.gz","wb9h");

    // make sure the open was successful
    if(!($myFile))
    {
            print("file could not be opened");
            exit;
    }

    for($index=0; $index<10; $index++)
    {
            // write a line to the file
            gzputs($myFile, "line $index\n");
```

```
        }

        // close the file
        gzclose($myFile);
?>
```

gzread

The gzread function is an alias to gzgets.

boolean gzrewind(integer file_handle)

The gzrewind function moves PHP's internal file pointer back to the beginning of a compressed file. It returns TRUE on success, FALSE if there is an
error.

```
<?
        /*
        ** print a file, then print the first line again
        */

        // open a local file
        if(!($myFile = gzopen("data.gz", "r")))
        {
                print("file could not be opened");
                exit;
        }

        while(!gzeof($myFile))
        {
                // read a line from the file
                $myLine = gzgetss($myFile, 255);
                print("$myLine <BR>\n");
        }

        gzrewind($myFile);
        $myLine = gzgetss($myFile, 255);
        print("$myLine <BR>\n");

        // close the file
        gzclose($myFile);
?>
```

integer gzseek(integer file_handle, integer offset)

This function works exactly like `fseek`, except that it operates on compressed files.

```
<?
    // open a file
    if(!($myFile = gzopen("data.gz", "r")))
    {
        print("file could not be opened");
        exit;
    }

    // jump 32 bytes into the file
    gzseek($myFile, 32);

    $myLine = gzgets($myFile, 255);
    print($myLine);

    // dump the rest of the file
    gzpassthru($myFile);

?>
```

integer gztell(integer file_handle)

Given a valid file handle, `gztell` returns the offset of PHP's internal file pointer.

```
<?
    // open a file
    if(!($myFile = gzopen("data.gz", "r")))
    {
        print("file could not be opened");
        exit;
    }

    $myLine = gzgets($myFile, 255);
    print($myLine);

    print("<HR>\n");
```

```
    print("File pointer at " . gztell($myFile) . " bytes");

    // close file
    gzclose($myFile);

?>
```

gzwrite

The gzwrite function is an alias to gzputs.

integer readgzfile(string filename, boolean use_include_path)

The readgzfile function operates identically to the readfile function, except that it expects the file to be compressed. The file is uncompressed on the fly and sent directly to the browser.

```
<?
    //dump uncompressed contents of
    //data.gz to browser
    readgzfile("data.gz");
?>
```

POSIX

Kristian Koehntopp added a module to PHP to support the POSIX.1 standard, also known as IEEE 1003.1. This standard describes functionality provided to user processes by an operating system. A few functions in this section are not part of the standard, but are commonly available in System V or BSD UNIX systems.

Many of these functions are available only to the root user. PHP scripts are executed by the owner of the Web server process, which is usually a special user for just this purpose. Running the Web server as root is unusual and dangerous. Anyone able to view a PHP file through the Web server would have arbitrary control over the system. Keep in mind, however, that PHP can be compiled as a stand-alone executable. In this case it can be used like any other scripting language.

These functions are wrappers for underlying C functions, usually named by the part after the `posix_` prefix. If you require detailed information, I suggest reading the man pages.

string posix_ctermid()

The `posix_ctermid` function returns the terminal path name.

```
<?
        print("Terminal Path Name: " . posix_ctermid() . "<BR>\n");
?>
```

string posix_getcwd()

The `posix_getcwd` function returns the current working directory.

```
<?
    print ("Current Working Directory: " . posix_getcwd() . "<BR>\n");
?>
```

integer posix_getegid()

The `posix_getegid` function returns the effective group ID of the calling process.

integer posix_geteuid()

The `posix_geteuid` function returns the effective user ID for the process running the PHP engine.

integer posix_getgid()

The `posix_getgid` function returns the ID of the current group.

array posix_getgrgid(integer group)

The `posix_getgrgid` function returns an array describing access to the group database. The elements of the returned array are `gid`, `members`, `name`, and an entry of each member of the group.

```
<?
    $group = posix_getgrgid(posix_getgid());
    print("Group: {$group['name']}<BR>\n");
?>
```

array posix_getgrnam(string group)

The `posix_getgrnam` function returns an array describing access to the group database. The elements of the returned array are `gid`, `members`, `name`, and an entry of each member of the group.

array posix_getgroups()

The `posix_getgroups` function returns supplementary group IDs.

string posix_getlogin()

Use `posix_getlogin` to get the login name of the user executing the PHP engine.

integer posix_getpgid()

The `posix_getpgid` function returns the group ID for the user executing the PHP engine.

integer posix_getpgrp()

The `posix_getpgrp` function returns the current process group ID.

integer posix_getpid()

The `posix_getpid` function returns the process ID.

integer posix_getppid()

The `posix_getppid` function returns the process ID of the parent process.

array posix_getpwnam(string user)

The posix_getpwnam function returns an array describing an entry in the user database. The elements of the array are dir, gecos, gid, name, passwd, shell, and uid.

array posix_getpwuid(integer user)

The posix_getpwuid function returns an array describing an entry in the user database based on a given user ID. The elements of the array are dir, gecos, gid, name, passwd, shell, and uid. These are the same elements returned by posix_getpwnam.

array posix_getrlimit()

The posix_getrlimit function returns an array describing system resource usage. The array contains elements that begin with hard or soft followed by a space and one of the following limit names: core, cpu, data, filesize, maxproc, memlock, openfiles, rss, stack, totalmem, virtualmem.

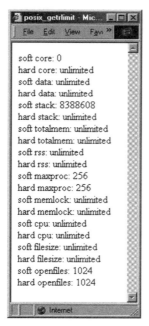

Figure 8-6 posix_getrlimit.

```
<?
      foreach(posix_getrlimit() as $key=>$value)
      {
            print("$key: $value<BR>\n");
      }
?>
```

Figure 8-6 Continued

integer posix_getsid()

The posix_getsid function returns the process group ID of the session leader.

integer posix_getuid()

The posix_getuid function returns the user ID of the user executing the PHP engine.

boolean posix_isatty (integer descriptor)

The posix_isatty function returns TRUE if the given file descriptor is a TTY.

boolean posix_kill(integer process, integer signal)

The posix_kill function sends a signal to a process.

boolean posix_mkfifo(string path, integer mode)

The posix_mkfifo function creates a FIFO file. The mode argument follows the same rules as chmod.

boolean posix_setgid(integer group)

Use posix_setgid to change the group for the current process. Only the root user may switch groups.

integer posix_setpgid(integer process, integer group)

The posix_setpgid function sets the process group ID for a given process.

integer posix_setsid()

The posix_setsid function creates a session and returns the process group ID.

boolean posix_setuid(integer user)

Use posix_setuid to change the user for the current process. Only the root user may change the user ID.

array posix_times()

The posix_times function returns an array of values on system clocks. The elements of the array are cstime, cutime, stime, ticks, and utime.

```
<?
      foreach(posix_times() as $key=>$value)
      {
            print("$key: $value<BR>\n");
      }
?>
```

string posix_ttyname(integer descriptor)

The `posix_ttyname` function returns the name of the terminal device.

array posix_uname()

The `posix_uname` function returns an array of information about the system. The elements of the array are `machine`, `nodename`, `release`, `sysname`, and `version`.

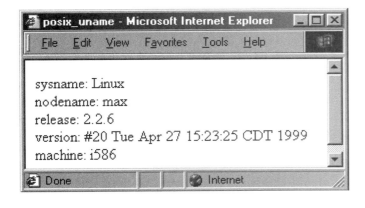

```
<?
        foreach(posix_uname() as $key=>$value)
        {
                print("$key: $value<BR>\n");
        }
?>
```

Figure 8-7 `posix_uname.`

Debugging

The debugging functions help you figure out just what the heck is going on with the inevitable broken script. Some of these functions make diagnostic information available to you inside your script. Others communicate with either a system log or a remote debugger. Practical approaches to debugging are addressed in Chapter 21, "Design."

assert(expression)

The assert function tests an expression. If the assertion is true, no action is taken and the script continues. If the assertion is false, behavior is dictated by the assertion options. By default, assertions are not active, which means they are simply ignored. Use `assert_options` to activate them.

Assertions are a nice way to add error checking to your code, especially paranoid checks that are useful during development but unneeded during production.

```
<?
    //create custom assertion function
    function failedAssertion($file, $line, $expression)
    {
        print("On line $line, in file '$file' ");
        print("the following assertion failed: '$expression'<BR>\n");
    }

    //turn on asserts
    assert_options(ASSERT_ACTIVE, TRUE);

    //bail on assertion failure
    assert_options(ASSERT_CALLBACK, "failedAssertion");

    //assert a FALSE expression
    assert(1 == 2);
?>
```

value assert_options(integer flag, value)

Use `assert_options` to get and set assert flags. Table 8.8 lists the flags and their meanings. The previous value is returned. Most of the options expect a boolean because they are either on or off. The exception is the option for setting the callback function. This option expects the name of a function to be called when an assertion fails. This function will be called with three arguments: the filename, the line number, and the expression that evaluated as FALSE.

value call_user_function(string function, ...)

Use `call_user_function` to execute a function you've defined. The function argument names the function. Arguments to be passed to the function follow.

Table 8.8 Assert Options	
Flag	*Description*
ASSERT_ACTIVE	Asserts are ignored unless activated with this option.
ASSERT_BAIL	Exits the script if assertion fails. FALSE by default.
ASSERT_CALLBACK	Registers a function to be called on failure. No function is registered by default.
ASSERT_QUIET_EVAL	Prints the expression passed to assert. FALSE by default.
ASSERT_WARNING	Prints a regular PHP warning message. TRUE by default.

value call_user_method(string method, string object, ...)

Use `call_user_method` to execute a method defined in an object. You are required to name a method and an object. Any arguments to pass to the method follow.

closelog()

The `closelog` function closes any connection to the system log. Calling it is optional, as PHP will close the connection for you when necessary. See `syslog` for an example of use.

boolean connection_aborted()

Use `connection_aborted` to test if a request for your script was aborted. The user may do this by clicking the stop button on the browser, or closing the browser completely. Ordinarily your script will stop executing when aborted. However, you may change this behavior with the `ignore_user_abort` function. You can also set abort handling using commands in `php.ini` or with an Apache directive.

```
<?
    //allow script continuation if aborted
    ignore_user_abort(TRUE);
```

```
//fake a long task
sleep(20);

//check for abort
if(connection_aborted())
{
     //write to log that the process was aborted
     openlog("TEST", LOG_PID | LOG_CONS, LOG_USER);
     syslog(LOG_INFO, "The fake task has been aborted!");
     closelog();
}
else
{
     print("Thanks for waiting!\n");
}
?>
```

integer connection_status()

The connection_status function returns an integer describing the status of the connection to the browser. The integer uses bitfields to signal whether a connection was aborted or timed out. That is, binary digits are flipped on to signal either of the conditions. The first bit signals whether the script aborted. The second signals whether the script reached its maximum execution time. Rather than using 1 or 2, you can use the convenient constants ABORTED and TIMEOUT. There's also a constant named NORMAL, which is set to zero, meaning no bitfields are turned on.

An alternative to connection_status is to use connect_aborted and connection_timeout, which each return TRUE or FALSE.

```
<?
     function cleanUp()
     {
          $status = connection_status();

          $statusMessage = date("Y-m-d H:i:s");
          $statusMessage .= " Status was $status. ";

          if($status & ABORTED)
          {
               $statusMessage .= "The script was aborted. ";
          }
```

```
        if($status & TIMEOUT)
        {
                $statusMessage .= "The script timed out. ";
        }

        $statusMessage .= "\n";
        //write status to log file
        error_log($statusMessage, 3, "status.log");
    }

    //set cleanUp to the shutdown function
    register_shutdown_function("cleanUp");

    //wait out the max execution time
    sleep(35);

    print("Fake task finished.\n");
?>
```

boolean connection_timeout()

The `connection_timeout` function returns TRUE when the current script has stopped because the maximum execution time was reached. It is really of use only inside a function you've registered as a shutdown function with `register_shutdown_function`. You can use `set_time_limit` to adjust the time a script is allowed to run. Alternatively, you may wish to use `connection_status`.

```
<?
    function cleanUp()
    {
        if(connection_timeout())
        {
                $statusMessage = date("Y-m-d H:i:s");
                $statusMessage .= " The script timed out. \n";

                //write status to log file
                error_log($statusMessage, 3, "status.log");
        }
    }
```

```
        //set cleanUp to the shutdown function
        register_shutdown_function("cleanUp");

        //wait out the max execution time
        while(TRUE);

        print("Fake task finished.\n");
?>
```

debugger_off()

The `debugger_off` function tells PHP to stop sending debugging information to the remote debugger.

```
<?
        debugger_off();
?>
```

boolean debugger_on(string host)

Use `debugger_on` to enable remote debugging. Diagnostic information will be sent to the specified host using the port set in `php.ini`, which is 7869 by default. Use of the remote debugger is discussed in Chapter 22, "Efficiency and Debugging."

```
<?
        debugger_on("127.0.0.1");
?>
```

boolean error_log(string message, integer type,
string destination, string extra_headers)

The `error_log` function sends an error message to one of four places depending on the `type` argument. The four values for the `type` argument are listed in Table 8.9. An alternative to `error_log` is the `syslog` function.

```
<?
        //send log message via email to root
        error_log("The error_log is working", 1, "root", "");
?>
```

Table 8.9 `error_log` Message Types	

Type	Description
0	Depending on the `error_log` configuration directive, the message is sent either to the system log or to a file.
1	The message is sent by email to the address specified by the destination argument. If the `extra_headers` argument is not empty, it is sent as headers to the email.
2	The message is sent through the remote debugging system. The destination argument specifies the `host` and `port` separated by a colon.
3	The message is appended to the file specified by the `destination` argument.

boolean extension_loaded(string extension)

Use `extension_loaded` to test for the presence of an extension.

```
<?
    if(extension_loaded("php_mysql.dll"))
    {
            print("php_mysql.dll is present");
    }
    else
    {
            print("php_mysql.dll is not present");
    }
?>
```

value func_get_arg(integer argument)

The `func_get_arg` function allows you to get by number an argument passed to a function you write. The first argument will be number zero. This allows you to write functions that take any number of arguments. The return value might be any type, matching the type of the argument being fetched. The `func_num_args` function returns the number of arguments available.

Chapter 4, "Functions," discusses functions, including writing functions that accept an unlimited number of arguments.

```
<?
        /*
        ** Function concat
        ** Input: any number of strings
        ** Output: string
        ** Description: input strings are put together in
        ** order and returned as a single string.
        */
        function concat()
        {
                //start with empty string
                $returnValue ="";

                //loop over each argument
                for($i=0; $i < func_num_args(); $i++)
                {
                        //add current argument to return value
                        $returnValue .= func_get_arg($i);
                }

                return($returnValue);
        }

        //prints "OneTwoThree"
        print(concat("One", "Two", "Three") . "<BR>\n");
?>
```

array func_get_args()

Use func_get_args to get an array containing all the arguments passed as
arguments to the function. The elements of the array will be indexed
with integers, starting with zero. This provides an alternative to using
func_get_arg and func_num_args.

```
<?
        /*
        ** Function gcd
        ** Input: any number of integers
        ** Output: integer
        ** Description: Returns the greatest common
        ** denominator from the input.
        */
        function gcd()
        {
```

```
/*
** start a smallest value and try every value
** until we get to 1, which is common to all
*/

$start = 2147483647;
foreach(func_get_args() as $arg)
{
        if(abs($arg) < $start)
        {
                $start = abs($arg);
        }
}

for($i=$start; $i > 1; $i--)
{
        //assume we will find a gcd
        $isCommon = TRUE;

        //try each number in the supplied arguments
        foreach(func_get_args() as $arg)
        {
                //if $arg divided by $i produces a
                //remainder, then we don't have a gcd
                if(($arg % $i) != 0)
                {
                        $isCommon = FALSE;
                }
        }

        //if we made it through the previous code
        //and $isCommon is still TRUE, then we found
        //our gcd
        if($isCommon)
        {
                break;
        }
}

        return($i);
}

//prints 5
print(gcd(10, 20, -35) . "<BR>\n");
?>
```

integer func_num_args()

The `func_num_args` function returns the number of arguments passed to a function. See the description of `func_get_arg` for an example of use.

boolean function_exists(string function)

Use `function_exists` to test that a function is available, either natively or defined previously by PHP code.

```
<?
    $function = "date";
    if(function_exists($function))
    {
        print($function . " exists");
    }
?>
```

object get_browser(string user_agent)

The `get_browser` function works with the `browscap.ini` (browser capabilities) file to report the capabilities of a browser. The `user_agent` argument is the text a browser identifies itself with during an HTTP transaction. If you leave out this argument, PHP uses `HTTP_USER_AGENT`, a variable created by PHP for you. The argument is matched against all the browsers in the `browscap.ini` file. When a match occurs, each of the capabilities becomes a property in the object returned.

The location of the `browscap.ini` file is specified in `php.ini` using the `browscap` directive. If the directive is not used, or PHP can't match a browser to an entry in your `browscap.ini` file, no error will be produced. However, the returned object will have no properties.

Microsoft provides a `browscap.ini` file for use with its Web server, but it is not freely distributable. In response, PHP has an official `browscap.ini` file. It may be found at <http://php.netvision.net.il/browscap/> and depends on contributions. At the time of this writing, it appeared to be abandoned. Alternatively, you may wish to get a `browscap.ini` from Web developer cyScape at <http://www.cyscape.com/asp/browscap/>. Be aware you are required to register first.

```
<?
    $browser = get_browser();
    print("You are using " . $browser->browser . "<BR>\n");
```

```
        if($browser->javascript)
        {
                print("Your browser supports JavaScript.<BR>\n");
        }
?>
```

string get_cfg_var(string variable)

The `get_cfg_var` function returns the value of the specified configuration variable. These are the variables specified in `php.ini` or in Apache's configuration files. You can get a report on all configuration information by calling the `phpinfo` function.

```
<?
    print("Scripts are allowed to run " .
        get_cfg_var("max_execution_time") .
        " seconds");
?>
```

string get_class(object variable)

The `get_class` function returns the name of the class for the given object.

```
<?
        class animal
        {
                var $name;
        }

        $gus = new animal;

        print("Gus is of type " . get_class($gus) . "<BR>\n");
?>
```

array get_class_methods(string class)

The `get_class_methods` function returns an array of the names of the methods for the given class.

```
<?
        class dog
        {
```

```
            var $name="none";
            var $sound="woof!";

            function speak()
            {
                    print($this->sound);
            }
    }

    $gus = new dog;
    $gus->name = "Gus";

    foreach(get_class_methods("dog") as $method)
    {
            print("$method<BR>\n");
    }
?>
```

array get_class_vars(string class)

The get_class_vars function returns an array containing properties of a class and their default values. Compare this function to get_object_vars.

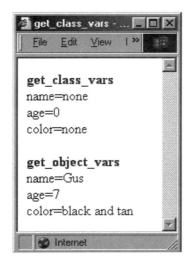

Figure 8-8 get_class_vars.

```
<?
    class animal
    {
            var $name="none";
            var $age=0;
            var $color="none";
    }

    $gus = new animal;
    $gus->name = "Gus";
    $gus->age = 7;
    $gus->color = "black and tan";

    print("<B>get_class_vars</B><BR>\n");
    foreach(get_class_vars("animal") as $key=>$val)
    {
            print("$key=$val<BR>\n");
    }

    print("<BR>\n");

    print("<B>get_object_vars</B><BR>\n");
    foreach(get_object_vars($gus) as $key=>$val)
    {
            print("$key=$val<BR>\n");
    }

?>
```

Figure 8-8 Continued

string get_current_user()

The `get_current_user` function returns the name of the user who owns the script being executed. This function isn't guaranteed to have any meaning under Windows 98.

```
<?
    print(get_current_user());
?>
```

string getcwd()

The `getcwd` function returns the name of the current working directory, including the full path.

```
<?
      print(getcwd());
?>
```

array get_extension_funcs(string extension)

Use `get_extension_funcs` to get an array of the names of functions created by an extension.

array get_loaded_extensions()

The `get_loaded_extensions` function returns an array of the names of the extensions available. This includes extensions compiled into PHP or loaded with `dl`. Another way to see this list is with `phpinfo`.

array get_object_vars(object data)

The `get_object_vars` function returns an array describing the properties of an object and their values. See `get_class_vars` for an example of use.

boolean highlight_file(string filename)

The `highlight_file` function prints a PHP script directly to the browser using syntax highlighting. HTML is used to emphasize parts of the PHP language in order to aid readability.

```
<?
      //highlight this file
      highlight_file(__FILE__);
?>
```

boolean highlight_string(string code)

The `highlight_string` function prints a string of PHP code to the browser using syntax highlighting.

```
<?
      //create some code
      $code = "print(\"a string\");";
```

```
        //highlight sample code
        highlight_string($code);
?>
```

string get_html_translation_table (integer table)

Use `get_html_translation_table` to get the table used by `htmlentities` and `htmlspecialchars`. By default the former is returned, but if `table` is 1, the table used by `htmlspecialchars` is returned.

```
<?
        $trans = get_html_translation_table(HTML_ENTITIES);

        print("<pre>");
        var_dump($trans);
        print("</pre>\n");
?>
```

integer get_magic_quotes_gpc()

The `get_magic_quotes_gpc` function returns the `magic_quotes_gpc` directive setting, which controls whether quotes are escaped automatically in user-submitted data.

```
<?
        if(get_magic_quotes_gpc() == 1)
        {
                print("magic_quotes_gpc is on");
        }
        else
        {
                print("magic_quotes_gpc is off");
        }
?>
```

integer get_magic_quotes_runtime()

The `get_magic_quotes_runtime` function returns the magic_quotes_ runtime directive setting, which controls whether quotes are escaped automatically in data retrieved from databases. You can use `set_magic_quotes_runtime` to change its value.

```
<?
    if(get_magic_quotes_runtime() == 1)
    {
            print("magic_quotes_runtime is on");
    }
    else
    {
            print("magic_quotes_runtime is off");
    }
?>
```

string get_parent_class(object variable)

The `get_parent_class` function returns the name of the parent class for an object.

```
<?
    class animal
    {
            var $name;
    }

    class dog extends animal
    {
            var $owner;
    }

    $gus = new dog;
    $gus->name = "Gus";
    //Gus is of type dog, which is of type animal
    print("$gus->name is of type " .
            get_class($gus) . ", which is of type ".
            get_parent_class($gus) . "<BR>\n");
?>
```

integer getlastmod()

The `getlastmod` function returns the date the executing script was last modified. The date is returned as a number of seconds since January 1, 1970. This is the same as calling `filemtime` on the current file.

```
<?
    printf("This script was last modified %s",
        date("m/d/y", getlastmod()));
?>
```

integer getmyinode()

The `getmyinode` function returns the inode of the executing script. Under Windows, zero is always returned. You can get the inode of any file using `fileinode`.

```
<?
    print(getmyinode());
?>
```

integer getmypid()

The `getmypid` function returns the process identifier of the PHP engine. It may not return anything under Windows 98.

```
<?
    print(getmypid());
?>
```

integer getmyuid()

The `getmyuid` function returns the user identifier of the owner of the script.

```
<?
    print(getmyuid());
?>
```

array getrusage(integer children)

The getrusage function is a wrapper for the C function of the same name. It reports information about the resources used by the calling process. If the children argument is 1, the function will be called with the RUSAGE_CHILDREN constant. You may wish to read the man page for more information.

```
<?
        //show CPU time used
        $rusage = getrusage(1);
        print($rusage["ru_utime.tv_sec"] . " seconds used.");
?>
```

boolean headers_sent()

The headers_sent function returns TRUE if HTTP headers have been sent. Headers must precede any content, so executing a print statement or placing text outside PHP tags will cause headers to be sent. Attempting to add headers to the stack after they're sent causes an error.

```
<?
        if(headers_sent())
        {
                print("Can't add more headers!<BR>\n");
        }
        else
        {
                header("X-Debug: It's OK to send a header");
        }
?>
```

boolean leak(integer bytes)

The leak function purposely leaks memory. It is useful mostly for testing the garbage-collecting routines of PHP itself. You might also use it to simulate lots of memory usage if you were stress-testing.

```
<?
        //leak 8 megs
        leak(8388608);
?>
```

boolean method_exists(object variable, string method)

The `method_exists` function returns TRUE when the named method exists in the specified object.

```
<?
    class animal
    {
        var $name;
    }

    class dog extends animal
    {
        var $owner;

        function speak()
        {
            print("woof!");
        }
    }

    $gus = new dog;
    $gus->name = "Gus";

    if(method_exists($gus, "speak"))
    {
        $gus->speak();
    }
?>
```

openlog(string identifier, integer option, integer facility)

The `openlog` function begins a connection to the system log and calls C's `openlog` function. It is not strictly required to call `openlog` before using `syslog`, but it may be used to change the behavior of the `syslog` function. You may wish to refer to the man page for `openlog` for more details. On Windows, emulation code is used to mimic UNIX functionality.

The `identifier` argument will be added to the beginning of any messages sent to the system log. Usually this is the name of the process or task being performed.

The `option` argument is a bitfield that controls toggling of miscellaneous options. Use a logical-or operator to combine the options you want. Table 8.10 lists the values available. Only the `LOG_PID` option has any effect under Windows.

Table 8.10   `openlog` Options

Constant	Description
LOG_PID	Add process identifier to each message.
LOG_CONS	If a message can't be sent to the log, send it to the system console.
LOG_ODELAY	Delay opening log until the first call to `syslog`. This is true by default.
LOG_NDELAY	Open the log immediately. Do not wait for first call to `syslog`.
LOG_NOWAIT	Do not wait for child processes. The use of this flag is discouraged.
LOG_PERROR	Log all messages to `stderr` as well.

The `facility` argument sets a default value for the source of the error—that is, from which part of the system the report comes. The argument is ignored under Windows. Table 8.11 lists the facilities available.

See `syslog` for an example of use.

Table 8.11   `openlog` Facilities

Constant	Facility
LOG_AUTH	Authorization
LOG_AUTHPRIV	Authorization Privileges
LOG_CRON	Cron
LOG_DAEMON	Daemon
LOG_KERN	Kernal
LOG_LPR	Printer
LOG_MAIL	Mail

(continued)

Constant	Facility
LOG_NEWS	News
LOG_SYSLOG	System Log
LOG_USER	User
LOG_UUCP	UNIX to UNIX protocol

phpcredits(integer flags)

The `phpcredits` function prints information about the major contributors to the PHP project. If the optional `flags` argument is left out, all information will be provided. Otherwise, you may combine the flags listed in Table 8.12 to choose a specific set of information. The `PHP_FULL_PAGE` constant will cause the credits to be surrounded with minimal tags for defining an HTML page.

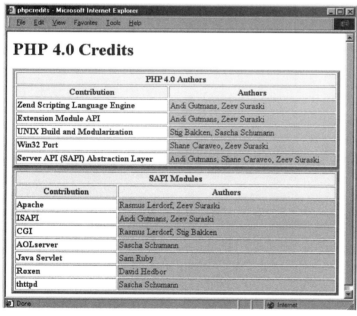

```
<?
      //display full credits
      phpcredits();
?>
```

Figure 8–9 `phpcredits`.

Table 8.12   Flags for `phpcredits`

CREDITS_FULLPAGE

CREDITS_GENERAL

CREDITS_MODULES

CREDITS_DOCS

boolean phpinfo(integer flags)

The `phpinfo` function sends a large amount of diagnostic information to the browser and returns TRUE. The `flags` argument is not required. By default all information is returned. You may use the flags listed in Table 8.13 with bitwise OR operators to choose specific information.

The complete set of information will contain

- PHP version
- Credits
- Operating system of the Web server
- Extensions compiled into PHP executable
- Every configuration variable
- Every environment variable
- Apache variables if running as an Apache module
- HTTP headers

Table 8.13   Flags for `phpinfo`

INFO_GENERAL

INFO_CREDITS

INFO_CONFIGURATION

INFO_MODULES

INFO_ENVIRONMENT

INFO_VARIABLES

INFO_LICENSE

Calling `phpinfo` is a good way to find out which environment variables are available to you.

```
<?
    phpinfo();
?>
```

string phpversion()

The `phpversion` function returns a string that describes the version of PHP executing the script.

```
<?
    print("PHP version" . phpversion() . "<BR>\n");
?>
```

print_r(expression)

The `print_r` function prints the value of an expression. If the expression is a string, integer, or double, the simple representation of it is sent to the browser. If the expression is an object or array, special notation is used to show indices or property names. Arrays and objects are explored recursively in the cases where objects or arrays are contained within each other.

```
<?
    //define some test variables
    $s = "a string";
    $a = array("x", "y", "z", array(1, 2, 3));

    //print a string
    print_r($s);
    print("\n");

    //print an array
    print_r($a);
    print("\n");
?>
```

show_source

Use show_source as an alias to highlight_file.

syslog(integer priority, string message)

The syslog function adds a message to the system log. It is a wrapper for C's function of the same name. The priority is an integer that stands for how severe the situation is. Under UNIX the priority may cause the system to take special measures. Priorities are listed in Table 8.14.

Under Windows NT, emulation code is used to simulate the UNIX functionality. Messages generated by the syslog function are added to the application log, which may be viewed with Event Viewer. The priority

Table 8.14   syslog Priorities

Constant	Priority	Description
LOG_EMERG	Emergency	This is a panic situation and the message may be broadcast to all users of the system. On Windows this is translated into a warning.
LOG_ALERT	Alert	This is a situation that demands being corrected immediately. It is translated into being an error on Windows.
LOG_CRIT	Critical	This is a critical condition that may be created by hardware errors. It is translated into being a warning on Windows.
LOG_ERR	Error	These are general error conditions. They are translated into warnings on Windows.
LOG_WARNING	Warning	These are warnings, less severe than errors.
LOG_NOTICE	Notice	A notice is not an error but requires more attention than an informational message. It is translated into a warning on Windows.
LOG_INFO	Information	Informational messages do not require that any special action be taken.
LOG_DEBUG	Debug	These messages are of interest only to debugging tasks. They are translated into warnings.

is used in two ways. First, it is translated into being either an error, a warning, or information. This determines the icon that appears next to the message in Event Viewer. It is also used to fill the Category column. The Event column will always be set to 2000 and the User column will be set to null.

```
<?
      openlog("TEST", LOG_PID | LOG_CONS, LOG_USER);
      syslog(LOG_INFO, "The log has been tested");
      closelog();
?>
```

var_dump(expression, …)

The `var_dump` function reports all information about a given variable. Information is printed directly to the browser. You may supply any number of variables separated by commas. The output of the command is well formatted, including indention for cases such as arrays containing other arrays. Arrays and objects are explored recursively.

```
<?
      //create a directory object
      $d = dir(".");

      //dump info about it
      var_dump($d)
?>
```

string zend_version()

Use `zend_version` to get the version of the Zend library.

```
<?
      print(zend_version());
?>
```

Session Handling

The functions in this section work with the session handling capabilities of PHP. They were added in PHP 4. To read more about their use, turn back to Chapter 7. That chapter also includes a complete example.

boolean session_decode(string code)

Use `session_decode` to read encoded session data and set the values of global variables in the session. This happens automatically when you start a session with `session_start`.

boolean session_destroy()

The `session_destroy` function eliminates all the data stored in the session. It does not destroy the session itself, however.

string session_encode()

The `session_encode` function returns a string that contains encoded information about the current session.

string session_id(string id)

Use `session_id` to get the value of the session identifier. If you wish to change the session identifier, supply the optional `id` argument. If you do, take care to do so before any output is sent to the browser, because the identifier is sent as a cookie.

boolean session_is_registered(string name)

The `session_is_registered` function returns TRUE if the specified variable is registered with the session.

string session_module_name(string name)

The `session_module_name` function returns the name of the module that handles session duties. This is the same value set by the `session.save_handler` directive inside `php.ini`. You can change the module name if you supply the optional `name` argument, but the only one available at the time of writing was the `files` module.

If you wish to implement your own handler in PHP, see the `session_set_save_handler` function.

string session_name(string name)

The `session_name` function returns the current name for the session variable. The session may be renamed with the optional `name` argument. This name is used as the name of the cookie that contains the session identifier. It's also used for the back-up GET variable. Consequently, if you wish to override the name of the session defined in `php.ini`, you must do so prior to registering any variables or starting the session.

boolean session_register(...)

The `session_register` function accepts any number of arguments, each of which may be a string or an array. Each argument names a global variable that will be attached to the session. Arrays passed as arguments will be traversed for elements. You can even pass multidimensional arrays. Each registered variable that is set when the script ends will be serialized and written into the session information. When the user returns with a later request, the variables will be restored.

string session_save_path(string path)

The `session_save_path` function returns the path in the file system used to save serialized session information. This is `/tmp` by default. The optional `path` argument will change the path. Keep in mind, the permissions for this directory must include read/write access for the Web server.

session_set_save_handler(string open, string close, string read, string write, string destroy, string garbage)

The `session_set_save_handler` function allows you to implement an alternative method for handling sessions. Each argument is the name of a function for handling a certain aspect of the session handling process. Unfortunately, at the time of this writing the code that implements this functionality was not finished. Consequently, I can describe the expected arguments, but I can't provide a working example. See Table 8.15.

boolean session_start()

Use `session_start` to activate a session. If no session exists, one will be created. Since this involves sending a cookie, you must call `session_start` before sending any text to the browser. You can avoid using this function by configuring PHP to automatically start sessions with each request. This is done with the `session.auto_start` directive in `php.ini`.

Once you start a session, PHP will begin watching the variables you register with `session_register`.

boolean session_unregister(string name)

Use `session_unregister` to remove a global variable from the session. It will not be saved with the session when the script ends.

Table 8.15   Functions for Use with `session_set_save_handler`

Function	Arguments
open	string SavePath, string SessionName
close	none
read	string Variable
write	string Variable, Value
destroy	none
garbage	integer MaximumLifetime

Shell Commands

This section describes functions that interact with the command shell in some way. Some of them execute other programs, and two of them read or write to environment variables.

string exec(string command, array output, integer return)

The `exec` function attempts to execute the `command` argument as if you had typed it in command shell. Nothing is echoed to the browser, but the last line of output from the execution is returned. If the optional `output` argument is supplied, each line of output will be added to the output argument as an array element. If the optional `return` argument is supplied, the variable is set to the return value of the command.

It is very dangerous to put any user-supplied information inside the command argument. Users may pass values in form fields that allow them to execute their own commands on your Web server. If you must execute a command based on user input, pass the information through the `escape-shellcmd` function, defined in Chapter 9.

Compare this function to `passthru` and `system`.

```
<?
    // get directory list for the root of C drive
    $LastLine = exec("dir C:\\", $AllOutput, $ReturnValue);

    print("Last Line: $LastLine <BR>\n");

    print("All Output:<BR>\n");
    for($index = 0; $index < count($AllOutput); $index++)
    {
        print("$AllOutput[$index] <BR>\n");
    }
    print("<BR><BR>\n");

    print("Return Value: $ReturnValue<BR>\n");
?>
```

string getenv(string variable)

The `getenv` function returns the value of the given environment variable or `false` if there is an error. PHP converts all environment variables into PHP variables, so this function is useful only in those rare instances when environment variables change after a script begins executing. If you need to set the value of an environment variable, use `putenv`.

```
<?
    print(getenv("PATH"));
?>
```

string passthru(string command, integer return)

The `passthru` function is similar to `exec` and `system`. The `command` argument is executed as if you typed it in a command shell. If you provide the optional `return` argument, it will be set with the return value of the command. All output will be returned by the `passthru` function and sent to the browser. The output will be sent as binary data. This is useful in situations where you need to execute a shell command that creates some binary file, such as an image. See Chapter 17, "Database Integration," for an application of this.

It is very dangerous to put any user-supplied information inside the command argument. Users may pass values in form fields that allow them to execute their own commands on your Web server. If you must allow this, pass the information through the `escapeshellcmd` function first.

putenv(string variable)

The `putenv` function sets the value of an environment variable. You must use syntax similar to that used by a command shell, as shown in the example below. To get the value of an environment variable, use `getenv`, or use `phpinfo` to dump all environment variables.

```
<?
    putenv("PATH=/local/bin;.");
?>
```

string system(string command, integer return)

The `system` function behaves identically to C's `system` function. It executes the `command` argument, sends the output to the browser, and returns the last line of output. If the `return` argument is provided, it is set with the return value of the command. If you do not wish for the output to be sent to the browser, use the `exec` function.

It is very dangerous to put any user-supplied information inside the `command` argument. Users may pass values in form fields that allow them to execute their own commands on your Web server. If you must allow this, pass the information through the `escapeshellcmd` function first.

```
<?
    // list files in directory
    print("<PRE>");
    system("ls -l");
    print("</PRE>");
?>
```

HTTP Headers

HTTP headers are special commands sent between the browser and Web server before the browser receives any content. Some of the headers let the server know which file the browser wants. Others may instruct the browser about the type of file it will soon be sent. To learn more about headers, refer to the HTTP specification that was originally described in RFC 1945. It and other documents may be found at the W3C site, which has a section devoted to the HTTP protocol <http://www.w3.org/Protocols/>. For an overview of how headers work with PHP, turn back to Chapter 7.

boolean header(string http_header)

The `header` function sends an HTTP header to the browser. It must be called before any output is sent to the browser, inside or outside PHP tags. You may wish to turn back to the description of HTTP connections in Chapter 7. Many different kinds of headers may be sent. Perhaps the most common is a location header, which redirects the browser to another URI.

Each time you call `header`, it is pushed onto a stack. If you are unfamiliar with the concept of a stack, think of it as a list of items placed one on top of another. When your script gets to the point of sending content to the browser, headers are pulled from the stack one at a time. This means headers are sent to the browser in reverse order.

Headers are also used to send cookies, but PHP's `setcookie` function is better suited for this purpose.

One common trick the `header` function provides is sending a user to another page, as demonstrated in the example below. Another is to force the browser to either download the file or display it in an OLE container. This is done by setting the `Content-type` header, which PHP defaults to `text/html`. Sending a value of `application/octet-stream` will cause most browsers to prompt the user for where to save the file. You can also use other MIME types to get the browser to run a helper application. For example, if you use `application/vnd.ms-excel`, a Windows machine with Microsoft Excel installed will launch Excel in an OLE container inside the browser window. In this case you don't need to send an actual Excel file. A simple tab-delimited file will be interpreted correctly.

```
<?
    // redirect request to another address
    header("Location: http://www.leonatkinson.com/");
?>
```

boolean setcookie(string name, string value, integer expire, string path, string domain, integer secure)

Use `setcookie` to send a cookie to the browser. Cookies are sent as headers during an HTTP connection. Since cookie headers are more complex than other headers, it is nice to have a function specifically for sending cookies. Keep in mind that all headers must be sent prior to any content. Also, calling `setcookie` does not create a PHP variable until the cookie is sent back by the browser on the next page load.

If `setcookie` is called with only the name argument, the cookie will be deleted from the browser's cookie database. Otherwise, a cookie will be created on the client browser with the name and value given.

The optional `expire` argument sets a time when the cookie will automatically be deleted by the browser. This takes the form of seconds since January 1, 1970. PHP converts this into Greenwich Mean Time and the proper form for the Set-Cookie header. If the expire argument is omitted, the browser will delete the cookie when the session ends. Usually this means when the browser application is shut down.

The `path` and `domain` arguments are used by the browser to determine whether to send the cookie. The hostname of the Web server is compared to the domain. If it is left empty, the complete hostname of the server setting the cookie is used. The path is matched against the beginning of the path on the server to the document. The cookie specification requires that domains contain two periods. This is to prevent scripts that get sent to every top-level domain (`.com`, `.edu`, `.net`). It also prevents a domain value of `leonatkinson.com`. Just remember to add a leading dot.

The `secure` argument is used to tell the browser to send the cookie only over secure connections which use Secure Socket Layers. Use a value of 1 to denote a secure cookie.

Like other headers, those created by the `setcookie` function are pushed onto a stack, which causes them to be sent in reverse order. If you set the same cookie more than once, the first call to `setcookie` will be executed last. Most likely, this isn't what you intend. Keep track of the value you intend to set as the value of the cookie and call `setcookie` once.

Netscape, which developed cookies, offers more information about them in a document titled *Persistent Client State: HTTP Cookies*. Its URL is

```
<http://developer.netscape.com/docs/manuals/communicator/
jsguide4/cookies.htm>.
```

How do you know if a browser accepts your cookie? The only way is to send one and test that it is returned on the next page request.

```
<?
    /*
    ** mark this site as being visited
    ** for the next 24 hours
    */
    setcookie ("HasVisitedLast24Hours", "Yes", time()+86400;
?>
```

Network I/O

The network I/O functions send information directly over the Internet Protocol, or they fetch information about Internet hosts.

boolean checkdnsrr(string host, string type)

The `checkdnsrr` function checks DNS records for a host. The `type` argument defines the type of records for which to search. Valid types are listed in Table 8.16.

If type is not specified, `checkdnsrr` checks for MX records. You may wish to read the man page for `named`, the Internet domain name server daemon.

```
<?
     if(checkdnsrr("clearink.com", "MX"))
     {
            print("clearink.com is a mail exchanger");
     }
?>
```

integer fsockopen(string hostname, integer port, integer error_number, string error_description, double timeout)

The `fsockopen` begins a network connection as a file stream, returning a file descriptor suitable for use by `fputs`, `fgets`, and other file-stream functions discussed earlier in this chapter. A connection is attempted to the `hostname` at the given port. The `hostname` may also be a numerical IP address. The `hostname` may also be the path to a UNIX domain socket, in which case `port` should be set to 0. Some operating systems, specifically Windows, don't support UNIX domain sockets.

Table 8.16	DNS Record Types
Type	*Description*
A	IP Address
ANY	Any records
CNAME	Canonical name
MX	Mail Exchanger
NS	Name Server
SOA	Start of a zone of authority

If an error occurs, FALSE is returned and the optional error_number and
error_description arguments are set. They must be passed by reference,
which means adding an ampersand (&) prior to the dollar sign. If the error
number returned is zero, an error occurred before PHP tried to connect.
This may indicate a problem initializing the socket.

The optional timeout argument will set the number of seconds PHP will
wait for a connection to be established. You may specify fractions of a second
as well, if you wish.

The pfsockopen adds persistence to the fsockopen functionality.

```php
<?
        //tell browser not to render this
        header("Content-type: text/plain");

        //try to connect to Web server,
        //timeout after 60 seconds
        $fp = fsockopen("www.clearink.com", 80,
                &$error_number, &$error_description,
                60);

        if($fp)
        {
                //set nonblocking mode
                set_socket_blocking($fp, FALSE);

                // tell server we want root document
                fputs($fp, "GET / HTTP/1.0");
                fputs($fp, "\r\n\r\n");

                while(!feof($fp))
                {
                        //print next 4K
                        print(fgets($fp, 4096));
                }

                //close connection
                fclose($fp);

        }
        else
        {
                //$connect was false
                print("An error occurred!<BR>\n");
                print("Number: $error_number<BR>\n");
```

```
                        print("Description: $error_description<BR>\n");
        }
?>
```

string gethostbyaddr(string ip_address)

The gethostbyaddr function returns the name of the host specified by the numerical IP address. If the host cannot be resolved, the address is returned.

```
<?
        print(gethostbyaddr("207.46.131.30"));
?>
```

string gethostbyname(string hostname)

The gethostbyname function returns the IP address of the host specified by its name. It is possible a domain name resolves to more than one IP address. To get each one, use gethostbyname1.

```
<?
        print(gethostbyname("www.php.net"));
?>
```

array gethostbynamel(string hostname)

The gethostbynamel function returns a list of IP addresses that a given hostname resolves to.

```
<?
        $hosts = gethostbynamel("www.microsoft.com");
        for($index = 0; $index < count($hosts); $index++)
        {
                print("$hosts[$index] <BR>\n");
        }
?>
```

boolean getmxrr(string host, array mxhost, array weight)

The getmxrr function gets mail-exchanger DNS records for a host. Hostnames will be added to the array specified by the mxhost argument. The optional `weight` array is assigned with the weight for each host. The return value signals whether the operation was successful.

Chapter 18 contains an example of using `getmxrr` to verify an email address.

```
<?
    //get mail-exchanger records for clearink.com
    getmxrr("clearink.com", $mxrecord, $weight);

    //display results
    for($index=0; $index < count($mxrecord); $index++)
    {
        print($mxrecord[$index]);
        print(" - ");
        print($weight[$index]);
        print("<BR>\n");
    }
?>
```

integer getprotobyname(string name)

The `getprotobyname` function returns the number associated with a protocol.

string getprotobynumber(integer protocol)

The `getprotobynumber` function returns the name of a protocol given its number.

integer getservbyname(string service, string protocol)

The `getservbyname` function returns the port used by a service. The `protocol` argument must be `tcp` or `udp`.

```
<?
    //check which port ftp uses
    $port = getservbyname("ftp", "tcp");

    print("port $port<BR>\n");
?>
```

string getservbyport(integer service, string protocol)

The `getservbyport` function returns the name of the service that uses a specified port. The `protocol` argument must be `tcp` or `udp`.

```
<?

    //check which service uses port 25
    $service = getservbyport(25, "tcp");

    print("$service<BR>\n");
?>
```

boolean mail(string recipient, string subject, string body, string additional_headers)

The `mail` function sends email. Under UNIX it runs the `sendmail` shell command. Under Windows it makes a connection to an SMTP server. The mail is sent to the address specified in the `recipient` argument. You may specify multiple recipients by separating them with commas. You must also provide a subject and a message body. Optionally, you may provide additional headers in the fourth argument. Each extra header should be separated by a single newline character. If the mail is sent successfully, `TRUE` is returned.

On Windows, `Date:` and `From:` headers are added to the message automatically, unless you supply them yourself.

There are a few directives in `php.ini` for configuring this function. For Windows you can set the name of the SMTP host using the `SMTP` directive, and you can set the default `From:` header with the `sendmail_from` directive. It's valid, of course, to point to an SMTP server on the localhost. For UNIX, you may specify the path to your `sendmail` executable, which may have an acceptable default compiled in already. You can't set up PHP on UNIX to send mail directly to a remote SMTP host. You can configure `sendmail` to relay messages to a specific host, but the instructions are outside the scope of this text.

See Chapter 18 for an example that sends attachments.

```
<?
    //define who is to receive the mail
```

```
//(in this case, root of the localhost)
$mailTo = "root@" . $SERVER_NAME;

//set the subject
$mailSubject = "Testing Mail";

//build body of the message
$mailBody = "This is a test of PHP's mail function. ";
$mailBody .= "It was generated by PHP version ";
$mailBody .= phpversion();

//add a from header
$mailHeaders = "From: php@$SERVER_NAME.com\n";

//send mail
if(mail($mailTo, $mailSubject, $mailBody, $mailHeaders))
{
        print("Mail successfull sent to $mailTo.");
}
else
{
        print("Mail could not be sent to $mailTo.");
}
?>
```

integer pfsockopen(string hostname, integer port, integer error_number, string error_description, double timeout)

The pfsockopen function operates identically to fsockopen, except that connections are cached. Connections opened with pfsockopen are not closed when a script terminates. They persist with the server process.

boolean set_socket_blocking(integer file_descriptor, boolean mode)

The set_socket_blocking function sets whether a file stream is blocking. In nonblocking mode, calls to functions that get information from the stream will return immediately with whatever data are in the input buffer. Blocking mode forces execution to halt until sufficient data are received.

FTP

The functions in this section allow you to make connections to FTP servers. FTP is the file transfer protocol. While the file functions allow you to open and manipulate remote files by specifying a URL instead of a local path, these functions operate directly with the FTP protocol. They offer a greater degree of control. They also allow you to get a list of files on the server. The FTP functions were added to PHP by Andrew Skalski.

boolean ftp_cdup(integer link)

The `ftp_cdup` function changes the working directory to the parent directory.

boolean ftp_chdir(integer link, string directory)

The `ftp_chdir` function moves the working directory to the specified directory.

integer ftp_connect(string host, integer port)

Use `ftp_connect` to begin an FTP connection. The `port` argument is optional. An FTP resource identifier will be returned if the connection is successful, FALSE otherwise. This ID is used in the rest of the FTP commands. Remember that once you connect, you must log in before you can issue any commands.

```
<?
    //connect to server
    if(!($ftp = ftp_connect("localhost")))
    {
        print("Unable to connect!<BR>\n");
        exit();
```

```php
}

print("Connected.<BR>\n");

//log in
if(!ftp_login($ftp, "anonymous", "corephp@localhost"))
{
        print("Unable to login!<BR>\n");
        exit();
}

print("Logged In.<BR>\n");

//print system type
print("System Type: " . ftp_systype($ftp) . "<BR>\n");

//make sure passive mode is off
ftp_pasv($ftp, FALSE);

//get working directory
print("Working Directory: " . ftp_pwd($ftp) . "<BR>\n");

//get files in raw format
print("Raw List:<BR>\n");
foreach(ftp_rawlist($ftp, ".") as $line)
{
        print("$line<BR>\n");
}
print("<BR>\n");

//move to pub directory
if(!ftp_chdir($ftp, "pub"))
{
        print("Unable to go to the pub directory!<BR>\n");
}

print("Moved to pub directory.<BR>\n");

//get a list of files
print("Files:<BR>\n");
foreach(ftp_nlist($ftp, ".") as $filename)
{
        print("$filename<BR>\n");
}
```

```
print("<BR>\n");

//return to root directory
if(!ftp_cdup($ftp))
{
       print("Failed to move up a directory!<BR>\n");
}

//close connection
ftp_quit($ftp);
?>
```

boolean ftp_delete(integer link, string path)

The ftp_delete function removes a file on the remote server. The link argument is as returned by ftp_connect. The path argument is the path on the remote server to the file to be deleted. See ftp_put for an example of use.

boolean ftp_fget(integer link, integer file, string filename, integer mode)

The ftp_fget function copies a remote file into an open file stream. You must create a file resource using fopen or a similar function to pass as the second argument. The mode argument should be set with one of two constants: FTP_ASCII or FTP_IMAGE. These are sometimes referred to as text or binary modes.

```
<?
    //connect to server
    if(!($ftp = ftp_connect("localhost")))
    {
           print("Unable to connect!<BR>\n");
           exit();
    }

    //log in
    if(!ftp_login($ftp, "anonymous", "corephp@localhost"))
    {
```

```
            print("Unable to login!<BR>\n");
            exit();
    }

    //open local file for writing
    $fp = fopen("/tmp/ftp_fget.test", "w");

    //save remote file in open file stream
    if(!ftp_fget($ftp, $fp, "data.txt", FTP_ASCII)))
    {
            print("Unable to get remote file!<BR>\n");
    }

    //close local file
    fclose($fp);

    //close connection
    ftp_quit($ftp);
?>
```

boolean ftp_fput(integer link, string remote, integer file, integer mode)

The ftp_fput function creates a file on the remote server from the contents of an open file stream. The link argument is as returned by ftp_connect. The remote argument is the path to the file to be created on the remote server. The file argument is a file identifier as returned by fopen or a similar function. The mode argument should be FTP_ASCII or FTP_IMAGE.

```
<?
    //connect to server
    if(!($ftp = ftp_connect("localhost"))
    {
            print("Unable to connect!<BR>\n");
            exit();
    }

    //log in
    if(!ftp_login($ftp, "anonymous", "corephp@localhost"))
    {
            print("Unable to login!<BR>\n");
            exit();
```

```
        }

        //open local file
        if(!($fp = fopen("/tmp/data.txt", "r"))
        {
                print("Unable to open local file!<BR>\n");
                exit();
        }

        //write file to remote server
        ftp_fput($ftp, "data.txt", $fp, FTP_ASCII);

        //close local file
        fclose($fp);

        //close connection
        ftp_quit($ftp);
?>
```

boolean ftp_get(integer link, string local, string remote, integer mode)

Use ftp_get to copy a file from the remote server to local filesystem. The link argument is as returned by ftp_connect. The local and remote arguments specify paths. The mode argument should use FTP_ASCII or FTP_IMAGE.

```
<?
    //connect to server
    if(!($ftp = ftp_connect("localhost")))
    {
            print("Unable to connect!<BR>\n");
            exit();
    }

    //log in
    if(!ftp_login($ftp, "anonymous", "corephp@localhost"))
    {
            print("Unable to login!<BR>\n");
```

```
            exit();
    }

    //save file to tmp directory
    ftp_get($ftp, "/tmp/data.bin", "/pub/data.bin", FTP_IMAGE);

    //close connection
    ftp_quit($ftp);
?>
```

boolean ftp_login(integer link, string username, string password)

Once you make a connection to an FTP server, you must use `ftp_login` to identify yourself. All three arguments are required, even if you are logging in anonymously. See `ftp_connect` for an example of use.

integer ftp_mdtm(integer link, string path)

The `ftp_mdtm` function returns the last modification time for the file named in the `path` argument.

```
<?
    //connect to server
    if(!($ftp = ftp_connect("localhost")))
    {
            print("Unable to connect!<BR>\n");
            exit();
    }

    //log in
    if(!ftp_login($ftp, "anonymous", "corephp@localhost"))
    {
            print("Unable to login!<BR>\n");
            exit();
    }

    //get the size of the README file
    print("Size: " . ftp_size($ftp, "README") . "<BR>\n");
```

```
            //get the last modification date
            print("Modified: " .
                    date("Y-m-d", ftp_mdtm($ftp, "README")) .
                    "<BR>\n");

            //close connection
            ftp_quit($ftp);
    ?>
```

string ftp_mkdir(integer link, string directory)

The ftp_mkdir function creates a directory on the remote server. FALSE is
returned if the directory cannot be created.

```
<?
    //connect to server
    if(!($ftp = ftp_connect("localhost")))
    {
            print("Unable to connect!<BR>\n");
            exit();
    }

    //log in
    if(!ftp_login($ftp, "anonymous", "corephp@localhost"))
    {
            print("Unable to login!<BR>\n");
            exit();
    }

    //create a new directory
    $result = ftp_mkdir($ftp, "corephp");
    if($result)
    {
            print("Created directory: $result<BR>\n");
    }
    else
    {
            print("Unable to create corephp directory!<BR>\n");
    }

    //remove corephp directory
    if(!ftp_rmdir($ftp, "corephp"))
    {
```

```
           print("Unable to remove corephp
directory!<BR>\n");
       }

       //close connection
       ftp_quit($ftp);
?>
```

array ftp_nlist(integer link, string directory)

The ftp_nlist function returns an array of files in the specified directory.

boolean ftp_pasv(integer link, boolean on)

Use ftp_pasv to turn passive mode on or off. It is off by default.

boolean ftp_put(integer link, string remote, string local, integer mode)

The ftp_put function copies a file from the local filesystem to the remote server. The link argument is as returned by ftp_connect. The local and remote arguments specify paths. The mode argument should be either FTP_ASCII or FTP_IMAGE.

```
<?
       //connect to server
       if(!($ftp = ftp_connect("localhost")))
       {
              print("Unable to connect!<BR>\n");
              exit();
       }

       //log in
       if(!ftp_login($ftp, "anonymous", "corephp@localhost"))
       {
              print("Unable to login!<BR>\n");
              exit();
       }

       //copy local file to remote server
```

```
        ftp_put($ftp, "/uploads/data.txt", "/tmp/data.txt",
FTP_ASCII);

        //remove remote file
        ftp_delete($ftp, "/uploads/data.txt");

        //close connection
        ftp_quit($ftp);
?>
```

string ftp_pwd(integer link)

The ftp_pwd function returns the name of the current directory. See ftp_connect for an example of use.

boolean ftp_quit(integer link)

Use ftp_quit to close an FTP connection.

array ftp_rawlist(integer link, string directory)

The ftp_rawlist returns the raw output of an ls -1 command on the given directory.

boolean ftp_rename(integer link, string original, string new)

The ftp_rename function changes the name of a file on the remote server.

boolean ftp_rmdir(integer link, string directory)

Use ftp_rmdir to remove a directory.

integer ftp_size(integer link, string path)

The `ftp_size` function returns the size of a remote file in bytes. If an error occurs, −1 is returned.

string ftp_systype(integer link)

The `ftp_systype` function returns the system type of the remote FTP server.

DATA FUNCTIONS

Topics in This Chapter

- Data Types, Constants, and Variables
- Arrays
- Hashing
- Strings
- Encoding and Decoding
- Encryption
- Regular Expressions
- PERL-compatible Regular Expressions

Chapter 9

The functions in this chapter manipulate data. They check the values of variables. They transform one type of data into another. They also deal with arrays. You may find it useful to turn back to Chapter 2, "Variables, Operators, and Expressions," and read the discussion on data types and variables.

Data Types, Constants, and Variables

These functions check the status of a variable, change its type, or return a value as a particular data type.

boolean define(string name, value, boolean non_case_sensitive)

The `define` function creates a constant, which is essentially a variable that may be set only once. The `value` argument may be a string, integer, double, or boolean. It may not be an array or object. The `non_case_sensitive` argument is optional. By default, constants are case sensitive, which is the same as with variables.

If the constant cannot be created for some reason, FALSE will be returned. If you wish to check that a constant is defined, use the defined function.

It is customary to name constants using all uppercase letters, as is the practice in C. This makes them stand out among other identifiers.

Because PHP allows for unquoted string literals, it is possible to write code that uses constants that do not exist, yet produces no error. When you are using constants to hold strings to be displayed on the page, this is simply an annoyance, because you can see the error right away. When used for values not displayed, it can be a frustrating source of bugs. If you discover a constant mysteriously evaluating to zero, check that the constant has been defined.

```
<?
    /*
    ** Database variables
    */
    define("DATABASE_HOST", "localhost");
    define("DATABASE_USER", "httpd");
    define("DATABASE_PASSWORD", "");
    define("DATABASE_NAME", "freetrade");

    print("Connecting to " . DATABASE_HOST . "<BR>\n");
?>
```

boolean defined(string constantname)

The defined function returns TRUE if a constant exists, FALSE otherwise.

```
<?
    define("THERMOSTAT","72 degrees");
    if(defined("THERMOSTAT"))
    {
        print("THERMOSTAT is " . THERMOSTAT);
    }
?>
```

double doubleval(expression)

The doubleval function returns its argument as a double. Chapter 2 discusses converting between data types. Related functions are strval and intval. It is an error to pass an array or object to doubleval.

```
<?
        $myNumber = "13.1cm";
        print(doubleval($myNumber));
?>
```

empty

This function is an alias for isset.

string gettype(expression)

The gettype function returns a string that describes the type of the variable
or expression. It will be one of the following values: array, class, double,
integer, object, resource, string, unknown type.

```
<?
        //integer
        printf("%s <BR>\n", gettype(11));

        //double
        printf("%s <BR>\n", gettype(7.3));

        //string
        printf("%s <BR>\n", gettype("hello"));
?>
```

integer intval(expression, integer base)

The intval function returns its argument as an integer. The optional base
argument instructs intval to use a numerical base other than ten.
    Chapter 2 discusses converting between types.

```
<?
        //drop extraneous stuff after decimal point
        print(intval("13.5cm") . "<BR>\n");

        //convert from hex
        print(intval("EE", 16));
?>
```

boolean is_array(expression)

The is_array function returns TRUE if the expression is an array, otherwise FALSE is returned.

```
<?
    $colors = array("red", "blue", "green");
    if(is_array($colors))
    {
        print("colors is an array");
    }
?>
```

boolean is_bool(expression)

Use is_bool to test whether an expression is a boolean.

boolean is_double(expression)

The is_double function returns TRUE if the expression is a double, FALSE otherwise.

```
<?
    $Temperature = 15.23;
    if(is_double($Temperature))
    {
        print("Temperature is a double");
    }
?>
```

is_float

The is_float function is an alias for the is_double function.

is_int

The is_int function is an alias for the is_integer function.

boolean is_integer(expression)

The `is_integer` function returns TRUE if the expression is an integer, FALSE otherwise.

```
<?
        $PageCount = 2234;
        if(is_integer($PageCount))
        {
                print("$PageCount is an integer");
        }
?>
```

is_long

The `is_long` function is an alias for the `is_integer` function.

boolean is_object(expression)

The `is_object` function returns TRUE if the expression is an object, FALSE otherwise.

```
<?
        class widget
        {
                var $name;
                var $length;
        }

        $thing = new widget;

        if(is_object($thing))
        {
                print("thing is an object");
        }

?>
```

boolean is_real(expression)

The `is_real` function is an alias for the `is_double` function.

boolean is_resource(variable)

This function returns TRUE if the given variable is a resource. A resource is an integer used to identify a system resource. An example is the return value of fopen.

boolean is_string(expression)

The is_string function returns TRUE if the expression is a string, FALSE otherwise.

```
<?
     $Greeting = "Hello";
     if(is_string($Greeting))
     {
          print("Greeting is a string");
     }
?>
```

boolean isset(variable)

The isset function returns TRUE if the variable has been given a value, or FALSE if the variable has never been on the left side of a set operator. In other words, it tests that the variable has been set with a value.

```
<?
     if(isset($Name))
     {
          print("Your Name is $Name");
     }
     else
     {
          print("I don't know your name");
     }
?>
```

boolean settype(variable, string type)

The settype function changes the type of a variable. The type is written as a string and may be one of the following: array, double, integer, object, string. If the type could not be set, FALSE is returned.

```
<?
      $myValue = 123.45;
      settype($myValue, "integer");
      print($myValue);
?>
```

string strval(expression)

The strval function returns its argument as a string.

```
<?
      $myNumber = 13;
      print(strval($myNumber));
?>
```

unset(variable)

The unset function destroys a variable, causing all memory associated with
the variable to be freed.

```
<?
      $list[0] = "milk";
      $list[1] = "eggs";
      $list[2] = "sugar";

      unset($list);

      if(!isset($list))
      {
            print("list has been cleared and has ");
            print(count($list));
            print(" elements");
      }
?>
```

Arrays

The functions in this section operate on arrays. Some of them sort the arrays;
some of them help you find and retrieve values from arrays. Chapter 5,
"Arrays," discusses arrays in depth.

array array(...)

The array function takes a list of values separated by commas and returns an array. This is especially useful for creating one-off arrays to be passed to functions. Elements will be added to the array as if you used empty square brackets, which means they are numbered consecutively starting at zero. You may use the => operator to specify index values.

```
<?
    //create an array
    $myArray = array(
        "Name"=>"Leon Atkinson",
        "Profession"=>array("Programmer", "Author"),
        "Residence"=>"Martinez, California"
        );
?>
```

array array_count_values(array data)

The array_count_values function returns counts for each distinct value in the data argument. The returned array is indexed by the values of the data argument. Although the example below uses an array of numbers, array_count_values will count the appearance of elements that contain any other data type.

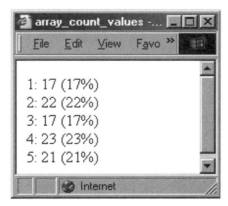

Figure 9-1   array_count_values.

```
<?
    //generate $sample_size random numbers
    //between 1 and 5
    $sample_size = 100;
    srand(time());
    for($i=0; $i<$sample_size; $i++)
    {
        $data[] = rand(1,5);
    }

    //count elements
    $count = array_count_values($data);

    //sort by keys
    ksort($count);

    //print out totals
    foreach($count as $key=>$value)
    {
        print("$key: $value (".(100 *
$value/$sample_size)."%)<BR>\n");
    }
?>
```

Figure 9–1 Continued

array array_flip(array data)

The array_flip function returns the data argument with the indices and
elements exchanged.

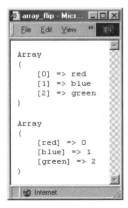

Figure 9–2 array_flip.

```
<?
        //create a test array
        $colors = array("red", "blue", "green");

        //show array like [0] => red
        print("<PRE>");
        print_r($colors);
        print("</PRE>\n");

        //flip indices for elements
        $colors = array_flip($colors);

        //show array like [red] => 0
        print("<PRE>");
        print_r($colors);
        print("</PRE>\n");
?>
```

Figure 9–2 Continued

array array_keys(array data, string value)

The array_keys function returns an array of the keys used in the data array. If the optional value argument is supplied, only the subset of indices that point the given element value are returned.

```
<?
        //create random test data with 0 or 1
        srand(time());
        for($i=0; $i<10; $i++)
        {
                $data[] = rand(0,1);
        }

        //print out the keys to 1's
        foreach(array_keys($data, 1) as $key)
        {
                print("$key<BR>\n");
        }
?>
```

array array_merge
(array data, array data, ...)

The `array_merge` function takes two or more arrays and returns a single array containing all elements. Elements indexed by integers are added to the new array one at a time, in most cases renumbering them. Elements indexed by strings retain their index values and are added as they are encountered in the input arrays. They may replace previous values. If you are unsure of the indices used in the merged arrays, you can use `array_values` to make sure all values are indexed by an integer.

```
<?
    function printElement($element)
    {
        print("$element<BR>\n");
    }

    //set up an array of color names
    $colors = array("red", "blue", "green");
    $more_colors = array("yellow", "purple", "orange");

    //merge arrays
    $all_colors = array_merge($colors, $more_colors);

    //print out all the values
    array_walk($all_colors, "printElement");
?>
```

boolean array_multisort(array data,
integer direction, ...)

The `array_multisort` function sorts arrays together, as if array were a column in a table. The `data` argument is an array and the `direction` argument is one of two constants: `SORT_ASC` or `SORT_DESC`. These stand for ascending and descending, respectively. If left out, the direction defaults to ascending order, which is smallest to largest. You may specify any number of arrays, but you must alternate between arrays and sort order constants as you do.

The way `array_multisort` works is similar to the way a relational database sorts the results of a join. The first element of each array is joined into

```
<?
        //create data
        $color = array("green", "green", "blue", "white", "white");
        $item = array("dish soap", "hand soap", "dish soap", "towel",
            "towel");
        $dept = array("kitchen", "bathroom", "kitchen", "kitchen",
            "bathroom");
        $price = array(2.50, 2.25, 2.55, 1.75, 3.00);

        //sort by department, item name, color, price
        array_multisort($dept, SORT_ASC,
                $item, SORT_ASC,
                $color, SORT_ASC,
                $price, SORT_DESC);

        //print sorted list
        for($i=0; $i < count($item); $i++)
        {
                print("$dept[$i] $item[$i] $color[$i] $price[$i]<BR>\n");
        }
?>
```

Figure 9–3 `array_multisort`.

a virtual row, and all elements in a row move together. The arrays are sorted by the first array. In the case where elements of the first array repeat, rows are sorted on the second row. Sorting continues as necessary.

array array_pad(array data, integer size, value padding)

The array_pad function adds elements to an array until it has the number of elements specified by the size argument. If the array is long enough already, no elements are added. Otherwise, the padding argument is used for the value of the new elements. If the size argument is positive, padding is added to the end of the array. If the size argument is negative, padding is added to the beginning.

```
<?
        //create test data
        $data = array(1,2,3);

        //add "start" to beginning of array
        $data = array_pad($data, -4, "start");

        //add "end" to end of array
        $data = array_pad($data, 5, "end");

        foreach($data as $value)
        {
                print("$value<BR>\n");
        }
?>
```

value array_pop(array stack)

The array_pop function returns the last element of an array, removing it from the array as well. The array_push function compliments it, and array_shift and array_unshift add and remove elements from the beginning of an array.

```
<?
        //set up an array of color names
        $colors = array("red", "blue", "green");

        $lastColor = array_pop($colors);
```

```
        //prints "green"
        print($lastColor . "<BR>\n");

        //shows that colors contains red, blue
        print("<PRE>");
        print_r($colors);
        print("</PRE>\n");
?>
```

boolean array_push(array stack, expression entry, ...)

The array_push function adds one or more values to the end of an array. It treats the array as a stack. Use array_pop to remove elements from the stack. The array_shift and array_unshift functions add and remove elements to the beginning of an array.

```
<?
        //set up an array of color names
        $colors = array("red", "blue", "green");

        //push two more color names
        array_push($colors, "purple", "yellow");

        //print out all the values
        //(red, blue, green, purple, yellow)
        print("<PRE>");
        print_r($colors);
        print("</PRE>\n".);
?>
```

array array_reverse(array data)

The array_reverse function returns the data argument with the elements in reverse order. The elements are not sorted in any way. They are simply in the opposite order.

```
<?
        //create test data
        $data = array(3, 1, 2, 7, 5);

        //reverse order
        $data = array_reverse($data);
```

```
        //print in reverse order
        //5, 7, 2, 1, 3
        print("<PRE>");
        print_r($data);
        print("</PRE>\n");
?>
```

value array_shift(array stack)

The `array_shift` function returns the first element of an array, removing it as well. This allows you to treat the array like a stack. The `array_unshift` function adds an element to the beginning of an array. Use `array_pop` and `array_push` to perform the same actions with the end of the array.

```
<?
        //set up an array of color names
        $colors = array("red", "blue", "green");

        $firstColor = array_shift($colors);

        //print "red"
        print($firstColor . "<BR>\n");

        //dump colors (blue, green)
        print("<PRE>");
        print_r($colors);
        print("</PRE>\n");
?>
```

array array_slice(array data, integer start, integer stop)

The `array_slice` function returns part of an array, starting with the element specified by the `start` argument. If you specify a negative value for `start`, the starting position will be that many elements before the last element. The optional `stop` argument allows you to specify how many elements to return or where to stop returning values. A positive value is treated as a maximum number of elements to return. A negative `stop` is used to count backward from the last element to specify the element at which to stop.

Compare this function to `array_merge` and `array_splice`.

```
<?
        function printElement($element)
        {
```

```
            print("$element<BR>\n");
    }

    //set up an array of color names
    $colors = array("red", "blue", "green",
            "purple", "cyan", "yellow");

    //get a new array consisting of a slice
    //from "green" to "cyan"
    $colors_slice = array_slice($colors, 2, 3);

    //print out all the values
    array_walk($colors_slice, "printElement");
?>
```

array_splice(array data, integer start, integer stop, array insert_data)

The array_splice function removes part of an array and inserts another in its place. The array passed is altered in place, not returned. Starting with the element specified by the start argument, elements are removed until the element specified by the stop argument is reached. If stop is left out, then removal continues until the end of the array. If stop is negative, it references from the end of the array backward. It is possible to specify start and stop values that do not actually remove any values. For instance, the stop value may be positive and less than start. This is a valid way to use array_splice to insert an array without removing any elements.

In place of any removed elements, the array passed as the insert_data argument is inserted if it is supplied. Declaring it is optional, as you may wish simply to remove some elements. If you wish to insert a single element into the array, you do not need to supply an array for insert_data.

Compare this function to array_merge and array_slice.

```
<?
    function printElement($element)
    {
            print("$element<BR>\n");
    }

    //set up an array of color names
    $colors = array("red", "blue", "green",
            "yellow", "orange", "purple");
```

```
        //remove green
        array_splice($colors, 2, 2);

        //insert "pink" after "blue"
        array_splice($colors, 2, 0, "pink");

        //insert "cyan" and "black" between
        //"orange" and "purple"
        array_splice($colors, 4, 0, array("cyan", "black"));

        //print out all the values
        array_walk($colors, "printElement");
?>
```

boolean array_unshift(array stack, expression entry, ...)

The array_unshift function adds one or more values to the beginning of an array, as if the array were a stack. Use array_shift to remove an element from the beginning of an array. Compare this function to array_pop and array_push, which operate on the end of the array.

```
<?
        function printElement($element)
        {
                print("$element<BR>\n");
        }

        //set up an array of color names
        $colors = array("red", "blue", "green");

        //push two more color names
        array_unshift($colors, "purple", "yellow");

        //print out all the values
        array_walk($colors, "printElement");
?>
```

array array_values(array data)

The array_values function returns just the array elements, re-indexed with integers.

```
<?
        //set up an array of color names
        $UserInfo = array("First Name"=>"Leon",
                "Last Name"=>"Atkinson",
                "Favorite Language"=>"PHP");

        //re-index using integers
        $UserInfo = array_values($UserInfo);

        //print out all the values and their
        //new indices
        for($n=0; $n < count($UserInfo); $n++)
        {
                print("($n) $UserInfo[$n]<BR>\n");
        }
?>
```

boolean array_walk(array data, string function)

The `array_walk` function executes the specified function on each element of the given array. The function must take exactly one element; otherwise an error message is generated. The array elements will be passed by reference, so any change made to them by the specified function will be permanent in the array. The function specified must be one you create, not a built-in PHP function.

```
<?
        $colors = array("red", "blue", "green");

        function printElement($element)
        {
                print("$element<BR>\n");
        }

        array_walk($colors, "printElement");
?>
```

arsort(array unsorted_array)

The `arsort` function sorts an array in reverse order by its values. The indices are moved along with the values. This sort is intended for associative arrays. Chapter 15, "Sorting, Searching, and Random Numbers," discusses sorting in depth.

```
<?
        // build array
        $users = array("bob"=>"Robert",
                "steve"=>"Stephen",
                "jon"=>"Jonathon");

        // sort array
        arsort($users);

        // print out the values
        for(reset($users); $index=key($users); next($users))
        {
                print("$index : $users[$index] <BR>\n");
        }
?>
```

asort(array unsorted_array)

The `asort` function sorts an array by its values. The indices are moved along with the values. This sort is intended for associative arrays. Chapter 15 discusses sorting in depth.

```
<?
        // build array
        $users = array("bob"=>"Robert",
                "steve"=>"Stephen",
                "jon"=>"Jonathon");

        // sort array
        asort($users);

        // print out the values
        for(reset($users); $index=key($users); next($users))
        {
                print("$index : $users[$index] <BR>\n");
        }
?>
```

array compact(...)

The `compact` function returns an array containing the names and values of variables named by the arguments. Any number of arguments may be passed, and they may be single string values or arrays of string values. Arrays containing other arrays will be recursively explored. The variables must be in the current scope. This function complements extract, which creates variables from an array.

```
<?
    //create some variables
    $name = "Leon";
    $language = "PHP";
    $color = "blue";
    $city = "Martinez";

    //get variables as array
    $variable = compact("name",
        array("city", array("language", "color")));

    //print out all the values
    print("<PRE>");
    print_r($variable);
    print("</PRE>\n");
?>
```

Figure 9–4 compact.

integer count(variable array)

The count function returns the number of elements in an array. If the variable has never been set, count returns zero. If the variable is not an array, count returns 1. Despite this added functionality, you should use the isset and is_array functions to determine the nature of a variable.

```
<?
        $colors = array("red", "green", "blue");
        print(count($colors));
?>
```

value current(array arrayname)

The current function returns the value of the current element pointed to by PHP's internal pointer. Each array maintains a pointer to one of the elements of an array. By default it points to the first element added to the array until it is moved by a function such as next or reset.

```
<?
        //create test data
        $colors = array("red", "green", "blue");

        //loop through array using current
        for(reset($colors); $value = current($colors); next($colors))
        {
                print("$value<BR>\n");
        }
?>
```

array each(array arrayname)

The each function returns a four-element array that represents the next value from an array. The four elements of the returned array (0, 1, key, and value) refer to the key and value of the current element. You may refer to the key with 0 or key, and to get the value use 1 or value. You may traverse an entire array by repeatedly using list and each, as in the example below.

```
<?
        //create test data
        $colors = array("red", "green", "blue");
```

```
        //loop through array using each
        //output will be like "0 = red"
        while(list($key, $value) = each($colors))
        {
                print("$key = $value<BR>\n");
        }
?>
```

end(array arrayname)

The end function moves PHP's internal array pointer to the array's last element. The reset function moves the internal pointer to the first element.

```
<?
        $colors = array("red", "green", "blue");
        end($colors);
        print(current($colors));
?>
```

array explode(string delimiter, string data)

The explode function creates an array from a string. The delimiter argument divides the data argument into elements. This function is safe for use with binary strings. The implode function will convert an array into a string.

```
<?
        /*
        ** convert tab-delimited list into an array
        */
        $data = "red\tgreen\tblue";
        $colors = explode("\t", $data);

        // print out the values
        for($index=0; $index < count($colors); $index++)
        {
                print("$index : $colors[$index] <BR>\n");
        }
?>
```

extract(array variables, integer mode, string prefix)

The `extract` function creates variables in the local scope based on elements in the `variables` argument. Elements not indexed by strings are ignored. The optional `mode` argument controls whether variables overwrite existing variables or are renamed to avoid a collision. The valid modes are listed in Table 9.1. If left out, `EXTR_OVERWRITE` mode is assumed. The `prefix` argument is required only if `EXTR_PREFIX_SAME` or `EXTR_PREFIX_ALL` modes are chosen. If used, the `prefix` argument and an underscore are added to the name of the extracted variable.

Compare this function to compact, which creates an array based on variables in the local scope.

```
<?
    $new_variables = array('Name'=>'Leon', 'Language'=>'PHP');

    $Language = 'English';

    extract($new_variables, EXTR_PREFIX_SAME, "collision");

    //print extracted variables
    print($Name . "<BR>\n");
    print($collision_Language . "<BR>\n");

?>
```

boolean in_array(value query, array data)

The `in_array` function returns TRUE if the `query` argument is an element of the `data` argument.

Table 9.1   **extract** Modes

Mode	Description
EXTR_OVERWRITE	Overwrite any variables with the same name.
EXTR_SKIP	Skip any variables with the same name.
EXTR_PREFIX_SAME	Add prefix to variables with same name.
EXTR_PREFIX_ALL	Prefix all variables.

```
<?
        //create test data
        $colors = array("red", "green", "blue");

        //test for the presence of green
        if(in_array("green", $colors))
        {
                print("Yes, green is present!");
        }
?>
```

string implode(array data, string delimiter)

The `implode` function transforms an array into a string. The elements are concatenated with the `delimiter` string separating them. To perform the reverse functionality, use `explode`.

```
<?
        /*
        ** convert an array into a comma-delimited string
        */
        $colors = array("red", "green", "blue");
        $colors = implode($colors, ",");

        print($colors);
?>
```

join

You may use `join` as an alias to the implode function.

value key(array arrayname)

The `key` function returns the index of the current element. Use `current` to find the value of the current element.

```
<?
        $colors = array("FF0000"=>"red",
                "00FF00"=>"green",
                "0000FF"=>"blue");

        for(reset($colors); $key = key($colors); next($colors))
        {
```

```
        print("$key is $colors[$key]<BR>\n");
    }
?>
```

boolean krsort(array data)

The krsort function sorts an array by its keys in reverse order—that is, largest values first. The element values are moved along with the keys. This is mainly for the benefit of associative arrays, since arrays indexed by integers can easily be traversed in order of their keys.

```
<?
    $colors = array("red"=>"FF0000",
        "green"=>"00FF00",
        "blue"=>"0000FF");

    // sort an array by its keys
    krsort($colors);

    // print out the values
    foreach($colors as $key=>$value)
    {
        print("$key : $value <BR>\n");
    }
?>
```

boolean ksort(array data)

The ksort function sorts an array by its keys, or index values. The element values are moved along with the keys. This is mainly for the benefit of associative arrays, since arrays indexed by integers can easily be traversed in order of their keys.

```
<?
    $colors = array("red"=>"FF0000",
        "green"=>"00FF00",
        "blue"=>"0000FF");

    // sort an array by its keys
    ksort($colors);

    // print out the values
    foreach($colors as $key=>$value)
```

```
        {
                print("$key : $value <BR>\n");
        }
?>
```

list(...)

The list function treats a list of variables as if they were an array. It may only be used on the left side of an assignment operator. It is useful for translating a returned array directly into a set of variables.

```
<?
        $colors = array("red", "green", "blue");

        //put first two elements of returned array
        //into key and value, respectively
        list($key, $value) = each($colors);

        print("$key: $value<BR>\n");
?>
```

value max(array arrayname) value max(...)

The max function returns the largest value from all the array elements. If all values are strings, then the values will be compared as strings. If any of the values is a number, only the integers and doubles will be compared numerically. The alternate version of the max function takes any number of arguments and returns the largest of them. With this use, you must supply at least two values.

To find the minimum value, use min.

```
<?
        $colors = array("red"=>"FF0000",
                "green"=>"00FF00",
                "blue"=>"0000FF");

        //prints FF0000
        print(max($colors) . "<BR>\n");

        //prints 13
        print(max("hello", "55", 13) . "<BR>\n");
```

```
        //prints 17
        print(max(1, 17, 3, 5.5) . "<BR>\n");
?>
```

value min(array arrayname) value min(...)

The min function returns the smallest value from all the array elements. If all values are strings, then the values will be compared as strings. If any of the values is a number, only the integers and doubles will be compared numerically. The alternate version of the min function takes any number of arguments and returns the smallest of them. You must supply at least two values.

```
<?
        $colors = array("red"=>"FF0000",
              "green"=>"00FF00",
              "blue"=>"0000FF");

        //prints 0000FF
        print(min($colors) . "<BR>\n");

        //prints 13
        print(min("hello", "55", 13) . "<BR>\n");

        //prints 1
        print(min(1, 17, 3, 5.5) . "<BR>\n");
?>
```

value next(array arrayname)

The next function moves PHP's array pointer forward one element. It returns the value at the new element. If the pointer is already at the end of the array, FALSE is returned.

```
<?
        $colors = array("red", "green", "blue");
        $my_color = current($colors);
        do
        {
              print("$my_color <BR>\n");
        }
        while($my_color = next($colors))
?>
```

pos

You may use pos as an alias to the current function.

value prev(array arrayname)

The prev function operates similarly to the next function with the exception that it moves backward through the array. The internal pointer to the array is moved back one element, and the value at that position is returned. If the pointer is already at the beginning, FALSE is returned.

```
<?
    $colors = array("red", "green", "blue");
    end($colors);
    $my_color = current($colors);
    do
    {
        print("$my_color <BR>\n");
    }
    while($my_color = prev($colors))
?>
```

array range(integer start, integer stop)

Use range to create an array containing every integer between the first argument and the second, inclusive.

```
<?
    $numbers = range(13, 19);

    //print out all the values
    foreach($numbers as $value)
    {
        print("$value<BR>\n");
    }
?>
```

value reset(array arrayname)

Use the reset function to move an array's internal pointer to the first element. The element in the first position is returned. Use end to set the pointer to the last element.

```
<?
    //create test data
    $colors = array("red", "green", "blue");

    //move internal pointer
    next($colors);

    //set internal pointer to first element
    reset($colors);

    //show which element we're at (red)
    print(current($colors));
?>
```

rsort(array unsorted_array)

The rsort function sorts an array in reverse order. As with other sorting functions, the presence of string values will cause all values to be treated as strings and the elements will be sorted alphabetically. If all the elements are numbers, they will be sorted numerically. The difference between rsort and arsort is that rsort discards any key values and reassigns elements with key values starting at zero. Chapter 15 discusses sorting in depth.

```
<?
    //create test data
    $colors = array("one"=>"orange", "two"=>"cyan",
        "three"=>"purple");

    //sort and discard keys
    rsort($colors);

    //show array
    foreach($colors as $key=>$value)
    {
        print("$key = $value<BR>\n");
    }
?>
```

shuffle(array data)

The shuffle function randomly rearranges the elements in an array. The srand function may be used to seed the random number generator, but as with the rand function, a seed based on the current time will be used if you do not provide a seed.

```
<?
        //create test data
        $numbers = range(1, 10);

        //rearrange
        shuffle($numbers);

        //print out all the values
        foreach($numbers as $value)
        {
                print("$value<BR>\n");
        }
?>
```

sizeof

This is an alias for the count function.

sort(array unsorted_array)

The sort function sorts an array by element values from lowest to highest. If any element is a string, all elements will be converted to strings for the purpose of comparison, which will be made alphabetically. If all elements are numbers, they will be sorted numerically. Like rsort, sort discards key values and reassigns elements with key values starting at zero. Chapter 15 discusses sorting in depth.

```
<?
//create test data
$colors = array("one"=>"orange", "two"=>"cyan", "three"=>"purple");

//sort and discard keys
sort($colors);

//show array
foreach($colors as $key=>$value)
{
        print("$key = $value<BR>\n");
}
?>
```

uasort(array unsorted_array, string comparison_function)

The uasort function sorts an array using a custom comparison function. The index values, or keys, move along with the element values, similar to the behavior of the asort function.

The comparison function must return a signed integer. If it returns zero, then two elements are considered equal. If a negative number is returned, the two elements are considered to be in order. If a positive number is returned, the two elements are considered to be out of order.

```
<?
    /*
    ** duplicate normal ordering
    */
    function compare($left, $right)
    {
        return($left - $right);
    }

    //create test data
    $some_numbers = array(
        "red"=>6,
        "green"=>4,
        "blue"=>8,
        "yellow"=>2,
        "orange"=>7,
        "cyan"=>1,
        "purple"=>9,
        "magenta"=>3,
        "black"=>5);

    //sort using custom compare
    uasort($some_numbers, "compare");

    //show sorted array
    foreach($some_numbers as $key=>$value)
    {
        print($key . "=" . $value . "<BR>\n");
    }
?>
```

uksort(array unsorted_array, string comparison_function)

The `uksort` function sorts an array using a custom comparison function. Unlike `usort`, the array will be sorted by the index values, not the elements. The comparison function must return a signed integer. If it returns zero, then two indices are considered equal. If a negative number is returned, the two indices are considered to be in order. If a positive number is returned, the two indices are considered to be out of order.

```
<?

    /*
    ** duplicate normal ordering
    */
    function compare($left, $right)
    {
        return($left - $right);
    }

    //create test data
    srand(time());
    for($i=0; $i<10; $i++)
    {
        $data[rand(1,100)] = rand(1,100);
    }

    //sort using custom compare
    uksort($data, "compare");

    //show sorted array
    foreach($data as $key=>$value)
    {
        print($key . "=" . $value . "<BR>\n");
    }
?>
```

usort(array unsorted_array, string compare_function)

The `usort` function sorts an array by element values using a custom comparison function. The function must return a signed integer. If it returns zero, then two elements are considered equal. If a negative number is returned, the two elements are considered to be in order. If a positive number is returned, the two elements are considered to be out of order.

```
<?
        /*
        ** duplicate normal ordering
        */
        function compare($left, $right)
        {
                return($left - $right);
        }

        //create test data
        srand(time());
        for($i=0; $i<10; $i++)
        {
                $data[rand(1,100)] = rand(1,100);
        }

        //sort using custom compare
        usort($data, "compare");

        //show sorted array
        foreach($data as $key=>$value)
        {
                print($key . "=" . $value . "<BR>\n");
        }
?>
```

Hashing

Hashing is the process of creating an index for a value using the value itself. The index is called a hash. Sometimes hashes are unique to values, but not always. Hashes can be used to make fast lookups, a method that PHP uses for keeping track of variables. Other times hashes are used like encryption. If the hashes of two strings match, you can assume the two strings match, as long as hash values are unique. In this way you can check passwords without ever decrypting the original password.

Some of the functions in this section are built into PHP. The others are part of Sascha Shumann's Mhash library. This library presents a universal interface to many hashing algorithms. Visit the home site to learn more about it <http://schumann.cx/mhash/>.

string md5(string text)

The md5 function produces a hash as described by RFC 1321. The function takes a string of any length and returns a 32-character identifier. It is theorized that the algorithm for the md5 function will produce unique identifiers for all strings.

```
<?
    print(md5("Who is John Galt?"));
?>
```

Figure 9–5 md5.

string metaphone(string word)

Use metaphone to produce a string that describes how a word sounds when spoken. This function is similar to soundex; however, it knows about how groups of letters are pronounced in English. Therefore it is more accurate. Compare this function to soundex and similar_text.

The metaphone algorithm, invented by Lawrence Philips, was first described in *Computer Language* magazine. You may find a discussion of metaphone at Scott Gasch's Algorithm Archive <http://perl.guru.org/alg/node131.html>.

```
<?
    print("Atkinson encodes as " . metaphone("Atkinson"));
?>
```

string mhash(integer hash, string data)

Use mhash to get a hash for a string. Hashing algorithms available at the time of writing are shown in Table 9.2.

Refer to the Mhash documentation for more information about each algorithm.

```
<?
    print(mhash(MHASH_GOST, "Who is John Galt?"));
?>
```

Table 9.2   Mhash Algorithms

MHASH_CRC32

MHASH_CRC32B

MHASH_GOST

MHASH_HAVAL

MHASH_MD5

MHASH_RIPEMD128

MHASH_RIPEMD160

MHASH_SHA1

MHASH_TIGER

integer mhash_count()

The mhash_count function returns the highest-numbered hash identifier. All hash algorithms are numbered from zero, so you can use this function and mhash_get_hash_name to get a complete list.

```
<?
    print("<TABLE BORDER=\"1\">\n");

    print("<TR>\n");
    print("<TH>Algorithm</TH>\n");
    print("<TH>Block Size</TH>\n");
    print("</TR>\n");

    for($i=0; $i <= mhash_count(); $i++)
```

```
        {
                print("<TR>\n");
                print("<TD>MHASH_" . mhash_get_hash_name($i) .
"</TD>\n");
                print("<TD>" . mhash_get_block_size($i) .
"</TD>\n");
                print("</TR>\n");
        }

        print("</TABLE>\n");
?>
```

integer mhash_get_block_size(integer hash)

The mhash_get_block_size function returns the block size used for a hash algorithm.

string mhash_get_hash_name(integer hash)

The mhash_get_hash_name function returns the name for a particular hash identifier.

int similar_text(string left, string right, reference percentage)

The similar_text function compares two strings and returns the number of characters they have in common. If present, the variable specified for the percentage argument will receive the percentage similarity. Compare this function to metaphone and soundex.

The algorithm used for similar_text is taken from a book by Ian Oliver called *Programming Classics: Implementing the World's Best Algorithms*. It's published by Prentice Hall, and you can find out more about it on the Prentice Hall PTR Web site <http://www.phptr.com/ptrbooks/ptr_0131004131.html>.

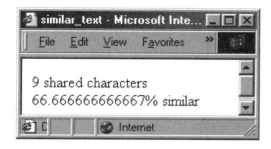

```
<?
    //create two strings
    $left = "Leon Atkinson";
    $right = "Vicky Atkinson";

    //test to see how similar they are
    $i = similar_text($left, $right, &$percent);

    //print results
    print($i . " shared characters<BR>\n");
    print($percent . "% similar<BR>\n");
?>
```

Figure 9–6 `similar_text`.

string soundex(string text)

The `soundex` function returns an identifier based on how a word sounds when spoken. Similar-sounding words will have similar or identical soundex codes. The soundex code is four characters and starts with a letter. Compare this function to the `similar_text` and the `metaphone` functions.

The soundex algorithm was described by Donald Knuth in Volume 3 of *The Art of Computer Programming*.

```
<?
    print(soundex("lion"));
    print("<BR>");
    print(soundex("lying"));
?>
```

Strings

For the most part, the string functions create strings from other strings or report about the properties of a string. The exception is the `eval` function, which executes a string as if it were a line of code in your PHP script.

array count_chars(string data, integer mode)
string count_chars(string data, integer mode)

The `count_chars` function analyzes a string by the characters present. The `mode` argument controls the return value. Modes 0, 1 and 2 return an array. Modes 3 and 4 return a string. If `mode` is left out, mode 0 is used.

If `mode` is 0, an array is returned indexed by ASCII codes, 0–255. Each element is set with the count for that character. If `mode` is 1, only the elements with count greater than zero are returned. If `mode` is 2, only the elements with count equal to zero are returned. Mode 3 returns a string containing each character appearing in the input string. Mode 4 contains a string containing all characters not appearing in the input string.

```
<?
//print counts for characters found
foreach(count_chars("Core PHP", 1) as $key=>$value)
{
        print("$key: $value<BR>\n");
}

//print list of characters found
print("Characters: '" . count_chars("Core PHP", 3) . "'<BR>\n");
?>
```

eval(string phpcode)

The `eval` function attempts to execute the `phpcode` argument as if it were a line in your PHP script. As with all strings, double quotes will cause the string to be evaluated for embedded strings and other special characters, so you may wish to use single quotes or escape dollar signs with backslashes.

In some ways, eval is like `include` or `require`. Beyond the obvious difference that `eval` works on strings instead of files, `eval` starts in a mode where it expects PHP code. If you need to switch to a mode where plain HTML is passed directly to the browser, you will need to insert a closing PHP tag (`?>`). Why would you ever want to execute `eval` on a string that contained plain HTML? Probably because the code was stored in a database.

Be extremely careful when calling `eval` on any string that contains data that at any time came from form variables. This includes database fields that were originally set through a form. When possible, use nested `$` operators instead of `eval`.

```
<?
       //Contrived example
       //eval() line could be replaced with $$varName = 1;
       $varName = "myValue";
       eval("\$$varName = 1;");
       print($myValue . "<BR>\n");

       //More realistic simulation of using eval
       //on data from a database
       $code_from_database = "<B><? print(date(\"Y-m-d\")); ?></B>";
       eval("?>" . $code_from_database);
?>
```

string sprintf(string format, ...)

The `sprintf` function operates identically to the `printf` function, except that instead of sending the assembled string to the browser, the string is returned. See the description of `printf` for a detailed discussion. This function offers an easy way to control the representation of numbers. Ordinarily PHP may print a double with no fraction

```
<?
       $x = 3.00;

       //print $x as PHP default
       print($x . "<BR>\n");

       //format value of $x so that
       //it show two decimals after
       //the decimal point
       $s = sprintf("%.2f", $x);
       print($s . "<BR>\n");
?>
```

string str_repeat(string text, integer count)

The str_repeat function returns a string consisting of the text argument repeated the number of times specified by the count argument.

```
<?
    print(str_repeat("PHP!<BR>\n", 10));
?>
```

integer strcasecmp(string first, string second)

The strcasecmp function operates identically to strcmp with the exception that upper- and lowercase letters are treated as being identical. Check out soundex, metaphone, and similar_text for alternative ways of comparing strings.

```
<?
    $first = "abc";
    $second = "aBc";

    if(strcasecmp($first, $second) == 0)
    {
        print("strings are equal");
    }
    else
    {
        print("strings are not equal");
    }
?>
```

strchr

This function is an alias to strstr.

integer strcmp(string first, string second)

The strcmp function compares the first string to the second string. A number less than zero is returned if the first string is less than the second. Zero is returned if they are equal. A number greater than zero is returned if the first string is greater than the second string. Comparisions are made by ASCII values. This function is safe for comparing binary data. Check out soundex, metaphone, and similar_text for alternative ways of comparing strings.

```
<?
     $first = "abc";
     $second = "xyz";

     if(strcmp($first, $second) == 0)
     {
            print("strings are equal");
     }
     else
     {
            print("strings are not equal");
     }
?>
```

integer strcspn(string text, string set)

The strcspn function returns the position of the first character in the text argument that is part of the set argument. Compare this function to strspn.

```
<?
     $text = "red cabbage";
     $set = "abc";
     $position = strcspn($text, $set);

     // prints 'red '
     print(substr($text, 0, $position));
?>
```

string stristr(string text, string substring)

The stristr function is a case-insensitive version of strstr, below. A portion of the text argument is returned starting from the first occurrence of the substring argument to the end.

```
<?
     $text = "Although he had help, Leon is the author of
this book.";

     print("Full text: $text <BR>\n");
     print("Looking for 'leon':" . stristr($text, "leon"));
?>
```

integer strlen(string text)

Use the strlen function to get the length of a string.

```
<?
    $text = "a short string";
    print("'$text' is " . strlen($text) . " characters long.");
?>
```

integer strpos(string data, string substring, integer offset)

The `strpos` function returns the position of the `substring` argument in the `data` argument. If the `substring` argument is not a string, it will be treated as an ASCII code. If the substring appears more than once, the position of the first occurrence is returned. If the substring doesn't exist at all, then FALSE is returned. The optional `offset` argument instructs PHP to begin searching after the specified position. Positions are counted starting with zero.

This function is a good alternative to `ereg` when you are searching for a simple string. It carries none of the overhead involved in parsing regular expressions. It is safe for use with binary strings.

```
<?
    $text = "Hello, World!";

    //check for a space
    if(strpos($text, 32))
    {
        print("There is a space in '$text'<BR>\n");
    }

    //find where in the string World appears
    print("World is at position " . strpos($text, "World") . "<BR>\n");
?>
```

strrchr

This is an alias for `strrpos`.

integer strrpos(string text, string character)

The `strrpos` function operates similarly to `strpos`. It returns the last occurrence of the second argument in the first. However, only the first character of the second argument is used. This function offers a very neat way of chopping off the last part of a path, as in the example below.

```
<?
    //set test string
    $path = "/usr/local/apache";

    //find last slash
    $pos = strrpos($path, "/");

    //print everything after the last slash
    print(substr($path, $pos+1));
?>
```

integer strspn(string text, string set)

The strspn function returns the position in the first character in the text argument that is not part of the set of characters in the set argument. Compare this function to strcspan.

```
<?
    $text = "cabbage";
    $set = "abc";
    $position = strspn($text, $set);

    // prints 'cabba'
    print(substr($text, 0, $position));
?>
```

string strstr(string text, string substring)

The strstr function returns the portion of the text argument from the first occurrence of the substring argument to the end of the string. If substring is not a string, it is assumed to be an ASCII code. ASCII codes are listed in Appendix B.

An empty string is returned when substring is not found in text. You can use it as a faster alternative to ereg if you test for an empty string, as in the example below. The stristr function is a case-insensitive version of this function.

```
<?
    $text = "Although this is a string, it's not very long.";
    if(strstr($text, "it") != "")
    {
        print("The string contains 'it'.<BR>/n");
    }
?>
```

string strtok(string line, string separator)

The `strtok` function pulls tokens from a string. The `line` argument is split up into tokens separated by any of the characters in the `separator` string. The first call to `strtok` must contain two arguments. Subsequent calls are made with just the `separator` argument, unless you wish to begin tokenizing another string. Chapter 16, "Parsing and String Evaluation," discusses this function in depth, including alternatives like `ereg`.

```
<?
    // create a demo string
    $line = "leon\tatkinson\tleon@clearink.com";

    // loop while there are still tokens
    for($token = strtok($line, "\t");
            $token != "";
            $token = strtok("\t"))
    {
            print("token: $token<BR>\n");
    }
?>
```

string substr(string text, integer start, integer length)

Use the `substr` function to extract a substring from the `text` argument. A string is returned that starts with the character identified by the `start` argument, counting from zero. If `start` is negative, counting will begin at the last character of the `text` argument instead of the first and work backward.

The number of characters returned is determined by the `length` argument or the beginning and end of the string. If `length` is negative, the returned string will end that many characters from the end of the string. In any case, if the combination of start and length calls for a string of negative length, a single character is returned.

This function is safe for use with binary strings.

```
<?
    $text = "My dog's name is Angus.";

    //print Angus
    print(substr($text, 17, 5));
?>
```

Encoding and Decoding

The functions in this section transform data from one form to another. This includes stripping certain characters, substituting some characters for others, and translating data into some encoded form.

string addcslashes(string text, string characters)

The addcslashes function returns the text argument after escaping characters in the style of the C programming language. Briefly, this means special characters are replaced with codes, such as \n replacing a newline character, and other characters outside ASCII 32–126 are replaced with backslash octal codes.

The optional characters argument may contain a list of characters to be escaped, which overrides the default of escaping all special characters. The characters are specified with octal notation. You may specify a range using two periods as in the example below.

```
<?
    $s = addcslashes($s, "\0..\37");
?>
```

string addslashes(string text)

The addslashes function returns the text argument with backslashes preceding characters that have special meaning in database queries. These are single quotes ('), double quotes ("), and backslashes themselves (\).

```
<?
    // add slashes to text
    $phrase = addslashes("I don't know");

    // build query
    $Query = "SELECT * ";
    $Query .= "FROM comment ";
    $Query .= "WHERE text like '%$phrase%'";

    print($Query);
?>
```

string base64_decode(string data)

The `base64_decode` function translates data from MIME base64 encoding into 8-bit data. Base64 encoding is used for transmitting data across protocols, such as email, where raw binary data would otherwise be corrupted.

```
<?
    $data = "VGhpcyBpcyBhIAptdWx0aS1saW51IG1lc3NhZ2UK";
    print(base64_decode($data));
?>
```

string base64_encode(string text)

The `base64_encode` function converts text, such as email, to a form that will pass through 7-bit systems uncorrupted.

```
<?
    $text = "This is a \nmulti-line message\n";
    print(base64_encode($text));
?>
```

string basename(string path)

The `basename` function returns only the filename part of a path. Directories are understood to be strings of numbers and letters separated by slash characters (/). When running on Windows, backslashes (\) are used as well. The flip side to this function is `dirname`, which returns the directory.

```
<?
 $path="/usr/local/bin/ls";
 print(basename($path));
?>
```

string bin2hex(string data)

The `bin2hex` function returns the `data` argument with each byte replaced by its hexadecimal representation. The numbers are returned in little-endian style. That is, the first digit is most significant.

```
<?
    //print book title in hex
    //436f726520504850502050726f6772616d6d696e67
    $s = "Core PHP Programming";
```

```
        $s = bin2hex($s);
        print($s);
?>
```

string chop(string text)

The chop function returns the text argument with any trailing whitespace removed. If you wish to remove both trailing and leading whitespace, use the trim function. If you wish to remove leading whitespace only, use ltrim. Whitespace includes spaces, tabs, and other nonprintable characters, including nulls (ASCII 0).

```
<?
        print("\"" .
                chop("This has whitespace    ") .
                "\"");
?>
```

string chr(integer ascii_code)

Use chr to get the character for an ASCII code. This function is helpful for situations where you need to use a nonprinting character that has no backslash code, or the backslash code is ambiguous. Imagine a script that writes to a formatted text file. Ordinarily you would use \n for an end-of-line marker. But the behavior may be different when your script is moved from Windows to Linux, because Windows uses a carriage return followed by a linefeed. If you wish to enforce that each line end with a linefeed only, you can use chr(10) as in the example below.

Of course, you may always use a backslash code to specify an ASCII code, as listed in Appendix A and discussed in Chapter 2. Another alternative to chr is sprintf. The %c code stands for a single character, and you may specify an ASCII value for the character. Additionally, some functions, such as ereg_replace, accept integers that are interpreted as ASCII codes.

If you need the ASCII code for a character, use ord. Appendix B lists ASCII codes.

```
<?
        //open a test file
        $fp = fopen("data.txt", "w");

        //write a couple of records that have
        //linefeeds for end markers
```

```
     fwrite($fp, "data record 1" . chr(10));
     fwrite($fp, "data record 2" . chr(10));

     //close file
     fclose($fp);
?>
```

string chunk_split(string data, integer length, string marker)

The `chunk_split` function returns the `data` argument after inserting an end-of-line marker at regular intervals. By default a carriage return and a linefeed are inserted every 76 characters. Optionally, you may specify a different length and a different marker string.

Sascha Schumann added this function specifically to break base64 codes up into 76-character chunks. Although `ereg_replace` can mimic this functionality, `chunk_split` is faster. It isn't appropriate for breaking prose between words. That is, it isn't intended for performing a soft wrap.

```
<?
     $encodedData = chunck_split(base64_encode($rawData));
?>
```

string convert_cyr_string(string text, string from, string to)

Use `convert_cyr_string` to convert a text in one Cyrillic character set to another. The `from` and `to` arguments are single-character codes listed in Table 9.3.

Table 9.3   Codes for `convert_cyr_String`

Code	Description
a,d	x-cp866
i	iso8859-5
k	koi8-r
m	x-mac-cyrillic
w	windows-1251

```
<?
      $new = convert_cyr_string($old, "a", "w");
?>
```

string dirname(string path)

The `dirname` function returns only the directory part of a path. The trailing slash is not included in the return value. Directories are understood to be separated by slashes (/). On Windows, backslashes (\) may be used, too. If you need to get the filename part of a path, use `basename`.

```
<?
      $path = "/usr/local/bin/ls";
      print(dirname($path));
?>
```

string escapeshellcmd(string command)

The `escapeshellcmd` function adds a backslash before any characters that may cause trouble in a shell command. This function should be used to filter user input before it is used in `exec` or `system`. Table 9.4 lists characters escaped by `escapeshellcmd`.

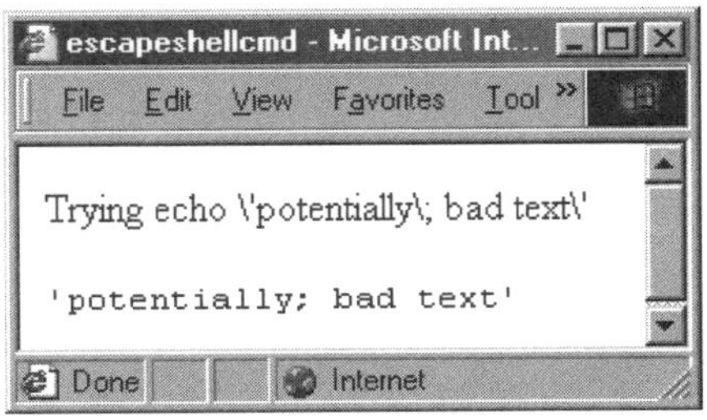

```
<?
      $cmd = "echo 'potentially; bad text'";
      $cmd = escapeshellcmd($cmd);

      print("Trying $cmd <BR>\n");

      print("<PRE>");
      system($cmd);
      print("</PRE>");
?>
```

Figure 9-7   `escapeshellcmd.`

Table 9.4 Characters Escaped by `escapeshellcmd`	
Character	*Description*
&	Ampersand
;	Semicolon
`	Left Tick
'	Single Quote
"	Double Quote
|	Vertical Bar
*	Asterisk
?	Question Mark
~	Tilde
<	Left Angle Bracket
>	Right Angle Bracket
^	Caret
(	Left Parenthesis
)	Right Parenthesis
[	Left Square Bracket
]	Right Square Bracket
{	Left Curly Brace
}	Right Curly Brace
$	Dollar Sign
\	Backslash
ASCII 10	Linefeed
ASCII 255	

string hebrev(string text, integer length)

Unlike English, Hebrew text reads right to left, which makes working with strings inconvenient at times. The `hebrev` function reverses the orientation of Hebrew text, but leaves English alone. Hebrew characters are assumed to be in the ASCII range 224 through 251, inclusive. The optional `length` argument specifies a maximum length per line. Lines that exceed this length are broken.

```
<?
     print(hebrev("Hebrew"));
?>
```

string hebrevc(string text, integer length)

The `hebrevc` function operates exactly like `hebrev`, except that `BR` tags are inserted before end-of-line characters.

string htmlentities(string text)

The `htmlentities` function returns the `text` argument with certain characters translated into HTML entities. Table 9.5 lists entities supported.

This list conforms to the ISO-8859-1 standard. The `nl2br` function is similar: it translates line breaks to `BR` tags. You can use `strip_tags` to remove HTML tags altogether.

```
<?
     $text = "Use <HTML> to begin a document.";
     print(htmlentities($text));
?>
```

string htmlspecialchars(string text)

The `htmlspecialchars` function works like `htmlentities`, except that a smaller set of entities are used. They are `amp`, `quot`, `lt`, and `gt`.

```
<?
     $text = "Use <HTML> to begin a document.";
     print(htmlspecialchars($text));
?>
```

integer ip2long(string address)

The `ip2long` function takes an IP address and returns an integer. This allows you to compress a 16-byte string into a 4-byte integer. Use `long2ip` to reverse the process.

Table 9.5   HTML Entities

aacute	eacute	macr	raquo
aacute	eacute	micro	reg
acirc	ecirc	middot	sect
acirc	ecirc	nbsp	shy
acute	egrave	not	sup1
aelig	egrave	ntilde	sup2
aelig	eth	ntilde	sup3
agrave	eth	oacute	szlig
agrave	euml	oacute	thorn
aring	euml	ocirc	thorn
aring	frac12	ocirc	times
atilde	frac14	ograve	uacute
atilde	frac34	ograve	uacute
auml	iacute	ordf	ucirc
auml	iacute	ordm	ucirc
brvbar	icirc	oslash	ugrave
ccedil	icirc	oslash	ugrave
ccedil	iexcl	otilde	uml
cedil	igrave	otilde	uuml
cent	igrave	ouml	uuml
copy	iquest	ouml	yacute
curren	iuml	para	yacute
deg	iuml	plusmn	yen
divide	laquo	pound	yuml

string long2ip(integer address)

Use `long2ip` to get the textual representation of an IP address. Use `ip2long` to reverse the process.

string ltrim(string text)

The `ltrim` function returns the text argument with any leading whitespace removed. If you wish to remove whitespace on the end of the string, use `chop`. If you wish to remove whitespace from the beginng and end, use `trim`. Whitespace includes spaces, tabs and other nonprintable characters, including nulls (ASCII 0).

```
<?
    $text = "   Leading whitespace";
```

```
      print("<PRE>" . ltrim($text) . "</PRE>");
?>
```

string nl2br(string text)

The `nl2br` function inserts `<BR>` before every newline in the text argument and returns the modified text.

```
<?
    $text = "line1\nline2\nline3\n";
    print(nl2br($text));
?>
```

string number_format(double value, integer precision, string decimal, string thousands)

The `number_format` function returns a formatted representation of the `value` argument as an integer with commas inserted to separate thousands. The optional `precision` argument specifies the number of digits after the

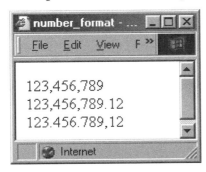

```
<?
        $test_number = 123456789.123456789;

        //add commas, drop any fraction
        print(number_format($test_number) . "<BR>\n");

        //add commas and limit to two digit precision
        print(number_format($test_number, 2) . "<BR>\n");

        //format for Germans
        print(number_format($test_number, 2, ",", ".") . "<BR>\n");
?>
```

Figure 9-8 `number_format`.

decimal point, which by default is zero. The optional `decimal` and `thousands` arguments must be used together. They override the default use of periods and commas for decimal points and thousands separators.

integer ord(string character)

The `ord` function returns the ASCII code of the first character in the character argument. This function allows you to deal with characters by their ASCII values, which often can be more convenient than using backslash codes, especially if you wish to take advantage of the order of the ASCII table. Refer to Appendix B for a complete table of ASCII codes.

If you need to find the character associated with an ASCII code, use the `chr` function.

```
<?
    /*
    ** Decompose a string into its ASCII codes.
    ** Test for codes below 32 because these have
    ** special meaning and we may not want to
    ** print them.
    */

    $text = "Line 1\nLine 2\n";

    print("ASCII Codes for '$text'<BR>\n");

    print("<TABLE>\n");

    for($i=0; $i < strlen($text); $i++)
    {
        print("<TR>");

        print("<TH>");
        if(ord($text[$i]) > 31)
        {
            print($text[$i]);
        }
        else
        {
            print("(unprintable)");
        }
        print("</TH> ");
```

```
            print(ord($text[$i]));
            print("</TD>");

            print("</TR>\n");
    }

    print("</TABLE>\n");
?>
```

string pack(string format, ...)

The pack function takes inspiration from the Perl function of the same name. It allows you to put data in a compact format readable on all platforms. Format codes in the first argument match with the arguments that follow it. The codes determine how the values are stored. An optional number, called the repeat count, may follow the format code. It specifies how many of the following arguments to use. The repeat count may also be *, which matches the remaining arguments. Some of the codes use the repeat count differently. Table 9.6 lists all the format codes and how they use the repeat count.

A string with the packed data is returned. Note that it will be in a binary form, unsuitable for printing. In the example below, I've printed out each byte of the packed data as hexadecimal codes.

```
<?
    //create some packed data
    $packedData = pack("ca10n", 65, "hello", 1970);

    //display ASCII code for each character
    print("<PRE>");
    for($i=0; $i<strlen($packedData); $i++)
    {
        print("0x" . dechex(ord($packedData[$i])) . " ");
    }
    print("</PRE>\n");

    //unpack the data
    $Data = unpack("cOne/a10Two/nThree", $packedData);

    //show all elements of the unpacked array
    while(list($key, $value) = each($Data))
    {
        print("$key = $value <BR>\n");
    }
?>
```

Table 9.6	Pack Codes	
Code	*Data Type*	*Description*
a	String	Repeat count is the number of characters to take from the string. If there are fewer characters in the string than specified by the repeat count, spaces are used to pad it out.
A	String	Repeat count is the number of characters to take from the string. If there are fewer characters in the string than specified by the repeat count, nulls (ASCII 0) are used to pad it out.
c	Integer	The integer will be converted to a signed character.
C	Integer	The integer will be converted to an unsigned character.
d	Double	The double will be stored in double-width floating-point format. Depending on your operating system, this is probably 8 bytes.
f	Double	The double will be converted to a single-width floating-point format. Depending on your operating system, this is probably 4 bytes.
h	String	The ASCII value of each character of the argument will be saved as two characters representing the ASCII code in hexadecimal, big-endian. The repeat count denotes the number of characters to take from the input.
H	String	The ASCII value of each character of the argument will be saved as two characters representing the ASCII code in hexadecimal, little-endian. The repeat count denotes the number of characters to take from the input.
i	Integer	The argument will be saved as an unsigned integer. Typically this is 4 bytes.
I	Integer	The argument will be saved as a signed integer. Typically this is 4 bytes, with one bit used for sign.
l	Integer	The argument is saved as an unsigned long, which is usually 8 bytes.
L	Integer	The argument is saved as a signed long, which is usually 8 bytes with one bit used for sign.

n	Integer	The argument is saved as an unsigned short, which is 2 bytes. The value is saved in a way that allows for safe unpacking on both little-endian and big-endian machines.
N	Integer	The argument is saved as an unsigned long, which is 8 bytes. The value is saved in a way that allows for safe unpacking on both little-endian and big-endian machines.
s	Integer	The argument is saved as an unsigned short, which is usually 2 bytes.
S	Integer	The argument is saved as a signed short, which is usually 2 bytes with one bit used for sign.
v	Integer	The argument is saved as an unsigned short in little-endian order.
V	Integer	The argument is saved as an unsigned long in little-endian order.
x	None	This format directive doesn't match with an argument. It writes a null byte.
X	None	This format directive causes the pointer to packed string to back up 1 byte.
@	None	This format directive moves the pointer to the absolute position specified by its repeat count. The empty space is padded with null bytes.

parse_str(string query)

The `parse_str` function parses the `query` argument as if it were an HTTP GET query. A variable is created in the current scope for each field in the query. You may wish to use this function on the output of `parse_url`.

```
<?
    $query = "name=Leon&occupation=Web+Engineer";
    parse_str($query);
    print("$name <BR>\n");
    print("$occupation <BR>\n");
?>
```

array parse_url(string query)

The `parse_url` function breaks an URL into an associative array with the following elements: `fragment`, `host`, `pass`, `path`, `port`, `query`, `scheme`, `user`. The query is not evaluated as with the `parse_str` function.

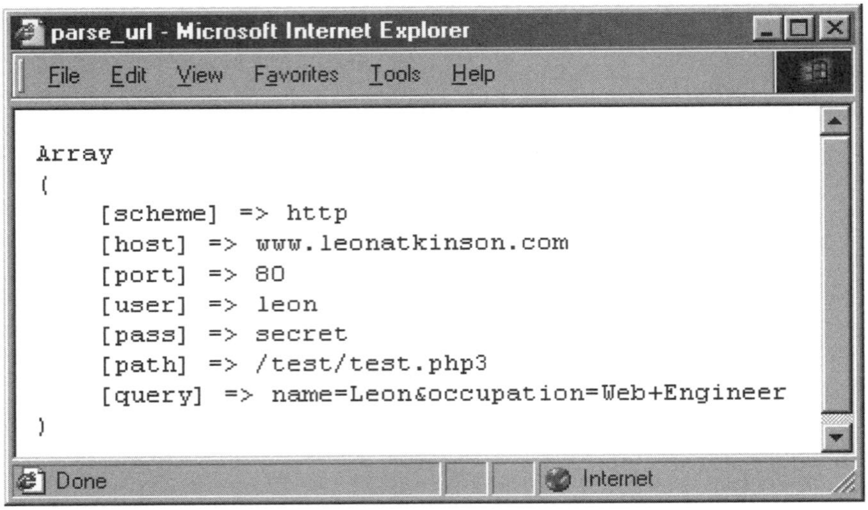

```
parse_url - Microsoft Internet Explorer
File   Edit   View   Favorites   Tools   Help

Array
(
    [scheme] => http
    [host] => www.leonatkinson.com
    [port] => 80
    [user] => leon
    [pass] => secret
    [path] => /test/test.php3
    [query] => name=Leon&occupation=Web+Engineer
)

Done                                    Internet
```

```php
<?
    $query = "http://leon:secret@www.leonatkinson.com:80";
    $query .= "/test/test.php3?";
    $query .= "name=Leon&occupation=Web+Engineer";
    $url = parse_url($query);
    for(reset($url); $index = key($url); next($url))
    {
        print("$index: $url[$index]<BR>\n");
    }
?>
```

Figure 9-9   `parse_url`.

string quoted_printable_decode(string text)

The `quoted_printable_decode` function converts a quoted string into 8-bit binary form. It reverses the action of the `quotemeta` function. That is, it removes backslashes preceding special characters. Table 9.7 lists these special characters.

Table 9.7 Meta Characters	
Character	*Description*
.	Period
\	Backslash
+	Plus
*	Asterisk
?	Question Mark
[	Left Square Bracket
]	Right Square Bracket
^	Caret
(	Left Parenthesis
)	Right Parenthesis
$	Dollar Sign

This function performs the same function as `imap_qprint` but does not require the IMAP extension.

```
<?
    $command = "echo 'hello\?'";
    print(quoted_printable_decode($command));
?>
```

string quotemeta(string command_text)

The `quotemeta` function returns the `command_text` argument with backslashes preceding special characters. These characters are listed in Table 9.7. Compare this function to `addslashes` and `escapeshellcmd`. If your intention is to ensure that user data will cause no harm when placed within a shell command, use `escapeshellcmd`.

The `quotemeta` function may be adequate for assembling PHP code passed to `eval`. Notice in the example below how characters with special meaning inside double quotes are escaped by quote meta, thus defeating an attempt at displaying the `password` variable.

```
<?
    //simulate user input
    $input = '$password';
```

```
//assemble safe PHP command
$cmd = '$text = "' . quotemeta($input) . '";';

//execute command
eval($cmd);

//print new value of $text
print($text);
?>
```

string rawurldecode(string url_text)

The `rawurldecode` function returns the `url_text` string translated from URL format into plain text. It reverses the action of `rawurlencode`. This function is safe for use with binary data. The `urldecode` function is not.

```
<?
    print(rawurldecode("mail%20leon%40clearink.com"));
?>
```

string rawurlencode(string url_text)

The `rawurlencode` function returns the `url_text` string translated into URL format. This format uses percent signs (`%`) to specify characters by their ASCII code, as required by the HTTP specification. This allows you to pass information in an URL that includes characters that have special meaning in URLs, such as the ampersand (`&`). This is discussed in detail in RFC 1738.

This function is safe for use with binary data. Compare this to `urlencode`, which is not.

```
<?
    print(rawurlencode("mail leon@clearink.com"));
?>
```

string serialize(value)

Use `serialize` to transform a value into an ASCII string that may be later turned back into the same value using the `unserialize` function. The serialized value may be stored in a file or a database for retrieval later. In fact, this function offers a great way to store complex data structures in a database without writing any special code.

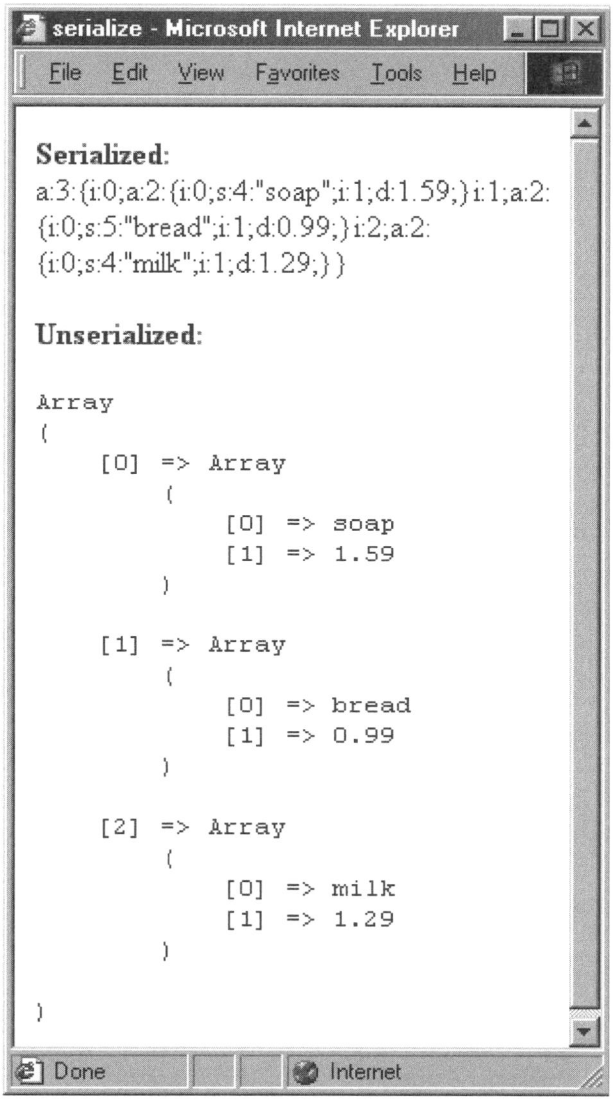

```
serialize - Microsoft Internet Explorer     _ □ ×

  File   Edit   View   Favorites   Tools   Help      

Serialized:
a:3:{i:0;a:2:{i:0;s:4:"soap";i:1;d:1.59;}i:1;a:2:
{i:0;s:5:"bread";i:1;d:0.99;}i:2;a:2:
{i:0;s:4:"milk";i:1;d:1.29;}}

Unserialized:

Array
(
    [0] => Array
        (
            [0] => soap
            [1] => 1.59
        )

    [1] => Array
        (
            [0] => bread
            [1] => 0.99
        )

    [2] => Array
        (
            [0] => milk
            [1] => 1.29
        )

)

 Done                        Internet
```

Figure 9–10 `serialize.`

```
<?
        //simulate a shopping basket as
        //a multi-dimensional array
        $Basket = array(
                array("soap", 1.59),
                array("bread", 0.99),
                array("milk", 1.29)
                );

        //serialize array
        $Data = serialize($Basket);

        //print out the data, just for fun
        print($Data . "<BR>\n");

        //unserialize the data
        $recoveredBasket = unserialize($Data);

        //show the contents
        print("Unserialized:<BR>\n");
        while(list($key, $value) = each($recoveredBasket))
        {
                print("$value[0] $value[1]<BR>\n");
        }
?>
```

Figure 9-10   Continued

string sql_regcase(string regular_expression)

The sql_regcase function translates a case-sensitive regular expression into a case-insensitive regular expression. This is unnecessary for use with PHP's built-in regular expression functions but can be useful when creating regular expressions for external programs such as databases.

```
<?
        //print [Mm][Oo][Zz][Ii][Ll][Ll][Aa]
        print(sql_regcase("Mozilla"));
?>
```

string str_replace(string target, string replacement, string text)

The `str_replace` function attempts to replace all occurrences of `target` in `text` with `replacement`. This function is safe for replacing strings in binary data. It's also a much faster alternative to `ereg_replace`. Note that `str_replace` is case sensitive.

```
<?
     $text = "Search results with keywords highlighted.";
     print(str_replace("keywords", "<B>keywords</B>", $text));
?>
```

string strip_tags(string text, string ignore)

The `strip_tags` function attempts to remove all SGML tags from the `text` argument. This includes HTML and PHP tags. The optional `ignore` argument may contain tags to be left alone. This function uses the same algorithm used by `fgetss`. If you want to preserve tags, you may wish to use `htmlentities`.

```
<?
     //create some test text
     $text = "<P><B>Paragraph One</B><P>Paragraph Two";

     //strip out all tags except paragraph and break
     print(strip_tags($text, "<P><BR>"));
?>
```

string stripcslashes(string text)

The `stripcslashes` function complements `addcslashes`. It removes backslash codes that conform to the C style. See `addcslashes`, above, for more details.

```
<?
     //create some test text
     $text = "Line 1\x0ALine 2\x0A";

     //convert backslashes to actual characters
     print(stripcslashes($text));
?>
```

string stripslashes(string text)

The `stripslashes` function returns the text argument with backslash encoding removed. It complements `addslashes`. By default, PHP is configured to add slashes to user input. Use `stripslashes` to remove slashes before sending submitted form fields to the browser.

```
<?
    $text = "Leon\'s Test String";

    print("Before: $text<BR>\n");
    print("After: " . stripslashes($text) . "<BR>\n");
?>
```

string strrev(string text)

The `strrev` function returns the text argument in reverse order.

```
<?
    print(strrev("abcdefg"));
?>
```

string strtolower(string text)

The `strtolower` function returns the `text` argument with all letters changed to lowercase. Other characters are unaffected. Locale affects which characters are considered letters, and you may find that letters with accents and umlauts are being ignored. You may overcome this by using `setlocale`, discussed in Chapter 11, "Time, Date, and Configuration Functions."

```
<?
    print(strtolower("Hello World"));
?>
```

string strtoupper(string text)

The `strtoupper` function returns the `text` argument with all letters changed to uppercase. Other characters are unaffected. Locale affects which characters are considered letters, and you may find that letters with accents and umlauts are being ignored. You may overcome this by using `setlocale`, discussed in Chapter 11.

```
<?
       print(strtoupper("Hello World"));
?>
```

string strtr(string text, string original, string translated)

When passed three arguments, the `strtr` function returns the `text` argument with characters matching the second argument changed to those in the third argument. If `original` and `translated` aren't the same length, the extra characters are ignored.

At the time of writing a second prototype for `strtr` was being planned that allows you to pass two arguments. The second argument must be an associative array. The indices specify strings to be replaced, and the values specify replacement text. If a substring matches more than one index, the longer substring will be used. The process is not iterative. That is, once substrings are replaced, they are not further matched.

This function is safe to use with binary strings.

```
<?
       $text = "Wow! This is neat.";
       $original = "!.";
       $translated = ".?";

       // turn sincerity into sarcasm
       print(strtr($text, $original, $translated));
?>
```

string substr_replace(string text, string replacement, integer start, integer length)

Use `substr_replace` to replace one substring with another. Unlike `str_replace`, which searches for matches, `substr_replace` simply removes a length of text and inserts the `replacement` argument. The arguments operate similarly to `substr`. The `start` argument is an index into the `text` argument with the first character numbered as zero. If `start` is negative, counting will begin at the last character of the `text` argument instead of the first.

The number of characters replaced is determined by the optional `length` argument or the ends of the string. If `length` is negative, the returned string will end as many characters from the end of the string. In any case, if the combination of `start` and `length` calls for a string of negative length, a single character is removed.

```
<?
    $text = "My dog's name is Angus.";

    //replace Angus with Gus
    print(substr_replace($text, "Gus", 17, 5));
?>
```

string trim(string text)

The `trim` function strips whitespace from both the beginning and end of a string. Compare this function to `ltrim` and `chop`. Whitespace includes spaces, tabs and other nonprintable characters, including nulls (ASCII 0).

```
<?
    $text = "   whitespace   ";
    print("\"" . trim($text) . "\"");
?>
```

string ucfirst(string text)

Use the `ucfirst` function to capitalize the first character of a string. Compare this function to `strtoupper` and `ucwords`. As with these other functions, your locale determines which characters are considered letters.

```
<?
    print(ucfirst("i forgot to capitalize something."));
?>
```

string ucwords(string text)

Use the `ucwords` function to capitalize every word in a string. Compare it to `strtoupper` and `ucfirst`. As with these other functions, your locale determines which characters are considered letters.

```
<?
    print(ucwords("core PHP programming"));
?>
```

array unpack(string format, string data)

The unpack function transforms data created by the pack function into an associative array. The format argument follows the same rules used for pack except that each element is separated by a slash to allow them to be named. These names are used as the keys in the returned associative array. See the pack example.

value unserialize(string data)

Use unserialize to transform serialized data back into a PHP value. The description of serialize has an example of the entire process.

string urldecode(string url_text)

The urldecode function returns the url_text string translated from URL format into plain text. It is not safe for binary data.

```
<?
    print(urldecode("mail%20leon%40clearink.com"));
?>
```

string urlencode(string url_text)

The urlencode function returns the url_text string translated into URL format. This format uses percent signs (%) to specify characters by their ASCII code. This function is not safe for use with binary data.

```
<?
    print(urlencode("mail leon@clearink.com"));
?>
```

Encryption

Encryption is the process of transforming information to and from an unreadable format. Some algorithms simply scramble text; others allow for reversing the process. PHP offers a wrapper to C's crypt function, plus an extension that wraps the mcrypt library.

The mcrypt functions rely on a library of the same name written by Nikos Mavroyanopoulos, which provides an advanced system for encrypting data. The URI for the project is `<ftp://argeas.cs-net.gr/pub/unix/mcrypt/>`. Sascha Schumann added mycrypt functionality to PHP.

Cryptography is a topic beyond the scope of this text. Some concepts discussed in this section require familiarity with advanced cryptographic theories. A great place to start learning about cryptography is the FAQ file for the sci.crypt Usenet newsgroup. The URI is `<http://www.faqs.org/faqs/cryptography-faq/>`. Another resource is a book Prentice Hall publishes called *Cryptography and Network Security: Principles and Practice* by William Stallings. The PHP manual suggests *Applied Cryptography* by Bruce Schneier.

string crypt(string text, string salt)

The `crypt` function encrypts a string using C's `crypt` function, which usually uses standard DES encryption, but depends on your operating system. The `text` argument is returned encrypted. The `salt` argument is optional. PHP will create a random `salt` value if one is not provided. You may wish to read the man page on `crypt` to gain a better understanding.

Note that data encrypted with the `crypt` function cannot be decrypted. The function is usually used to encrypt a password that is saved for when authorization is necessary. At that time, the password is asked for, encrypted, and compared to the previously encrypted password.

Depending on your operating system, alternatives to DES encryption may be available. The `salt` argument is used to determine which algorithm to use. A two-character salt is used for standard DES encryption. A nine-character salt specifies extended DES. A twelve-character salt specifies MD5 encryption. And a sixteen-character salt specifies the blowfish algorithm.

When PHP is compiled, available algorithms are incorporated. The following constants will hold TRUE or FALSE values you can use to determine the availability of the four algorithms: CRYPT_STD_DES, CRYPT_EXT_DES, CRYPT_MD5, CRYPT_BLOWFISH.

```
<?
    $password = "secret";

    if(CRYPT_MD5)
    {
        $salt = "leonatkinson";
        print("Using MD5: ");
```

```
        }
        else
        {
                $salt = "cp";
                print("Using Standard DES: ");
        }

        print(crypt($password, $salt));
?>
```

string mcrypt_create_iv(integer size, integer source)

Use `mcrypt_create_iv` to create an initialization vector. The size should match the encryption algorithm and should be set using `mcrypt_get_block_size`. The source argument can be one of three constants. `MCRYPT_DEV_RANDOM` uses random numbers from `/dev/random`. `MCRYPT_DEV_URANDOM` uses random numbers from `/dev/urandom`. `MCRYPT_RAND` uses random numbers from the `rand` function, which means you ought to seed it first with `srand`.

string mcrypt_cbc(integer algorithm, string key, string data, integer mode, string initialization_vector)

The `mcrypt_cbc` function encrypts a string using cipher block chaining. This method is best suited to encrypting whole files. The algorithm argument is one of the constants listed in Table 9.8. The `mode` argument can be either `MCRYPT_DECRYPT` or `MCRYPT_ENCRYPT`. An initialization vector is optional. Remember that if you encrypt using one, you must use the same one to decrypt.

```
<?
        //set up test data
        $message = "This message is sensitive.";
        $key = "secret";

        //encrypt message
        $code = mcrypt_cbc(MCRYPT_BLOWFISH_128, $key, $message, MCRYPT_ENCRYPT);

        //pring decrypted message
        print(mcrypt_cbc(MCRYPT_BLOWFISH_128, $key, $code, MCRYPT_DECRYPT));
?>
```

mcrypt_cfb(integer algorithm, string key, string data, integer mode, string initialization_vector)

The `mcrypt_cfb` function encrypts a string using cipher feedback. This method is best suited to encrypting streams. However, PHP's mcrypt interface does not support stream ciphers at the time of this writing. The algorithm argument is one of the constants listed in Table 9.8. The `mode` argument can be either `MCRYPT_DECRYPT` or `MCRYPT_ENCRYPT`. An initialization vector is required. You must use the same one to decrypt.

mcrypt_ecb(integer algorithm, string key, string data, integer mode)

The `mcrypt_ecb` function encrypts a string using the electronic codebook method, which is good for encryption of short, irregular data. The algorithm argument is one of the constants listed in Table 9.8. The `mode` argument can be either `MCRYPT_DECRYPT` or `MCRYPT_ENCRYPT`.

```
<?
    //set up test data
    $message = "This message is sensitive.";
    $key = "secret";

    //encrypt message
    $code = mcrypt_ecb(MCRYPT_BLOWFISH_128, $key, $message, MCRYPT_ENCRYPT);

    //pring decrypted message
    print(mcrypt_ecb(MCRYPT_BLOWFISH_128, $key, $code, MCRYPT_DECRYPT));
?>
```

integer mcrypt_get_block_size(integer algorithm)

Use `mcrypt_get_block_size` to find the block size for a given encryption algorithm. Use one of the constants listed in Table 9.8. See `mcrypt_get_cipher_name` for an example of use.

string mcrypt_get_cipher_name(integer algorithm)

Use `mcrypt_get_cipher_name` to get the name of an encryption algorithm. Use one of the constants listed in Table 9.8.

```
<?
     //create array of encryption algorithms
     $algorithm = array(
          3DES, 3WAY, BLOWFISH_128, BLOWFISH_192, BLOWFISH_256,
          BLOWFISH_448, CAST_128, CAST_256, DES, GOST, IDEA, LOKI97,
          RC2_1024, RC2_128, RC2_256, RC4, RC6_128, RC6_192, RC6_256,
          RIJNDAEL_128, RIJNDAEL_192, RIJNDAEL_256, SAFERPLUS,
          SAFER_128, SAFER_64, SERPENT_128, SERPENT_192, SERPENT_256,
          TWOFISH_128, TWOFISH_192, TWOFISH_256, XTEA);

     print("<TABLE BORDER=\"1\">\n");

     print("<TR>\n");
     print("<TH>Name</TH>\n");
     print("<TH>Block Size</TH>\n");
     print("<TH>Key Size</TH>\n");
     print("</TR>\n");


     //loop over each one
     foreach($algorithm as $value)
     {
          print("<TR>\n");
          print("<TD>" . mcrypt_get_cipher_name($value) . "</TD>");
          print("<TD>" . mcrypt_get_block_size($value) . "</TD>");
          print("<TD>" . mcrypt_get_key_size($value) . "</TD>");
          print("</TR>\n");
     }

     print("</TABLE>\n");
?>
```

integer mcrypt_get_key_size(integer algorithm)

Use mcrypt_get_key_size to find the key size for a given encryption algorithm. Use one of the constants listed in Table 9.8. See mcrypt_get_cipher_name for an example of use.

mcrypt_ofb(integer algorithm, string key, string data, integer mode, string initialization_vector)

The mcrypt_ofb function encrypts a string using output feedback. This method is another method suited to stream ciphers. The algorithm argument is one of the constants listed in Table 9.8. The mode argument can be either MCRYPT_DECRYPT or MCRYPT_ENCRYPT. An initialization vector is required. You must use the same one to decrypt.

```
<?
       //set up test data
       $message = "This message is sensitive.";
       $key = "secret";
       $iv = mcrypt_create_iv(
              mcrypt_get_block_size(MCRYPT_BLOWFISH_128),
              MCRYPT_DEV_RANDOM);


       //encrypt message
       $code = mcrypt_ofb(MCRYPT_BLOWFISH_128, $key, $mes-
       sage, MCRYPT_ENCRYPT, $iv);

       //pring decrypted message
       print(mcrypt_ofb(MCRYPT_BLOWFISH_128, $key, $code,
       MCRYPT_
       DECRYPT, $iv));
?>
```

Table 9.8   Encryption Algorithms

MCRYPT_3DES
MCRYPT_3WAY
MCRYPT_BLOWFISH_128
MCRYPT_BLOWFISH_192
MCRYPT_BLOWFISH_256
MCRYPT_BLOWFISH_448
MCRYPT_CAST_128
MCRYPT_CAST_256
MCRYPT_DES
MCRYPT_GOST
MCRYPT_IDEA
MCRYPT_LOKI97
MCRYPT_RC2_1024
MCRYPT_RC2_128
MCRYPT_RC2_256
MCRYPT_RC4
MCRYPT_RC6_128
MCRYPT_RC6_192

(continued)

```
MCRYPT_RC6_256
MCRYPT_RIJNDAEL_128
MCRYPT_RIJNDAEL_192
MCRYPT_RIJNDAEL_256
MCRYPT_SAFERPLUS
MCRYPT_SAFER_128
MCRYPT_SAFER_64
MCRYPT_SERPENT_128
MCRYPT_SERPENT_192
MCRYPT_SERPENT_256
MCRYPT_TWOFISH_128
MCRYPT_TWOFISH_192
MCRYPT_TWOFISH_256
MCRYPT_XTEA
```

Regular Expressions

Regular expressions offer a powerful way to test strings for the presence of patterns. They use a language all their own to describe patterns, a language that consists mostly of symbols. PHP has several functions that use regular expressions. You may wish to turn to Chapter 16, which describes regular expressions in detail.

boolean ereg(string pattern, string text, array matches)

The `ereg` function evaluates the pattern argument as a regular expression and attempts to find matches in the `text` argument. If the optional `matches` argument is supplied, each match will be added to the array. TRUE is returned if at least one match is made, FALSE otherwise.

The first element in the `matches` array, with an index of zero, will contain the match for the entire regular expression. Subsequent elements of `matches` will contain the matches for subexpressions. These are the expressions enclosed in parentheses in the example.

This function is discussed in depth in Chapter 16.

```
<?
        // show User Agent
        print("User Agent: $HTTP_USER_AGENT<BR>\n");

        // try to parse User Agent
        if(ereg("^(.+)/([0-9])\.([0-9]+)",
                $HTTP_USER_AGENT, $matches))
        {
                print("Full match: $matches[0]<BR>\n");
                print("Browser: $matches[1]<BR>\n");
                print("Major Version: $matches[2]<BR>\n");
                print("Minor Version: $matches[3]<BR>\n");
        }
        else
        {
                print("User Agent not recognized");
        }
?>
```

string ereg_replace(string pattern, string replacement, string text)

Use `ereg_replace` to replace substrings within the `text` argument. Each time the pattern matches a substring within the text argument, it is replaced with the replacement argument. The `text` argument is unchanged, but the altered version is returned.

If the pattern contains subexpressions in parentheses, the `replacement` argument may contain a special code for specifying which subexpression to replace. The form is to use two backslashes followed by a single digit, zero through nine. Zero matches the entire expression; one through nine each match the first nine subexpressions, respectively. Subexpressions are numbered left to right, which accounts for nested subexpressions.

Regular expressions are discussed in depth in Chapter 16.

```
<?
        // swap newlines for break tags
        $text = "line1\nline2\nline3\n";
        print(ereg_replace("\n", "<BR>", $text));

        print("<HR>\n");

        //mix up these words
        $text = "one two three four";
        print(ereg_replace("([a-z]+) ([a-z]+) ([a-z]+) ([a-z]+)",
                "\\4 \\2 \\1 \\3", $text));
?>
```

Figure 9–11 `ereg_replace.`

boolean eregi(string pattern, string text, array matches)

The `eregi` function operates identically to `ereg` with the exception that letters are matched with no regard for upper or lower case.

Regular expressions are discussed in depth in Chapter 16.

string eregi_replace(string pattern, string replacement, string text)

The `eregi_replace` function operates identically to `ereg_replace` with the exception that letters are matched with no regard for upper or lower case.

array split(string pattern, string text, integer limit)

The split function returns an array of substrings from the text argument. The pattern argument will be used as a field delimiter. The optional limit argument sets the maximum number of elements to return. There is no case-insensitive version of split.

Compare this function to explode, which uses a simple string to delimit substrings. Regular expression processing is slower than straight string matching, so use explode when you can.

```
<?
       $paragraph = "This is a short paragraph. Each ";
       $paragraph .= "sentence will be extracted by ";
       $paragraph .= "the split function. As a ";
       $paragraph .= "result, you will be amazed!";

       $sentence = split("[\.\!\?]", $paragraph);

       for($index = 0; $index < count($sentence); $index++)
       {
              print("$index. $sentence[$index] <BR>\n");
       }
?>
```

Perl-Compatible Regular Expressions

Andrei Zmievski added support to PHP for Perl-compatible regular expressions. Expressions are surrounded by delimiters, which are usually / or | characters, but can be any printable character other than a number, letter, or backslash. After the second delimiter, you may place one or more modifiers. These are letters that change the way the regular expression is interpreted.

For the most part, the functions in this section comply with the way regular expressions work in Perl 5. There are a few very specific differences. They are narrow enough that you probably won't run into them, and they may not make much sense without explaining regular expressions in detail. If you're curious, read the excellent notes in the PHP manual available online <http://www.php.net/manual/html/ref.pcre.html>.

array preg_grep(string pattern, array data)

The preg_grep function compares the elements of the data argument that match the given pattern.

boolean preg_match(string pattern, string text, array matches)

The preg_match function is the equivalent of ereg. It evaluates the pattern argument as a regular expression and attempts to find matches in the text argument. If the optional matches argument is supplied, each match will be added to the array. TRUE is returned if at least one match is made, FALSE otherwise.

The first element in the matches array, with an index of zero, will contain the match for the entire regular expression. Subsequent elements of matches will contain the matches for subexpressions. These are the expressions enclosed in parentheses in the example.

```
<?
    // show User Agent
    print("User Agent: $HTTP_USER_AGENT<BR>\n");

    // try to parse User Agent
    if(preg_match("/^(.+)/([0-9])\.([0-9]+)/",
        $HTTP_USER_AGENT, $matches))
    {
        print("Full match: $matches[0]<BR>\n");
        print("Browser: $matches[1]<BR>\n");
        print("Major Version: $matches[2]<BR>\n");
        print("Minor Version: $matches[3]<BR>\n");
    }
    else
    {
        print("User Agent not recognized");
    }
?>
```

integer preg_match_all (string pattern, string text, array matches, integer order)

The preg_match_all function operates similarly to preg_match. A pattern is evaluated against the text argument, but instead of stopping when a match is found, subsequent matches are sought. The matches argument is

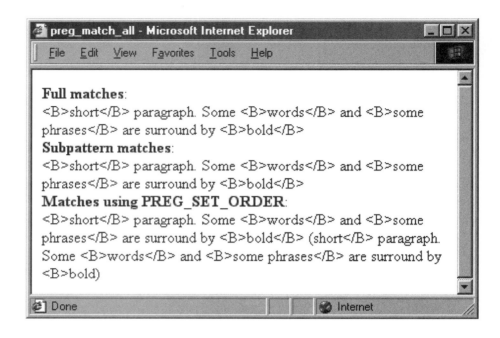

```
<?
     //create test data
     $paragraph = "This is a <B>short</B> paragraph. Some ";
     $paragraph .= "<B>words</B> and <B>some phrases</B> ";
     $paragraph .= "are surround by <B>bold</B> tags. ";

     /*
     ** use PREG_MATCH_ORDER to find bold words
     */
     preg_match_all("|<[^>]+>(.*)</[^>]+>|", $paragraph,
            $match, PREG_MATCH_ORDER);

     //print full matches
     print("<B>Subpattern matches</B>:<BR>\n");
     for($i=0; $i < count($match[0]); $i++)
     {
            print(htmlentities($match[0][$i]) . "<BR>\n");
     }

     print("<B>Subpattern matches</B>:<BR>\n");
     for($i=0; $i < count($match[1]); $i++)
```

Figure 9-12 `preg_match_all.`

```
    {
            print(htmlentities($match[0][$i]) . "<BR>\n");
    }

    /*
    ** use PREG_SET_ORDER to find bold words
    */
    preg_match_all("|<[^>]+>(.*)</[^>]+>|", $paragraph,
            $match, PREG_SET_ORDER);

    foreach($match as $m)
    {
            print(htmlentities($m[0]));

            for($i=1; $i < count($m); $i++)
            {
                    print(" (".htmlentities($m[$i]).")");
            }

            print("<BR>\n");
    }
?>
```

Figure 9–12   Continued

required and will receive a two-dimensional array. The method for filling this array is determined by the order argument. It may be set with two constants, either PREG_PATTERN_ORDER, the default, or PREG_SET_ORDER. The number of matches against the full pattern is returned.

If PREG_PATTERN_ORDER is used, the first element of the matches array will contain an array of all the matches against the full pattern. The other elements of the array will contain arrays of matches against subpatterns.

If PREG_SET_ORDER is used, each element of the matches array contains an array organized like those created by preg_match. The first element is the entire matching string. Each subsequent element contains the match against the subpattern for that match.

string preg_quote(string text)

The preg_quote function returns text with backslashes inserted before character that have special meaning to the functions in this section. The special characters are:

```
    . \\ + * ? [ ^ ] $ ( ) { } = ! < > | :
```

string preg_replace(string pattern, string replacement, string text)

The `preg_replace` function is equivalent to `ereg_replace`. Each time the pattern matches a substring within the text argument, it is replaced with the replacement argument. The `text` argument is unchanged, but the altered version is returned.

If the pattern contains subexpressions in parentheses, the `replacement` argument may contain a special code for specifying which subexpression to replace. The form is to use two backslashes followed by a single digit, zero through nine. Zero matches the entire expression; one through nine each match the first nine subexpressions, respectively. Subexpressions are numbered left to right, which accounts for nested subexpressions.

```
<?
        // swap newlines for break tags
        $text = "line1\nline2\nline3\n";
        print(preg_replace("|\n|", "<BR>", $text));

        print("<HR>\n");

        //mix up these words
        $text = "one two three four";
        print(preg_replace("|([a-z]+) ([a-z]+) ([a-z]+) ([a-z]+)|",
                "\\4 \\2 \\1 \\3", $text));
?>
```

array preg_split(string pattern, string text, integer limit)

The `preg_split` function returns an array of substrings from the text argument. The `pattern` argument will be used as a field delimiter. The optional `limit` argument sets the maximum number of elements to return. This function is equivalent to `split`.

```
<?
        $paragraph = "This is a short paragraph. Each ";
        $paragraph .= "sentence will be extracted by ";
        $paragraph .= "the preg_split function. As a ";
        $paragraph .= "result, you will be amazed!";
```

```
$sentence = preg_split("/[\.\!\?]/", $paragraph);

for($index = 0; $index < count($sentence); $index++)
{
        print("$index. $sentence[$index] <BR>\n");
}
?>
```

MATHEMATICAL FUNCTIONS

Topics in This Chapter

- Common Math
- Random Numbers
- Arbitrary-Precision Numbers

Chapter 10

The math functions fall into three categories: common mathematical operations, random numbers, and special functions for handling numbers of arbitrary precision.

Common Math

The functions in this section offer most of the common mathematical operations that are part of arithmetic, geometry, and trigonometry. Most of these functions work on either doubles or integers. The return type will be the same as the argument. Unless a specific type is called for, I've written "number" to indicate that either an integer or a double is expected.

number abs(number value)

The `abs` function returns the absolute value of a number. This is the number itself if it's positive, or the number multiplied by negative one (–1) if negative.

```
<?
     //prints 13
     print(abs(-13));
?>
```

double acos(double value)

The acos function returns the arc cosine of the value argument. Trying to find the arc cosine of a value greater than one or less than negative one is undefined.

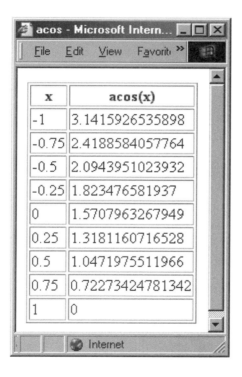

```
<?
     // print acos values from -1 to 1
     print("<TABLE BORDER=\"1\">\n");
     print("<TR><TH>x</TH><TH>acos(x)</TH></TR>\n");

     for($index = -1; $index <= 1; $index += 0.25)
     {
```

Figure 10-1   acos.

```
      print("<TR>\n");
      print("<TD>$index</TD>\n");
      print("<TD>" . acos($index) . "</TD>\n");
      print("</TR>\n");
   }

   print("</TABLE>\n");
?>
```

Figure 10–1   Continued

double asin(double value)

The asin function returns the arc sine of the value argument. Trying to find the arc sine of a value greater than one or less than negative one is undefined.

```
<?
   // print asin values from -1 to 1
   print("<TABLE BORDER=\"1\">\n");
   print("<TR><TH>x</TH><TH>asin(x)</TH></TR>\n");

   for($index = -1; $index <= 1; $index += 0.25)
   {
      print("<TR>\n");
      print("<TD>$index</TD>\n");
      print("<TD>" . asin($index) . "</TD>\n");
      print("</TR>\n");
   }

   print("</TABLE>\n");
?>
```

double atan(double value)

The atan function returns the arc tangent of the value argument.

```
<?
   // print atan values from -1 to 1
   print("<TABLE BORDER=\"1\">\n");
   print("<TR><TH>x</TH><TH>atan(x)</TH></TR>\n");

   for($index = -1; $index <= 1; $index += 0.25)
```

```
     {
       print("<TR>\n");
       print("<TD>$index</TD>\n");
       print("<TD>" . atan($index) . "</TD>\n");
       print("</TR>\n");
     }

     print("</TABLE>\n");
?>
```

double atan2(double x, double y)

The atan2 function returns the angle portion in radians of the polar coordinate specified by the Cartesian coordinates.

```
<?
     //print 0.40489178628508
     print(atan2(3, 7));
?>
```

string base_convert(string value, int base, int new_base)

The base_convert function converts a number from one base to another. Some common bases have their own functions.

```
<?
     //convert hex CC to decimal
     print(base_convert("CC", 16, 10));
?>
```

integer bindec(string binary_number)

The bindec function returns the integer value of a binary number written as a string. PHP uses 32-bit signed integers. The binary numbers are little-endian, which means the least significant bit is to the right. The first bit is the sign bit.

```
<?
        // print largest integer
        print("Largest Integer: ");
        print(bindec("1111111111111111111111111111111"));

        print("<BR>\n");

        // print smallest integer
        print("Smallest Integer: ");
        print(bindec("10000000000000000000000000000000"));
        print("<BR>\n");
?>
```

Figure 10–2 `bindec`.

integer ceil(double value)

The `ceil` function returns the ceiling of the argument, which is the smallest integer greater than the argument.

```
<?
        //print 14
        print(ceil(13.2));
?>
```

double cos(double angle)

The `cos` function returns the cosine of an angle expressed in radians.

```
<?
        //prints 1
        print(cos(2 * pi()));
?>
```

string decbin(integer value)

The decbin function returns a binary representation of an integer as a string.

```
<?
    //prints 11111111
    print(decbin(255));
?>
```

string dechex(integer value)

The dechex function returns the hexadecimal representation of the value argument as a string.

```
<?
    //prints ff
    print(dechex(255));
?>
```

string decoct(integer value)

The decoct function returns the octal representation of the value argument as a string.

```
<?
    //prints 377
    print(decoct(255));
?>
```

double deg2rad(double angle)

The deg2rad function returns the radians that correspond to angle argument, specified in degrees.

```
<?
    //prints 1.5707963267949
    print(deg2rad(90));
?>
```

double exp(double power)

The exp function returns the natural logarithm raised to the power of the argument.

```
<?
        //prints 20.085536923188
        print(exp(3));
?>
```

integer floor(double value)

The `floor` function returns the floor of the argument, which is the integer part of the argument.

```
<?
        //prints 13
        print(floor(13.2));
?>
```

integer hexdec(string hexadecimal_number)

The `hexdec` function converts a string that represents a hexadecimal number into an integer. Preceding the number with "0x" is optional.

```
<?
        print(hexdec("FF"));
        print("<BR>\n");
        print(hexdec("0x7FAD"));
        print("<BR>\n");
?>
```

double log(double value)

The `log` function returns the natural logarithm of the `value` argument.

```
<?
        //prints 3.0022112396517
        print(log(20.13));
?>
```

double log10(double value)

The `log10` function returns the decimal logarithm of its argument.

```
<?
        //prints 3.2494429614426
        print(log10(1776));
?>
```

integer octdec(string octal_number)

The `octdec` function returns the integer value of a string representing an octal number.

```
<?
     //prints 497
     print(octdec("761"));
?>
```

double pi()

The `pi` function returns the approximate value of pi. Alternatively, you may use the `M_PI` constant.

```
<?
     //prints 3.1415926535898
     print(pi() . "<BR>\n");

     //prints 3.1415926535898
     print(M_PI . "<BR>\n");
?>
```

double pow(double base, double power)

Use the `pow` function to raise the `base` argument to the power indicated by the second argument.

```
<?
     //print 32
     print(pow(2, 5));
?>
```

double rad2deg(double angle)

The `deg2rad` function returns the degrees that correspond to given radians specified in the `angle` argument.

```
<?
     //print 90.00021045915
     print(rad2deg(1.5708));
?>
```

double round(double value)

The round function returns the argument rounded to the nearest integer.

```
<?
        //prints 1
        print(round(1.4)  .  "<BR>\n");

        //prints 1
        print(round(1.5)  .  "<BR>\n");

        //prints 2
        print(round(1.6)  .  "<BR>\n");
?>
```

double sin(double angle)

The sin function returns the sine of the angle. The angle is assumed to be in radians.

```
<?
        //prints 1
        print(sin(0.5 * M_PI));
?>
```

double sqrt(double value)

Use sqrt to find the square root of a number.

```
<?
        //prints 9
        print(sqrt(81.0));
?>
```

double tan(double angle)

The tan function returns the tangent of an angle. The angle is expected to be expressed in radians.

```
<?
        //prints 1.5574077246549
        print(tan(1));
?>
```

Random Numbers

The following functions help you generate pseudorandom numbers. There are wrappers for the randomizing functions offered by your operating system, and there are functions based on the Mersenne Twister algorithm. The Mersenne Twister functions are faster and return numbers with a much better distribution suitable for cryptographic applications. The algorithm was developed by Makoto Matsumoto and Takuji Nishimura. You can read more about it on their Web page <http://www.math.keio.ac.jp/~matumoto/emt.html>. Pedro Melo refactored an implementation by Shawn Cokus in order to add support to PHP.

integer getrandmax()

The `getrandmax` function returns the maximum random number that may be returned by the `rand` function.

```
<?
  print(getrandmax());
?>
```

integer mt_getrandmax()

The `mt_getrandmax` function returns the maximum random number that may be returned by the `mt_rand` function.

```
<?
  print(mt_getrandmax());
?>
```

double lcg_value()

The `lcg_value` function returns a number between 0 and 1 using an algorithm called a linear congruential generator, or LCG. This is a common method for generating pseudorandom numbers. The generator is seeded with the process identifier.

integer mt_rand(integer min, integer max)

The `mt_rand` function uses the Mersenne Twister algorithm to return a number between the two optional arguments, inclusive. If left out, zero and the integer returned by the `mt_getrandmax` function will be used. Use `mt_srand` to seed the Mersenne Twister random number generator.

```
<?
    //seed the generator
    mt_srand(time());

    //get ten random numbers from 1 to 100
    for($index = 0; $index < 10; $index++)
    {
      print(mt_rand(1, 100) . "<BR>\n");
    }
?>
```

mt_srand()

The `mt_srand` function seeds the Mersenne Twister random number generator. It is best to call this function once before using the `mt_rand` function.

integer rand(integer lowest, integer highest)

The `rand` function returns a number between the two optional arguments, inclusive. If left out, zero and the integer returned by the `getrandmax` function will be used. Use the `srand` function to seed the random number generator.

```
<?
    srand(time());

    //get ten random numbers from -100 to 100
    for($index = 0; $index < 10; $index++)
    {
      print(rand(-100, 100) . "<BR>\n");
    }
?>
```

srand(integer seed)

The `srand` function seeds the random number generator. It is best to call this function once before using the `rand` function.

string tempnam(string directory, string prefix)

The `tempnam` function returns the complete path to a unique temporary filename. This guarantees you will not overwrite an existing file. You must take the responsibility to create and then destroy the file.

The `directory` argument specifies a directory to put the file in, but it will be discarded if a default temporary directory is defined in an environment variable. Under UNIX this variable is called TMPDIR. Under Windows it is called TMP.

You must also specify a prefix for the file, but you may pass an empty string. It's a good idea to pass a meaningful prefix, which will allow you to distinguish between temporary files created by different processes. Note that no suffix is added to the file. Under Windows you may want to add `.tmp` or some other file extension.

An empty string is returned on failure. This function is similar to `uniqid`.

```
<?
    $myFile = tempnam("C:\temp", "data");
    if(strlen($myFile) > 0)
    {
      print($myFile);
    }
    else
    {
      print("Couldn't make temporary name");
    }
?>
```

string uniqid(string prefix, boolean use_lcg)

The `uniqid` function joins the prefix argument to a random series of numbers and letters, which are generated based on the system clock. The prefix may be up to 114 characters long and the unique string is always 13 characters long.

If the optional `use_lcg` argument is TRUE, nine additional characters will be added to the end of the return string These characters are generated by the same algorithm used by the `lcg_value` function, so they will be a period followed by eight digits. Because the `lcg_value` function seeds itself with the process ID, turning on this flag may not actually add much randomness.

Compare this function to `tempnam`.

```
<?
  print(uniqid("data"));
?>
```

Arbitrary-Precision Numbers

Doubles are usually sufficiently precise for any numerical analysis you may wish to perform. However, PHP offers a way to work with numbers of much higher precision. The functions in this section use strings to store very long floating-point numbers. They each use a scale value that is the number of digits to the right of the decimal point. The `scale` argument that appears in all of the functions is optional and will override the default scale. The `bcscale` function, described in Chapter 11, "Date, Time, and Configuration Functions," sets the default scale.

These functions are activated when PHP is compiled. They are part of the binary distribution for windows, but they are not activated by default for other operating systems. If PHP reports these functions as being unrecognized, you may need to recompile PHP using the –enable-bcmath option.

string bcadd(string left, string right, integer scale)

The `bcadd` function adds `left` to `right`.

```
<?
    print(bcadd("1.234567890", "9.87654321", 10));
?>
```

integer bccomp(string left, string right, integer scale)

The `bccomp` function compares left to right. If they are equal, zero is returned. If left is less than right, –1 is returned. If `left` is greater than `right`, 1 is returned.

```
<?
       print(bccomp("12345","1.111111111111", 10));
?>
```

string bcdiv(string left, string right, integer scale)

Use bcdiv to divide left by right.

```
<?
       print(bcdiv("12345", "98754", 10));
?>
```

string bcmod(string left, string right)

The bcmod function finds the modulus of the division of left by right.

```
<?
       print(bcmod("66394593", "133347"));
?>
```

string bcmul(string left, string right, integer scale)

Use bcmul to multiply the left argument and the right argument.

```
<?
       print(bcmul("66394593", "133347", 10));
?>
```

string bcpow(string value, string exponent, integer scale)

The bcpow function raises the value argument to the power of the exponent argument. If the exponent is not an integer, the fractional part will be chopped off.

```
<?
       print(bcpow("66394593", "3", 10));
?>
```

string bcsqrt(string value, integer scale)

The bcsqrt function returns the square root of the value argument.

```
<?
    print(bcsqrt("1234.567", 10));
?>
```

string bcsub(string left, string right, integer scale)

Use the bcsub function to subtract the right argument from the left argument.

```
<?
    print(bcsub("1234.4842", "88.6674"));
?>
```

TIME, DATE, AND CONFIGURATION FUNCTIONS

Topics in This Chapter

- Time and Date
- Alternative Calendars
- Configuration

Chapter 11

The functions in this section fall into three categories: time and date, alternative calendars, and configuration. The time and date functions are standard for any programming language. They allow you to get the current date in several formats. The calendar functions manipulate dates in various calendars, including ancient and obscure calendars. The configuration functions offer a way to change the configuration of PHP on a per-script basis.

Time and Date

All the time functions work off the UNIX epoch, which is January 1, 1970. Dates are expressed as seconds since the epoch. This makes it easy to refer to dates with integers. When a function calls for seconds since the epoch, I've referred to it as a timestamp.

boolean checkdate(integer month, integer day, integer year)

The checkdate function returns TRUE if a date is valid, FALSE otherwise. A day is considered valid if the year is between 0 and 32,767, the month is between 1 and 12, and lastly, if the day is within the allowable days for that month.

```
<?
     if(checkdate(2,18,1970))
     {
            print("It is a good day");
     }
?>
```

string date(string format, integer timestamp)

The date function returns a string describing the date of the timestamp according to the format argument. Letters in the format argument are replaced with parts of the date or time. Any characters not understood as codes are passed along in place. Format codes are listed in Table 11.1.

The timestamp argument is optional. If left out, the current time will be used. The timestamp is interpreted as being in local time.

```
<?
     //prints something like
     //03:59 PM Monday January 1st, 2001
     print(date("h:i A l F dS, Y"));
?>
```

array getdate(integer timestamp)

The getdate function returns an associative array with information about the given date. This array is described in Table 11.2. The timestamp argument is the number of seconds since January 1, 1970. If left out, the current time is used.

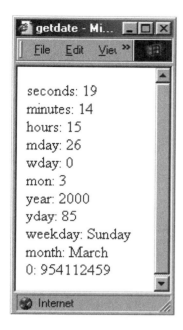

```
<?
        //get current date
        $dateInfo = getdate();

        //show all element of return array
        foreach($dateInfo as $key=>$value)
        {
                print("$key: $value<BR>\n");
        }
?>
```

Figure 11-1   `getdate.`

array gettimeofday()

The `gettimeofday` function returns an associative array containing information about the current time. This is a direct interface to the C function of the same name. The element of the returned array are listed in Table 11.3.

```
<?
        $timeOfDay = gettimeofday();

        foreach($timeOfDay as $key=>$value)
        {
                print("$key = $value<BR>\n");
        }
?>
```

Figure 11–2   `gettimeofday`.

Table 11.1	`date` Format Codes

Code	Description
a	am or pm
A	AM or PM
B	Swatch Beat time
d	Day of the month with leading zeroes
D	Day of the week as a three-letter abbreviation
F	Name of the month
h	Hour from 01 to 12
H	Hour from 00 to 23
g	Hour from 1 to 12 (no leading zeroes)
G	Hour from 0 to 23 (no leading zeroes)
i	Minutes
j	Day of the month with no leading zeroes

(continued)

Table 11.1   Continued

Code	Description
l	Day of the week
L	1 if leap year, 0 otherwise
m	Month number from 01 to 12
M	Abbreviated month name (Jan, Feb, . . .)
n	Month number from 1 to 12 (no leading zeroes)
s	Seconds 00 to 59
S	Ordinal suffix for day of the month (1st, 2nd, 3rd)
t	Number of days in the month
U	Seconds since the epoch
y	Year as two digits
Y	Year as four digits
z	Day of the year from 0 to 365
Z	Timezone offset in seconds (-43,200 to 43,200)

Table 11.2   Elements in `getdate` Array

Element	Description
hours	Hour in 24-hour format
mday	Day of the month
minutes	Minutes for the hour
mon	Month as a number
month	Full name of the month
seconds	Seconds for the minute
wday	Day of the week as a number from 0 to 6
weekday	Name of the day of the week
yday	Day of the year as a number
year	Year
0	Timestamp

Table 11.3	Elements of the Array Returned by `gettimeofday`	
Element	*Meaning*	
sec	Seconds	
usec	Microseconds	
minuteswest	Minutes West of Greenwich	
dsttime	Type of DST correction	

string gmdate(string format, integer timestamp)

The `gmdate` function operates identically to the `date` function except that, rather than return the time for the local time zone, Greenwich Mean Time is returned.

```
<?
    print("Local: ");
    print(date("h:i A l "));
    print(date("F dS, Y"));
    print("<BR>\n");

    print("GMT: ");
    print(gmdate("h:i A l "));
    print(gmdate("F dS, Y"));
    print("<BR>\n");
?>
```

string gmstrftime(string format, integer timestamp)

The `gmstrftime` function operates identically to `strftime` except that the timestamp is translated into Greenwich Mean Time. The same format codes defined in Table 11.4 are used in the `format` argument.

```
<?
    print(gmstrftime("%A, %c", mktime(0, 0, 0, 1, 1,
    1970)));
?>
```

Table 11.4	Codes Used by `strftime`

Code	*Description*
%a	Abbreviated weekday name
%A	Full weekday name
%b	Abbreviated month name
%B	Full month name
%c	Preferred date and time representation
%d	Two-digit day of the month with zero-fill
%H	Hour on the 24-hour clock with zero-fill
%I	Hour on the 12-hour clock
%j	Three-digit day of the year with zero-fill
%m	Month number from 1 to 12
%M	Minutes
%p	Equivalent representation of *am* or *pm*
%S	Seconds
%U	Week number with week one starting with the first Sunday of the year
%W	Week number with week one starting with the first Monday of the year
%w	Day of the week as a number with Sunday being zero
%x	Preferred date representation
%X	Preferred time representation
%y	Two-digit year with zero-fill
%Y	Four-digit year
%Z	Time zone
%%	A literal % character

string microtime()

The `microtime` function returns a string with two numbers separated by a space. The first number is microseconds on the system clock. The second is the number of seconds since January 1, 1970.

```
<?
    //print microtime
    print("Start: ". microtime() . "<BR>\n");

    //sleep for a random time
    usleep(rand(100,5000));

    //print microtime
    print("Stop: " . microtime() . "<BR>\n");
?>
```

integer mktime(integer hour, integer minute, integer second, integer month, integer day, integer year)

The `mktime` function returns a timestamp for a given date, the number of seconds since January 1, 1970. All the arguments are optional and, if left out, the appropriate value for the current time will be used. If an argument is out of range, `mktime` will account for the surplus or deficit by modifying the other time units. For example, using 13 for the `month` argument is equivalent to January of the following year. This makes `mktime` an effective tool for adding arbitrary time to a date.

```
<?
    print("Fifty Hours from Now: ");
    print(date("h:i A l F dS, Y", mktime(date("h")+50)));
    print("<BR>\n");
?>
```

string strftime(string format, integer timestamp)

The strftime function returns a date in a particular format. If the optional timestamp argument is left out, the current time will be used. Language-dependent strings will be set according to the current locale, which may be changed with the setlocale function. The format string may contain codes that have special meaning and begin with a percentage sign. Other characters are passed through unchanged. See Table 11.4 for a list of format codes.

```
<?
        //prints something like
        //Monday, 01/01/01 16:04:12
        print(strftime("%A, %c"));
?>
```

integer strtotime(string date, integer now)

The strtotime function attempts to parse a string containing date and time, returning the timestamp for it. If partial information is provided in the date argument, the missing information will be drawn from the now argument. You may leave out the now argument to use the current time.

```
<?
        //create a reason description
        //of a date
        $time = "Feb 18, 1970 3AM";

        //get its timestamp
        $ts = strtotime($time);

        //print it to verify that it worked
        print(date("h:i A l F dS, Y", $ts));
?>
```

integer time()

Use time to get the current timestamp.

```
<?
        print(time());
?>
```

Alternative Calendars

PHP offers a powerful way to convert dates from one calendar system to another. In order to do this, you must first convert a date into a Julian Day Count. You then convert that integer back into a date according to another calendar.

These functions require the calendar extension. You may load it dynamically, or compile it into PHP.

integer easter_date(integer year)

Use `easter_date` to get the timestamp for midnight on Easter for a given year.

```
<?
    print(easter_date(2000));
?>
```

integer easter_days(integer year)

The `easter_days` function returns the number of days after March 21 on which Easter falls for the given year.

```
<?
    print(easter_days(2000));
?>
```

integer frenchtojd(integer month, integer day, integer year)

The `frenchtojd` function returns the Julian Day Count for the given French Republican calendar date.

```
<?
    $jdc = frenchtojd(1,1,1);
    print(jdtogregorian($jdc));
?>
```

integer gregoriantojd(integer month, integer day, integer year)

The `gregoriantojd` function returns the Julian Day Count for the given Gregorian date.

```
<?
    $jdc = gregoriantojd(1,1,1);
    print(jdtogregorian($jdc));
?>
```

value jddayofweek(integer julian_day, integer mode)

The `jddayofweek` function returns either an integer or a string, depending on the mode. Modes are listed in Table 11.5.

```
<?
    $jdc = gregoriantojd(1,1,1);
    print(jddayofweek($jdc, 1));
?>
```

Table 11.5   Calendar Day Modes

Mode	*Description*
0	Return the day of the week as a number from zero to 6, zero being Sunday.
1	Return the day of the week as a name using the English name from the Gregorian calendar.
2	Returns the abbreviated name of the day of the week using the English name from the Gregorian calendar.

string jdmonthname(integer julian_day, integer mode)

The jdmonthname function returns the name of the month for a particular day. The mode argument specifies which calendar to draw month names from. Modes are listed in Table 11.6.

```
<?
        $jdc = gregoriantojd(1,1,1800);
        print(jdmonthname($jdc, 0) . "<BR>\n");
        print(jdmonthname($jdc, 1) . "<BR>\n");
        print(jdmonthname($jdc, 2) . "<BR>\n");
        print(jdmonthname($jdc, 3) . "<BR>\n");
        print(jdmonthname($jdc, 4) . "<BR>\n");
        print(jdmonthname($jdc, 5) . "<BR>\n");
?>
```

string jdtofrench(integer julian_day)

The jdtofrench function returns the date on the French Republican calendar for a Julian Day Count.

```
<?
        $jdc = gregoriantojd(1,1,1800);
        print(jdtofrench($jdc));
?>
```

Table 11.6	Month-Name Modes
Mode	Calendar
0	Gregorian, abbreviated
1	Gregorian, full
2	Julian, abbreviated
3	Julian, full
4	Jewish
5	French Republican

string jdtogregorian(integer julian_day)

Use the `jdtogregorian` function to convert a Julian Day Count to a Gregorian date.

```
<?
      $jdc = jewishtojd(1,1,1);
      print(jdtogregorian($jdc));
?>
```

string jdtojewish(integer julian_day)

The `jdtojewish` function returns the Jewish calendar date for the given Julian Day Count.

```
<?
      $jdc = gregoriantojd(1,1,1);
      print(jdtojewish($jdc));
?>
```

string jdtojulian(integer julian_day)

Use the `jdtojulian` function to get the Julian date for a Julian Day Count.

```
<?
      $jdc = gregoriantojd(1,1,1);
      print(jdtojulian($jdc));
?>
```

integer jewishtojd(integer month, integer day, integer year)

The `jewishtojd` function returns a Julian Day Count for the given Jewish calendar date.

```
<?
      $jdc = jewishtojd(1,1,1);
      print(jdtogregorian($jdc));
?>
```

integer juliantojd(integer month, integer day, integer year)

Use the `juliantojd` function to get the Julian Day Count for a Julian calendar date.

```
<?
    $jdc = juliantojd(1,1,1);
    print(jdtogregorian($jdc));
?>
```

Configuration

The following functions affect the operation of PHP. Some of them alter configuration variables. Others cause a script to stop executing for a period of time.

boolean bcscale(integer scale)

The `bcscale` function sets the default scale for the functions that perform math on arbitrary-precision numbers. The scale is the number of digits after the decimal point. See the section on arbitrary-precision numbers in Chapter 10, "Mathematical Functions."

```
<?
    //use ten digits
    bcscale(10);
?>
```

clearstatcache()

Calling C's `stat` function may take a considerable amount of time. To increase performance, PHP caches the results of each call. When you use a function that relies on `stat`, the information from the cache is returned. If information about a file changes often, you may need to clear the stat cache.

The functions that use the stat cache are: stat, file_exists, fileatime, filectime, fileinode, filegroup, fileowner, fileperms, filesize, filetype.

```
<?
        //make sure info isn't cached
        clearstatcache();

        //get size of this file
        print(filesize(__FILE__));
?>
```

define_syslog_variables()

The `define_syslog_variables` function emulates the configuration directive of the same name. It causes the constants for use with the system log to be created as variables. The functions that interact with the system log are `closelog`, `openlog`, and `syslog`.

```
<?
define_syslog_variables();
?>
```

boolean dl(string extension)

Use the `dl` function to load a dynamic extension module. The function returns `FALSE` if the module could not be loaded. The path to these modules is set in `php.ini`, so you need type only the name of the module file.

```
<?
        //load windows mysql module
        dl("php_mysql.dll");

        //show diagnostics
        phpinfo();
?>
```

integer error_reporting(integer level)

The `error_reporting` function sets the level of error reporting and returns the previous value. The `level` argument is a bitfield, so use the bitwise OR operator (|) to put together the type of error reporting you would like. By default PHP uses a level of seven, which is Errors, Warnings, and Parser Errors. Refer to Table 11.7, which lists error levels.

Table 11.7	Error Levels	
Value	*Name*	*Description*
1	Errors	Unrecoverable errors that cause execution of the script to halt.
2	Warnings	Recoverable errors where incorrect values are passed to functions, but script execution continues.
4	Parser Errors	Errors generated by the parser, halting execution.
8	Notice	A warning about a condition that may or may not be an error, such as getting the value of a variable before setting it.
16	Core Error	Error conditions reported by the operating system
32	Core Warning	Warnings reported by the operating system.

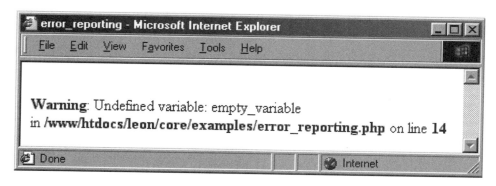

```
<?
        //empty variable, but no notice
        print($empty_variable);
        //turn on notices
        error_reporting(error_reporting(0) | 8);
        //empty variable, notice message
        print($empty_variable);
?>
```

Figure 11–3   error_reporting.

boolean ignore_user_abort(boolean ignore)

Calling ignore_user_abort with a TRUE value for the ignore argument will cause PHP to continue executing even when the remote client abruptly closes the connection. The previous setting is returned. You may call ignore_user_abort with no argument, in which case no change is made.

```
<?
    function fakeProcess($name)
    {
        print("Start of fake process.<BR>\n");
        flush();
        sleep(10);
        print("End of fake process.<BR>\n");

        //write message to log
        $statusMessage = date("Y-m-d H:i:s") . " Fake
        process $name completed\n";
        error_log($statusMessage, 3, "status.log");
    }

    //finish script even if user
    //aborts execution
    ignore_user_abort(TRUE);

    fakeProcess("one");

    //allow aborts again
    ignore_user_abort(FALSE);

    fakeProcess("two");
?>
```

string ini_alter(string directive, string value)

Use ini_alter to override the value of one of the directives in the php.ini file. The setting is for your script only. The file itself is not changed.

string ini_get(string directive)

The ini_get function returns the value of one of the directives in the php.ini file.

```
<?
        //see what SMTP is now
        print(ini_get("SMTP") . "<BR>\n");

        //change to bogus value
        ini_alter("SMTP", "mail.corephp.com");
        print(ini_get("SMTP") . "<BR>\n");

        //return to original
        ini_restore("SMTP");
        print(ini_get("SMTP") . "<BR>\n");
?>
```

ini_restore(string directive)

The ini_restore function returns the named directive to the value in the php.ini file. See ini_get for an example of use.

magic_quotes_runtime

You may use magic_quotes_runtime as an alias to set_magic_quotes_runtime.

register_shutdown_function(string function)

Use register_shutdown_function to cause PHP to execute a function after it has parsed the entire script, including anything outside PHP tags. The shutdown function will also be executed in the event of an error, time-out, or user abort.

Keep in mind that the shutdown function may be called after the connection to the browser has been shut down, in which case using print makes little sense. In other words, this isn't a good way to debug.

You may register more than one shutdown function. Each will be executed in the order they were registered.

```
<?
        function shutdown()
        {
                print("<!- Script Terminated ->\n");
```

```
        }

        register_shutdown_function("shutdown");
?>
```

integer set_magic_quotes_runtime(boolean setting)

Use `set_magic_quotes_runtime` to change whether quotes are escaped in data pulled from a database. The original value is returned.

```
<?
        //turn off magic_quotes_runtime
        set_magic_quotes_runtime(0);
?>
```

string setlocale(string category, string locale)

The `setlocale` function modifies the locale information for PHP and returns the new locale specification. FALSE is returned if an error occurs. The locale determines things such as whether to use a comma or a period in floating-point numbers. Locale does not affect how you write PHP scripts, only the output of some functions.

If the `category` argument is an empty string, the values for the categories will be set from environment variables. If the category argument is zero, the current setting will be returned. Otherwise, a category from Table 11.8 should be chosen.

This function wraps the C function of the same name, so it's a good idea to check out the man page. PHP accepts some categories that have no effect on PHP itself. Also, PHP does not necessarily accept all the valid categories your operating system offers.

Location codes differ with operation systems. In general they take the form of `language_country`—that is, a language code followed by an optional underscore and a country code. If you are using Windows, Visual C's help file lists all the languages and countries.

```
<?
        // change locale in Windows NT
        print("Changing to Russian: ");
        print(setlocale(LC_ALL, "russian"));
        print("<BR>\n");
        print("Dos vedanya!");
?>
```

Table 11.8 Categories for `setlocale`	
Category	*Description*
LC_ALL	All aspects of locale
LC_COLLATE	Comparison of strings (not used by PHP)
LC_CTYPE	Conversion and classification of characters
LC_MONETARY	Monetary formatting (not used by PHP)
LC_NUMERIC	Number separation
LC_TIME	Time formatting

set_time_limit(integer seconds)

Use `set_time_limit` to override the default time a script is allowed to run, which is usually set to 30 seconds inside `php.ini`. If this limit is reached, an error occurs and the script stops executing. Setting the seconds argument to zero causes the time limit to be disabled.

Each time the `set_time_limit` function is called, the counter is reset to zero. This means that calling `set_time_limit(30)` gives you a fresh 30 seconds of execution time.

The time-limit functionality does not operate in Windows. Scripts will execute until finished.

```
<?
  // allow this script to run forever
  set_time_limit(0);
?>
```

sleep(integer seconds)

The `sleep` function causes execution to pause for the given number of seconds.

```
<?
    print(microtime());
    sleep(3);
    print("<BR>\n");
    print(microtime());
?>
```

usleep(integer microseconds)

The `usleep` function causes execution to pause for the given number of microseconds. There are a million microseconds in a second.

```
<?
    print(microtime());
    usleep(30);
    print("<BR>\n");
    print(microtime());
?>
```

IMAGE FUNCTIONS

Topics in This Chapter

- Analyzing Images
- Creating JPEG, PNG, and WBMP Images

Chapter 12

The majority of the image functions draw their functionality from the GD library, free software for manipulating images. These require the GD extension to be loaded, via `php3.ini` or the `dl` function. The four functions in the first section of this chapter are not part of the GD extension and should always be available to you.

The GD library was created at Boutell.com, a company that has contributed several Open Source tools to the Web community. The library historically supported GIF image creation, but in 1999 this functionality was pulled in favor of PNG format files. The compression algorithm used in GIF creation is patented, which means permission must be granted to software authors who use it. PNG, on the other hand, is an open specification. It also happens to be technically superior to GIF. Support for PNG was added to the fourth generations of the two most popular browsers, Netscape Navigator and Microsoft Internet Explorer, so using PNG is feasible. In early 2000, support for JPEG and WBMP images was added to GD.

The GD library's home on the Web is <http://www.boutell.com/gd/>. The URL for PNG's home page is <http://www.cdrom.com/pub/png/>.

Two of the functions in this section require a special library to deal with TrueType fonts: `imagettfbbox` and `imagettftext`. Likewise, the functions that work with PostScript fonts require their own library. Consequently, these functions may not be available to you, depending on how PHP was compiled.

Chapter 19, "Generating Graphics," makes use of the functions in this chapter to explore some practical uses.

Analyzing Images

These functions are part of PHP's core and do not require loading an extension.

string gamma_correct_tag(string color, double original, double new)

The gamma_correct_tag function adjusts an HTML color from one gamma to another. Video display hardware is given a gamma rating that describes relatively how bright images appear. Identical images appear lighter on Macintosh hardware than on the typical Wintel clone. The W3C has a nice discussion about color spaces that includes information about gamma values: <http://www.w3.org/Graphics/Color/sRGB.html>.

```
<?
    //go from Windows gamma to Macintosh gamma
    $color = gamma_correct_tag("#CC0000", 2.2, 1.571);

    print("<FONT COLOR=\"$color\">");
    print("Sample Text");
    print("</FONT>");
?>
```

array getimagesize(string filename, array image_info)

The getimagesize function returns a four-element array that tells you the image size of the given filename. The contents of this array are listed in Table 12.1. The file must be a graphic file in one of three formats: GIF, JPEG, or PNG.

The optional image_info argument will be set with additional information from the file. At the time of this writing, this array is set with APP markers 0–15 from JPEG files. One of the most common is APP13, which is an International Press Telecommunications Council (IPTC) block. These blocks are used to communicate information about electronic media released to

Table 12.1	Array Elements for `getimagesize`
Element	*Description*
0	Width in pixels
1	Height in pixels
2	Image Type (GIF = 1, JPG = 2, PNG = 3)
3	String like "height=150 width=200", usable in IMG tag
bits	Bits per sample for jpegs
channels	Samples per pixel for jpegs

news agencies. They are stored in binary form, so to decode them you must use the `iptcparse` function. You can find out more about the IPTC at their Web site: <http://www.iptc.org/iptc/>.

Note that the `image_info` argument must be passed by reference, which means it must be preceded by an ampersand.

```
<?
    $image_file = "php.jpg";
    $image_size = getimagesize($image_file, &$image_info);
    print("<IMG SRC=\"$image_file\" $image_size[3]><BR>\n");

    //show information if it exists
    while(list($key, $value) = each($image_info))
    {
        print($key . "<BR>\n");
    }
?>
```

string iptcembed(string iptc, string file, integer spool)

The `iptcembed` function adds IPTC blocks to JPEG files. By default the blocks are added to the file, and the modified file is returned. The `spool` argument allows you to change this behavior. If the `spool` flag is 1 or 2, then the modified JPEG will be sent directly to the browser. If the `spool` flag is 2, the JPEG will not be returned as a string.

array iptcparse(string iptc_block)

The iptcparse function takes an IPTC block and returns an array containing all the tags in the block. See the description of getimagesize to see how to get IPTC blocks.

Creating JPEG, PNG, and WBMP Images

All the functions in this section require the GD library. If you haven't compiled it as part of your PHP module, either load it automatically by editing php3.ini, or use the dl function. Some of these functions also require other libraries, which allow you to use font files.

To get started you can use either imagecreate to start with a blank graphic, or a function such as imagecreatefrompng to load a PNG from a file. Coordinates in these functions treat (0, 0) to be the top-left corner and refer to pixels. Likewise, any size arguments refer to pixels.

When creating images with these functions, you can't simply decide to output an image in the middle of a script that outputs HTML. You must create a separate script that sends a content-type header. All the examples illustrate this idea.

For functions that use fonts, there are five built-in fonts numbered 1, 2, 3, 4, and 5. You may also load fonts, which will always have identifiers greater than five.

boolean imagearc(integer image, integer center_x, integer center_y, integer width, integer height, integer start, integer end, integer color)

Use imagearc to draw a section of an ellipse. The first argument specifies a valid image. The ellipse is centered at center_x and center_y. The height and width are set by the respective arguments in pixels. The start and end points of the curve are given in degrees. Zero degrees is at 3 o'clock and proceeds counterclockwise.

```
<?
/*
** cut out a circular view of an image
*/
```

```php
//attempt to open image, suppress error messages
if(!($image = @imagecreatefrompng("php.png")))
{
        //error, so create an error image and exit
        $image = imagecreate(200,200);
        $colorWhite = imagecolorallocate($image, 255, 255, 255);
        $colorBlack = imagecolorallocate($image, 0, 0, 0);
        imagefill($image, 0, 0, $colorWhite);
        imagestring($image, 4, 10, 10, "Couldn't load image!",
        $colorBlack);
        header("Content-type: image/jpeg");
        imagejpeg($image);
        exit();
}

//create a color to be transparent, hopefully
//not already in the image
$colorMagenta = imagecolorallocate($image, 255, 0, 255);

//draw a circle
imagearc($image,
        100, 50,
        100, 100,
        0, 360,
        $colorMagenta);

//fill outside of circle with Magenta
imagefilltoborder($image, 0, 0, $colorMagenta, $colorMagenta);

//turn magenta transparent
imagecolortransparent($image, $colorMagenta);

//send image to browser
header("Content-type: image/png");
imagepng($image);
?>
```

boolean imagechar(integer image, integer font, integer x, integer y, string character, integer color)

The imagechar function draws a single character at the given pixel. The font argument can be a loaded font or one of the five built-in fonts. The character will be oriented horizontally—that is, left to right. The x and y coordinates refer to the top-left corner of the letter.

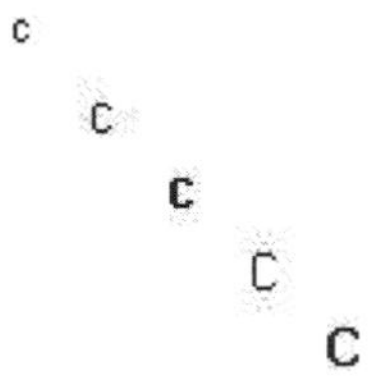

```
<?
    /*
    ** Draw 'C' in each of the built-in fonts
    */

    //create white square
    $image = imagecreate(200,200);
    $colorBlack = imagecolorallocate($image, 0, 0, 0);
    $colorWhite = imagecolorallocate($image, 255,255,255);
    imagefill($image, 0, 0, $colorWhite);

    //draw a C in each built-in font
    imagechar($image, 1, 0, 0, "C", $colorBlack);
    imagechar($image, 2, 20, 20, "C", $colorBlack);
    imagechar($image, 3, 40, 40, "C", $colorBlack);
    imagechar($image, 4, 60, 60, "C", $colorBlack);
    imagechar($image, 5, 80, 80, "C", $colorBlack);

    //send image
    header("Content-type: image/jpeg");
    imagejpeg($image);
?>
```

Figure 12-1   `imagechar`.

boolean imagecharup(integer image, integer font, integer x, integer y, string character, integer color)

The `imagecharup` function operates identically to `imagechar`, except that the character is oriented vertically, bottom to top.

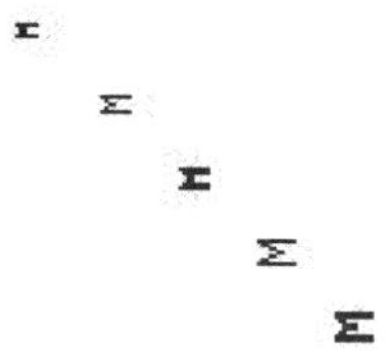

ꭇ

Σ

ꭇ

Σ

Σ

```
<?
    /*
    ** Draw vertical 'M' in each of the built-in fonts
    */

    //create white square
    $image = imagecreate(200,200);
    $colorBlack = imagecolorallocate($image, 0, 0, 0);
    $colorWhite = imagecolorallocate($image, 255,255,255);
    imagefill($image, 0, 0, $colorWhite);

    //draw an M in each built-in font
    imagecharup($image, 1, 10, 10, "M", $colorBlack);
    imagecharup($image, 2, 30, 30, "M", $colorBlack);
    imagecharup($image, 3, 50, 50, "M", $colorBlack);
    imagecharup($image, 4, 70, 70, "M", $colorBlack);
    imagecharup($image, 5, 90, 90, "M", $colorBlack);

    //send image
    header("Content-type: image/gif");
    imagejpeg($image);
?>
```

Figure 12-2   `imagecharup`.

integer imagecolorallocate(integer image, integer red, integer green, integer blue)

The `imagecolorallocate` function allocates a color in the given image. The color is specified by the amount of red, green, and blue. An identifier is returned for referring to this color in other functions.

```
<?
        /*
        ** Draw Red, Green, Blue circles
        */

        //create white square
        $image = imagecreate(200,200);
        $colorWhite = imagecolorallocate($image, 255,255,255);
        $colorRed = imagecolorallocate($image, 255, 0, 0);
        $colorGreen = imagecolorallocate($image, 0, 255, 0);
        $colorBlue = imagecolorallocate($image, 0, 0, 255);
        imagefill($image, 0, 0, $colorWhite);

        //make red circle
        imagearc($image, 50, 50, 100, 100, 0, 360, $colorRed);
        imagefilltoborder($image, 50, 50, $colorRed, $colorRed);

        //make green circle
        imagearc($image, 100, 50, 100, 100, 0, 360, $colorGreen);
        imagefilltoborder($image, 100, 50, $colorGreen, $colorGreen);

        //make blue circle
        imagearc($image, 75, 75, 100, 100, 0, 360, $colorBlue);
        imagefilltoborder($image, 75, 75, $colorBlue, $colorBlue);

        //send image
        header("Content-type: image/jpeg");
        imagejpeg($image);
?>
```

integer imagecolorat(integer image, integer x, integer y)

The imagecolorat function returns the index of the color at the specified pixel. All images have a palette of arbitrary colors referred to by integers.

```
<?
        /*
        ** Change a color
        */

        //attempt to open image, suppress error messages
```

```
if(!($image = @imagecreatefromjpeg("php_lang.jpg")))
{
        //error, so create an error image and exit
        $image = imagecreate(200,200);
        $colorWhite = imagecolorallocate($image, 255, 255, 255);
        $colorBlack = imagecolorallocate($image, 0, 0, 0);
        imagefill($image, 0, 0, $colorWhite);
        imagestring($image, 4, 10, 10, "Couldn't load image!",
        $colorBlack);
        header("Content-type: image/jpeg");
        imagejpeg($image);
        exit();
}

//get the color at (10,10)
$colorIndex = imagecolorat($image, 10, 10);

//change that color to red
imagecolorset($image, $colorIndex, 255, 0, 0);

//send image
header("Content-type: image/jpeg");
imagejpeg($image);
?>
```

integer imagecolorclosest(integer image, integer red, integer green, integer blue)

The imagecolorclosest function returns the index of the color in the given image closest to the given color. Colors are treated as three-dimensional co-ordinates, and closeness is defined by the distance between two points.

```
<?
    /*
    ** Compare closest color to real color
    */

    //attempt to open image, suppress error messages
    if(!($image = @imagecreatefromjpeg("php_lang.jpg")))
    {
        //error, so create an error image and exit
        $image = imagecreate(200,200);
```

```
        $colorWhite = imagecolorallocate($image, 255, 255, 255);
        $colorBlack = imagecolorallocate($image, 0, 0, 0);
        imagefill($image, 0, 0, $colorWhite);
        imagestring($image, 4, 10, 10, "Couldn't load image!",
        $colorBlack);
        header("Content-type: image/jpeg");
        imagejpeg($image);
        exit();
}

//find index of color closest to pure magenta
$magentaIndex = imagecolorclosest($image, 255, 0, 255);

//get RGB values
$colorArray = imagecolorsforindex($image, $magentaIndex);

//allocate closest color
$colorMagenta = imagecolorallocate($image,
        $colorArray["red"],
        $colorArray["green"],
        $colorArray["blue"]);

//draw a square
imagefilledrectangle($image, 10, 10, 100, 100, $colorMagenta);

//send image
header("Content-type: image/jpeg");
imagejpeg($image);
?>
```

integer imagecolorexact(integer image, integer red, integer green, integer blue)

Use the imagecolorexact function to find the index of the color in the given image that matches the given color exactly. If the color doesn't exist, negative one (–1) is returned.

```
<?
        /*
        ** Check that an image contains black
        ** If so, change all black to cyan.
        */
```

```
      //attempt to open image, suppress error messages
      if(!($image = @imagecreatefromjpeg("php_lang.jpg")))
      {
            //error, so create an error image and exit
            $image = imagecreate(200,200);
            $colorWhite = imagecolorallocate($image, 255, 255, 255);
            $colorBlack = imagecolorallocate($image, 0, 0, 0);
            imagefill($image, 0, 0, $colorWhite);
            imagestring($image, 4, 10, 10, "Couldn't load image!",
            $colorBlack);
            header("Content-type: image/jpeg");
            imagejpeg($image);
            exit();
      }

      //find index of black
      $blackIndex = imagecolorexact($image, 0, 0, 0);

      if($blackIndex >= 0)
      {
            //make all black areas cyan
            imagecolorset($image, $blackIndex, 0, 255, 255);
      }

      //send image
      header("Content-type: image/jpeg");
      imagejpeg($image);
?>
```

integer imagecolorresolve(integer image, integer red, integer green, integer blue)

The imagecolorresolve function returns a color identifier based on a specified color. If the color does not exist in the image's palette, it will be added. In the event that the color cannot be added, an identifier for the closest color will be returned.

```
<?
      /*
      ** Attempt to draw a magenta square
      */

      //attempt to open image, suppress error messages
      if(!($image = @imagecreatefromjpeg("php_lang.jpg")))
      {
```

```
            //error, so create an error image and exit
            $image = imagecreate(200,200);
            $colorWhite = imagecolorallocate($image, 255, 255, 255);
            $colorBlack = imagecolorallocate($image, 0, 0, 0);
            imagefill($image, 0, 0, $colorWhite);
            imagestring($image, 4, 10, 10, "Couldn't load image!",
            $colorBlack);
            header("Content-type: image/jpeg");
            imagejpeg($image);
            exit();
        }

        $colorMagenta = imagecolorresolve($image, 255, 0, 255);

        // draw a square
        imagefilledrectangle($image, 10, 10, 50, 50, $colorMagenta);

        //send ima
        header("Content-type: image/jpeg");
        imagejpeg($image);
    ?>
```

boolean imagecolorset(integer image, integer index, integer red, integer green, integer blue)

The `imagecolorset` function sets the color at the given index to the specified color. For an example of use, see the example for the `imagecolorat` function.

array imagecolorsforindex(integer image, integer index)

The `imagecolorsforindex` function returns an associative array with the red, green, and blue elements of the color for the specified color index.

```
        <?
            /*
            ** Show RGB values for a color
            */

            //attempt to open image, suppress error messages
            if(!($image = @imagecreatefromjpeg("php_lang.jpg")))
```

```
        {
                //error, so create an error image and exit
                $image = imagecreate(200,200);
                $colorWhite = imagecolorallocate($image, 255, 255, 255);
                $colorBlack = imagecolorallocate($image, 0, 0, 0);
                imagefill($image, 0, 0, $colorWhite);
                imagestring($image, 4, 10, 10, "Couldn't load image!",
                $colorBlack);
                header("Content-type: image/jpeg");
                imagejpeg($image);
                exit();
        }

        //get the color at (100,100)
        $colorIndex = imagecolorat($image, 100, 100);

        //get RGB values
        $colorParts = imagecolorsforindex($image, $colorIndex);

        //display RGB values
        printf("RGB: " .
                $colorParts["red"] . ", " .
                $colorParts["green"] . ", " .
                $colorParts["blue"]);
?>
```

integer imagecolorstotal(integer image)

The imagecolorstotal function returns the number of colors in the given image.

```
<?
        /*
        ** Find number of colors in an image
        */

        //attempt to open image, suppress error messages
        if(!($image = @imagecreatefromjpeg("php_lang.jpg")))
        {
                //error, so print error message
                print("Couldn't load image!");
        }
        else
        {
                print("Total Colors: " . imagecolorstotal
```

```
                ($image));
        }
?>
```

integer imagecolortransparent (integer image, integer color)

The imagecolortransparent function sets the given color transparent. The color argument is as returned by the imagecolorallocate functions.

```
<?
    /*
    ** Create a red image with a transparent
    ** square cut out of it.
    */

    //create red square
    $image = imagecreate(200,200);
    $colorRed = imagecolorallocate($image, 255, 0, 0);
    $colorBlue = imagecolorallocate($image, 0, 0, 255);
    imagefill($image, 0, 0, $colorRed);

    //draw a smaller blue square
    imagefilledrectangle($image, 30, 30, 70, 70, $colorBlue);

    //make blue transparent
    imagecolortransparent($image, $colorBlue);

    //send image
    header("Content-type: image/png");
    imagepng($image);
?>
```

integer imagecopyresized(integer destination, integer source, integer destination_x, integer destination_y, integer source_x, integer source_y, integer destination_width, integer destination_height, integer source_width, integer source_height)

The imagecopyresized function copies a portion of the source image into the destination image. If the destination width and height are different than the source width and height, the clip will be stretched or shrunk. It is possible to copy and paste into the same image, but if the destination and source overlap, there will be unpredictable results.

```
<?
        /*
        ** Put PHP logo into field of red
        ** and resize it to 180x180
        */

        //create red square
        $image = imagecreate(200,200);
        $colorRed = imagecolorallocate($image, 255, 0, 0);
        imagefill($image, 0, 0, $colorRed);

        //attempt to open image, suppress error messages
        if(!($image2 = @imagecreatefromjpeg("php_lang.jpg")))
        {
                //error, so create an error image and exit
                $image = imagecreate(200,200);
                $colorWhite = imagecolorallocate($image, 255, 255, 255);
                $colorBlack = imagecolorallocate($image, 0, 0, 0);
                imagefill($image, 0, 0, $colorWhite);
                imagestring($image, 4, 10, 10, "Couldn't load image!",
                $colorBlack);
                header("Content-type: image/jpeg");
                imagejpeg($image);
                exit();
        }

        //drop image2 into image, and stretch or squash it
        imagecopyresized($image, $image2, 10, 10, 0, 0,
                180, 180, imagesx($image2), imagesy($image2));

        //send image
        header("Content-type: image/jpeg");
        imagejpeg($image);
?>
```

integer imagecreate(integer width, integer height)

The imagecreate function returns an image identifier of the specified width and height. This identifier is used in many of the other image functions.

```
<?
        /*
        ** Create a red square
```

```
        */

        //create red square
        $image = imagecreate(200,200);
        $colorRed = imagecolorallocate($image, 255, 0, 0);
        imagefill($image, 0, 0, $colorRed);

        //send image
        header("Content-type: image/jpeg");
        imagejpeg($image);
    ?>
```

integer imagecreatefromjpeg(string filename)

Use imagecreatefromjpeg to load a JPEG image from a file.

```
<?
    //attempt to open image, suppress error messages
    if(!($image = @imagecreatefromjpeg("php_lang.jpg")))
    {
        //error, so create an error image and exit
        $image = imagecreate(200,200);
        $colorWhite = imagecolorallocate($image, 255, 255, 255);
        $colorBlack = imagecolorallocate($image, 0, 0, 0);
        imagefill($image, 0, 0, $colorWhite);
        imagestring($image, 4, 10, 10, "Couldn't load image!",
        $colorBlack);
        header("Content-type: image/jpeg");
        imagejpeg($image);
        exit();
    }

    //send image
    header("Content-type: image/jpeg");
    imagejpeg($image);
?>
```

integer imagecreatefrompng(string filename)

Use imagecreatefrompng to load a PNG image from a file.

```
    <?
        //load an image and display it
        $image = imagecreatefrompng("php.png");
```

```
        header("Content-type: image/png");
        imagepng($image);
?>
```

boolean imagedashedline(integer image, integer start_x, integer start_y, integer end_x, integer end_y, integer color)

The `imagedashedline` function draws a dashed line from the start point to the end point. The `color` argument is a color identifier returned by `image-colorallocate`. Use `imageline` to draw a solid line.

Figure 12–3   `imagedashedline`.

```
<?
        /*
        ** Show image with a dashed line
        */

        //create yellow square
        $image = imagecreate(200,200);
        $colorBlue = imagecolorallocate($image, 0, 0, 255);
        $colorYellow = imagecolorallocate($image, 255, 255, 0);
        imagefill($image, 0, 0, $colorYellow);

        //draw dashed line in blue
        imagedashedline($image, 10, 10, 150, 130, $colorBlue);

        //send image
        header("Content-type: image/jpeg");
        imagejpeg($image);
?>
```

boolean imagedestroy(integer image)

Use the `imagedestroy` function to clear memory associated with the specified image. Most of the time you will not need this function. PHP will clean up when your script ends.

```
<?
    /*
    ** Create an image, then free its memory
    */

    //create blue square
    $image = imagecreate(200,200);
    $colorBlue = imagecolorallocate($image, 128, 128, 255);
    imagefill($image, 0, 0, $colorBlue);

    //send image
    header("Content-type: image/jpeg");
    imagejpeg($image);

    //free memory associated with image
    imagedestroy($image);
?>
```

boolean imagefill(integer image, integer x, integer y, integer color)

The `imagefill` function performs a flood fill at the given point with the given color. The `color` argument must be as returned by `imagecolorallo-cate`. Starting at the given point, pixels are changed to the specified color. The coloring spreads out, continuing until a color different from the one at the specified point is encountered. See the description of `imagearc` for an example of use. See `imagefilltoborder` for an alternative.

boolean imagefilledpolygon(integer image, array points, integer number, integer color)

The `imagefilledpolygon` function creates a polygon with its inside filled with the specified color. The `points` argument is an array of x and y values for each point: Each point uses two array elements. The `number` argument reports how many points to use from the array.

```
<?
    /*
    ** Draw a black triangle
    */

    //create red square
    $image = imagecreate(200,200);
    $colorRed = imagecolorallocate($image, 255, 0, 0);
    $colorBlack = imagecolorallocate($image, 0, 0, 0);
    imagefill($image, 0, 0, $colorRed);

    //set up three points of the triangle
    $points = array(100, 10, 50, 60, 150, 60);

    //draw triangle
    imagefilledpolygon($image,
        $points, count($points)/2,
        $colorBlack);

    //send image
    header("Content-type: image/jpeg");
    imagejpeg($image);
?>
```

Figure 12–4   `imagefilledpolygon.`

```
<?
    /*
    ** Draw a black square
    */

    //create green square
    $image = imagecreate(200,200);
    $colorGreen = imagecolorallocate($image, 128, 255,
    128);
    $colorBlack = imagecolorallocate($image, 0, 0, 0);
    imagefill($image, 0, 0, $colorRed);

    //draw a black rectangle
    imagefilledrectangle($image,
        10, 10, 90, 90,
        $colorBlack);

    //send image
    header("Content-type: image/jpeg");
    imagejpeg($image);
?>
```

Figure 12–5 `imagefilledrectangle.`

boolean imagefilledrectangle(integer image, integer top_left_x, integer top_left_y, integer bottom_right_x, integer bottom_right_y, integer color)

The `imagefilledrectangle` function draws a filled rectangle based on the top-left and bottom-right corners.

boolean imagefilltoborder(integer image, integer x, integer y, integer border_color, integer color)

The `imagefilltoborder` function will flood-fill an area bounded by the `border_color` argument. The flood fill will begin at the given coordinate. See imagecolorallocate for an example.

integer imagefontheight(integer font)

The `imagefontheight` function returns the height in pixels of the specified font, which may be a built-in font (1–5) or a font loaded with `imagefont-load`.

```
<?
    /*
    ** Create image just the right size for text
    */

    $Text = "Core PHP Programming";
    $Font = 5;
    $Width = imagefontwidth($Font) * strlen($Text);
    $Height = imagefontheight($Font);

    //create green square
    $image = imagecreate($Width, $Height);
    $colorGreen = imagecolorallocate($image, 128, 255, 128);
    $colorBlack = imagecolorallocate($image, 0, 0, 0);
    imagefill($image, 0, 0, $colorRed);

    //add text in black
    imagestring($image, $Font, 0, 0, $Text, $colorBlack);

    //send image
```

```
        header("Content-type: image/jpeg");
        imagejpeg($image);
?>
```

integer imagefontwidth(integer font)

The `imagefontwidth` function returns the width in pixels of the specified font, which may be a built-in font (1–5) or a font loaded with `imagefont-load`. See `imagefontheight` for an example.

boolean imagegammacorrect(integer image, double original, double new)

The `imagegammacorrect` function changes the gamma for an image. Video display hardware is given a gamma rating that describes relatively how bright images appear. Identical images appear lighter on Macintosh hardware than on the typical Wintel clone. Each color in the palette of the image will be adjusted to the new gamma.

At the time of this writing, imagegammacorrect was not part of PHP 4, although it was part of PHP 3.

```
<?
    //attempt to open image, suppress error messages
    if(!($image = @imagecreatefromjpeg("php_lang.jpg")))
    {
        //error, so create an error image and exit
        $image = imagecreate(200,200);
        $colorWhite = imagecolorallocate($image, 255, 255, 255);
        $colorBlack = imagecolorallocate($image, 0, 0, 0);
        imagefill($image, 0, 0, $colorWhite);
        imagestring($image, 4, 10, 10, "Couldn't load image!",
        $colorBlack);
        header("Content-type: image/jpeg");
        imagejpeg($image);
        exit();
    }

    //adjust gamma, display
    imagegammacorrect($image, 2.2, 1.571);

    //send image
    header("Content-type: image/jpeg");
    imagejpeg($image);
?>
```

boolean imageinterlace(integer image, boolean on)

Use `imageinterlace` to set an image as interlaced or not. If the change is successful, TRUE is returned.

Interlaced images are stored so that they appear progressively rather than all at once. JPEGs marked as interlaced are called progressive JPEGs, in fact. While most browsers support interlaced GIFs, many do not support interlaced PNGs or progressive JPEGs. You can read more on the subject in the GD library's manual.

```
<?
    /*
    ** Create interlaced image
    */

    //create red square
    $image = imagecreate(200,200);
    $colorRed = imagecolorallocate($image, 255, 0, 0);
    imagefill($image, 0, 0, $colorRed);

    //set as interlaced
    imageinterlace($image, TRUE);

    //send image
    header("Content-type: image/jpeg");
    imagejpeg($image);
?>
```

boolean imagejpeg(integer image, string filename, integer quality)

The `imagejpeg` function either sends an image to the browser or writes it to a file. If a filename is provided, a JPEG file is created. Otherwise, the image is sent directly to the browser. The optional `quality` argument determines the compression level used in the image, and should range from 0 (lowest quality) to 10 (highest quality).

```
<?
    /*
    ** create a blue square, save to disk
```

```
*/

//create image if it doesn't exist,
//or it's older than an hour
if(!file_exists("blue_square.jpg") OR
     (filectime("blue_square.jpg") < (time() - 3600)))
{
     //send debugging info
     print("<!—creating image—>\n");

     //create a blue square
     $image = imagecreate(200, 100);
     $colorBlue = imagecolorallocate($image, 128, 128, 255);
     $colorWhite = imagecolorallocate($image, 255, 255, 255);
     imagefill($image, 0, 0, $colorBlue);

     //add file creation time to image
     imagestring($image, 4, 10, 10,
          date("Y-m-d H:i:s"),
          $colorWhite);

     //write it to a file
     imagejpeg($image, "blue_square.jpg");
}

//print image tag that show image
print("<IMG SRC=\"blue_square.jpg\" " .
     "HEIGHT=\"100\" WIDTH=\"200\" BORDER=\"0\">");
?>
```

boolean imageline(integer image, integer start_x, integer start_y, integer end_x, integer end_y, integer color)

Like imagedashedline, imageline draws a line from the starting point to the ending point. In this case, the line is solid.

```
<?
        /*
        ** Draw solid black line
        */

        //create cyan square
        $image = imagecreate(200,200);
        $colorCyan = imagecolorallocate($image, 0, 255, 255);
        $colorBlack = imagecolorallocate($image, 0, 0, 0);
        imagefill($image, 0, 0, $colorCyan);

        //draw solid, black line
        imageline($image, 10, 10, 150, 130, $colorBlack);

        //send image
        header("Content-type: image/jpeg");
        imagejpeg($image);
?>
```

Figure 12-6 `imageline`.

integer imageloadfont(string filename)

The `imageloadfont` function loads a font and returns a font identifier that may be used with the other font functions. The fonts are stored as bitmaps in a special format. The PHP 3 distribution contained a Perl script for converting X11 .bdf files to PHP's format.

The code that loads fonts is architecture dependent. Table 12.2 shows the structure of a font file for systems that use 32-bit integers. Use this if you wish to create your own font files.

Table 12.2	PHP Font File Format	

Position	Length	Description
0	4	Number of characters in the font
4	4	ASCII value of first character
8	4	Width in pixels for each character
12	4	Height in pixels for each character
16	variable	Each pixel uses 1 byte, so this field should be the product of the number of characters, the width, and the height.

```php
<?
    /*
    ** Load a font and display some text
    */

    //create red square
    $image = imagecreate(200,200);
    $colorRed = imagecolorallocate($image, 255, 0, 0);
    $colorBlack = imagecolorallocate($image, 0, 0, 0);
    imagefill($image, 0, 0, $colorRed);

    //load font
    if(!($myFont = imageloadfont("myFont")))
    {
        print("Unable to load font!");
        exit();
    }

    //draw some text with loaded font
    imagestring($image, $myFont, 10, 10,
        "Hello World!", $colorBlack);

    //send image
    header("Content-type: image/jpeg");
    imagejpeg($image);
?>
```

boolean imagepng(integer image, string filename)

The `imagepng` function either sends an image to the browser or writes it to a file. If a filename is provided, a PNG file is created. Otherwise, the image is sent directly to the browser. This latter method is used in most of the examples in this section.

boolean imagepolygon(integer image, array points, integer number, integer color)

The `imagepolygon` function behaves identically to the `imagefilledpolygon` function with the exception that the polygon is not filled. The `points` argument is an array of integers, two for each point of the polygon. A line will be drawn from each point in succession and from the last point to the first point.

```
<?
        /*
        ** Draw a hollow black triangle
        */

        //create red square
        $image = imagecreate(200,200);
        $colorRed = imagecolorallocate($image, 255, 0, 0);
        $colorBlack = imagecolorallocate($image, 0, 0, 0);
        imagefill($image, 0, 0, $colorRed);

        //set points of triangle
        $points = array(100, 10, 50, 60, 150, 60);
```

Figure 12–7 `imagepolygon`.

```
        //draw a black triangle
        imagepolygon($image,
            $points, count($points)/2,
            $colorBlack);

        //send image
        header("Content-type: image/jpeg");
        imagejpeg($image);
    ?>
```

Figure 12–7   Continued

array imagepsbbox(string text, integer font_identifier, integer size, integer spacing, integer letting, double angle)

The `imagepsbbox` function returns an array containing a pair of coordinates that specify a bounding box that would surround a theoretical string of text. The first two numbers are the x and y values of the lower-left corner. The second pair of numbers specify the upper-right corner.

The `font_identifier` is an integer returned by `imagepsloadfont`. The `size` argument is in pixels. The `spacing` argument controls vertical spacing between lines of text. The `letting` argument controls horizontal spacing between characters. Both are expressed in units of 1/1000th of an em-square, and are added to the default spacing or leading for a font. They may be positive or negative. The `angle` argument specifies a number of degrees to rotate from normal left-to-right orientation.

See `imagepstext`, below, for an example.

integer imagepscopyfont(integer font_identifier)

The `imagepscopyfont` function copies a font loaded with `imagepsload-font` into another font identifier. This allows you to have an original version of the font in memory and another copy you've stretched or slanted.

```
<?
    /*
    ** Draw text using a Postscript font
    ** Draw normal, stretched and slanted
    */

    //set parameters for text
```

```php
$font_file = "ComputerModern-Roman";
$size = 20;
$angle = 0;
$text = "PHP";
$antialias_steps = 16;
$spacing = 0;
$letting = 0;

//create red square
$image = imagecreate(300, 300);
$colorRed = imagecolorallocate($image, 0xFF, 0x00, 0x00);
$colorBlack = imagecolorallocate($image, 0, 0, 0);
imagefill($image, 10, 10, $colorRed);

//Load font
if(!($myFont = imagepsloadfont($font_file)))
{
      print("Unable to load font!");
      exit();
}

//make extended font
$myFontExtended = imagepscopyfont($myFont);
imagepsextendfont($myFont, 1.5);

//make slanted font
$myFontSlanted = imagepscopyfont($myFont);
imagepsslantfont($myFont, 1.5);

//write normal text
imagepstext($image, $text, $myFont, $size,
      $colorBlack, $colorRed,
      0, 0, $spacing, $letting,
      $angle, $antialias_steps);

//write extended text
imagepstext($image, $text, $myFont, $size,
      $colorBlack, $colorRed,
      0, $size, $spacing, $letting,
      $angle, $antialias_steps);

//write slanted text
imagepstext($image, $text, $myFont, $size,
      $colorBlack, $colorRed,
      0, $size*2, $spacing, $letting,
```

```
        $angle, $antialias_steps);

    //unload fonts
    imagepsfreefont($myFont);
    imagepsfreefont($myFontExtended);
    imagepsfreefont($myFontSlanted);

    //send image
    header("Content-type: image/jpeg");
    imagejpeg($image);
?>
```

imagepsencodefont(string filename)

Use `imagepsencodefont` to change the encoding vector used to match ASCII characters to PostScript font images. By default, PostScript fonts only have characters for the first 127 ASCII values. See `imagepstext`, below, for an example.

imagepsextendfont(integer font_identifier, double extension_factor)

The `imagepsextendfont` function stretches or compresses a PostScript font. The normal width of the font will be multiplied by the `extension_factor`. See `imagepscopyfont` for an example. Multiple calls to this function are not cumulative, they just change the extension. If you want to set the font back to normal width, use a factor of one.

imagepsfreefont(integer font_identifier)

The `imagepsfreefont` function removes a PostScript font from memory. Generally you do not need to do this. PHP will unload fonts when your script ends. See `imagepstext`, below, for an example.

imagepsslantfont(integer font_identifier, double slant_factor)

Use `imagepsslantfont` to pitch the font forward or backwards. Sometimes this is referred to as italics. The `font_identifier` is an integer returned by `imagepsloadfont`. The `slant_factor` operates similarly to the extension_factor in the imagepsextendfont function. Values greater than one will cause the top of the font to pitch to the right. Values less than one will cause the top of the font to pitch to the left.

integer imagepsloadfont(string filename)

Use imagepsloadfont to load a PostScript font. A font identifier will be returned for use in with the other PostScript functions. If the load fails, FALSE is returned. See imagepstext, below, for an example.

array imagepstext(integer image, string text, integer font_identifer, integer size, integer foreground, integer background, integer x, integer y, integer spacing, integer letting, double angle, integer antialias_steps)

The imagepstext function draws a string of text into an image using a PostScript font. The image argument is an integer as returned by imagecreate or imagecreatefrompng. The font_identifier argument is a value returned by the imagepsloadfont function. The size argument specifies the height in number of pixels. The foreground and background arguments are color identifiers. The x and y arguments specify the bottom-left corner from where to begin drawing. The spacing argument controls vertical spacing between lines of text. The letting argument controls horizontal spacing between characters. Both are expressed in units of 1/1000th of an em-square and are added to the default spacing or leading for a font. They may be positive or negative. The angle argument specifies a number of degrees to rotate from normal left-to-right orientation. The antialias_steps argument specifies how many colors to use when antialiasing, or smoothing. Two values are valid: 4 and 16. The last four arguments are optional.

The returned array contains two pairs of coordinates specifying the lower-left corner and upper-right corner of the bounding box, respectively.

```
<?
    /*
    ** Draw text using a Postscript font
```

```
** Make the image the correct size
*/

//set parameters for text
$font_file = "ComputerModern-Roman";
$size = 20;
$angle = 0;
$text = "PHP";
$antialias_steps = 16;
$spacing = 0;
$letting = 0;

//Load font
if(!($myFont = imagepsloadfont($font_file)))
{
      print("Unable to load font!");
      exit();
}

//set encoding
imagepsencodefont("IsoLatin1.enc");

//get bounding box
$Box = imagepsbbox($text, $myFont, $size, $spacing, $letting,
$angle);

//create an image with ten extra pixels
$image = imagecreate($Box[1]+10, $Box[3]+10);
$colorRed = imagecolorallocate($image, 0, 0, 0);
$colorBlack = imagecolorallocate($image, 0, 0, 0);
imagefill($image, 10, 10, $colorRed);

//write the text
imagepstext($image, $text, $myFont, $size,
      $colorBlack, $colorRed,
      0, 0, $spacing, $letting,
      $angle, $antialias_steps);

//unload font
imagepsfreefont($myFont);

//send image
header("Content-type: image/jpeg");
imagejpeg($image);
?>
```

imagerectangle(integer image, integer top_left_x, integer top_left_y, integer bottom_right_x, integer bottom_right_y, integer color)

The imagerectangle function draws a rectangle based on the top-left and bottom-right corners. The inside of the rectangle will not be filled as it is with the imagefilledrectangle function.

```
<?
    /*
    ** Draw a hollow black rectangle
    */

    //create yellow square
    $image = imagecreate(200,200);
    $colorYellow = imagecolorallocate($image, 255, 255, 0);
    $colorBlack = imagecolorallocate($image, 0, 0, 0);
    imagefill($image, 0, 0, $colorYellow);

    //draw a black rectangle
    imagerectangle($image, 10, 10, 150, 150, $colorBlack);

    //send image
    header("Content-type: image/jpeg");
    imagejpeg($image);
?>
```

boolean imagesetpixel(integer image, integer x, integer y, integer color)

The imagesetpixel function sets a single pixel to the specified color.

```
<?
    /*
    ** Draw 100 black dots
    */

    //create yellow square
    $image = imagecreate(100, 100);
    $colorYellow = imagecolorallocate($image, 255, 255, 0);
    $colorBlack = imagecolorallocate($image, 0, 0, 0);
```

```
imagefill($image, 0, 0, $colorYellow);

//draw 100 random black dots
srand(time());
for($i=0; $i < 100; $i++)
{
        imagesetpixel($image, rand(0, 99), rand(0, 99), $color-
        Black);
}

//send image
header("Content-type: image/jpeg");
imagejpeg($image);
?>
```

boolean imagestring(integer image, integer font, integer x, integer y, string text, integer color)

The imagestring function draws the given text at the specified point. The top-left part of the string will be at the specified point. The font argument may be a built-in font or one loaded by imageloadfont.

Hello World!

```
<?
    /*
    ** Print "Hello, World!" in black
    */

    //create yellow square
    $image = imagecreate(150, 50);
    $colorYellow = imagecolorallocate($image, 255, 255, 0);
    $colorBlack = imagecolorallocate($image, 0, 0, 0);
    imagefill($image, 0, 0, $colorYellow);
```

Figure 12–8 imagestring.

```
        //draw some text with loaded font
        imagestring($image, 4, 10, 10, "Hello World!", $colorBlack);

        //send image
        header("Content-type: image/jpeg");
        imagejpeg($image);
?>
```

Figure 12–8   Continued

boolean imagestringup(integer image, integer font, integer x, integer y, string text, integer color)

The imagestringup function draws a string oriented vertically instead of horizontally. Otherwise it works identically to imagestring.

```
<?
        /*
        ** Write "Hello, World!" vertically
        */

        //create blue square
        $image = imagecreate(50, 200);
        $colorBlue = imagecolorallocate($image, 128, 128,
        255);
        $colorBlack = imagecolorallocate($image, 0, 0, 0);
        imagefill($image, 0, 0, $colorYellow);

        //draw some text with loaded font
        imagestringup($image, 4, 10, 150, "Hello World!",
        $colorBlack);

        //send image
        header("Content-type: image/jpeg");
        imagejpeg($image);
?>
```

integer imagesx(integer image)

The `imagesx` function returns the width in pixels of the specified image.

```php
<?
    /*
    ** Put a rectangle in the center of any image
    */

    //attempt to open image, suppress error messages
    if(!($image = @imagecreatefromjpeg("php_lang.jpg")))
    {
        //error, so create an error image and exit
        $image = imagecreate(200,200);
        $colorWhite = imagecolorallocate($image, 255, 255, 255);
        $colorBlack = imagecolorallocate($image, 0, 0, 0);
        imagefill($image, 0, 0, $colorWhite);
        imagestring($image, 4, 10, 10, "Couldn't load image!",
        $colorBlack);
        header("Content-type: image/jpeg");
        imagejpeg($image);
    }

    //find center
    $centerX = intval(imagesx($image)/2);
    $centerY = intval(imagesy($image)/2);

    $colorGreen = imagecolorallocate($image, 0, 255, 0);

    //draw a green rectangle in center
    imagefilledrectangle($image,
        ($centerX-15), ($centerY-15),
        ($centerX+15), ($centerY+15),
        $colorGreen);

    //send image
    header("Content-type: image/jpeg");
    imagejpeg($image);
?>
```

Table 12.3	Array Returned by `imagettfbbox`
Array Pair	*Corner*
0, 1	Lower-Left
2, 3	Lower-Right
4, 5	Upper-Right
6, 7	Upper-Left

integer imagesy(integer image)

The `imagesy` function returns the height in pixels of the specified image.

array imagettfbbox(integer point_size, integer angle, string font, string text)

The `imagettfbbox` function returns an array of points that describe a bounding box around text to be drawn by the `imagettftext` function. The points are relative to the leftmost point on the baseline. The array elements correspond to the lower-left, lower-right, upper-right, and upper-left corners, in that order, as shown in Table 12.3.

This function may not be available, depending on the libraries available when PHP was compiled.

boolean imagettftext(integer image, integer point_size, integer angle, integer x, integer y, integer color, string font, string text)

The `imagettftext` function uses a TrueType font to draw a string of text. The x and y arguments refer to the leftmost position of the baseline. The text will radiate from that point at the given angle, which should be from 0 to 360. An angle of zero represents normal right-to-left text. The `font` argument is the full path to a .ttf file.

This function may not be available, depending on the libraries available when PHP was compiled.

```php
<?
        /*
        ** Draw text using a TrueType font
        ** Also, draw a box around the text.
        */

        //set parameters for text
        $size = 40;
        $angle = 30;
        $startX = 50;
        $startY = 100;

        //create red square
        $image = imagecreate(200, 200);
        $colorRed = imagecolorallocate($image, 255, 0, 0);
        $colorBlack = imagecolorallocate($image, 0, 0, 0);
        imagefill($image, 10, 10, $colorRed);

        //get bounding box
        $Box = imagettfbbox($size, $angle, "comic.ttf", "PHP");

        //move bounding box to starting point (100,100)
        for($index = 0; $index < count($Box); $index += 2)
        {
                $Box[$index] += $startX;
                $Box[$index+1] += $startY;
        }

        //draw bounding box
        imagepolygon($image, $Box, count($Box)/2, $colorBlack);

        //write the text
        imagettftext($image, $size, $angle,
                $startX, $startY, $colorBlack,
                "comic.ttf", "PHP");

        //send image
        header("Content-type: image/jpeg");
        imagejpeg($image);
?>
```

boolean imagewbmp(integer image, string filename)

The `imagewbmp` function either sends an image to the browser or writes it to a file. If a filename is provided, a WAP (Wireless Application Protocol) bitmap file is created. Otherwise, the image is sent directly to the browser. This function is similar to `imagepng` and `imagejpeg`.

DATABASE FUNCTIONS

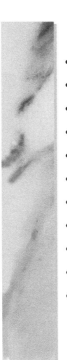

Topics in This Chapter

- dBase
- DBM-style Database Abstraction
- filePro
- Informix
- InterBase
- mSQL
- MySQL
- ODBC
- Oracle
- Postgres
- Sybase

Chapter 13

PHP offers support for many databases. Open source relational databases are well represented, as are many commercial products. If native support for a database doesn't exist, it's likely you may use ODBC with an appropriate driver. Chapter 17, "Database Integration," discusses strategies for using databases with PHP-powered sites.

Most of the functions in this section rely on an extension module. These may be loaded either in the `php.ini` file or the `dl` function, but most likely are compiled into PHP. Typically Windows requires use of the first method and other operating systems require the second.

While this chapter describes the PHP functions that communicate with various systems, it does not pursue introducing the intricacies of all the systems. I can't possibly include a full tutorial on SQL within this book. If you have chosen a database for integration with PHP, I assume you will take the time to learn about that database. I am a big fan of MySQL and have found the online documentation to be great. Additionally, several books are available about MySQL.

dBase

The following functions work on dBase files, which typically end with a .dbf extension. If you are using the precompiled version for Windows, you will need to load the dBase extension by editing php.ini or using the dl function. The extension is likely called php_dbase.dll but was unavailable at the time of this writing. On other operating systems it's easy to compile dBase support into PHP.

The dBase functionality in PHP is somewhat limited. Index and memo fields are not supported. Neither is any kind of locking. The dBase functionality in PHP is meant to be a means of importing data from what has become somewhat of a lowest common denominator in data exchange.

Jim Winstead added dBase support to PHP.

boolean dbase_add_record(integer database, array record)

The dbase_add_record function adds a record to the database specified by a database identifier returned by dbase_open. The record array contains an element for each field in the database, in order and starting at zero. If the correct number of fields is not supplied, FALSE is returned.

```
<?
    //open connection to database
    $db = dbase_open("customer.dbf", 2);

    //create record to be added
    $newRecord = array("John Smith", 100.00, "19980901", "Y");

    //add record
    dbase_add_record($db, $newRecord);

    //close connection
    dbase_close($db);
?>
```

boolean dbase_close(integer database)

The dbase_close function closes a database. See other functions in this section for examples of use.

integer dbase_create(string filename, array fields)

The `dbase_create` function creates a dBase database. The fields argument is an array of arrays that describe fields. Each array may have up to four elements. In order, they are `name`, `type`, `length`, and `precision`. Type is a single character. Some types require length, and precision; others do not. See Table 13.1.

If a database is successfully created, a database identifier is returned; otherwise `FALSE` is returned.

```
<?
        // create field definition
        $fields = array(
              array("Name", "C", 32),
              array("Balance", "N", 8, 2),
              array("Birthday", "D"),
              array("Commercial", L));

        $db = dbase_create("customer.dbf", $fields);

        dbase_close($db);
?>
```

boolean dbase_delete_record(integer database, integer record)

The `dbase_delete_record` function marks a record for deletion. The record will remain in the database until `dbase_pack` is called.

Table 13.1   dBase Field Types

Type	Code	Description
Boolean	L	This type does not have a length or a precision.
Date	D	Dates are stored in YYYYMMDD format and do not use length or precision.
Number	N	The length property refers to the total number of digits in the number and the precision refers to the number of digits after the decimal point.
String	C	The length property specifies how many characters are stored in the field. The precision property is not used.

```
<?
        //open connection to database
        $db = dbase_open("customer.dbf", 2);

        //mark record for deletion
        dbase_delete_record($db, 2);

        //close connection
        dbase_close($db);
?>
```

array dbase_get_record(integer database, integer record)

The `dbase_get_record` function returns the fields of a record in an array.
The first field will be numbered zero. In addition, an element indexed by
`deleted` will contain 1 if the row was marked for deletion. Records are numbered from one.

```
<?
        //connect to database
        $db = dbase_open("customer.dbf", 2);

        //get some information about database
        $numRecords = dbase_numrecords($db);
        $numFields = dbase_numfields($db);

        // get every record
        for($index = 1; $index <= $numRecords; $index++)
        {
                //get a record
                $record = dbase_get_record($db, $index);

                print("<H3>Record $index</H3>\n");

                //loop over fields
                for($index2 = 0; $index2 < $numFields; $index2++)
                {
                        print("<B>Field $index2:</B>");
                        print($record[$index2]);
                        print("<BR>\n");
                }

                //print deletion status
```

```
            print("<B>Deleted:</B> ");
            print($record["deleted"]);
            print("<BR>\n");
      }

      //close connection
      dbase_close($db);
?>
```

array dbase_get_record_with_names(integer database, integer record)

This function behaves like `dbase_get_record`, except that instead of being indexed by integers, fields are indexed by their names.

```
<?
      //connect to database
      $db = dbase_open("customer.dbf", 2);

      // get every record
      for($index = 1; $index <= dbase_numrecords($db); $index++)
      {
            $record = dbase_get_record_with_names($db, $index);
            print("<H3>Record $index</H3>\n");

            //loop over fields
            while(list($key, $value) = each($record))
            {
                  print("<B>Field $key: $value</B><BR>\n");
            }
      }

      //close connection
      dbase_close($db);
?>
```

integer dbase_numfields(integer database)

The `dbase_numfields` function returns the number of fields for the given database. See the description of `dbase_get_record` for an example of its use.

integer dbase_numrecords(integer database)

The dbase_numrecords function returns the number of records in the database. See the description of dbase_get_record for an example of its use.

integer dbase_open(string filename, integer mode)

Use dbase_open to get a dbase identifier. This integer is needed for identifying which database to operate on. The mode may be 0 for read-only, 1 for write-only, or 2 for allowing both reading and writing. FALSE is returned if the database cannot be opened. The other examples in this section demonstrate dbase_open.

boolean dbase_pack(integer database)

When rows are deleted in a dbase database, they are simply marked for deletion. Use the dbase_pack function to permanently remove these rows, thus packing the database.

```
<?
        //connect to database
        $db = dbase_open("customer.dbf", 2);

        //removed rows marked for deletion
        dbase_pack($db);

        //close connection
        dbase_close($db);
?>
```

boolean dbase_replace_record(integer database, array record, integer record_number)

Use dbase_replace_record to change the contents of a record. The record argument must have one element for each field defined in the database. Record numbers start counting at one.

```
<?
        $db = dbase_open("customer.dbf", 2);

        $Record = array("John Smith", 200.00, "19990901", "Y");
```

```
        dbase_replace_record($db, $Record, 1);

        dbase_close($db);
?>
```

DBM-style Database Abstraction

The DBA functions abstract communications with databases that conform to the style of Berkeley DB database systems. Rather than storing complex records, a DBM database simply stores key/value pairs. This is similar to an associative array.

The functions in this section replace a set of functions that allow just one type of DBM database. These new functions allow for choosing the underlying system from within your PHP code rather than compiling PHP for a single DBM implementation. You choose a type of database when you open a connection, and the rest of the functions perform accordingly. Sascha Schumann added these functions to PHP.

dba_close(integer link)

The dba_close function closes a link to a database. The link argument is an integer returned by the dba_open or dba_popen functions. If you choose not to close a database connection, PHP will close it for you.

boolean dba_delete(string key, integer link)

The dba_delete function removes an entry from a database. You must supply both the key and a valid link to a database, as supplied by dba_open or dba_popen. The success of the delete is returned as a boolean.

```
<?
        // open database in write mode
        $db = dba_popen('inventory', 'w', 'gdbm');

        if($db)
        {
                //check for record
                if(dba_exists('3', $db))
                {
```

```
                    // remove item 3
                    dba_delete('3', $db);
            }
            else
            {
                    print('Record does not exist');
            }

            // close database
            dba_close($db);
        }
        else
        {
            print('Database does not exist');
        }
    ?>
```

boolean dba_exists(string key, integer link)

The dba_exists function tests for the presence of a key. The link argument must be an integer returned by the dba_open or dba_popen functions. The description of dba_delete has an example of using dba_exists.

string dba_fetch(string key, integer link)

Use the dba_fetch function to retrieve a record.

```
<?
    // open database in write mode
    $db = dba_popen('inventory', 'r', 'gdbm');

    if($db)
    {
        //loop over each record
        for($key = dba_firstkey($db); $key; $key=dba_nextkey($db))
        {
            print("$key = ");

            //fetch this record
            print(dba_fetch($key, $db));

            print("<BR>\n");
        }
    }
```

```
        else
        {
                print('Database does not exist');
        }
?>
```

string dba_firstkey(integer link)

The `dba_firstkey` function returns the first key in the database. If the database is empty, `FALSE` will be returned. As the example for `dba_fetch` shows, `dba_firstkey` and `dba_nextkey` may be used to traverse the entire database.

boolean dba_insert(string key, string value, integer link)

Use `dba_insert` to add a record to the database. The success of the insert is returned. Trying to insert a record that already exists is not allowed. If you need to update a record, use `dba_replace`.

```
<?
    // open database in write mode
    $db = dba_popen('inventory', 'w', 'gdbm');

    if($db)
    {
        //check for record
        if(dba_exists('3', $db))
        {
                //item 3 exists, set inventory to 150
                dba_replace('3', '150', $db);
        }
        else
        {
                //item 3 doesn't exists, insert it
                dba_insert('3', '150', $db);
        }

        // close database
        dba_close($db);
    }
    else
```

```
        {
                print('Database does not exist');
        }
?>
```

string dba_nextkey(integer link)

The `dba_nextkey` function returns the next key from the database. When there are no keys left, `FALSE` is returned. The description of `dba_fetch` shows a typical use of `dba_nextkey` and `dba_firstkey` together.

integer dba_open(string filename, string mode, string type, ...)

Use `dba_open` to establish a link to a dbm-style database. A positive integer will be returned if the open is successful, `FALSE` if it fails. The `filename` argument is simply the path to a database. The `mode` argument can be one of four characters that control input and output of data. Table 13.2 lists the four modes.

The `type` argument chooses the underlying database engine. Table 13.3 describes the four types. You may also supply any number of optional arguments that will be passed directly to the underlying engine.

When your script finishes executing, the database link will close automatically. You may choose to close it sooner with `dba_close`, and this may save some small amount of memory. Contrast this function to `dba_popen`, which attempts to reuse links.

Table 13.2   DBA Open Modes

Mode	Description
c	If the database doesn't exist, it will be created. Reads and writes may be performed.
n	If the database doesn't exist, it will be created. If it does exist, all records will be deleted. Reads and writes may be performed.
r	Only reads may be performed.
w	Reads and writes may be performed. If the file does not exist, an error occurs.

Table 13.3	DBA Database Engine Codes

Code	*Description*
dbm	This code represents the original style of DBM database as developed at Berkeley.
ndbm	This code stands for a newer version of the DBM standard with less restrictions than dbm.
gdbm	The GNU Database Manager is the result of project by GNU. You can download gdbm from the GNU FTP server `<ftp://ftp.gnu.org/gnu/gdbm>`.
db2	This code stands for a database package developed by Sleepycat software that is based on the original Berkeley source code. In fact, the founders wrote the original DBM at Berkeley. You can get more information and download software at their Web site: `<http://www.sleepycat.com/>`.
cdb	CDB is a package for creating constant databases—that is, databases that are read created and read from only. This offers a performance advantage with the tradeoff being that none of the writing functions work. To download the sofware, visit `<ftp://koobera.math.uic.edu/www/cdb.html>`.

boolean dba_optimize(integer link)

Use `dba_optimize` to optimize a database, which usually consists of eliminating gaps between records created by deletes. This function returns TRUE on success. Some underlying engines do not support optimizations, in which case this function will have no effect.

```
<?
        // open database in write mode
        $db = dba_popen('inventory', 'w', 'gdbm');

        if($db)
        {
                //optimize database
                dba_optimize($db);

                // close database
                dba_close($db);
```

```
        }
        else
        {
                print('Database does not exist');
        }
?>
```

integer dba_popen(string filename, string mode, string type, ...)

The dba_popen function behaves identically to dba_open with one difference: Links are not closed. They remain with the process until the process ends. When you call dba_popen, it first tries to find an existing link. Failing that, it will create a new link. You never call dba_close on a link returned by dba_popen.

Since the links are pooled on per-process basis, this functionality offers no benefit when using PHP as a stand-alone executable. When used as an Apache module, there may be some small performance benefit due to the unique way Apache uses child processes.

boolean dba_replace(string key, string value, integer link)

Use dba_replace to update the value of an existing record. As with the other DBA functions, a valid link as returned by dba_open or dba_popen should be used for the link argument. See the description of dba_insert for an example using dba_replace.

boolean dba_sync(integer link)

The dba_sync function will synchronize the view of the database in memory and its image on the disk. As you insert records, they may be cached in memory by the underlying engine. Other processes reading from the database will not see these new records until synchronization.

```
<?
        // open database in write mode
        $db = dba_popen('inventory', 'w', 'gdbm');

        if($db)
        {
```

```
        for($n=1; $n<=10; $n++)
        {
                //insert row
                dba_insert($n, '', $db);

                //synchronize
                dba_sync($db);
        }

        // close database
        dba_close($db);
    }
    else
    {
        print('Database does not exist');
    }
?>
```

filePro

filePro is a relational database by fP Technologies. There are versions for win32 and SCO UNIX. PHP only supports reading from filePro databases. Further information can be found at the filePro Web site <http://www.fptechnologies.com/>. To enable filePro functions dynamically, use the dl function to load the appropriate extension. You can also compile filePro support into the PHP module. Chad Robinson wrote the filePro extension.

boolean filepro(string directory)

The filepro function starts a connection to a map file. Information about the database is stored in memory and used by the other FilePro functions.

```
<?
    //get information about database
    filepro("/fp/store");

    print("<TABLE>");

    //create headers that contain
```

```
        //field names, type, width
        print("<TR>\n");
        for($col=1; $col <= filepro_fieldcount(); $col++)
        {
                print("<TH>");
                print(filepro_fieldname($col));
                print(" ");
                print(filepro_fieldtype($col));
                print(" ");
                print(filepro_fieldwidth($col));
                print("</TH>");
        }
        print("</TR>\n");


        //loop over each row
        for($row=1; $row <= filepro_rowcount(); $row++)
        {
                print("<TR>\n");

                //output fields
                for($col=1; $col <= filepro_fieldcount(); $col++)
                {
                        print("<TD>");
                        print(filepro_retrieve($row, $col));
                        print("</TD>");
                }

                print("</TR>\n");
        }

        print('</TABLE>');

?>
```

integer filepro_fieldcount()

Use `filepro_fieldcount` to find the number of fields. See the `filepro` example above.

string filepro_fieldname(integer field_number)

The `filepro_fieldname` function returns the name of the field for the given field number. See the `filepro` example above.

string filepro_fieldtype(integer field_number)

The `filepro_fieldtype` function returns the edit type for the given field number. See the `filepro` example above.

string filepro_retrieve(integer row, integer field)

The `filepro_retrieve` function returns the value for the specified field on the specified row. See the `filepro` example above.

integer filepro_rowcount()

Use `filepro_rowcount` to find the number of rows. See the `filepro` example above.

integer filepro_fieldwidth(integer field_number)

Use the `filepro_fieldwidth` function to find the width of the specified field. See the `filepro` example above.

Informix

Informix makes several specialized relational database servers for Windows NT and UNIX. Like Oracle and Sybase, Informix products are intended for demanding situations. I can't begin to discuss the unique features of Informix database servers, but you can learn more about them at their home site <http://www.informix.com/>.

PHP includes support for two parts of the Informix API, ODS and IUS. The functions that begin with `ifx_`, such as `ifx_pconnect`, are part of ODS and should be available to you. The IUS functions begin with `ifxus_`, such as `ifxus_create_slob`. These will be available only if you have IUS libraries. Keep in mind that ODBC drivers for Informix are available, so you could pursue using PHP's ODBC functions instead.

Jouni Ahto, Christian Cartus, and Danny Heijl collaborated to create the Informix extension.

integer ifx_affected_rows(integer result)

The `ifx_affected_rows` function returns the number of rows selected, inserted, updated, or deleted, depending on the query. If the query was a select, the number is only an estimate. You can use this function on a result identifier returned by `ifx_prepare` in order to avoid executing queries that will return large result sets.

boolean ifx_blobinfile_mode(integer mode)

Use `ifx_blobinfile` function to control how to work with blobs. If `mode` is 0, blobs are saved in memory. If `mode` is 1, blobs are saved to disk.

boolean ifx_byteasvarchar(integer mode)

Use `ifx_byteasvarchar` to control how byte blobs are returned in queries. If `mode` is 0, blob IDs are returned. If `mode` is 1, blob contents are returned.

boolean ifx_close(integer link)

The `ifx_close` function closes a database connection created by `ifx_connect`. If the optional `link` argument is left out, the last-opened connection is closed.

integer ifx_connect(string database, string user, string password)

The `ifx_connect` function returns a connection to an Informix database. All of the arguments are optional and will draw their values from the `php.ini` file if necessary. If a connection cannot be established, `FALSE` is returned. If you attempt to connect again after successfully connecting, the original connection identifier is returned. The connection will be closed automatically when the script ends, but you can close it manually with `ifx_close`. The `ifx_pconnect` function creates a persistent connection.

integer ifx_copy_blob(integer blob)

The `ifx_copy_blob` function makes a copy of an existing blob and returns the identifier to the new blob.

integer ifx_create_blob(integer type, integer mode, string data)

The `ifx_create_blob` function creates a blob in the database. The `type` argument can be 1 for text or 0 for byte. The `mode` argument is set to 0 if the `data` argument contains data to place in the blob. The mode is set to 1 if the `data` argument is a path to a file.

```
<?
    //connect to database
    if(!($dbLink = ifx_pconnect("mydb@ol_srv1", "leon", "secret"))
    {
        print("Unable to connect!<BR>\n");
        exit();
    }

    //create blob and add to array
    $blob[] = ifx_create_blob(0, 0, "This is a message");

    //insert message
    $Query = "INSERT INTO message " .
        "VALUES (3,'My Title', ?)";

    if(!($result = ifx_query($Query, $dbLink, $blob))
    {
        print("Unable to insert message!<BR>\n");

        //print Informix error message
        print(ifx_error() . "<BR>\n");
        print(ifx_errormsg() . "<BR>\n");
    }

    //free result identifier
    ifx_free_result($result);

    //close connection
    ifx_close($dbLink);
?>
```

integer ifx_create_char(string data)

The `ifx_create_char` function creates a character object. An identifier for the character object is returned.

boolean ifx_do(integer result)

The ifx_do function executes a query prepared with ifx_prepare. The re-sult argument must be as returned by ifx_prepare.

string ifx_error()

Use ifx_error to fetch the error produced by the last query. The first char-acter of the returned string is a flag reporting the type of condition. A space means no error. E is an error. N means no more data is available. W is a warn-ing. A ? signals an unknown error condition. If anything other than a space is returned in the first character, the string will contain extra information, in-cluding an error code.

See ifx_create_blob for an example of use.

string ifx_errormsg(integer error)

Use ifx_errormsg to fetch a description of an error given its code. This is the same numerical code returned by the ifx_error function. If no error code is supplied, the description of the last error is returned.

array ifx_fetch_row(integer result, integer position)
array ifx_fetch_row(integer result, string position)

The ifx_fetch_row function returns a row from a result set after executing a select. The returned array will contain elements named in the query in-dexed by column names. If cursor type was set using IFX_SCROLL, then you may use the position argument. This can be an integer, or one of these strings: FIRST, NEXT, LAST, PREVIOUS, CURRENT. See ifx_prepare for an example of use.

array ifx_fieldproperties(integer result)

The ifx_fieldproperties function returns an array containing informa-tion about each column in a result set. The elements of the array are indexed by the column names. Each element contains a list of properties separated by semicolons. The parts of this string are type, length, precision, scale, and a flag for whether the column can be null. The type is one of the strings listed in `ifx_fieldtypes`, below.

array ifx_fieldtypes(integer result)

The `ifx_fieldtypes` function returns an array describing the type for each column in the result set. Possible values are SQLBOOL, SQLBYTES, SQLCHAR, SQLDATE, SQLDECIMAL, SQLDTIME, SQLFLOAT, SQLINT, SQLINT8, SQLINTERVAL, SQLLVARCHAR, SQLMONEY, SQLNCHAR, SQL-NVCHAR, SQLSERIAL, SQLSERIAL8, SQLSMFLOAT, SQLSMINT, SQLTEXT, SQLUDTFIXED, SQLVCHAR. The returned array is indexed by the names of the columns.

boolean ifx_free_blob(integer blob)

The `ifx_free_blob` function deletes the specified blob from the database.

boolean ifx_free_char(integer character)

The `ifx_free_char` function deletes a character object from the database.

boolean ifx_free_result(integer result)

The `ifx_free_result` function frees memory associated with a result set. See `ifx_pconnect` for an example of use.

string ifx_get_blob(integer blob)

The `ifx_get_blob` function returns the contents of a blob.

string ifx_get_char(integer character)

The `ifx_get_char` function returns the contents of a character object.

array ifx_getsqlca(integer result)

The `ifx_getsqlca` function returns an array of the values in the `sqlerrd` struct from the underlying Informix API.

integer ifx_htmltbl_result(integer result, string options)

The `ifx_htmltbl_result` function prints an HTML table containing all the rows in the result set. The optional `options` argument will be placed inside the table tag. See `ifx_pconnect` for an example of use.

boolean ifx_nullformat(integer mode)

When mode is 0, `ifx_nullformat` will cause all null columns to be returned as empty strings. If mode is 1, they are returned as NULL, a four-character string.

integer ifx_num_fields(integer result)

The `ifx_num_fields` function returns the number of columns in the result set.

integer ifx_num_rows(integer result)

Use `ifx_num_rows` to get the exact number of rows already fetched for a result set. To get an approximate number of rows in a result set, use `ifx_affected_rows`.

integer ifx_pconnect(string database, string user, string password)

The `ifx_pconnect` function is similar to `ifx_connect`, except that connections are not closed until the Web server process ends. Persistent links remain available for subsequent connection attempts by other scripts.

```
<?
    //connect to database
    if(!($dbLink = ifx_pconnect("mydb@ol_srv1", "leon", "secret"))
    {
        print("Unable to connect!<BR>\n");
        exit();
    }
```

```
        //treat blobs as varchars
        ifx_textasvarchar(TRUE);

        //get a record from the message table
        $Query = "SELECT Title, Body FROM message " .
                "WHERE ID = 3 ";
        if(!($result = ifx_query($Query, $dbLink))
        {
                print("Unable to query message table!<BR>\n");
        }

        //print results in HTML table
        ifx_htmltbl_result($result);

        //free result identifier
        ifx_free_result($dbLink);

        //close connection
        ifx_close($dbLink);
?>
```

integer ifx_prepare(string query, integer link, integer cursor_type, array blob_id)

The ifx_prepare function parses a query but does not execute it. Otherwise it operates identically to ifx_query, described below. To execute the query, use ifx_do.

```
<?
        //connect to database
        if(!($dbLink = ifx_pconnect("mydb@ol_srv1", "leon", "secret"))
        {
                print("Unable to connect!<BR>\n");
                exit();
        }

        //get message about PHP
        $Query = "SELECT ID, Title FROM message " .
                "WHERE Title like '%PHP%' ";
        if(!($result = ifx_prepare($Query, $dbLink, IFX_SCROLL))
        {
                print("Unable to query message table!<BR>\n");
```

```
        }

        if(ifx_affectedrows($result) < 100)
        {
                //execute query
                ifx_do($result);

                //fetch each row, print a link
                while($row = ifx_fetch_row($result, "NEXT"))
                {
                        print("<A HREF=\"get.php?id={$row["ID"]}\">");
                        print("{$row["Title"]}</A><BR>\n");
                }
        }
        else
        {
                print("Too many results to display on one page.<BR>\n");
        }

        //free result identifier
        ifx_free_result($dbLink);

        //close connection
        ifx_close($dbLink);
?>
```

integer ifx_query(string query, integer link, integer cursor_type, array blob_id)

The `ifx_query` function executes a query and returns a result identifier, which most of the other Informix functions require. The `link` argument is as returned by `ifx_pconnect`, but if you leave it out, the last link established will be used. If the query is a select, you may use the `IFX_SCROLL` and `IFX_HOLD` constants for the cursor type.

If performing an update or insert, you may use a `?` in the query and match it to an entry in the `blob_id` argument. Each entry must be a value returned by `ifx_create_blob`. Selects that return blob columns will return blob identifiers by default, but you can override this functionality with `ifx_textasvarchar`.

Note that both `cursor_type` and `blob_id` are optional. The `ifx_query` function will allow you to specify an array of blob identifiers for the third argument. See `ifx_create_blob` for an example of use.

boolean ifx_textasvarchar(integer mode)

Use `ifx_textasvarchar` to control how text blobs are returned in queries. If `mode` is 0, blob IDs are returned. If `mode` is 1, blob contents are returned. See `ifx_pconnect` for an example of use.

boolean ifx_update_blob(integer blob, string data)

The `ifx_update_blob` function changes the contents of a blob.

boolean ifx_update_char(integer character, string data)

The `ifx_update_char` function changes the contents of a character object.

ifxus_close_slob

You can use `ifxus_close_slob` as an alias for `ifxus_free_slob`.

integer ifxus_create_slob(integer mode)

Use `ifxus_create_slob` to create a slob object. The object identifier is returned. The modes listed in Table 13.4 may be combined with | operators.

Table 13.4 Informix Slob Modes	
Value	*Informix API Constant*
1	LO_RDONLY
2	LO_WRONLY
4	LO_APPEND
8	LO_RDWR
16	LO_BUFFER
32	LO_NOBUFFER

boolean ifxus_free_slob(integer slob)

The `ifxus_free_slob` function deletes a slob object.

integer ifxus_open_slob(integer slob, integer mode)

Use `ifxus_open_slob` to get an identifier for an existing slob object. The modes listed in Table 13.4 may be combined with | operators.

string ifxus_read_slob(integer slob, integer bytes)

The `ifxus_read_slob` function returns data from the specified slob object. The `bytes` argument specifies the number of bytes to return.

integer ifxus_seek_slob(integer slob, integer mode, integer offset)

The `ifxus_seek_slob` function moves the current cursor position within a slob object. The `mode` argument controls where the offset is applied. If `mode` is 0, `offset` is applied to the beginning. If `mode` is 1, `offset` is applied to the current position. If `mode` is 2, `offset` is applied to the end of the slob object.

integer ifxus_tell_slob(integer slob)

The `ifxus_tell_slob` function returns the current position of a cursor inside a slob object.

integer ifxus_write_slob(integer slob, string data)

The `ifxus_write_slob` function writes data to an open slob object. The number of bytes written is returned.

InterBase

InterBase is a full-featured database that spent much of its life as closed-source and proprietary. In January 2000, Inprise released InterBase under an open source license, allowing everyone access to the source code. Inter-

Base is the first opensource database to be compliant with the SQL 92 standard. Under commercial development for more than 16 years, InterBase compares favorably to Oracle, Sybase, and IBM's DB2. This section discusses the PHP functions for communicating with InterBase, but a tutorial on InterBase itself is out of scope. Apart from the extensive documentation on the InterBase site `<http://www.interbase.com/>`, you may find useful information in books about Borland's C++ compiler or Delphi.

InterBase support was added to PHP by Jouni Ahto. Later work was done by Andrew Avdeev and Ivo Panacek. At the time of writing, InterBase functions in PHP were not complete, but the recent change in licensing will probably encourage developers. You also have the option of using the ODBC functions.

boolean ibase_blob_add(integer blob, string data)

The `ibase_blob_add` function adds data to a blob. You must create the blob first with `ibase_blob_create`.

boolean ibase_blob_cancel(integer blob)

Use `ibase_blob_cancel` to discard a blob you have created with `ibase_blob_create`.

boolean ibase_blob_close(integer blob)

The `ibase_blob_close` function writes changes made to a blob to the database.

integer ibase_blob_create(integer link)

The `ibase_blob_create` function creates a new blob. The `link` argument is optional and will default to the last-opened connection. A blob identifier is returned.

boolean ibase_blob_echo(string blob)

The `ibase_blob_echo` function prints the contents of the named blob to the browser.

string ibase_blob_get(integer blob, integer bytes)

Use `ibase_blob_get` to get the specified number of bytes from a blob.

integer ibase_blob_import(integer file)
integer ibase_blob_import(integer link, integer file)

The `ibase_blob_import` function creates a blob and places the contents of an open file into it. The file argument must be a file identifier as returned by `fopen`. You may call `ibase_blob_import` with or without an open link. The file is closed after the import. The blob identifier is returned.

object ibase_blob_info(string blob)

Use `ibase_blob_info` to get information about a blob. An object is returned with the following properties: `isnull`, `length`, `maxseg`, `numseg`, `stream`.

integer ibase_blob_open(string blob)

Use `ibase_blob_open` to get a blob identifier for an existing blob.

boolean ibase_close(integer link)

Use `ibase_close` to close a connection created by `ibase_connect`. If a link is not specified, the last opened link will be closed. The default transaction will be committed, and other transactions will be rolled back.

boolean ibase_commit(integer link)

The `ibase_commit` function commits the default transaction on the specified link, or the last link if none is specified.

integer ibase_connect(string path, string user, string password)

Use `ibase_connect` to connect to an InterBase database. You must specify a path to database file. The `user` and `password` arguments may be omitted.

They default to those set in `php.ini` using the `ibase.default_user` and `ibase.default_password` directives.

A connection identifier is returned that is used by most of the other functions in this section. When the script ends, the connection will be closed for you, but you can close it manually with `ibase_close`. A second connection attempt to the same database as the same user will return the same connection identifier.

Compare this function to `ibase_pconnect`.

string ibase_errmsg()

Use `ibase_errmsg` to get the last error message. `FALSE` is returned when no error message is available.

integer ibase_execute(integer query, value bind, …)

Use `ibase_excute` to execute a query prepared with `ibase_prepare`. If the query contained ? placeholders, you must supply matching bind values following the query identifier. A result identifier is returned if executing a select query.

object ibase_fetch_object(integer result, integer blob)

The `ibase_fetch_object` function returns an object that contains a property for each column in the next result row. The name of the property will match the name of the column. The `blob` argument is optional. If set to `IBASE_TEXT`, blob columns will be returned as text. Otherwise the blob identifier is returned. `FALSE` is returned when no rows remain.

array ibase_fetch_row(integer result, integer blob)

The `ibase_fetch_row` function operates identically to `ibase_fetch_object` except that an array is returned. Instead of being referenced by name, columns are referenced by number, starting with 0.

array ibase_field_info(integer result, integer field)

Use `ibase_field_info` to get information about a column in a result set. An associative array is returned containing the following elements: `alias`, `length`, `name`, `relation`, `type`.

boolean ibase_free_query(integer query)

Use `ibase_free_query` to free memory associated with a prepared query.

boolean ibase_free_result(integer result)

Use `ibase_free_result` to free memory associated with a result set.

integer ibase_num_fields(integer result)

The `ibase_num_fields` function returns the number of fields in a result set.

ibase_pconnect(string path, string user, string password, string character_set)

The `ibase_pconnect` function works similarly to `ibase_connect`. The difference is that connections are not closed by PHP or by your script. They persist with the server process to be reused when later script executions need identical connections.

integer ibase_prepare(string query)
integer ibase_prepare(integer link, string query)

Use `ibase_prepare` to prepare a query for later execution with `ibase_execute`. If you leave out the `link` argument, the last-opened link will be used. A query identifier is returned.

integer ibase_query(string query, value bind, ...)
integer ibase_query(integer link, string query, value bind, ...)

The `ibase_query` function executes a query on an open connection. You may skip the link identifier, causing the last-opened connection to be used. If the query contains ? placeholders, you must match them with bind values

that follow the `query` argument. A result identifier is returned. It is used
with functions such as `ibase_fetch_row`.

```
<?
    //connect to database
    if(!($dbLink = ibase_connect("mydatabase.gdb", "leon", "secret"))
    {
        print("Unable to connect!<BR>\n");
        exit();
    }

    //begin transaction
    $dbTran = ibase_trans(IBASE_DEFAULT, $dbLink);

    //insert a message using bind parameters
    $Query = "INSERT INTO message " .
        "VALUES (?, ?, ?) ";

    if(!($result = ibase_query($dbLink, $Query, $inputID, $inputTi-
    tle, $inputBody))
    {
        print("Unable to insert row!<BR>\n");
        exit();
    }

    //release memory
    ibase_free_result($result);


    //dump table
    print("<TABLE BORDER=\"1\">\n");
    $Query = "SELECT * FROM message ";

    if(!($result = ibase_query($dbLink, $Query))
    {
        print("Unable to query table!<BR>\n");
        exit();
    }

    //print headers
    print("<TR>\n");
    for($i=0; $i<ibase_num_fields($result); $i++)
    {
        $info = ibase_field_info($result, $i);
        print("<TH>{$info["name"]}</TH>\n");
```

```
        }
        print("</TR>\n");

        //get all rows
        while($row = ibase_fetch_row($result))
        {
                print("<TR>\n");
                for($i=0; $i<ibase_num_fields($result); $i++)
                {
                        print("<TD>$row[$i]</TD>\n");
                }
                print("</TR>\n");
        }

        print("</TABLE>\n");

        //release memory
        ibase_free_result($result);

        //commit transaction
        ibase_commit($dbTran);

        //close connection
        ibase_close($dbLink);
?>
```

boolean ibase_rollback(integer link)

The ibase_rollback function causes a transaction to roll back. The default transaction on the specified link is rolled back. The last link will be used if none is specified.

boolean ibase_timefmt(string format)

Use ibase_timefmt to set the format for datetime columns. The format string should follow the rules of strftime. The default format is "%m/%d/%Y %H:%M:%S". The strftime function is described in Chapter 11, "Time, Date, and Configuration Functions."

integer ibase_trans(integer flags, integer link)

The ibase_trans function returns a transaction identifier. The flags can be any combination of the constants listed in Table 13.5. Use | to combine

Table 13.5	InterBase Constants

IBASE_COMMITED

IBASE_CONSISTENCY

IBASE_DEFAULT

IBASE_NOWAIT

IBASE_READ

IBASE_TEXT

IBASE_TIMESTAMP

them. IBASE_DEFAULT matches InterBase read, write, snapshot, and wait properties. The link argument is optional. The last connection established will be used if it's left out.

mSQL

The functions in this section communicate with mSQL, a database that implements a subset of SQL. The official site is at <http://www.hughes.com.au/>. A site supporting Windows versions of mSQL is at <http://blnet.com/msqlpc/>.

There are a handful of mSQL functions that exist simply for backward compatibility. I have chosen to leave them out. Only some of them are documented in the official PHP 3 manual. Their use is described in the PHP 2 documentation. For reference they are msql, msql_createdb, msql_db-name, msql_dropdb, msql_freeresult, msql_listdbs, msql_list-fields, msql_listtables, msql_numfields, msql_numrows, msql_selectdb, msql_tablename.

Two mSQL extensions exist, one for mSQL version 1 and one for version 2. You must load the appropriate extension to enable the functions in this section. Zeev Suraski wrote both mSQL extensions.

integer msql_affected_rows(integer link)

The msql_affected_rows function returns the number of rows involved in the previous query made on the given link. The link argument must be an integer returned by `msql_connect` or `msql_pconnect`. For an example of use, see `msql_db_query`, below.

boolean msql_close(integer link)

The `msql_close` function closes the link to a database. If the link argument is left out, the last-opened link is closed. Only links opened by `msql_connect` may be closed. Using this function is not strictly necessary, since all nonpersistent links are automatically closed when a script ends. For an example of use, see `msql_db_query`, below.

integer msql_connect(string host, string username, string password)

The `msql_connect` function attempts to connect to the mSQL server at the specified host. If the host argument is left out, the local host will be assumed. A link identifier is returned. In the case where an open link exists, it will be returned rather than establishing a second link. The connection is automatically closed at the end of the script.

You may add a colon and a port number to the `host` argument.

boolean msql_create_db(string database, integer link)

The `msql_create_db` function attempts to create a database. The `link` argument is optional. If left out, the last-opened link will be used.

```
<?
    $Link = msql_connect("msql.clearink.com");
    msql_create_db("store", $Link);
    msql_close($Link);
?>
```

boolean msql_data_seek(integer result, integer row)

Use `msql_data_seek` to move the internal row pointer to the specified row in a result set. The `result` argument is as returned by `msql_query`.

```
<?
        $Link = msql_connect("msql.clearink.com");
        msql_select_db("store", $Link);

        $Result = msql_query("SELECT Name FROM customer", $Link);

        // jump to tenth customer
        msql_data_seek($Result, 10);

        $Row = msql_fetch_row($Result);

        print($Row[0]);

        msql_close($Link);
?>
```

integer msql_db_query(string database, string query, integer link)

The msql_db_query function is identical to msql_query except that it specifies a database rather than using the database selected with msql_select_db. The query is executed in the specified database and a result identifier is returned.

```
<?
        $Link = msql_connect("msql.clearink.com");
        $Query = "DELETE FROM customer";
        $Result = msql_db_query("store", $Query, $Link);

        $RowsAffected = msql_affected_rows($Link);
        print($RowsAffected . " rows deleted.");

        msql_close($Link);
?>
```

boolean msql_drop_db(string database, integer link)

The msql_drop_db function removes an entire database from the server. The link argument is optional and, if omitted, the last connection opened will be used.

```
<?
    $Link = msql_connect("msql.clearink.com");

    if(msql_drop_db("store", $Link))
    {
        print("Database deleted!");
    }
    else
    {
        print("Database not deleted: ");
        print(msql_error());
    }

    msql_close($Link);
?>
```

string msql_error()

Use `msql_error` to retrieve the last error message returned by an mSQL function. See `msql_drop_db`, above, for an example of use.

array msql_fetch_array(integer result, integer type)

The `msql_fetch_array` function returns an array of the data for the current row. The `result` argument is as returned by `msql_query`. By default, result columns are returned in two elements each: one referenced by number and one referenced by field name. The optional `type` argument controls which elements are created. `MSQL_NUM` signals that only numbered elements be created. `MSQL_ASSOC` signals that only named elements be created. If you want both, you can explicitly request it with `MSQL_BOTH`.

Compare this function to `msql_fetch_row` and `msql_fetch_object`.

```
<?
    $Link = msql_connect("msql.clearink.com");
    msql_select_db("store", $Link);

    $Query = "SELECT * FROM customer";
    $Result = msql_query($Query, $Link);

    //fetch each row
    while($Row = msql_fetch_array($Result, MSQL_ASSOC))
    {
        print($Row["FirstName"] . "<BR>\n");
    }
```

```
        msql_close($Link);
?>
```

object msql_fetch_field(integer result, integer field)

The `msql_fetch_field` function returns an object with properties that describe the specified field. The `field` argument may be left out, and the next unfetched field will be returned. The properties of the object are listed in Table 13.6.

```
<?
        $Link = msql_connect("msql.clearink.com");
        msql_select_db("store", $Link);

        $Query = "SELECT * FROM item i, SKU s ";
        $Query .= "WHERE i.SKU = s.ID ";
        $Result = msql_query($Query, $Link);

        // get description of each field
        while($Field = msql_fetch_field($Result))
        {
                print("Name: " . $Field->name . "<BR>\n");
                print("Table: " . $Field->table . "<BR>\n");
                print("Not Null: " . $Field->not_null . "<BR>\n");
                print("Primary Key: " . $Field->primary_key "<BR>\n");
                print("Unique: " . $Field->unique . "<BR>\n");
                print("Type: " . $Field->type . "<BR>\n<BR>\n");
        }

        msql_close($Link);
?>
```

Table 13.6   Properties of `msql_fetch_field` **Object**

Property	Description
name	Name of the column
not_null	TRUE if the column cannot be null
primary_key	TRUE if the column is a primary key
table	Name of the table the column is from
type	Datatype of the column
unique	TRUE if the column is a unique key

object msql_fetch_object(integer result)

The `msql_fetch_object` function returns an object with a property for each column of the resulting row. Each call to `msql_fetch_object` gets the next row from the results, or returns FALSE when there are none left.

```
<?
        $Link = msql_connect("msql.clearink.com");
        msql_select_db("store", $Link);

        $Query = "SELECT * FROM item";
        $Result = msql_query($Query, $Link);

        while($Row = msql_fetch_object($Result))
        {
                print("$Row->ID: $Row->Name<BR>\n");
        }

        msql_close($Link);
?>
```

array msql_fetch_row(integer result)

The `msql_fetch_row` function returns an array with one element for each resulting column. FALSE is returned when no results are left. Columns are referenced by integers starting at zero. Compare this function to `msql_fetch_array` and `msql_fetch_object`.

```
<?
        $Link = msql_connect("msql.clearink.com");
        msql_select_db("store", $Link);

        $Query = "SELECT * FROM item";
        $Result = msql_query($Query, $Link);

        while($Row = msql_fetch_row($Result))
        {
                print($Row[0] . ": " . $Row[1] . "<BR>\n");
        }

        msql_close($Link);
?>
```

boolean msql_field_seek(integer result, integer field)

Use `msql_field_seek` to move the internal field pointer to the specified field.

```
<?
    $Link = msql_connect("msql.clearink.com");
    msql_select_db("store", $Link);

    $Query = "SELECT * FROM item i, SKU s ";
    $Query .= "WHERE i.SKU = s.ID ";
    $Result = msql_query($Query, $Link);

    // get description of each field
    // starting with the third
    msql_field_seek($Result, 2);

    while($Field = msql_fetch_field($Result))
    {
        print("Name: " . $Field->name . "<BR>\n");
        print("Table: " . $Field->table . "<BR>\n");
        print("Not Null: " . $Field->not_null ."<BR>\n");
        print("Primary Key: " . $Field->primary_key "<BR>\n");
        print("Unique: " . $Field->unique . "<BR>\n");
        print("Type: " . $Field->type . "<BR>\n<BR>\n");
    }

    msql_close($Link);
?>
```

string msql_fieldflags(integer result, integer field)

The `msql_fieldflags` function returns all the flags turned on for the specified field. These may be primary key, unique, and not null.

```
<?
    $Link = msql_connect("msql.clearink.com");
    msql_select_db("store", $Link);

    $Query = "SELECT * FROM item";
    $Result = msql_query($Query, $Link);
```

```
        print("Field 0 flags are " . msql_fieldflags($Result, 0));

        msql_close($Link);
?>
```

integer msql_fieldlen(integer result, integer field)

The `msql_fieldlen` function returns the length of the specified field.

```
<?
        $Link = msql_connect("msql.clearink.com");
        msql_select_db("store", $Link);

        $Query = "SELECT * FROM item";
        $Result = msql_query($Query, $Link);

        print("Field 0 length is " . msql_fieldlen($Result, 0));

        msql_close($Link);
?>
```

string msql_fieldname(integer result, integer field)

The `msql_fieldname` function returns the name of the specified field.

```
<?
        $Link = msql_connect("msql.clearink.com");
        msql_select_db("store", $Link);

        $Query = "SELECT * FROM item";
        $Result = msql_query($Query, $Link);

        print("Field 0 is " . msql_fieldname($Result, 0));

        msql_close($Link);
?>
```

string msql_fieldtable(integer result, integer field)

The `msql_fieldtable` function returns the name of the table for the specified field.

```
<?
        $Link = msql_connect("msql.clearink.com");
        msql_select_db("store", $Link);

        $Query = "SELECT * FROM item";
        $Result = msql_query($Query, $Link);

        print("Field 0 is from " . msql_fieldtable($Result, 0));

        msql_close($Link);
?>
```

string msql_fieldtype(integer result, integer field)

The `msql_fieldtype` function returns the type of the specified field.

```
<?
        $Link = msql_connect("msql.clearink.com");
        msql_select_db("store", $Link);

        $Query = "SELECT * FROM item";
        $Result = msql_query($Query, $Link);

        print("Field 0 is " . msql_fieldtype($Result, 0));

        msql_close($Link);
?>
```

boolean msql_free_result(integer result)

When a script ends, all results are freed. If memory is a concern while your script is running, use `msql_free_result`.

```
<?
        $Link = msql_connect("msql.clearink.com");
        msql_select_db("store", $Link);

        $Query = "INSERT INTO store VALUES (0, 'Martinez')";
        $Result = msql_query($Query, $Link);

        msql_free_result($Result);

        msql_close($Link);
?>
```

integer msql_list_dbs(integer link)

The `msql_list_dbs` function returns a result identifier as if the database were queried with `msql_query`. Any of the functions for fetching rows or fields may be used to get the names of the databases. The `link` argument is optional. If left out, the last-opened connection will be used.

```
<?
        $Link = msql_connect("msql.clearink.com");
        msql_select_db("store", $Link);

        $Result = msql_list_dbs($Link);
        while($row_array = msql_fetch_row($Result))
        {
                print($row_array[0] . "<BR>\n");
        }

        msql_close($Link);
?>
```

integer msql_list_fields(string database, string tablename, integer link)

The `msql_list_fields` function returns a result identifier as if the database were queried with `msql_query`. Any of the functions for fetching rows or fields may be used to get the names of the fields. The `link` argument is optional. If left out, the last-opened connection will be used.

```
<?
        $Link = msql_connect("msql.clearink.com");
        msql_select_db("store", $Link);

        $Result = msql_list_fields("store", "item", $Link);
        while($row_array = msql_fetch_row($Result))
        {
                print($row_array[0] . "<BR>\n");
        }

        msql_close($Link);
?>
```

integer msql_list_tables(string database, integer link)

The msql_list_tables function returns a result identifier as if the database were queried with msql_query. Any of the functions for fetching rows or fields may be used to get the names of the fields. The link argument is optional. If left out, the last-opened connection will be used.

```
<?
        $Link = msql_connect("msql.clearink.com");
        msql_select_db("store", $Link);

        $Result = msql_list_tables("store", $Link);
        while($row_array = msql_fetch_row($Result))
        {
                print($row_array[0] . "<BR>\n");
        }

        msql_close($Link);
?>
```

integer msql_num_fields(integer result)

Use msql_num_fields to get the number of fields in a result set.

```
<?
        $Link = msql_connect("msql.clearink.com");
        msql_select_db("store", $Link);

        $Query = "SELECT * FROM item i, SKU s ";
        $Query .= "WHERE i.SKU = s.ID ";
        $Result = msql_query($Query, $Link);

        print(msql_num_fields($Result));

        msql_close($Link);
?>
```

integer msql_num_rows(integer result)

The msql_num_rows function returns the number of rows in the result set.

```
<?
        $Link = msql_connect("msql.clearink.com");
        msql_select_db("store", $Link);

        $Query = "SELECT * FROM item i, SKU s ";
        $Query .= "WHERE i.SKU = s.ID ";
        $Result = msql_query($Query, $Link);

        print(msql_num_rows($Result));

        msql_close($Link);
?>
```

integer msql_pconnect(string host)

The msql_pconnect function is identical to the msql_connect function except that the connection will not be closed when the script ends. This has meaning only when PHP is compiled as an Apache module. These are called persistent links because they live as long as the server process.

```
<?
        $Link = msql_pconnect("localhost");
?>
```

integer msql_query(string query, integer link)

Use msql_query to execute a query. The database used will be the one specified in a call to the msql_select_db function. The link argument is optional. The last connection made will be used if it is left out.

msql_regcase

This is an alias to sql_regcase, described in Chapter 9, "Data Functions."

string msql_result(integer result, integer row, string field)

The msql_result function returns a single field value for the given row. The field argument can be interpreted in two ways. If it is a number, it will be used as a field offset, starting with zero. Otherwise, it will be considered to be a column name.

The `msql_result` function is relatively slow. Its use should be avoided in favor of faster functions such as `msql_fetch_array`.

```
<?
        $Link = msql_connect("msql.clearink.com");
        msql_select_db("store", $Link);

        $Query = "SELECT * FROM item i, SKU s ";
        $Query .= "WHERE i.SKU = s.ID ";
        $Result = msql_query($Query, $Link);

        $numRows = msql_num_rows($Result);

        for($index = 0; $index < $numRows; $index++)
        {
                $item_ID = msql_result($Result, $index, "item.ID");
                $item_Name = msql_result($Result, $index, "item.Name");

                print("$item_ID: $item_Name<BR>\n");
        }

        msql_close($Link);
?>
```

boolean msql_select_db(string database, integer link)

Use `msql_select_db` to select the database against which to make queries. As with most other mSQL functions, the link identifier is not required.

MySQL

MySQL is a relational database with a license that allows you to use it cost-free for most noncommercial purposes. It shares many features with mSQL because it was originally conceived as a faster, more flexible replacement. Indeed, MySQL has delivered on these goals. It easily outperforms even commercial databases. Not surprisingly, MySQL is the database of choice for many PHP developers.

To find out more about MySQL, as well as obtain source code and binaries, visit the Web site at `<http://www.mysql.com/>`. There are plenty of mirrors to aid your download speed. Be sure to check out the excellent on-line manual.

As with mSQL, there were MySQL functions in PHP2 that are still supported in PHP3, but their use is discouraged. I've chosen to leave these functions out of the reference. The functions I've left out are mysql, mysql_createdb, mysql_dbname, mysql_dropdb, mysql_fieldflags, mysql_fieldlen, mysql_fieldname, mysql_fieldtable, mysql_fieldtype, mysql_freeresult, mysql_listdbs, mysql_listfields, mysql_listtables, mysql_numfields, mysql_numrows, mysql_selectdb, mysql_tablename.

The MySQL extension was written by Zeev Suraski.

integer mysql_affected_rows(integer link)

The mysql_affected_rows function returns the number of rows affected by the last query made to the specified database connection link. If the link argument is omitted, the last-opened connection is assumed. If the last query was an unconditional delete, zero will be returned. If you want to know how many rows were returned by a select statement, use mysql_num_rows.

```
<?
    //connect to server as freetrade user, no password
    $dbLink = mysql_pconnect("localhost", "freetrade", "");

    //select the 'freetrade' database
    mysql_select_db("freetrade", $dbLink);

    //update some invoices
    $Query = "UPDATE invoice " .
        "SET Active = 'Y' " .
        "WHERE ID < 100 ";
    $dbResult = mysql_query($Query, $dbLink);

    //let user know how many rows were updated
    $AffectedRows = mysql_affected_rows($dbLink);
    print("$AffectedRows rows updated.<BR>\n");
?>
```

boolean mysql_change_user(string user, string password, string database, integer link)

Use mysql_change_user to change the user for a database connection. The database and link arguments are optional. If left out, the current database and the link last opened are used. If the user cannot be changed, the current connection remains open with the original user. This function requires MySQL version 3.23.3 or newer.

```
<?
        //connect to server as freetrade user, no password
        $dbLink = mysql_pconnect("localhost", "freetrade", "");

        //select the 'freetrade' database
        mysql_select_db("freetrade", $dbLink);

        //switch to admin user
        mysql_change_user("admin", "secret", "freetrade", $dbLink);
?>
```

boolean mysql_close(integer link)

Use `mysql_close` to close the connection to a database. The connect must have been opened with `mysql_connect`. Use of this function is not strictly necessary, as all nonpersistent links are closed automatically when the script finishes. The `link` argument is optional, and when it's left out, the connection last opened is closed.

```
<?
        // open connection
        $Link = mysql_connect("localhost", "httpd", "");

        // close connection
        mysql_close($Link);
?>
```

integer mysql_connect(string host, string user, string password)

The `mysql_connect` function begins a connection to a MySQL database at the specified host. If the database is on a different port, follow the hostname with a colon and a port number. You may alternatively supply a colon and the path to a socket if connecting to localhost. This might be written as `local-host:/tmp/sockets/mysql`. All the arguments are optional and will default to localhost, the name of the user executing the script, and an empty string, respectively. The user executing the script is typically httpd, the Web server.

Connections are automatically closed when a script finishes execution, though they may be closed earlier with `mysql_close`. If you attempt to open a connection that is already open, a second connection will not be made. The identifier of the previously open connection will be returned.

FALSE is returned in the event of an error.

```
<?

//establish connection
if(!($dbLink = mysql_connect("localhost:3606", "freetrade", "")))
{
        print("mysql_connect failed!<BR>\n");
}

//select database
if(!(mysql_select_db("freetrade", $dbLink)))
{
        print("mysql_select_db failed!<BR>\n");
        print(mysql_errno() . ": ");
        print(mysql_error() . "<BR>\n");
}
?>
```

boolean mysql_create_db(string database, integer link)

Use mysql_create_db to create a new database. Note that you must open a connection with an account that has permission to create databases. If you leave out the link argument, the last-opened connection will be used.

```
<?
        // open connection
        $dbLink = mysql_connect("localhost", "admin", "secret");

        //create database
        mysql_create_db("garbage", $dbLink);
?>
```

boolean mysql_data_seek(integer result, integer row)

The mysql_data_seek function moves the internal row pointer of a result set to the specified row. Use this function with mysql_fetch_row to jump to a specific row. The result argument must have been returned from mysql_query or a similar function.

```
<?
      //connect to server as freetrade user, no password
      $dbLink = mysql_pconnect("localhost", "freetrade", "");

      //select the 'freetrade' database
      mysql_select_db("freetrade", $dbLink);

      //get states from tax table
      $Query = "SELECT State " .
           "FROM tax ";
      $dbResult = mysql_query($Query, $dbLink);

      //jump to fifth row
      mysql_data_seek($dbResult, 4);

      //get row
      $row = mysql_fetch_row($dbResult);

      //print state name
      print($row[0]);
?>
```

integer mysql_db_query(string database, string query, integer link)

The mysql_db_query function executes a query on the specified database and returns a result identifier. If the link argument is omitted, the last-opened link will be used, or a new one will be created if necessary.

```
<?
      //connect to server as freetrade user, no password
      $dbLink = mysql_pconnect("localhost", "freetrade", "");

      //truncate session table
      $Query = "DELETE FROM session ";
      $dbResult = mysql_db_query("freetrade", $Query, $dbLink);
?>
```

boolean mysql_drop_db(string database, integer link)

Use mysql_drop_db to delete a database. If the link argument is omitted, the last-opened link will be used.

```
<?
        //open connection
        $dbLink = mysql_connect("localhost", "admin", "secret");

        //drop garbage database
        if(mysql_drop_db("garbage", $dbLink))
        {
                print("Database dropped.<BR>");
        }
        else
        {
                print("Database drop failed!<BR>");
        }
?>
```

integer mysql_errno(integer link)

The mysql_errno function returns the error number of the last database action. If the optional link identifier is left out, the last connection will be assumed.

```
<?
        //connect to server as freetrade user, no password
        $dbLink = mysql_pconnect("localhost", "freetrade", "");

        //select the 'freetrade' database
        mysql_select_db("freetrade", $dbLink);

        //try to execute a bad query (missing fields)
        $Query = "SELECT FROM tax ";
        if(!($dbResult = mysql_query($Query, $dbLink)))
        {
                // get error and error number
                $errno = mysql_errno($dbLink);
                $error = mysql_error($dbLink);

                print("ERROR $errno: $error<BR>\n");
        }
?>
```

string mysql_error(integer link)

Use mysql_error to get the textual description of the error for the last database action. If the optional link identifier is left out, the last connection will be assumed.

array mysql_fetch_array(integer result, integer type)

The `mysql_fetch_array` function returns an array that represents all the fields for a row in the result set. Each call produces the next row until no rows are left, in which case `FALSE` is returned. By default, each field value is stored twice: once indexed by offset starting at zero and once indexed by the name of the field. This behavior can be controlled with the `type` argument. If the `MYSQL_NUM` constant is used, elements will be indexed by field numbers only. If the `MYSQL_ASSOC` constant is used, elements will be index by field names only. You can also use `MYSQL_BOTH` to force the default.

Compare this function to `mysql_fetch_object` and `mysql_fetch_row`.

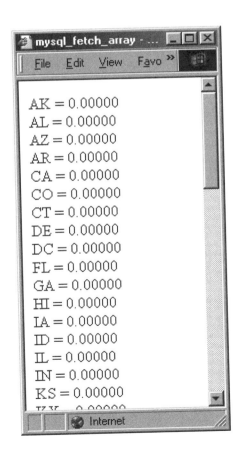

Figure 13-1 `mysql_fetch_array.`

```
<?
    //connect to server as freetrade user, no password
    $dbLink = mysql_pconnect("localhost", "freetrade", "");

    //select the 'freetrade' database
    mysql_select_db("freetrade", $dbLink);

    //get rates from tax table
    $Query = "SELECT State, Rate " .
        "FROM tax ";
    $dbResult = mysql_query($Query, $dbLink);

    // get each row
    while($row = mysql_fetch_array($dbResult, MYSQL_ASSOC))
    {
        // print state and rate
        print("{$row["State"]} = {$row["Rate"]}<BR>\n");
    }
?>
```

Figure 13–1   Continued

object mysql_fetch_field(integer result, integer field)

Use the `mysql_fetch_field` function to get information about a field in a result set. Fields are numbered starting with zero. The return value is an object with properties described in Table 13.7.

If the `field` argument is left out, the next field in the set will be returned. This behavior allows you to loop through each field easily.

Table 13.7   Properties of `mysql_fetch_field` Object

Property	Description
blob	TRUE if the column is a blob
max_length	Maximum length
multiple_key	TRUE if the column is a nonunique key
name	Name of the column
not_null	TRUE if the column cannot be null
numeric	TRUE if the column is numeric
primary_key	TRUE if the column is a primary key

(continued)

Property	Description
table	Name of the table
type	Type of the column
unique_key	TRUE if the column is a unique key
unsigned	TRUE if the column is unsigned
zerofill	TRUE if the column is zero-filled

```php
<?
    //connect to server as freetrade user, no password
    $dbLink = mysql_pconnect("localhost", "freetrade", "");

    //select the 'freetrade' database
    mysql_select_db("freetrade", $dbLink);

    //get everything from address table
    $Query = "SELECT * " .
        "FROM address a, user u " .
        "WHERE u.Address = a.ID ";
    $dbResult = mysql_query($Query, $dbLink);

    // get description of each field
    while($Field = mysql_fetch_field($dbResult))
    {
        print("$Field->table, $Field->name, $Field->type<BR>\n");
    }
?>
```

array mysql_fetch_lengths(integer result)

Use mysql_fetch_lengths to get an array of the maximum lengths for each of the fields in a result set.

```php
<?
    //connect to server as freetrade user, no password
    $dbLink = mysql_pconnect("localhost", "freetrade", "");

    //select the 'freetrade' database
    mysql_select_db("freetrade", $dbLink);

    //get everything from address table
    $Query = "SELECT * " .
        "FROM address ";
```

```
$dbResult = mysql_query($Query, $dbLink);

//get field lengths
$lengths = mysql_fetch_lengths($dbResult);

//print length of the third column
print($lengths[2]);
?>
```

object mysql_fetch_object(integer result)

The `mysql_fetch_object` function is similar to `mysql_fetch_array` and `mysql_fetch_row`. Instead of an array, it returns an object. Each field in the result set is a property in the returned object. Each call to `mysql_fetch_object` returns the next row, or `FALSE` if there are no rows remaining. This allows you to call `mysql_fetch_object` in the test condition of a while loop to get every row.

```
<?
    //connect to server as freetrade user, no password
    $dbLink = mysql_pconnect("localhost", "freetrade", "");

    //select the 'freetrade' database
    mysql_select_db("freetrade", $dbLink);

    //get unique cities from address table
    $Query = "SELECT DISTINCT City, StateProv " .
        "FROM address ";
    $dbResult = mysql_query($Query, $dbLink);

    // get each row
    while($row = mysql_fetch_object($dbResult))
    {
        // print name
        print("$row->City, $row->StateProv<BR>\n");
    }
?>
```

array mysql_fetch_row(integer result)

The `mysql_fetch_row` function returns an array that represents all the fields for a row in the result set. Each call produces the next row until no rows are left, in which case `FALSE` is returned. Each field value is indexed numerically, starting with zero. Compare this function to `mysql_` `fetch_array` and `mysql_fetch_object`. There isn't much difference in performance between these three functions.

```
<?
    //connect to server as freetrade user, no password
    $dbLink = mysql_pconnect("localhost", "freetrade", "");

    //select the 'freetrade' database
    mysql_select_db("freetrade", $dbLink);

    //get unique cities from address table
    $Query = "SELECT City, StateProv " .
        "FROM address ";
    $dbResult = mysql_query($Query, $dbLink);

    //get each row
    while($row = mysql_fetch_row($dbResult))
    {
        // print city, state
        print("$row[0], $row[1]<BR>\n");
    }
?>
```

string mysql_field_flags(integer result, integer field)

Use `mysql_field_flags` to get a description of the flags on the specified field. The flags are returned in a string and separated by spaces. The flags you can expect are `auto_increment`, `binary`, `blob`, `enum`, `multiple_key`, `not_null`, `primary_key`, `timestamp`, `unique_key`, `unsigned`, and `zero-fill`. Some of these flags may be available only in the newest versions of MySQL. See `mysql_list_fields` for an example of use.

integer mysql_field_len(integer result, integer field)

Use `mysql_field_len` to get the maximum number of characters to expect from a field. The fields are numbered from zero. See `mysql_list_fields` for an example of use.

string mysql_field_name(integer result, integer field)

Use `mysql_field_name` to get the name of a column. The `field` argument is an offset numbered from zero. See `mysql_list_fields` for an example of use.

boolean mysql_field_seek(integer result, integer field)

The `mysql_field_seek` function moves the internal field pointer to the specified field. The next call to `mysql_fetch_field` will get information from this field. See `mysql_list_fields` for an example of use.

```
<?
    //connect to server as freetrade user, no password
    $dbLink = mysql_pconnect("localhost", "freetrade", "");

    //select the 'freetrade' database
    mysql_select_db("freetrade", $dbLink);

    // get everything from address table
    $Query = "SELECT * " .
        "FROM address ";
    $dbResult = mysql_query($Query, $dbLink);

    //skip to second field
    mysql_field_seek($dbResult, 1);

    //get description of each field
    while($Field = mysql_fetch_field($dbResult))
    {
        print("$Field->table, $Field->name, $Field->type<BR>\n");
    }
?>
```

string mysql_field_table(integer result, integer field)

The `mysql_field_table` function returns the name of the table for the specified field. If an alias is used, as in the example below, the alias is returned.

```
<?
    //connect to server as freetrade user, no password
    $dbLink = mysql_pconnect("localhost", "freetrade", "");

    //select the 'freetrade' database
    mysql_select_db("freetrade", $dbLink);
```

```
//get everything from user table
//get everything from address table
$Query = "SELECT * " .
       "FROM address a, user u " .
       "WHERE u.Address = a.ID ";
$dbResult = mysql_query($Query, $dbLink);

$Fields = mysql_num_fields($dbResult);
for($i = 0; $i < $Fields; $i++)
{
       print(mysql_field_table($dbResult, $i) . "<BR>\n");
}
?>
```

string mysql_field_type(integer result, integer field)

Use mysql_field_type to get the type of a particular field in the result set.

boolean mysql_free_result(integer result)

Use mysql_free_result to free any memory associated with the specified result set. This is not strictly necessary, as this memory is automatically freed when a script finishes executing.

```
<?
     // connect to server
     $Link = mysql_connect("localhost", "httpd", "");

     // select the 'store' database
     mysql_select_db("store", $Link);

     // get everything from customer table
     $Query = "SELECT * FROM customer ";
     $Result = mysql_query($Query, $Link);

     // free result set
     mysql_free_result($Result);
?>
```

integer mysql_insert_id(integer link)

After inserting into a table with an auto_increment field, the mysql_insert_id function returns the ID assigned to the inserted row. If the link argument is left out, the most recent connection will be used.

```
<?
    //connect to server as freetrade user, no password
    $dbLink = mysql_pconnect("localhost", "freetrade", "");

    //select the 'freetrade' database
    mysql_select_db("freetrade", $dbLink);

    //insert a row
    $Query = "INSERT INTO user (Login, Password) " .
            "VALUES('leon', 'secret') ";
    $dbResult = mysql_query($Query, $dbLink);

    //get id
    print("ID is " . mysql_insert_id($dbLink));
?>
```

integer mysql_list_dbs(integer link)

The mysql_list_dbs function queries the server for a list of databases. It returns a result pointer that may be used with mysql_fetch_row and similar functions.

```
<?
    //connect to server as freetrade user, no password
    $dbLink = mysql_pconnect("localhost", "freetrade", "");

    //get list of databases
    $dbResult = mysql_list_dbs($dbLink);

    //get each row
    while($row = mysql_fetch_row($dbResult))
    {
        // print name
        print($row[0] . "<BR>\n");
    }
?>
```

integer mysql_list_fields(string database, string table, integer link)

The `mysql_list_fields` function returns a result pointer to a query on the list of fields for a specified table. The result pointer may be used with any of the functions that get information about columns in a result set: `mysql_field_flags`, `mysql_field_len`, `mysql_field_name`, `mysql_field_type`. The `link` argument is optional.

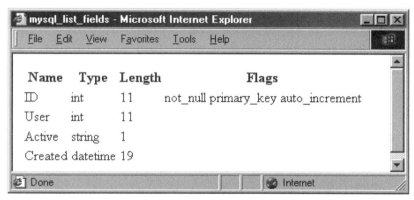

```
<?
    //connect to server
    $dbLink = mysql_pconnect("localhost", "freetrade", "");

    //get list of fields
    $dbResult = mysql_list_fields("freetrade", "invoice", $dbLink);

    //start HTML table
    print("<TABLE>\n");
    print("<TR>\n");
    print("<TH>Name</TH>\n");
    print("<TH>Type</TH>\n");
    print("<TH>Length</TH>\n");
    print("<TH>Flags</TH>\n");
    print("</TR>\n");

    //loop over each field
    for($i = 0; $i < mysql_num_fields($dbResult); $i++)
    {
        print("<TR>\n");
```

Figure 13-2 `mysql_list_fields`.

```
        print("<TD>" . mysql_field_name($dbResult, $i) . "</TD>\n");
        print("<TD>" . mysql_field_type($dbResult, $i) . "</TD>\n");
        print("<TD>" . mysql_field_len($dbResult, $i) . "</TD>\n");
        print("<TD>" . mysql_field_flags($dbResult, $i) . "</TD>\n");

        print("</TR>\n");
    }

    //close HTML table
    print("</TABLE>\n");
?>
```

Figure 13-2   Continued

integer mysql_list_tables(string database, integer link)

Use `mysql_list_tables` to get a result pointer to a list of tables for a speci-fied database. The result pointer may be used in any of the functions for fetching rows from a result set. The `link` argument is optional.

```
<?
        //connect to server as freetrade user, no password
        $dbLink = mysql_pconnect("localhost", "freetrade", "");

        //get list of tables
        $dbResult = mysql_list_tables("freetrade", $dbLink);

        //get each row
        while($row = mysql_fetch_row($dbResult))
        {
                //print name
                print($row[0] . "<BR>\n");
        }
?>
```

integer mysql_num_fields(integer result)

The `mysql_num_fields` function returns the number of fields in a result set. See `mysql_list_fields` for an example of use.

integer mysql_num_rows(integer result)

The `msyql_num_rows` function returns the number of rows in a result set. See `mysql_result` for an example of use.

integer mysql_pconnect(string host, string user, string password)

The `mysql_pconnect` function operates like `mysql_connect` except that the connection will be persistent. That is, it won't be closed when the script ends. The connection will last as long as the server process lasts, so that if a connection is attempted later from the same process, the overhead of opening a new connection will be avoided.

A link identifier is returned. This identifier is used in many of the other functions in this section.

```
<?
    //open persistent connection
    $dbLink = mysql_pconnect("localhost", "freetrade", "");
?>
```

integer mysql_query(string query, integer link)

Use `mysql_query` to execute a query. If the `link` argument is omitted, the last connection made is used. If there has been no previous connection, PHP will connect to the local host. If the query performs an insert, delete, or update, a boolean value will be returned. Select queries return a result identifier. See `mysql_fetch_object` for an example of use.

string mysql_result(integer result, integer row, string field)

The `mysql_result` function returns the value of the specified field in the specified row. The `field` argument may be a number, in which case it is considered a field offset. It may also be the name of a column, either with the table name or without. It could also be an alias.

In general, this function is very slow. It's better to use `mysql_fetch_row` or a similar function.

```
<?
    //connect to server as freetrade user, no password
    $dbLink = mysql_connect("localhost", "freetrade", "");

    //select the 'freetrade' database
    mysql_select_db("freetrade", $dbLink);
```

```
// get everything from customer table
$Query = "SELECT * FROM " .
        "user u " .
        "WHERE u.Login like 'A%' ";
$dbResult = mysql_query($Query, $dbLink);

// get number of rows
$rows = mysql_num_rows($dbResult);

for($i = 0; $i < $rows; $i++)
{
        $name = mysql_result($dbResult, $i, "u.Login");
        print("$name<BR>\n");
}
?>
```

boolean mysql_select_db(string database, integer link)

Use `mysql_select_db` to select the default database. Most of the other examples in this section use `mysql_select_db`.

ODBC

Open Database Connectivity (ODBC) has become an industry standard for communicating with a database. The model is simple. Client software is designed to use an ODBC API. Vendors write drivers that implement this API on the client side and talk natively to their database on the server side. This allows application developers to write one application that can communicate with many different databases simply by changing the driver, which is an external file.

ODBC uses SQL as its language for communicating with any database, even when the database isn't relational. Microsoft offers drivers that allow you to query text files and Excel workbooks. A good place to start learning more about ODBC is Microsoft's page at <http://www.microsoft.com/data/odbc/>.

Microsoft has offered free ODBC drivers for some time, but only for their operating systems. ODBC drivers for UNIX are harder to come by. Most database manufacturers offer drivers, and there are third parties, like Inter-solv, that sell optimized drivers for both Windows and UNIX platforms.

Most of the database with native support in PHP can also be accessed via ODBC. There are also numerous databases that can only be accessed via ODBC by PHP. Two that others have tried are Solid and Empress.

Stig Bakken, Andreas Karajannis and Frank Kromann have contributed to the creation of the ODBC extension.

boolean odbc_autocommit(integer connection, boolean on)

The odbc_autocommit function sets whether queries are automatically com-mitted when executed. By default this is on. The connection argument is an integer returned by the odbc_connect or odbc_pconnect functions. This function has to be used intelligently, as not all ODBC drivers support com-mits and rollbacks.

```
<?
        $Connection = odbc_connect("store", "sa", "sa");

        // turn off autocommit
        odbc_autocommit($Connection, FALSE);
?>
```

boolean odbc_binmode(integer result, integer mode)

Use odbc_binmode to set the way binary columns return data for a result set. When binary data are returned by the driver, each byte is represented by hexadecimal codes. By default, PHP will convert these codes into raw binary data. If you have to use the odbc_longreadlen function to set the maximum length of long data to anything other than zero, then the modes in Table 13.8 apply. If the maximum read length is zero, the data are always converted to raw binary data.

```
<?
        // get a GIF from a database and send it to browser

        // connect to database
        $Connection = odbc_connect("store", "admin", "secret");
```

Table 13.8 ODBC Binary Data Modes	
Mode	*Description*
ODBC_BINMODE_PASSTHRU	Pass through as binary data
ODBC_BINMODE_RETURN	Return as hexadecimal codes
ODBC_BINMODE_CONVERT	Return with data converted to a string

```
        // execute query
        $Query = "SELECT picture ";
        $Query .= "FROM employee ";
        $Query .= "WHERE id=17 ";
        $Result = odbc_do($Connection, $Query);

        // make sure binmode is set for binary pass through
        odbc_binmode($Result, ODBC_BINMODE_PASSTHRU);

        // make sure longreadlen mode
        // is set for echo to browser
        odbc_longreadlen($Result, 0);

        // get the first row, ignore the rest
        odbc_fetch_row($Result);

        // send header so browser knows it's a gif
        header("Content-type: image/gif");

        // get the picture
        odbc_result($Result, 1);
?>
```

odbc_close(integer connection)

Use odbc_close to close a connection to a database. If there are open transactions for the connection, an error will be returned and the connection will
not be closed.

```
<?
        // connect to database
        $Connection = odbc_connect("store", "guest", "guest");

        // execute query
```

```
$Query = "SELECT price ";
$Query .= "FROM catalog ";
$Query .= "WHERE id=10 ";
$Result = odbc_do($Connection, $Query);

odbc_fetch_row($Result)

$price = odbc_result($Result, 1);

print("$price<BR>\n");

odbc_close($Connection);
?>
```

odbc_close_all()

The `odbc_close_all` function closes every connection you have open to ODBC data sources. Like `odbc_close`, it will report an error if you have an open transaction on one of the connections.

```
<?
    // connect to database three times
    $Connection1 = odbc_connect("store", "guest", "guest");
    $Connection2 = odbc_connect("store", "guest", "guest");
    $Connection3 = odbc_connect("store", "guest", "guest");

    // close all the connections
    odbc_close_all();
?>
```

boolean odbc_commit(integer connection)

Use `odbc_commit` to commit all pending actions for the specified connection. If automatic commit is turned on, as is default, this function has no effect. Also, make sure your driver supports transactions before using this function.

```
<?
    // connect to database
    $Connection = odbc_connect("store", "guest", "guest");

    // turn off autocommit
    odbc_autocommit($Connection, FALSE);
```

```
// put everything on sale
$Query = "UPDATE catalog ";
$Query .= "SET price = price * 0.9 ";
$Result = odbc_do($Connection, $Query);

// commit
if(odbc_commit($Connection))
{
        print("Commit successful!<BR>\n");
}

odbc_close($Connection);
?>
```

integer odbc_connect(string dsn, string user, string password, integer cursor_type)

Use odbc_connect to connect to an ODBC data source. A connection identifier is returned, which is used by most of the other functions in this section.
The user and password arguments are required, so if your driver does not
require them, pass empty strings. The optional cursor_type argument
forces the use of a particular cursor so that you may avoid problems with
some ODBC drivers. Using the SQL_CUR_USE_ODBC constant for cursor type
may avoid problems with calling stored procedures or getting row numbers.

string odbc_cursor(integer result)

Use odbc_cursor to fetch the name of a cursor for a result set.

```
<?
    // connect to database
    $Connection = odbc_connect("store", "guest", "guest");

    // execute query
    $Query = "SELECT name, price ";
    $Query .= "FROM catalog ";
    $Result = odbc_do($Connection, $Query);

    print("Cursor: " . odbc_cursor($Result) . "<BR>\n");

    while(odbc_fetch_row($Result))
    {
        $name = odbc_result($Result, 1);
```

```
        $price = odbc_result($Result, 2);

        print("$name: $price<BR>\n");
    }

    odbc_close($Connection);
?>
```

integer odbc_do(integer connection, string query)

Use odbc_do to execute a query on a connection. A result identifier is returned, and is used in many of the other functions for fetching result data.

integer odbc_exec(integer connection, string query)

The odbc_exec function is an alias for odbc_do.

integer odbc_execute(integer result, array parameters)

The odbc_execute function executes a prepared statement. The result argument is an identifier returned by odbc_prepare. The parameters argument is an array that must be passed by reference and will be set with the value of the result columns. See odbc_prepare for an example of use.

integer odbc_fetch_into(integer result, array fields)
integer odbc_fetch_into(integer result, integer row, array fields)

The odbc_fetch_into function gets the specified row for the specified result set and puts the columns into the fields array. The fields argument must be passed by reference. The number of columns in the result set is returned. The row argument may be omitted, in which case the next row in the set is returned.

```
<?
    // connect to database
```

```
        $Connection = odbc_connect("store", "guest", "guest");

        // execute query
        $Query = "SELECT name, price ";
        $Query .= "FROM catalog ";
        $Result = odbc_do($Connection, $Query);

        while(odbc_fetch_into($Result, &$fields))
        {
                $name = $fields[0];
                $price = $fields[1];
                print("$name: $price<BR>\n");
        }

        odbc_close($Connection);
?>
```

boolean odbc_fetch_row(integer result, integer row)

Use `odbc_fetch_row` to get a row of data from a result set. The data for the row is stored in internal memory, ready to be retrieved with the `odbc_result` function. The `row` argument is optional and, if left out, the next available row will be returned. FALSE will be returned when there are no more rows in the result set. See the `odbc_result` function for an example of use.

integer odbc_field_len(integer result, integer field)

Use `odbc_field_len` to get the length of a field in a result set. Fields are numbered starting with one.

```
<?
        // connect to database
        $Connection = odbc_connect("store", "guest", "guest");

        // execute query
        $Query = "SELECT name, price ";
        $Query .= "FROM catalog ";
        $Result = odbc_do($Connection, $Query);

        print(odbc_field_len($Result, 1));

        odbc_close($Connection);
?>
```

string odbc_field_name(integer result, integer field)

Use `odbc_field_name` to get the name of a field in a result set. Fields are numbered starting with one.

```
<?
        // connect to database
        $Connection = odbc_connect("store", "guest", "guest");

        // execute query
        $Query = "SELECT name, price ";
        $Query .= "FROM catalog ";
        $Result = odbc_do($Connection, $Query);

        print(odbc_field_name($Result, 1));

        odbc_close($Connection);
?>
```

string odbc_field_type(integer result, integer field)

Use `odbc_field_type` to get the type of a field in a result set. Fields are numbered starting with one.

```
<?
        // connect to database
        $Connection = odbc_connect("store", "guest", "guest");

        // execute query
        $Query = "SELECT name, price ";
        $Query .= "FROM catalog ";
        $Result = odbc_do($Connection, $Query);

        print(odbc_field_type($Result, 1));

        odbc_close($Connection);
?>
```

boolean odbc_free_result(integer result)

Use `odbc_free_result` to free the memory associated with the result set. This is not strictly necessary, but it's a good idea if you are worried about running out of memory. If autocommit is disabled and you free a result set before calling `odbc_commit`, the transaction will be rolled back.

```
<?
        // connect to database
        $Connection = odbc_connect("store", "guest", "guest");

        // execute query
        $Query = "SELECT name, price ";
        $Query .= "FROM catalog ";
        $Result = odbc_do($Connection, $Query);

        // free the result set
        odbc_free_result($Result);

        odbc_close($Connection);
?>
```

boolean odbc_longreadlen(integer result, integer length)

Use `odbc_longreadlen` to set the maximum length for values of any columns of type long. This includes binary columns such as `longvarbinary`. By default the maximum length is zero, which has the special meaning of causing fetched columns to be echoed to the browser. Any other positive number will cause returned values to be truncated to the specified length.

Note that it is not always apparent that a field is considered to be a long by the ODBC driver. For example, a memo column in Microsoft Access is a long. Data appearing in the wrong place are a sign of fetching a long where you didn't expect it. One strategy to avoid these problems is to always call `longreadlen`.

See `odbc_binmode` for an example of use.

integer odbc_num_fields(integer result)

Use `odbc_num_fields` to find the number of fields in the result set.

```
<?
        // connect to database
        $Connection = odbc_connect("store", "guest", "guest");

        // execute query
        $Query = "SELECT name, price ";
        $Query .= "FROM catalog ";
        $Result = odbc_do($Connection, $Query);
```

```
        print(odbc_num_fields($Result));

        odbc_close($Connection);
?>
```

integer odbc_num_rows(integer result)

The `odbc_num_rows` function returns the number of rows in the set, or the number of rows affected by a delete or insert if the driver supports it.

```
<?
        // connect to database
        $Connection = odbc_connect("store", "guest", "guest");

        // execute query
        $Query = "SELECT name, price ";
        $Query .= "FROM catalog ";
        $Result = odbc_do($Connection, $Query);

        print(odbc_num_rows($Result));

        odbc_close($Connection);
?>
```

integer odbc_pconnect(string dsn, string user, string password)

The `odbc_pconnect` function operates similarly to `odbc_connect`. A connection is attempted to the specified Data Source Name (DSN) and a connection identifier is returned. The connection should not be closed with `odbc_close`. It will persist as long as the Web server process. The next time a script executes `odbc_pconnect`, PHP will first check for existing connections.

```
<?
        // connect to database
        $Connection = odbc_pconnect("store", "guest", "guest");
?>
```

integer odbc_prepare(integer connection, string query)

The `odbc_prepare` function parses a query and prepares it for execution. A result identifier that may be passed to `odbc_execute` is returned. Preparing statements can be more efficient than making the driver reparse statements. This is usually the case where you have many rows to insert into the same table. To specify a value to be filled in later, use a question mark.

```
<?
        // connect to database
        $Connection = odbc_connect("store", "guest", "guest");

        // prepare query
        $Query = "INSERT INTO catalog (ID, Name, Price) ";
        $Query .= "VALUES(?, ?, ?) ";
        $Result = odbc_prepare($Connection, $Query);

        // insert
        // 0, 2000 Calendar, 20.00
        // 1, 2001 Calendar, 20.50
        // 2, 2002 Calendar, 21.00
        for($index = 2000; $index <= 2002; $index++)
        {
                $values[0] = $index-2000;
                $values[1] = "$index Calendar";
                $values[2] = 20.00 + (0.50 * ($index-2000));

                odbc_execute($Result, $values);
        }

        odbc_close($Connection);
?>
```

string odbc_result(integer result, string field)

Use odbc_result to get the value of a field for the current row. Fields may be referenced by number or name. If by using numbers, start counting fields with 1. If you specify a field by name, do not include the table name.

This function is affected by the settings controlled by odbc_binmode and odbc_longreadlen. An important fact to keep in mind is that while in most cases the value of the field will be returned, fields that contain long data will be echoed to the browser instead by default. Use odbc_longreadlen to change this behavior.

```
<?
        // connect to database
        $Connection = odbc_connect("store", "guest", "guest");
```

```
        // execute query
        $Query = "SELECT name, price ";
        $Query .= "FROM catalog ";
        $Result = odbc_do($Connection, $Query);

        while(odbc_fetch_row($Result))
        {
        $name = odbc_result($Result, 1);
        $price = odbc_result($Result, 2);
                print("$name: $price<BR>\n");
        }

        odbc_close($Connection);
?>
```

integer odbc_result_all(integer result, string format)

The `odbc_result_all` function will dump all the rows for a result set to the browser. The number of rows is returned. The dumped rows will be formatted in a table. The field names will be printed in a header row with TH tags. The optional `format` argument will be inserted inside the initial table tag so that you may set table attributes.

```
<?
        // connect to database
        $Connection = odbc_connect("store", "guest", "guest");

        // execute query
        $Query = "SELECT name, price ";
        $Query .= "FROM catalog ";
        $Result = odbc_do($Connection, $Query);

        // dump all results
        odbc_result_all($Result, "BORDER=1");

        odbc_close($Connection);
?>
```

boolean odbc_rollback(integer connection)

Use `odbc_rollback` to abandon all pending transactions. By default all queries are automatically committed, but this behavior may be modified with `odbc_autocommit`. Not all databases support transactions.

```
<?
        // connect to database
        $Connection = odbc_connect("store", "guest", "guest");

        // turn off autocommit
        odbc_autocommit($Connection, FALSE);

        // put everything on sale
        $Query = "UPDATE catalog ";
        $Query .= "SET price = price * 0.9 ";
        $Result = odbc_do($Connection, $Query);

        // rollback
        odbc_rollback($Connection);

        odbc_close($Connection);
?>
```

integer odbc_setoption(integer id, integer function, integer option, integer parameter)

The odbc_setoption function changes the configuration of the ODBC driver for an entire connection or a single result set. Its purpose is to allow access to any ODBC setting in order to avoid problems with buggy ODBC drivers. To use this function, you ought to understand ODBC in greater detail than the average user. You will need to know the values of the various options available to you.

The id argument is either a connection identifier or a result set identifier. Since odbc_setoption wraps two C API functions, SQLSetConnectOption and SQLSetStmtOption, you must specify which to use with the function argument. The option argument is an integer that identifies one of the many options available on the ODBC driver. The parameter argument is the value to use with the option.

Oracle

Oracle is one of the most popular relational databases in the world. It is an industrial-strength engine preferred by large corporations using databases of exceeding complexity. Oracle database administrators are scarce and command high salaries. A full explanation of working with Oracle is far beyond the scope of this text. Fortunately you will find many books about Oracle for sale, as well as free documentation on the Oracle Web site. In particular, I recommend *Oracle Call Interface Programmer's Guide*, which exists in several versions. I found it at the following URL `<http://technet.oracle.com/doc/server.804/a58234/toc.htm>`. This document describes the Oracle Call Interface which PHP uses.

PHP supports two generations of Oracle libraries, Version 7 and Version 8. The functions that use Oracle 7 begin with `ora_`, such as `ora_logon`. The functions that work with Oracle 8 begin with `oci`, such as `ocilogon`. The Oracle 8 library supports connecting to older Oracle databases. I've included descriptions of the older functions because it's possible you're in the situation of not having access to the newer libraries. Aside from compiling Oracle support into PHP, you may also load an extension using the `dl` function.

The Oracle 7 functions require two environment variables to be set: `ORACLE_HOME` and `ORACLE_SID`. They are most likely not set for your Web server, so you must use the `putenv` function to set them. You will notice code to accomplish this in the examples below.

Thies Arntzen, Stig Bakken, Mitch Golden, Andreas Karajannis, and Rasmus Lerdorf contributed to the Oracle 7 extension. Oracle 8 support was added to PHP by Stig Bakken and Thies Arntzen.

Table 13.9 lists constants created by the Oracle 8 Extension.

When Oracle is installed, it creates a test user. The login is `scott` and the password is `tiger`. I'll take advantage of this in the examples below.

boolean ocibindbyname (integer statement, string placeholder, reference variable, integer length, integer type)

The `ocibindbyname` function binds an Oracle placeholder to a PHP variable. You must supply a valid statement identifier as created by `ociparse`, the name of the placeholder, a reference to a PHP variable, and the maximum length of the bind data. You may use a value of –1 to use the length of the variable passed as the `variable` argument.

The optional `type` argument specifies a data type and is necessary if you wish to bind to an abstract data type. Use one of the following constants to set the data type: `OCI_B_BLOB`, `OCI_B_CFILE`, `OCI_B_CLOB`, `OCI_B_FILE`, `OCI_B_ROWID`. Make sure you use `ocinewdescriptor` before binding to an abstract data type. You also need to use –1 for the `length` argument.

Table 13.9   All Oracle 8 Constants

OCI_ASSOC

OCI_BOTH

OCI_B_BFILE

OCI_B_BIN

OCI_B_BLOB

OCI_B_CFILEE

OCI_B_CLOB

OCI_B_CURSOR

OCI_B_ROWID

OCI_COMMIT_ON_SUCCESS

OCI_DEFAULT

OCI_DESCRIBE_ONLY

OCI_DTYPE_FILE

OCI_DTYPE_LOB

OCI_DTYPE_ROWID

OCI_D_FILE

OCI_D_LOB

OCI_D_ROWID

OCI_EXACT_FETCH

OCI_NUM

OCI_RETURN_LOBS

OCI_RETURN_NULLS

SQLT_BFILEE

SQLT_BLOB

SQLT_CFILEE

SQLT_CLOB

SQLT_RDD

```
<?
      //set-up data to insert
      $NewEmployee = array(
            array(8001, 'Smith', 'Clerk'),
            array(8002, 'Jones', 'Analyst'),
            array(8003, 'Atkinson', 'President')
            );

      //connect to database
      $Connection = ocilogon("scott", "tiger");

      //assemble query
      $Query = "INSERT INTO emp (EMPNO, ENAME, JOB, HIREDATE) ";
      $Query .= "VALUES (:empno, :ename, :job, SYSDATE ) ";
      $Query .= "RETURNING ROWID INTO :rowid ";

      //parse query
      $Statement = ociparse($Connection, $Query);

      //create descriptor the abstract data type
      $RowID = ocinewdescriptor($Connection, OCI_D_ROWID);

      //bind input and output variables
      ocibindbyname($Statement, ":empno", &$EmployeeNumber, 32);
      ocibindbyname($Statement, ":ename", &$EmployeeName, 32);
      ocibindbyname($Statement, ":job", &$Job, 32);
      ocibindbyname($Statement, ":rowid", &$RowID, -1, OCI_B_ROWID);


      //loop over each new employee
      while(list($key, $EmployeeInfo) = each($NewEmployee))
      {
            list($EmployeeNumber, $EmployeeName, $Job) = $EmployeeInfo;

            //execute query, do not automatically commit
            ociexecute($Statement, OCI_DEFAULT);

            print("$EmployeeNumber has ROWID $RowID<BR>\n");
      }

      //free the statement
      ocifreestatement($Statement);

      //undo the inserts
      //Normally, you won't do this, if we undo the inserts
```

```
        //each time, we can run the example over and over
        ocirollback($Connection);

        //close connection
        ocilogoff($Connection);
?>
```

boolean ocicancel(integer statement)

The ocicancel function fetches the next row from a statement. Internally it calls the OCIStmtFetch function, which is part of OCI, specifying zero for the number of rows. In every other way, it is identical to ocifetch.

boolean ocicolumnisnull(integer statement, value column)

Use ocicolumnisnull to test whether a column is null. You may specify columns by number, in which case columns are numbered starting with 1, or you may specify columns by name. See ocifetch for an example of use.

string ocicolumnname(integer statement, integer column)

The ocicolumnname function returns the name of a column given the column number. Columns are numbered starting with 1. See ocifetch for an example of use.

integer ocicolumnsize(integer statement, value column)

The ocicolumnsize function returns the size of a column. You may specify columns by number, in which case columns are numbered starting with 1, or you may specify columns by name. See ocifetch for an example of use.

value ocicolumntype(integer statement, integer column)

Use ocicolumntype to get the type of the specified column. You may specify columns by number, in which case columns are numbered starting with 1, or you may specify columns by name. The name of the type will be returned if it is one of the following: BFILE, BLOB, CHAR, CLOB, DATE, LONG RAW, LONG, NUMBER, RAW, REFCURSOR, ROWID, VARCHAR. Otherwise, an integer code from the data type will be returned. See ocifetch for an example of use.

boolean ocicommit(integer connection)

The ocicommit function commits all previous statements executed on the connection. By default, statements are committed when executed. You can override this functionality when you call ociexecute, by specifying a mode.

boolean ocidefinebyname(integer statement, string column, reference variable, integer type)

The ocidefinebyname function associates a column with a PHP variable. When the statement is executed, the value of the column will be copied into the variable. The statement argument must be an integer returned by ociparse. The column name must be written in upper case, otherwise Oracle will not recognize it. Unrecognized column names do not produce errors. Since the variable you pass in ocidefinebyname will be modified, you need to pass it by reference. That mean preceding it with an ampersand (&).

The type argument appears to be necessary only if you are attaching to an abstract data type, such as a ROWID. Abstract data types require ocinewdescriptor be used prior to ocidefinebyname. If the type argument is left out, the variable will be set as a null-terminated string.

```
<?
    //connect to database
    $Connection = ocilogon("scott", "tiger");

    //assemble query
    $Query = "SELECT ENAME, HIREDATE ";
    $Query .= "FROM emp ";
    $Query .= "WHERE JOB='CLERK' ";

    //parse query
    $Statement = ociparse($Connection, $Query);

    //associate two columns with variables
    ocidefinebyname($Statement, "ENAME", &$EmployeeName);
    ocidefinebyname($Statement, "HIREDATE", &$HireDate);

    //execute query
```

```
ociexecute($Statement);

//fetch each row
while(ocifetch($Statement))
{
        print("$EmployeeName was hired $HireDate<BR>\n");
}

//free the statement
ocifreestatement($Statement);

//close connection
ocilogoff($Connection);
?>
```

array ocierror(integer identifier)

If an error has occurred, the ocierror function returns an associative array that describes it. If no error has occurred, FALSE is returned. The identifier argument may be either a statement identifier or a connection identifier. The returned array will have two elements, code and message. You may also call ocierror with no argument to get information about a failed login. See ocifetch for an example of use.

boolean ociexecute(integer statement, integer mode)

Use ociexecute to execute a statement. The mode argument is optional. It controls whether the statement will be committed after execution. By default, OCI_COMMIT_ON_EXECUTE is used. If you do not wish to commit the transaction immediately, use OCI_DEFAULT. See ocifetch for an example of use.

boolean ocifetch(integer statement)

The ocifetch function prepares the next row of data to be read with ociresult. When no rows remain, FALSE is returned.

```
<?
        //connect to database
        $Connection = ocilogon("scott", "tiger");
```

```php
//assemble query
$Query = "SELECT * ";
$Query .= "FROM emp ";

//parse query
$Statement = ociparse($Connection, $Query);

//execute query
ociexecute($Statement);

//check that the query executed sucessfully
if($Error = ocierror($Statement))
{
      print($Error["code"] . ": " . $Error["message"] . "<BR>\n");
      exit;
}

//start HTML table
print("<TABLE>\n");

//build headers from column information
print("<TR>\n");
for($i=1; $i <= ocinumcols($Statement); $i++)
{
      print("<TH>");

      //print a line like "<TH>ENAME VARCHAR2(10)</TH>"
      print(ocicolumnname($Statement, $i) . " ");
      print(ocicolumntype($Statement, $i));
      print("(" . ocicolumnsize($Statement, $i) . ")");

      print("</TH>\n");
}
print("</TR>\n");


//fetch each row
while(ocifetch($Statement))
{
      print("<TR>\n");

      //loop over each column
      for($i=1; $i <= ocinumcols($Statement); $i++)
      {
            //print a line like "<TD>SMITH</TD>"
```

```
                print("<TD>");
                if(ocicolumnisnull($Statement, $i))
                {
                        print("(null)");
                }
                else
                {
                        print(ociresult($Statement, $i));
                }
                print("</TD>\n");
        }

        print("</TR>\n");
    }

    //close table
    print("</TABLE>\n");

    //free the statement
    ocifreestatement($Statement);

    //close connection
    ocilogoff($Connection);
?>
```

boolean ocifetchinto(integer statement, reference data, integer mode)

Use ocifetchinto to get the next row of data from an executed statement and place it in an array. The data argument will contain an array that by default will be indexed by integers starting with 1. The optional mode argument controls how the array is indexed. You may add the constants listed in Table 13.10 to get the features you desire.

Table 13.10   Constants for Use with ocifetchinto

Constant	Description
OCI_ASSOC	Return columns indexed by name
OCI_NUM	Return columns indexed by number
OCI_RETURN_NULLS	Create elements for null columns
OCI_RETURN_LOBS	Return values of LOBs instead of descriptors

```
<?
    //connect to database
    $Connection = ocilogon("scott", "tiger");

    //assemble query
    $Query = "SELECT * ";
    $Query .= "FROM emp ";

    //parse query
    $Statement = ociparse($Connection, $Query);

    //execute query
    ociexecute($Statement);

    //check that the query executed sucessfully
    if($Error = ocierror($Statement))
    {
        print($Error["code"] . ": " . $Error["message"] . "<BR>\n");
        exit;
    }

    //start HTML table
    print("<TABLE>\n");


    //fetch each row
    while(ocifetchinto($Statement, $Data,
          OCI_NUM + OCI_RETURN_NULLS + OCI_RETURN_LOBS))
    {
        print("<TR>\n");

        //loop over each column
        while(list($key, $value) = each($Data))
        {
            //print a line like "<TD>SMITH</TD>"
            print("<TD>$value</TD>\n");
        }

        print("</TR>\n");
    }

    //close table
    print("</TABLE>\n");

    //free the statement
```

```
        ocifreestatement($Statement);

        //close connection
        ocilogoff($Connection);
?>
```

integer ocifetchstatement(integer statement, reference data)

The `ocifetchstatement` function places an array with all the result data in the `data` argument and returns the number of rows. The `data` array is indexed by the names of the columns. Each element is an array itself which is indexed by integers starting with zero. Each element in this subarray corresponds to a row.

```
<?
        //connect to database
        $Connection = ocilogon("scott", "tiger");

        //assemble query
        $Query = "SELECT * ";
        $Query .= "FROM emp ";

        //parse query
        $Statement = ociparse($Connection, $Query);

        //execute query
        ociexecute($Statement);

        print("<TABLE>\n");

        //fetch all rows into array
        if($Rows = ocifetchstatement($Statement, &$Data))
        {
                while(list($key, $value) = each($Data))
                {
                        print("<TR>\n");

                        //name of column
                        print("<TH>$key</TH>\n");

                        //print data
                        for($i=0; $i < $Rows; $i++)
```

```
                    {
                          print("<TD>$value[$i]</TD>\n");
                    }

                    print("</TR>\n");
               }
      }

      print("</TABLE>\n");

      //free the statement
      ocifreestatement($Statement);

      //close connection
      ocilogoff($Connection);
?>
```

boolean ocifreecursor(integer cursor)

Use `ocifreecursor` to free the memory associated with a cursor you created with `ocinewcursor`.

boolean ocifreestatement(integer statement)

Use `ocifreestatement` to free the memory associated with a statement. The `statement` argument is an integer returned by `ociparse`.

ociinternaldebug(boolean on)

The `ociinternaldebug` function controls whether debugging information is generated. The debug output will be sent to the browser. It is off by default, of course.

boolean ocilogoff(integer connection)

Use `ocilogoff` to close a connection.

integer ocilogon(string user, string password, string sid)

The `ocilogon` function establishes a connection to an Oracle database. The identifier it returns is used to create statements, cursors, and descriptors.

The `user` and `password` arguments are required. The optional `sid` argument specifies the server; if it is left out, the `ORACLE_SID` environment variable will be used.

If you attempt to create a second connection to the same database, you will not really get another connection. This means that commits or rollbacks affect all statements created by your script. If you want a separate connection, use `ocinlogon` instead.

integer ocinewcursor(integer connection)

Use `ocinewcursor` to create a cursor. The cursor identifier that is returned is similar to a statement identifier. Use `ocifreecursor` to free the memory associated with a cursor. You can use a cursor to get the data returned by a stored procedure.

```
<?
//open connection
$Connection = ocilogon("scott", "tiger");

//create cursor
$Cursor = ocinewcursor($Connection);

//create statement that calls a stored procedure
$Query = "BEGIN ";
$Query .= "docalculation(:price); ";
$Query .= "END; ";
$Statement = ociparse($Connection, $Query);

//bind placeholder to cursor
ocibindbyname($Statement, "price", &$Cursor, -1, OCI_B_CURSOR);

//execute statement
ociexecute($Statement);

//execute cursor
ociexecute($Cursor);

//loop over results in cursor
while(ocifetchinto($Cursor, &$Results))
{
        print("$Results<BR>\n");
}
```

```
    //free memory for cursor
    ocifreecursor($Cursor);

    //free memory for statement
    ocifreestatement($Statement);

    //close connection
    ocilogoff($Connection);
?>
```

string ocinewdescriptor(integer connection, integer type)

The ocinewdescriptor function allocates memory for descriptors and LOB locators. The type defaults to being a file, but you may specify OCI_D_FILE, OCI_D_LOB, or OCI_D_ROWID. See ocibindbyname for an example of use.

integer ocinlogon(string user, string password, string sid)

The ocinlogon function establishes a unique connection to an Oracle database. The identifier it returns is used to create statements, cursors, and descriptors. The user and password arguments are required. The optional sid argument specifies the server, and if left out, the ORACLE_SID environment variable will be used.

Compare this function to ocilogon and ociplogon.

integer ocinumcols(integer statement)

The ocinumcols function returns the number of columns in a statement. See ocifetch for an example of use.

integer ociparse(integer connection, string query)

The ociparse function creates a statement from a query. It requires a valid connection identifier.

integer ociplogon(string user, string password, string sid)

The `ociplogon` function establishes a persistent connection to an Oracle database. These connections exist as long as the server process. When you request a persistent connection, you may get a connection that already exists, thus saving the overhead of establishing a connection.

The returned identifier is used to create statements, cursors, and descriptors. The `user` and `password` arguments are required. The optional `sid` argument specifies the server, and if left out, the `ORACLE_SID` environment variable will be used.

Compare this function to `ocilogon` and `ocinlogon`.

string ociresult(integer statement, value column)

Use `ociresult` to get the value of a column on the current row. The column may be identified by number or name. Columns are numbered starting with 1. Results are returned as strings, except in the case of LOBs, ROWIDs, and FILEs. See `ocifetch` for an example of use.

boolean ocirollback(integer connection)

Use `ocirollback` to issue a rollback operation on the given connection. By default, calls to `ociexecute` are committed automatically, so be sure to override this functionality if you wish to use `ocirollback`.

Keep in mind that if you used `ocilogon` or `ociplogon` to get more than one connection, they may not be unique. Therefore issuing a rollback will affect all statements. To avoid this situation use `ocinlogon` instead.

integer ocirowcount(integer statement)

The `ocirowcount` function returns the number of rows affected by an update, insert, or delete.

string ociserverversion(integer connection)

Use `ociserverversion` to get a string describing the version of the server for a connection.

integer ocisetprefetch(integer statement, integer size)

The `ociprefetch` function sets the size of a buffer that Oracle uses to prefetch results into. The `size` argument will be multiplied by 1024 to set the actual number of bytes.

string ocistatementtype(integer statement)

Use `ocistatementtype` to get a string that describes the type of the statement. The types you can expect are ALTER, BEGIN, CREATE, DECLARE, DELETE, DROP, INSERT, SELECT, UNKNOWN, and UPDATE.

boolean ora_bind(integer cursor, string variable, string parameter, integer length, integer type)

The `ora_bind` function binds a PHP variable to a parameter in an Oracle query. This causes data to flow between the two entities. You must call `ora_parse` before binding any variables. The `type` parameter is optional. It specifies whether data may go only into or out of the Oracle parameter. By default, data may go both ways. The type may be defined using the following constants: ORA_BIND_IN, ORA_BIND_INOUT, ORA_BIND_OUT.

```
<?
    //in case these aren't set for httpd
    putenv("ORACLE_HOME=/usr/local/oracle7");
    putenv("ORACLE_SID=ORCL");

    //connect to server
    $Connection = ora_logon("scott", "tiger");

    //open cursor
    $Cursor = ora_open($Connection);

    $Query = "DECLARE php_in INTEGER; ";
    $Query .= "BEGIN ";
    $Query .= ":php_out := :php_in + 3; ";
    $Query .= "END;";

    //parse query
    ora_parse($Cursor, $Query);
```

```
ora_bind($Cursor, "input", ":php_in", 11, ORA_BIND_IN);
ora_bind($Cursor, "output", ":php_out", 11, ORA_BIND_OUT);

$input = 10;

//execute query
ora_exec($Cursor);

print("$output<BR>\n");

//close the oracle cursor
ora_close($Cursor);

//disconnect.
ora_logoff($Connection);
?>
```

boolean ora_close(integer cursor)

The `ora_close` function closes a connection opened by `ora_open`. See `ora_bind` for an example of use.

string ora_columnname(integer cursor, integer column)

The `ora_columnname` function returns the name of the specified column. Columns are numbered from zero. See `ora_exec` for an example of use.

integer ora_columnsize(integer cursor, string column)

The `ora_columnsize` function returns the size of the specified column. Columns are numbered from zero. Alternatively, you may specify a column by its name. See `ora_exec` for an example of use.

string ora_columntype(integer cursor, integer column)

The `ora_columntype` function returns the data type of the specified column. Columns are numbered from zero. Alternatively, you may specify a column by its name. The type will be one of the following: CHAR, CURSOR, DATE, LONG, LONG RAW, NUMBER, ROWID, VARCHAR, VARCHAR2. See ora_exec for an example of use.

boolean ora_commit(integer connection)

The ora_commit function commits all the pending transactions on the connection. By default, all transactions are committed after a call to ora_exec.

boolean ora_commitoff(integer connection)

Use ora_commitoff to turn off automatic commits. By default, PHP commits each transaction.

boolean ora_commiton(integer connection)

Use ora_commiton to turn on automatic commits. By default, PHP commits each transaction.

integer ora_do(integer connection, string query)

The ora_do function executes a query on the given connection. PHP takes care of creating a cursor, parsing the query, and executing it. A cursor identifier is returned.

```
<?
        //in case these aren't set for httpd
        putenv("ORACLE_HOME=/usr/local/oracle7");
        putenv("ORACLE_SID=ORCL");

        // connect to server
        if($Connection = ora_logon("scott", "tiger"))
        {
                $Query = "SELECT ENAME ";
                $Query .= "FROM emp ";
                $Query .= "WHERE ENAME LIKE 'SMI%' ";

                if($Cursor = ora_do($Connection, $Query))
                {
                        ora_fetch($Cursor);

                        print(ora_columnname($Cursor, 0) . "<BR>\n");
```

```
                        // Close the Oracle cursor
                        ora_close($Cursor);
                }

                // disconnect.
                ora_logoff($Connection);
        }
?>
```

string ora_error(integer identifier)

The `ora_error` function returns a string that describes the error for the last command sent to the Oracle database. The identifier may be either a connection identifier or a cursor identifier.

The message takes the form of xxx-nnnnn, where xxx tells you where the error came from and nnnnn tells you the error number. If you want to look up a description of the error, you can use Oracle's `oerr` command. See `ora_exec` for an example of use.

integer ora_errorcode(integer identifier)

The `ora_errorcode` function returns the error number for the last command sent to the Oracle server. The identifier may be either a connection identifier or a cursor identifier. See `ora_exec` for an example of use.

boolean ora_exec(integer cursor)

The `ora_exec` function executes a query previously parsed by the `ora_parse` function. Compare this function to `ora_do`.

```
<?
    //in case these aren't set for httpd
    putenv("ORACLE_HOME=/usr/local/oracle7");
    putenv("ORACLE_SID=ORCL");

    function reportError($id, $message)
    {
        print("$message<BR>\n");

        print("Error Code: " . ora_errorcode($id) . "<BR>\n");
```

```
                print("Error Message: " . ora_error($id) . "<BR>\n");
}


//connect to server
if(!($Connection = ora_logon("scott", "tiger")))
{
        print("Could not connect to database!<BR>\n");
        exit;
}

//open cursor
if(!($Cursor = ora_open($Connection)))
{
        reportError($Connection, "Cursor could not be opened!");
        exit;
}

$Query = "SELECT * ";
$Query .= "FROM emp ";

//parse query
if(!ora_parse($Cursor, $Query))
{
        reportError($Cursor, "Statement could not be parsed!");
        exit;
}

// execute query
if(!ora_exec($Cursor))
{
        reportError($Cursor, "Statement could not be executed!");
        exit;
}

//start table
print("<TABLE BORDER=\"1\">\n");

//print header row that describes each column
print("<TR>\n");

for($i = 0; $i < ora_numcols($Cursor); $i++)
{
        print("<TH>");

        // get column info
```

```
                print(ora_columnname($Cursor, $i) . ": ");
                print(ora_columntype($Cursor, $i) . " ");
                print("(" . ora_columnsize($Cursor, $i) . ")");

                print("</TH>\n");
        }

        print("</TR>\n");

        // get each row
        while(ora_fetch($Cursor))
        {
                print("<TR>\n");

                //loop over each column
                for($i = 0; $i < ora_numcols($Cursor); $i++)
                {
                        print("<TD>");

                        // get column
                        print(ora_getcolumn($Cursor, $i));

                        print("</TD>\n");
                }

                print("</TR>\n");

        }

        //close table
        print("</TABLE>\n");

        print("<BR>\n");
        print("Rows: " . ora_numrows($Cursor));
        print("<BR>\n");

        // Close the Oracle cursor
        ora_close($Cursor);

        // disconnect.
        ora_logoff($Connection);
?>
```

boolean ora_fetch(integer cursor)

The `ora_fetch` function causes a row from an executed query to be fetched into the cursor. This allows you to call `ora_getcolumn`. See `ora_exec` for an example of use.

integer ora_fetch_into(integer cursor, reference fields, integer flags)

The `ora_fetch_into` function gets the next row from the cursor and puts it into the `fields` argument, which must be passed by reference. Fields will contain an array indexed by numbers, starting with zero. The number of fields fetched is returned. The optional `flags` argument is a bit field that uses two constants, `ORA_FETCHINTO_ASSOC` and `ORA_FETCHINTO_NULLS`. The first instructs `ora_fetch_into` to create array elements named by their database fields. The second allows causes null columns to be represented as empty strings.

```
<?
        //in case these aren't set for httpd
        putenv("ORACLE_HOME=/usr/local/oracle7");
        putenv("ORACLE_SID=ORCL");


        //connect to server
        if(!($Connection = ora_logon("scott", "tiger")))
        {
                print("Could not connect to database!<BR>\n");
                exit;
        }

        $Query = "SELECT EMPNO ";
        $Query .= "FROM emp ";

        if(!($Cursor = ora_do($Connection, $Query)))
        {
                print("Cursor could not be opened!<BR>\n");
                print("Error Code: " . ora_errorcode($Connection) . "<BR>\n");
                print("Error Message: " . ora_error($Connection) . "<BR>\n");
                exit;
        }
```

```
while(ora_fetch_into($Cursor, &$Column))
{
        print("$Column[0]<BR>\n");
}

// Close the Oracle cursor
ora_close($Cursor);

// disconnect.
ora_logoff($Connection);
?>
```

string ora_getcolumn(integer cursor, integer column)

The `ora_getcolumn` function returns the value of the column for the current row. Columns are indexed starting with zero. Long columns are limited to 64K. See `ora_exec` for an example of use.

boolean ora_logoff(integer connection)

Use `ora_logoff` to disconnect from the database server. See `ora_exec` for an example of use.

integer ora_logon(string user, string password)

The `ora_logon` function begins a connection with an Oracle database server. A connection identifier is returned. See `ora_exec` for an example of use. As stated at the beginning of this section, you must define environment variables that specify the server in order to make a successful connection.

integer ora_numcols(integer cursor)

The `ora_numcols` function returns the number of columns for a query that has been executed. See `ora_exec` for an example of use.

integer ora_numrows(integer cursor)

The `ora_numrows` function returns the number of rows in the result set for an executed query. See `ora_exec` for an example of use.

integer ora_open(integer connection)

The `ora_open` function opens a cursor for the given connection. See `ora_exec` for an example of use.

boolean ora_parse(integer cursor, string query)

The `ora_parse` function parses a query and readies it for execution. See `ora_exec` for an example of use.

integer ora_plogon(string user, string password)

The `ora_plogon` function returns a connection identifier. A persistent connection will be created. It will last as long as the server process. Later calls to either `ora_logon` or `ora_plogon` will find persistent connections and use them instead of creating new ones. Connections created with `ora_plogon` should not be used with `ora_logoff`.

boolean ora_rollback(integer connection)

The `ora_rollback` function performs a rollback on the given connection. Automatic commits must be turned off first.

Postgres

Postgres was originally developed at the University of California, Berkeley. It introduced many of the advanced object-relational concepts becoming popular in commercial databases. PostgreSQL is the most current incarnation of Postgres and is considered to be version 6. It implements almost all of the SQL specification. Best of all, it's free.

As with other sections in this chapter, the descriptions of the functions can't stand alone. You will have to study PostgreSQL to fully understand how they work. More information may be found at the official PostgreSQL Web site at <http://www.postgresql.org/>.

Zeev Suraski wrote the original Postgres extension. Jouni Ahto added support for large objects.

boolean pg_close(integer connection)

Use `pg_close` to close a connection to a PostgreSQL database. See `pg_exec` for an example of use.

integer pg_cmdtuples(integer result)

The `pg_cmdtuples` function returns the number of instances affected by the last query. This includes DELETE, INSERT, and UPDATE statements, but not SELECT statements.

```
<?
    //connect to database
    $Connection = pg_connect("", "", "", "", "leon");

    $Query = "INSERT INTO item ";
    $Query .= "VALUES ('hammer', 15.00) ";

    //execute query
    $Result = pg_exec($Connection, $Query);

    //tell user how many rows were inserted
    print(pg_cmdtuples($Result) . " rows inserted.<BR>\n");

    //close connection
    pg_close($Connection);
?>
```

integer pg_connect(string connection)
integer pg_connect(string host, string port, string database)
integer pg_connect(string host, string port, string options, string database)
integer pg_connect(string host, string port, string options, string tty, string database)

The `pg_connect` function returns a connection identifier to a PostgreSQL database. The prototype displayed above is actually only one of several configurations for the arguments.

If you provide only one argument, then it is assumed to be a connection string. This should be in the style expected by PostgreSQL. If you provide three arguments, `pg_connect` expects host, port, and database, in that order. If you provide four arguments, `pg_connect` expects host, port, options, and database. Finally, you may provide all five arguments in the order described in the last prototype. If blanks are used for any argument, a sensible default will be used.

Compare this function to `pg_pconnect`. See `pg_exec` for an example of use.

string pg_dbname(integer connection)

Use `pg_dbname` to get the name of the current database. See `pg_exec` for an example of use.

string pg_errormessage(integer connection)

The `pg_errormessage` function returns the error message for the last database action. See `pg_exec` for an example of use.

integer pg_exec(integer connection, string query)

The `pg_exec` function executes a query on the given connection. A result identifier is returned.

```
<?
    //connect to database
    if(!($Connection = pg_connect("", "", "", "", "leon")))
    {
        print("Could not establish connection.<BR>\n");
        exit;
    }
```

```php
//print information about connection
print("Connection established<BR>\n");
print("Host: " . pg_host($Connection) . "<BR>\n");
print("Port: " . pg_port($Connection) . "<BR>\n");
print("Database: " . pg_dbname($connection) . "<BR>\n");
print("Options: " . pg_options($connection) . "<BR>\n");
print("<BR>\n");

//create query
$Query = "SELECT * ";
$Query .= "FROM item";

//execute query
if(!($Result = pg_exec($Connection, $Query)))
{
      print("Could not execute query: ");
      print(pg_errormessage($Connection));
      print("<BR>\n");
      exit;
}


// print each row in a table
print("<TABLE>\n");

// print header row
print("<TR>\n");

for($Field=0; $Field < pg_numfields($Result); $Field++)
{
      print("<TD>");

      print(pg_fieldname($Result, $Field) . " ");
      print(pg_fieldtype($Result, $Field));
      print("(" . pg_fieldsize($Result, $Field) . ")");

      print("</TD>\n");
}
print("</TR>\n");

//loop through rows
for($Row=0; $Row < pg_numrows($Result); $Row++)
{
      print("<TR>\n");
```

```
        for($Field=0; $Field < pg_numfields($Result); $Field++)
        {
                print("<TD>");

                if(pg_fieldisnull($Result, $Row, $Field))
                {
                        $price = "NULL";
                }
                else
                {
                        print(pg_result($Result, $Row, $Field));
                }

                print("</TD>\n");
        }

        print("</TR>\n");
    }

    print("</TABLE>\n");

    // free the result and close the connection
    pg_freeresult($Result);
    pg_close($Connection);
?>
```

array pg_fetch_array(integer result, integer row)

The pg_fetch_array function returns an array containing every field value for the given row. The values are indexed by number, starting with zero, and by column name. Each call to pg_fetch_array returns the next row, or FALSE when no rows remain. Compare this function to pg_fetch_object and pg_fetch_row.

```
<?
    //connect to database
    if(!($Connection = pg_connect("", "", "", "", "leon")))
    {
            print("Could not establish connection.<BR>\n");
            exit;
    }

    //create query
```

```
$Query = "SELECT * ";
$Query .= "FROM item";

//execute query
if(!($Result = pg_exec($Connection, $Query)))
{
        print("Could not execute query: ");
        print(pg_errormessage($Connection));
        print("<BR>\n");
        exit;
}

//loop over each row
while($Row = pg_fetch_array($Result, $Row))
{
        print($Row["Name"] . "<BR>\n");
}

// free the result and close the connection
pg_freeresult($Result);
pg_close($Connection);
?>
```

object pg_fetch_object(integer result, integer row)

The pg_fetch_object function returns an object with a property for every field. Each property is named after the field name. Each call to pg_fetch_object returns the next row, or FALSE when no rows remain. Compare this function to pg_fetch_array and pg_fetch_row.

```
<?
//connect to database
if(!($Connection = pg_connect("", "", "", "", "leon")))
{
        print("Could not establish connection.<BR>\n");
        exit;
}

//create query
$Query = "SELECT * ";
$Query .= "FROM item";

//execute query
if(!($Result = pg_exec($Connection, $Query)))
```

```
      {
              print("Could not execute query: ");
              print(pg_errormessage($Connection));
              print("<BR>\n");
              exit;
      }

      //loop over each row
      while($Row = pg_fetch_object($Result, $Row))
      {
              print("$Row->Name<BR>\n");
      }

      // free the result and close the connection
      pg_freeresult($Result);
      pg_close($Connection);
?>
```

array pg_fetch_row(integer result, integer row)

The pg_fetch_row function returns the values of all the fields in a row. The fields may are indexed by their field number, starting with zero. Each call to pg_fetch_object returns the next row, or FALSE when no rows remain. Compare this function to pg_fetch_array, and pg_fetch_object.

```
<?
      //connect to database
      if(!($Connection = pg_connect("", "", "", "", "leon")))
      {
              print("Could not establish connection.<BR>\n");
              exit;
      }

      //create query
      $Query = "SELECT * ";
      $Query .= "FROM item";

      //execute query
      if(!($Result = pg_exec($Connection, $Query)))
      {
              print("Could not execute query: ");
              print(pg_errormessage($Connection));
              print("<BR>\n");
              exit;
```

```
}

//loop over each row
while($Row = pg_fetch_row($Result, $Row))
{
        print("$Row[0]<BR>\n");
}

// free the result and close the connection
pg_freeresult($Result);
pg_close($Connection);
?>
```

boolean pg_fieldisnull(integer result, integer row, string field)

The pg_fieldisnull function returns TRUE if the specified field is NULL. Fields are counted from 0. See pg_exec for an example of use.

string pg_fieldname(integer result, integer field)

The pg_fieldname function returns the name of the field in the result set specified by the field number, which starts counting at zero. See pg_exec for an example of use.

integer pg_fieldnum(integer result, string field)

The pg_fieldnum function returns the number of the field given its name. Numbering begins with 0. If an error occurs, negative one (–1) is returned.

```
<?
    print(pg_fieldnum($Result, "name"));
?>
```

integer pg_fieldprtlen(integer result, integer row, string field)

The pg_fieldprtlen function returns the printed length of a particular field value. You may specify the field either by number, starting at zero, or by name.

```
<?
        print(pg_fieldprtlen($Result, $Row, 2));
?>
```

integer pg_fieldsize(integer result, string field)

The `pg_fieldsize` function returns the size of the field, which may be specified by name or number. Fields are numbered from zero. See `pg_exec` for an example of use.

string pg_fieldtype(integer result, string field)

The `pg_fieldtype` function returns the type of the specified field. The `field` argument may be a number or a name. Fields are numbered starting with zero. See `pg_exec` for an example of use.

boolean pg_freeresult(integer result)

The `pg_freeresult` function frees any memory associated with the result set. Ordinarily it is not necessary to call this function, as all memory will be cleared when the script ends. See `pg_exec` for an example of use.

integer pg_getlastoid()

The `pg_getlastoid` function returns the object ID (OID) of the last object inserted into a table if the last call to `pg_exec` was an INSERT statement. Negative one (–1) is returned if there is an error.

```
<?
        //connect to database
        $Connection = pg_connect("", "", "", "", "leon");

        $Query = "INSERT INTO item (name, price) ";
        $Query .= "VALUES ('hammer', 15.00)";

        $Result = pg_exec($Connection, $Query);

        print("ID of inserted item: " . pg_getlastoid() . "<BR>\n");

        pg_close($Connection);
?>
```

string pg_host(integer connection)

The pg_host function returns the name of the host for the connection. See pg_exec for an example of use.

pg_loclose(integer file)

The pg_loclose function closes a large object. The file argument is a file identifier returned by pg_loopen. See pg_loopen for an example of use.

integer pg_locreate(integer connection)

The pg_locreate function creates a large object and returns the OID. The object is created with both read and write access.

```
<?
    $Object = pg_locreate($Connection);
?>
```

integer pg_loopen(integer connection, integer object, string mode)

The pg_loopen function opens a large object. The object argument is a valid large object ID and the mode may be one of r, w, rw. A file identifier is returned.

```
<?
    $Object = pg_locreate($Connection);
    $File = pg_loopen($Connection, $Object, "r");
    pg_loclose($File);
?>
```

string pg_loread(integer file, integer length)

The pg_loread function returns the large object as a string. The length argument specifies a maximum length to return.

```
<?
    $Object = pg_locreate($Connection);
    $File = pg_loopen($Connection, $Object, "r");
    $Contents = pg_loread($File, 4096);
?>
```

pg_loreadall(integer file)

The pg_loreadall function reads an entire large object and sends it directly to the browser.

```
<?
        $File = pg_loopen($Connection, $Object, "r");
        pg_loreadall($File);
?>
```

pg_lounlink(integer file, integer object)

Use pg_lounlink to delete a large object.

```
<?
        $Object = pg_locreate($Connection);
        $File = pg_loopen($Connection, $Object, "r");
        pg_lounlink($File, $Object);
?>
```

pg_lowrite(integer file, string buffer)

The pg_lowrite function writes the named buffer to the large object.

```
<?
        $Object = pg_locreate($Connection);
        $File = pg_loopen($Connection, $Object, "w");
        pg_lowrite($File, "some text");
?>
```

integer pg_numfields(integer result)

The pg_numfields function returns the number of fields in the result set. See pg_exec for an example of use.

integer pg_numrows(integer result)

Use pg_numrows to get the number of rows in the result set. See pg_exec for an example of use.

string pg_options(integer connection)

The pg_options function returns the options used when the connection was opened. See pg_exec for an example of use.

integer pg_pconnect(string host, string port, string options, string tty, string database)

The pg_pconnect function operates identically to pg_connect, except that a persistent connection is created. This connection will last as long as the server process, so it may be recycled. This saves the overhead time of opening a connection.

```
<?
        $Connection = pg_pconnect("", "", "", "", "leon");
?>
```

integer pg_port(integer connection)

The pg_port function returns the port number used in the pg_connect function. See pg_exec for an example of use.

string pg_result(integer result, integer row, string field)

Use pg_result to get the value of a specific field in a result set. Rows and fields are numbered from zero, but fields may also be specified by name. See pg_exec for an example of use.

string pg_tty(integer connection)

The pg_tty function returns the tty name used for debugging and supplied with the pg_connect function. See pg_exec for an example of use.

Sybase

Sybase offers an industrial-strength database that stands among other big competitors such as Oracle, Informix, and IBM's DB2. Unlike these other databases, Sybase is more available to developers with small budgets because of partnerships with application vendors. InterShop's electronic commerce server comes with a Sybase database. Microsoft's SQL Server 6.5 is a dressed-up version of Sybase. In fact, PHP's Sybase functions are able to connect to SQL Server databases. For the sake of code readability, there are function aliases for all the Sybase functions that start with `mssql_` instead of `sybase_`, but I've left them out of the reference to save space. Table 13.11 lists all `mssql_` aliases.

When support for Sybase is compiled for PHP, one of two libraries may be used. One is the older DB-Library. The other is its replacement, Client-Library. These two libraries are not compatible with each other, so PHP has special code to adapt either of them into a single set of functions. Consequently, some of these functions are present when using DB-Library and not

Table 13.11 MSSQL Functions

```
mssql_close
mssql_connect
mssql_data_seek
mssql_fetch_array
mssql_fetch_field
mssql_fetch_object
mssql_fetch_row
mssql_field_length
mssql_field_name
mssql_field_seek
mssql_field_type
mssql_free_result
mssql_get_last_message
mssql_min_error_severity
mssql_min_message_severity
mssql_num_fields
mssql_num_rows
mssql_pconnect
mssql_query
mssql_result
mssql_select_db
```

when using Client-Library. Also, it is possible to compile PHP for Windows using an MSSQL library. This library is really just the DB-Library, but the PHP extension creates only `mssql_` functions. It also contains three functions unavailable in the Sybase extension: `mssql_field_length`, `mssql_field_name`, and `mssql_field_type`.

Sybase's home page is <http://www.sybase.com/>. If you want to learn more about the two libraries, check out the online documentation

```
<http://sybooks.sybase.com/onlinebooks/group-
cn/cng1110e/ctref/@Generic__BookView>.
```

Tom May and Zeev Suraski both contributed to the sybase extension.

integer sybase_affected_rows(integer link)

Use `sybase_affected_rows` to get the number of rows affected by the last delete, insert, or update statement on a given connection. If the optional link argument is left out, the most recently opened connection will be used. Note that this function is not useful for determining the number of rows returned by a select statement. Also, this function is available only when using Client-Library.

```
<?
        //open connection as admin
        $Link = sybase_pconnect("db1", "sa", "sa");

        //use the store database
        sybase_select_db("store", $Link);

        //take 10% off all items that cost
        //more than ten dollars
        $Query = "UPDATE item ";
        $Query .= "SET Price = Price * 0.90 ";
        $Query .= "WHERE Price > 10.00 ";
        $Result = sybase_query($Query, $Link);

        //get number of rows changed
        $RowsChanged = sybase_affected_rows($Link);

        print("$RowsChanged prices updated.<BR>\n");

        //close connection
        sybase_close($Link);
?>
```

boolean sybase_close(integer link)

The `sybase_close` function closes a connection to a database. Its use is not strictly necessary, since PHP will close connections for you when your script ends. You can leave out the `link` argument, and the last connection to be opened will be closed.

integer sybase_connect(string server, string user, string password)

The `sybase_connect` function returns a connection identifier based on the `server`, `user` and `password` arguments. The server must be a valid server name as defined in the interfaces file. All the arguments are optional, and if left out, PHP will use sensible defaults. Connections created with `sybase_connect` will be closed automatically when your script completes. Compare this function with `sybase_pconnect`.

boolean sybase_data_seek(integer result, integer row)

The `sybase_data_seek` function moves the internal row pointer for a result to the specified row. Rows are numbered starting with zero. Use this function with `sybase_fetch_array`, `sybase_fetch_object` or `sybase_fetch_row` to move arbitrarily among the result set.

```
<?
    //move to sixth row
    sybase_data_seek($Result, 5);
?>
```

array sybase_fetch_array(integer result)

The `sybase_fetch_array` function returns an array that contains the values of all the fields for the next row. Each call to `sybase_fetch_array` gets the next row in the result set, or returns FALSE if no rows remain.

Each field is returned in two elements. One is indexed by the field number, starting with zero. The other is indexed by the name of the field. Compare this function to `sybase_fetch_object` and `sybase_fetch_row`.

```
<?
        //connect
        $Link = sybase_pconnect();

        //use the store database
        sybase_select_db("store", $Link);

        //get all items
        $Result = sybase_query("SELECT * FROM item ");

        print("<TABLE BORDER=\"1\">\n");

        //get rows
        while($Row = sybase_fetch_array($Result))
        {
                print("<TR>\n");

                print("<TD>" . $Row["Name"] . "</TD>\n");

                print("<TD>" . $Row["Price"] . "</TD>\n");

                print("</TR>\n");
        }

        print("</TABLE>\n");

?>
```

object sybase_fetch_field(integer result, integer field)

The sybase_fetch_field function returns an object that describes a field in the result set. The field argument is optional. If left out, the next field is returned. The object contains the properties described in Table 13.12. See sybase_result for an example of use.

object sybase_fetch_object(integer result)

The sybase_fetch_object function returns an object with a property for each of the fields in the next row. Each call to sybase_fetch_object gets the next row in the result set, or returns FALSE if no rows remain. Compare this function to sybase_fetch_array and sybase_fetch_row.

Table 13.12 `sybase_fetch_field` Object Properties	
Property	*Description*
`column_source`	The name of the table the column belongs to.
`max_length`	The maximum size of the field.
`name`	Name of the column.
`numeric`	If the column is numeric, this property will be true (1).

```
<?
      //connect
      $Link = sybase_pconnect();

      //use the store database
      sybase_select_db("store", $Link);

      //get all items
      $Result = sybase_query("SELECT * FROM item ");

      print("<TABLE BORDER=\"1\">\n");

      //get rows
      while($Row = sybase_fetch_object($Result))
      {
            print("<TR>\n");

            print("<TD>$Row->Name</TD>\n");

            print("<TD>$Row->Price</TD>\n");

            print("</TR>\n");
      }

      print("</TABLE>\n");

?>
```

array sybase_fetch_row(integer result)

The `sybase_fetch_row` function returns an array of all the field values for the next row. The fields are indexed by integers starting with zero. Each call to `sybase_fetch_row` gets the next row in the result set, or returns FALSE if no rows remain. Compare this function to `sybase_fetch_array` and `sybase_fetch_object`.

```
<?
        //connect
        $Link = sybase_pconnect();

        //use the store database
        sybase_select_db("store", $Link);

        //get all items
        $Result = sybase_query("SELECT * FROM item ");

        print("<TABLE BORDER=\"1\">\n");

        //get rows
        while($Row = sybase_fetch_array($Result))
        {
                print("<TR>\n");

                print("<TD>" . $Row[0] . "</TD>\n");

                print("<TD>" . $Row[1] . "</TD>\n");

                print("</TR>\n");
        }

        print("</TABLE>\n");
?>
```

boolean sybase_field_seek(integer result, integer field)

The `sybase_field_seek` function moves the internal field pointer to the specified field. Fields are numbered starting with zero. If you leave out the `field` argument, the internal pointer will be moved to the next field. This is the same internal pointer used by `sybase_fetch_field`.

```
<?
        // go back to first field
        sybase_field_seek($result, 0);
?>
```

boolean sybase_free_result(integer result)

The `sybase_free_result` function frees memory associated with a result set. It is not strictly necessary to call this function. All memory is freed when a script finishes executing.

string sybase_get_last_message()

The `sybase_get_last_message` function returns the last message from the Sybase database. This function is not available if you're using Client-Library instead of DB-Library.

```
<?
    print(sybase_get_last_message());
?>
```

sybase_min_client_serverity(integer severity)

This function is available only when using Client-Library. It sets the minimum severity for messages sent from the client interface to be turned into PHP error messages.

sybase_min_error_severity(integer severity)

Use `sybase_min_error_severity` to set the minimum severity level for errors to be turned into PHP error messages. This function is available only when using DB-Library.

sybase_min_message_severity(integer severity)

Use `sybase_min_message_severity` to set the minimum severity level for messages to be turned into PHP error messages. This function is available only when using DB-Library.

sybase_min_server_severity(integer severity)

This function is available only when using Client-Library. It sets the minimum level for messages from the server interface to cause PHP error messages to be generated.

integer sybase_num_fields(integer result)

The `sybase_num_fields` function returns the number fields in the given result set. See `sybase_result` for an example of use.

integer sybase_num_rows(integer result)

The `sybase_num_rows` function returns the number of rows in a result set. See `sybase_result` for an example of use.

integer sybase_pconnect(string server, string username, string password)

The `sybase_pconnect` function is identical to `sybase_connect`, except that connections created with this function persist after the script ends. The connection lasts as long as the server process does, so if the process executes another PHP script, the connection will be reused. Connections created with `sybase_pconnect` should not be closed with `sybase_close`.

integer sybase_query(string query, integer connection)

The `sybase_query` function executes a query on the given connection and returns a result identifier. This is used by many of the other functions in this section. If the connection argument is left out, the last opened connection is used.

string sybase_result(integer result, integer row, string field)

The `sybase_result` function returns the value of a particular field, identified by row and field. The `field` argument may be an integer or the name of a field. Fields and rows are numbered starting with zero. If performance is an issue, considering using `sybase_fetch_row`, which is much faster.

```
<?
    //connect using defaults
    $Link = sybase_connect();

    //use the store database
    sybase_select_db("store", $Link);

    //get all items
    $Result = sybase_query("SELECT * FROM item ");

    print("<TABLE BORDER=\"1\">\n");

    //header row
    $Fields = sybase_num_fields($Result);
```

```
        for($i = 0; $i < $Fields; $i++)
        {
                $Field = sybase_fetch_field($Result);

                print("<TR>\n");
                print("<TH>");
                print($Field->column_source);
                print(".");
                print($Field->name);
                print("(");
                print($Field->max_length);
                print(")");
                print("</TH>\n");
                print("</TR>\n");
        }

        // data rows
        $Rows = sybase_num_rows($Result);
        for($n = 0; $n < $Rows; $n++)
        {
                print("<TR>\n");

                for($i = 0; $i < $Fields; $i++)
                {
                        print("<TD>");
                        print(sybase_result($Result, $n, $i));
                        print("</TD>\n");
                }

                print("</TR>\n");
        }

        print("</TABLE>\n");

        sybase_free_result($Result);

        sybase_close($Link);
?>
```

boolean sybase_select_db(string database, integer connection)

The sybase_select_db function selects the database to use on the database server. If the connection argument is omitted, the last connection created will be used. See sybase_fetch_array for an example.

MISCELLANEOUS FUNCTIONS

Chapter 14

The functions in this section do not fit neatly into any other section of the functional reference. They are not available by default when compiling PHP, and most of them require extra libraries. While none are essential to building PHP scripts, some are quite useful in the right context. Because you may not be familiar with all the technologies in this chapter, I've attempted to give a brief synopsis and links to Web sites where you can learn more.

The list of extensions is growing rapidly. A few didn't make it into this edition of the book for several reasons. Some are very specialized, and perhaps not of general interest. Others are relatively immature, so I couldn't rely on them not to change. Most of them are documented in the online manual, and people, myself included, are working on documenting the others. It is likely that several new extensions will be created between the time this text is finished and when they become available. The extensions that I know exist and have chosen not to cover are: CyberCash, DAV, DOM, FDF, Hyperwave, ICAP, MCAL, NIS, PDF, Readline, Recode.

Apache

The functions in this section are available only when PHP is compiled as a module for the Apache Web server.

object apache_lookup_uri(string uri)

The `apache_lookup_uri` function evaluates a URI, or Universal Resource Identifier, and returns an object containing properties describing the URI. This function is a wrapper for a function that's part of the Apache Web Server's API: sub_req_lookup_uri. Consequently, you must be running PHP as an Apache module in order to use this function. The exact meaning of most of the returned object's properties is beyond this text. They mirror the properties of Apache's `request_rec` structure. The `sub_req_lookup_uri` function is contained in Apache's `http_request.c` source file, and the comments there may satisfy the truly curious.

Table 14.1 lists the properties of the returned object.

Table 14.1   Properties of the Object Returned by `apache_lookup_uri`

allowed

args

boundary

byterange

bytes_sent

clength

content_type

filename

handler

method

mtime

no_cache

no_local_copy

path_info

request_time

send_bodyct

status

status_line

the_request

unparsed_uri

uri

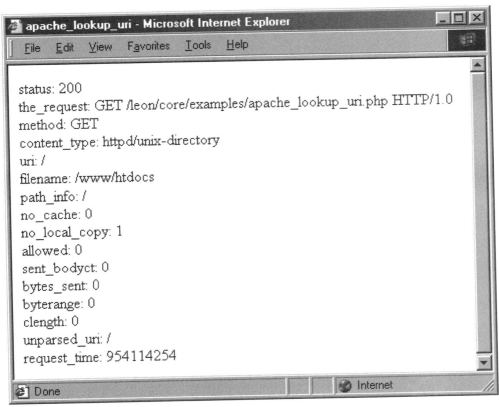

```
<?
        foreach((array)apache_lookup_uri("/") as $key=>$val)
        {
                print("$key: $val<BR>\n");
        }
?>
```

Figure 14-1   `apache_lookup_uri.`

string apache_note(string name, string value)

The `apache_note` function allows you to fetch and set values in Apache's note table. The current value of the named entry is returned. If the optional `value` argument is present, then the value of the entry will be changed to the supplied value. The notes table exists for the duration of the request made to the Apache Web Server and is available to any modules activated during the request. This function allows you to communicate with other Apache modules. One possible use of this functionality is the passing of information to the logging module.

Like `apache_lookup_uri`, the `apache_note` function deals with request records inside the Apache API. And like `apache_lookup_uri`, this function is available only when PHP is run as an Apache module. This function is a wrapper for the `table_get` and `table_set` functions that are part of the Apache API.

```
<?
     apache_note("session_id", $session_id);
?>
```

array getallheaders()

The `getallheaders` function returns every header sent by both the server and the browser. Some of these are turned into environment variables, which are then made available as variables inside your PHP script. Since this function relies on the Apache API, it is available only when you run PHP as an Apache module.

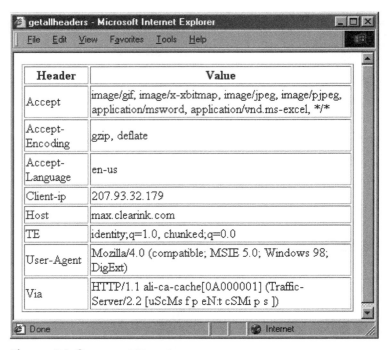

Header	Value
Accept	image/gif, image/x-xbitmap, image/jpeg, image/pjpeg, application/msword, application/vnd.ms-excel, */*
Accept-Encoding	gzip, deflate
Accept-Language	en-us
Client-ip	207.93.32.179
Host	max.clearink.com
TE	identity;q=1.0, chunked;q=0.0
User-Agent	Mozilla/4.0 (compatible; MSIE 5.0; Windows 98; DigExt)
Via	HTTP/1.1 ali-ca-cache[0A000001] (Traffic-Server/2.2 [uScMs f p eN:t cSMi p s])

Figure 14–2   `getallheaders`.

```
<?
     //start table
     print("<TABLE BORDER=\"1\">\n");
     print("<TR>\n");
     print("<TH>Header</TH>\n");
     print("<TH>Value</TH>\n");
     print("</TR>\n");

     //loop over headers
     foreach(getallheaders() as $header=>$value)
     {
          print("<TR>\n");
          print("<TD>$header</TD>\n");
          print("<TD>$value</TD>\n");
          print("</TR>\n");
     }

     //close table
     print("</TABLE>\n");
?>
```

Figure 14–2 Continued

boolean virtual(string filename)

The `virtual` function is available only when PHP is an Apache module. It is equivalent to writing `<!— #include virtual filename—>`, which is an Apache subrequest. You may wish to refer to the Apache documentation to learn more. Use the `include` and `require` functions if you want to parse a PHP script. `FALSE` is returned on error.

```
<?
     virtual("ssi-example.shtml");
?>
```

Aspell

The Aspell library is used to verify the spelling of a word. It is the result of an open source project run by Kevin Atkinson. The official Web site is <http://metalab.unc.edu/kevina/aspell/>. In order for PHP to use Aspell, the functions must be loaded as an extension. At the time of this writing, no win32 extension existed for Aspell, so its functionality is available to UNIX users only. Mark Musone added Aspell support to PHP.

integer aspell_new(string dictionary, string personal_words)

Use aspell_new to load a dictionary into the system. An identifier is returned that must be used in subsequent calls to Aspell functions. The second argument is optional and specifies a personal dictionary.

```
<?
//create a test sentence
$text = "Thiss sentense haz some spelling erors.";

//load dictionary
$aspell_link = aspell_new('english');

//tokenize sentence
for($word = strtok($text, ' ');
      $word != ''; $word = strtok(' '))
{
      //check for unrecognized words
      if(!aspell_check($aspell_link, $token))
      {
            //try checking raw version
            if(!aspell_check_raw($aspell_link, $token))
            {
                  //word not recognized, get suggestions
                  $suggestion = aspell_suggest($aspell_link, $token);

                  print("<B>Unrecognized word:</B>
                  $token<BR>\n");

                  while(list($index, $word) = each($suggestion))
```

```
                                     {
                                         print("$val<BR>\n");
                                     }

                                     print("<BR>\n");
                         }
                 }
         }
?>
```

boolean aspell_check(integer link, string word)

The `aspell_check` function returns `true` if the word argument is found in the dictionary specified by the `link` argument. This function attempts to trim extraneous characters before validating the spelling.

boolean aspell_check_raw(integer link, string word)

This function behaves like `aspell_check`, except that it makes no attempt to trim extraneous characters.

array aspell_suggest(integer link, string word)

The `aspell_suggest` function returns an array of suggested spellings for a word. The `link` argument is an integer returned by the `aspell_new` function.

COM

The component object model (COM) is a framework that allows sharing of executable modules without recompiling. If you have used Windows for any time at all, you are aware of dynamic-link libraries (DLLs), collections of functions a program can load on demand. Many programs can share a DLL, which goes a long way toward the principle of reuse. Unfortunately, DLLs that work well with some programming languages don't work at all with others. COM seeks to solve this problem. COM objects are accessible by C++, Visual Basic, Java, and PHP.

A tutorial on COM is beyond the scope of this text, of course. Microsoft's list of "noteworthy" books about COM is relatively long <http://www.microsoft.com/com/tech/com.asp>. However, you could keep busy just reading the articles online. You might read *Dr. GUI's Gentle Guide to COM* first <http://www.microsoft.com/com/news/drgui.asp>.

To use a COM object in PHP, you first load it with `com_load`. After that, you can invoke methods with `com_invoke`, and you get and set properties with `com_propget` and `com_propset`.

Zeev Suraski added COM support to PHP.

com_get

Use `com_get` as an alias for `com_propget`.

value com_invoke(integer object, string method, argument, argument, …)

The `com_invoke` function invokes a method on a COM object. You must specify a valid object resource identifier and the name of a method. If the method takes arguments, you list them after the method name.

integer com_load(string module, string server)

The `com_load` function loads the named COM object and returns a resource identifier to be used by the other COM functions. The optional `server` argument allows you to specify a remote server. FALSE is returned when the load fails. The module is named by its ProgID.

```
<?
    //load object
    if(!($beeper = com_load("BeepCntMod.BeepCnt")))
    {
        print("Could not load object!<BR>\n");
        exit();
    }

    //print current value of count
    print(com_propget($beeper, "Count") . "<BR>\n");

    //change count
    com_propset($beeper, "Count", 6);
```

```
        //make a beep
        com_invoke($beeper, "Beep");
?>
```

value com_propget(integer object, string property)

The com_propget function returns the value of a property on a COM object.

com_propput

Use com_propput as an alias for com_propset.

boolean com_propset(integer object, string property, value data)

The com_propset function changes the value of a property.

com_set

Use com_set as an alias for com_propset.

Gettext

The Gettext functions are based on work by the GNU Translation Project. They aim to make it easier to write programs that send messages to users in their preferred language. You can read more about gettext on the GNU site <http://www.gnu.org/software/gettext/gettext.html>. The PHP functions are wrappers for the gettext library. Detailed documentation is available on the Web <http://www.gnu.org/manual/gettext/index.html>. The Gettext functions rely on translation tables. These are usually given either .po or .mo extensions and are collected into directories. There is a global area for these files, but you can override that directory using bindtextdomain.

The Gettext functions were added to PHP by Alex Plotnick.

string bindtextdomain(string domain, string directory)

The `bintextdomain` function sets the path for a domain.

string dcgettext(string domain, string message, int category)

The `dcgettext` function allows you to override the current domain for a single message lookup, and it also allows you to specify a category. The gettext manual questions the usefulness of this function.

string dgettext(string domain, string message)

The `dgettext` function allows you to override the current domain for a single message lookup.

string gettext(string message)
string _(string message)

The Gettext function attempts to return a translated string. The `message` argument is used as both the key to the translation table and the default text if a translation is not found. The underscore character is an alias for the `gettext` function to help reduce cluttering your code.

```
<?
        //set language to Spanish
        putenv("LANG=es");

        //specify location of translation tables
        bindtextdomain("error_messages", "./locale");

        //choose domain
        textdomain("error_messages");

        //print a test message
        print(gettext("This book is named Core PHP Programming"));
?>
```

string textdomain(string domain)

The `textdomain` function sets the domain to search within when calls are made to `gettext`. The domain is usually the name of your application. The previous domain is returned. If you just want to get the current setting, pass an empty string. The default domain is called `messages`.

IMAP

IMAP is the Internet Message Access Protocol. It was developed in 1986 at Stanford University; however, it has been overshadowed by less sophisticated mail protocols, such as POP (Post Office Protocol). IMAP allows the user to manipulate mail on the server as if it existed locally.

PHP implements IMAP 4, the latest incarnation described in RFC 1730. More information may be obtained at `<http://www.imap.org/>`, the IMAP Connection.

IMAP support may be compiled directly into PHP or loaded as an extension. The extension has benefited from the work of many authors: Kaj-Michael Lang, Rasmus Lerdorf, Rex Logan, Mark Musone, Antoni Pamies Olive, Zeev Suraski, and Brian Wang.

string imap_8bit(string text)

The `imap_8bit` function converts an 8-bit string into a quote-printable string.

```
<?
    $qtext = imap_8bit($text);
?>
```

array imap_alerts()

The `imap_alerts` function returns all the alerts generated by IMAP functions as an array and clears the stack of alerts.

integer imap_append(integer stream, string mailbox, string message, string flags)

The `imap_append` function appends a message to a mailbox. The `stream` argument is an integer returned by `imap_open`. The `flags` argument is optional.

```
<?
    $mailbox = imap_open("{mail.server.com}INBOX", "leon","password");
    imap_append($mailbox, "INBOX", "This is a message");
    imap_close($mailbox);
?>
```

string imap_base64(string text)

Use imap_base64 to decode base64 text. This routine is part of the IMAP extension; base64_decode is a built-in PHP function that offers the same functionality.

```
<?
    $clear_text = imap_base64($encoded_text);
?>
```

string imap_binary(string text)

Use imap_binary to convert an 8-bit string into a base64 string.

```
<?
    $base64_text = imap_binary($clear_text);
?>
```

string imap_body(integer stream, integer message, integer flags)

The imap_body function returns the body of the specified message. The optional flags argument is a bit field that accepts the constants listed in Table 14.2. You can use the | operator to combine them.

Table 14.2   imap_body Flags

Constant	Description
FT_INTERNAL	Return the body using local line-end characters instead of CRLF.
FT_NOT	Do not fetch header lines.
FT_PEEK	Do not mark this message being read.
FT_PREFETCHTEXT	Fetch the text when getting the header.
FT_UID	The message argument is a UID.

```
<?
    // get first message and print it
    $mailbox = imap_open("{mail.server.com}INBOX", "leon", "password");
    $message = imap_body($mailbox, FT_INTERNAL);
    imap_close($mailbox);

    print($message);
?>
```

object imap_bodystruct(integer stream, integer message, integer section)

The `imap_bodystruct` function returns an object describing the structure of a body section. The object will contain the following properties: `bytes`, `description`, `disposition`, `dparameters`, `encoding`, `id`, `ifdescription`, `ifdisposition`, `ifdparameters`, `ifid`, `ifparameters`, `ifsubtype`, `lines`, `parameters`, `subtype`, `type`. The elements such as `ifsubtype` that begin with `if` are booleans that signal whether the similarly named elements are present.

object imap_check(integer stream)

The `imap_check` function returns information about the current mailbox in the form of an object. Table 14.3 lists the properties of the object. If the connection has timed out, `FALSE` is returned.

Table 14.3 Return Elements for `imap_check`	
Property	**Description**
Date	Date of the most recent message
Driver	Driver being used
Mailbox	Name of the mailbox
Nmsgs	Number of messages
Recent	Number of recent messages

```
<?

    //check for new messages

    $mailbox = imap_open("{mail.server.com}INBOX", "leon","secret");

    // Check messages
    $check = imap_check($mailbox);
    print($check->Date,"<br>\n");
    print("Connection Type: ",$check->Driver,"<br>\n");
    print("Mbox: ",$check->Mailbox,"<br>\n");
    print("Number Messages: ",$check->Nmsgs);
    print("Recent: ",$check->Recent,"<br>\n");

    // show headers for messages
    $nMessages=imap_num_msg($mailbox);
    for($index=1; $index <= $nMesssages ; $index++)
    {
        $header = imap_header($mailbox, $index);
        print($header->date . "<BR>\n");
        print($header->to . "<BR>\n");
        print($header->from . "<BR>\n");
        print($header->cc . "<BR>\n");
        print($header->replyTo . "<BR>\n");
        print($header->subject . "<BR>\n");
        print("<BR>\n");
print("<PRE>");
        print(imap_body($mbox,$i));
        print("</PRE>\n<HR>\n");
    }

    imap_close($mbox);
?>
```

string imap_clearflag_full(integer stream, string sequence, string flag, string options)

The imap_clearflag_full function deletes a flag on a sequence of messages. The options argument, if supplied, may be set to ST_UID, which signals that the sequence argument contains UIDs instead of message numbers.

```
<?
    $mailbox = imap_open("{news.server.com/nntp:119}", "leon", "password");
```

```
    imap_clearflag_full($mailbox, "12-15", "U", ST_UID);
    imap_close($mailbox);
?>
```

boolean imap_close(integer stream, integer flags)

Use `imap_close` to close a connection to a mailbox. The stream argument is an integer returned by `imap_open`. The optional `flags` argument may be set to CL_EXPUNGE, which will cause the mailbox to be expunged before closing.

imap_create

You may use `imap_create` as an alias for `imap_createmailbox`.

boolean imap_createmailbox(integer stream, string mailbox)

Use `imap_createmailbox` to create a mailbox.

```
<?
    // create a mailbox called PHP List
    $mailbox = imap_open("{mail.server.com}INBOX", "leon","password");
    imap_createmailbox($mailbox, "PHP List");
    imap_close($mailbox);
?>
```

boolean imap_delete(integer stream, integer message)

The `imap_delete` function marks a message for deletion. Use `imap_expunge` to cause the message to be permanently deleted.

```
<?
    // delete message number 3
    $mailbox = imap_open("{mail.server.com}INBOX", "leon","password");
    imap_delete($mailbox, 3);
    imap_close($mailbox);
?>
```

boolean imap_deletemailbox(integer stream, string mailbox)

The `imap_deletemailbox` function deletes the named mailbox.

```
<?
    // delete a mailbox
    $mailbox = imap_open("{mail.server.com}INBOX",
        "leon","password");
    imap_deletemailbox($mailbox, "PHP List");
    imap_close($mailbox);
?>
```

array imap_errors()

Use `imap_errors` to get an array of all errors generated by IMAP functions, removing them from an internal stack. You can use `imap_last_error` to get just the last error.

boolean imap_expunge(integer stream)

Use `imap_expunge` to remove all messages marked for deletion.

```
<?
//expunge messages
$mailbox = imap_open("{mail.server.com}INBOX", "leon", "password");
imap_expunge($mailbox);
imap_close($mailbox);
?>
```

array imap_fetch_overview(integer stream, integer message)

The `imap_fetch_overview` function returns an array that gives an overview of a message's headers. The array contains the following elements: answered, date, deleted, draft, flagged, from, message_id, msgno, recent, references, seen, size, subject, uid.

string imap_fetchbody(integer stream, integer message, integer part, integer flags)

The `imap_fetchbody` function gets a specific part of a message. The body parts are encoded in base64 and must be passed through `imap_base64` to be viewed as clear text. The `flags` argument accepts the flags described in Table 14.2.

```
<?
    // get first part of first message
    $mailbox=imap_open("{mail.server.com}INBOX", "leon", "password");
    $part1 = imap_fetchbody($mailbox, 1, 1);
    imap_close($mailbox);
?>
```

string imap_fetchheader(integer stream, integer message, integer flags)

Use `imap_fetchheader` to get the complete RFC 822 header text for a message. The `flags` argument is a bitfield that takes the following constants: `FT_UID`, `FT_INTERNAL` and `FT_PREFETCHTEXT`. The `FT_UID` and `FT_INTERNAL` constants have the same meaning as when used with the `imap_body` function. The `FT_PREFETCHTEXT` constant causes the message body to be fetched at the same time.

```
<?
    $mailbox=imap_open("{mail.server.com}INBOX", "leon", "password");
    print(imap_fetchheader($mailbox, 1, FT_PREFETCHTEXT));
    imap_close($mailbox);
?>
```

object imap_fetchstructure(integer stream, integer message)

The `imap_fetchstructure` returns an object with information about the specified message. Table 14.4 lists the properties of this object.

| Table 14.4 | `imap_fetchstructure` Properties |

Property	Datatype
type	Integer
encoding	Integer
ifsubtype	Boolean
subtype	String
ifdescription	Boolean
description	String
ifid	Boolean
id	String
lines	Integer
bytes	Integer
ifdisposition	Boolean
disposition	String
ifdparameters	Boolean
dparameters	Array of Objects
ifparameters	Boolean
parameters	Array of Objects
parts	Array of Objects

```
<?
    // get structure for first message
    $mailbox = imap_open("{mail.server.com}INBOX", "leon", "password");
    $structure = imap_fetchstructure($mailbox, 1);
    imap_close($mailbox);
?>
```

imap_fetchtext

You may use `imap_fetchtext` as an alias for `imap_body`.

array imap_getmailboxes(integer stream, string reference, string pattern)

The `imap_getmailboxes` function returns detailed information about mailboxes in the form of an array of objects. The `reference` argument is an IMAP server in the normal form: "{server:port}". The `pattern` argument controls which mailboxes are returned. An asterisk (*) matches all mailboxes, and a percentage symbol (%) matches all mailboxes at a particular level.

The returned objects contain three properties: `name`, `delimiter`, and `attributes`, a bitfield that may be tested against the constants listed in Table 14.5.

```
<?
    $mailbox = imap_open("{mail.server.com}INBOX", "leon", "password");
    $boxes = imap_getmailboxes($mailbox, "{mail.server.com:25}", "*");
    imap_close($mailbox);

    for(list($box) = each($boxes))
    {
        print("$box->name <BR>\n");
    }
?>
```

array imap_getsubscribed(integer stream, string reference, string pattern)

This function returns subscribed mailboxes. The `reference` and `pattern` arguments are optional.

Table 14.5　Constants in the `attributes` Property	
Constant	**Description**
LATT_NOINFERIORS	The mailbox contains no other mailboxes.
LATT_NOSELECT	The mailbox is a container only and cannot be opened.
LATT_MARKED	The mailbox is marked.
LATT_UNMARKED	The mailbox is unmarked.

object imap_header(integer stream, integer message, integer from_length, integer subject_length)

The imap_header function returns an object with properties matching message headers. The from_length and subject_length arguments are optional. These values govern the fetchfrom and fetchsubject properties, respectively. Table 14.6 lists the properties of the returned object.

Table 14.6 `imap_header` Properties

Property	Description
Answered	A if answered, blank otherwise.
bcc	Array of objects with the following properties: adl, host, mailbox, personal.
bccaddress	Full bcc: line, limited to 1024 characters.
cc	Array of objects with the following properties: adl, host, mailbox, personal.
ccaddress	Full cc: line, limited to 1024 characters.
Date	Date for the message.
date	Date for the message.
Deleted	D if marked for deletion, blank otherwise.
Draft	X if a draft, blank otherwise.
fetchfrom	The from: line limited by the from_length argument.
fetchsubject	The subject: line limited by the subject_length argument.
Flagged	F if flagged, blank otherwise.
followup_to	Full followup_to: line, limited to 1024 characters.
from	Array of objects with the following properties: adl, host, mailbox, personal.
fromaddress	Full from: line, limited to 1024 characters.
in_reply_to	The in_reply_to: line.
MailDate	Mail date

message_id	Unique ID assigned by mail server.
Msgno	Message number
newsgroups	The newsgroups: line.
Recent	
references	The references line.
remail	
reply_to	Array of objects with the following properties: adl, host, mailbox, personal.
reply_toaddress	The entire reply_to: line, limited to 1024 characters.
return_path	Array of objects with the following properties: adl, host, mailbox, personal.
return_pathaddress	The entire return_path: line, limited to 1024 characters.
sender	Array of objects with the following properties: adl, host, mailbox, personal.
senderaddress	The entire sender: line, limited to 1024 characters.
Size	Size of the message.
subject	Subject of the message.
Subject	Subject of the message.
to	Array of objects with the following properties: adl, host, mailbox, personal.
toaddress	The entire to: line, limited to 1024 characters.
udate	Timestamp
Unseen	U if the message is unread, blank otherwise.

```
<?
    $mailbox = imap_open("{mail.server.com}INBOX", "leon", "password");
    $header = imap_header($mailbox, 1);
    print("Subject: " . $header->subject);
    imap_close($mailbox);
?>
```

imap_headerinfo

The imap_headerinfo function is an alias for imap_header.

array imap_headers(integer stream)

The `imap_headers` function returns an array of strings, one element per message. Each string summarizes the headers for the message.

```
<?
    $mailbox = imap_open("{mail.server.com}INBOX", "leon", "password");
    $headers = imap_headers($mailbox);
    for($index = 0; $index < count($headers); $index++)
    {
        print($headers[$index] . "<BR>\n");
    }
    imap_close($mailbox);
?>
```

string imap_last_error()

Use `imap_last_error` to get the last error generated by an IMAP function.

imap_list

The `imap_list` function is an alias to `imap_listmailbox`.

imap_list_full

The `imap_list_full` function is an alias to `imap_getmailboxes`.

array imap_listmailbox(integer stream)

Use `imap_listmailbox` to get the name of every mailbox in an array.

```
<?
    $mailbox=imap_open("{mail.server.com}INBOX", "leon","password");
    $mailboxes = imap_listmailbox($mailbox);
    for($index = 0; $index < count($mailboxes); $index++)
    {
        print($mailboxes[$index] . "<BR>\n");
    }
    imap_close($mailbox);
?>
```

imap_listscan

The `imap_listscan` function is an alias for `imap_scanmailbox`.

integer imap_mail(string to, string subject, string message, string headers, string cc, string bcc, string rpath)

The `imap_mail` function is an alternative to the `mail` function. The difference is the arguments for specific headers.

string imap_mail_compose(array envelope, array body)

The `imap_mail_compose` function returns a MIME message given arrays describing the envelope and body. The `envelope` argument may contain the following elements: `bcc`, `cc`, `date`, `from`, `message_id`, `reply_to`, `return_path`, `to`. The `body` argument may contain the following elements: `bytes`, `contents.data`, `encoding`, `id`, `lines`, `md5`, `subtype`, `type`.

boolean imap_mail_copy(integer stream, string list, string mailbox, integer flags)

The `imap_mail_copy` function copies messages into another mailbox. The list of messages can be a list of messages or a range. The optional `flags` argument is a bitfield that may be set with `CP_UID`, which specifies that the list contains UIDs, or `CP_MOVE`, which instructs the function to delete the original messages after copying. This last functionality may be accomplished with the `imap_mail_move` function.

```
<?
    $mailbox = imap_open("{mail.server.com}INBOX", "leon", "password");
    imap_mail_copy($mailbox, "OLD", "17");
    imap_close($mailbox);
?>
```

boolean imap_mail_move(integer stream, string list, string mailbox)

The `imap_mail_move` function moves messages from the current mailbox to a new mailbox. The list of messages can be a list of messages or a range.

```
<?
$mailbox = imap_open("{mail.server.com}INBOX", "leon", "password");
imap_mail_move($mailbox, "OLD", "17");
imap_close($mailbox);
?>
```

object imap_mailboxmsginfo(integer stream)

Use `imap_mailboxmsginfo` to return information about the current mailbox. The object will have the properties listed in Table 14.7.

```
<?
$mailbox = imap_open("{mail.server.com}INBOX", "leon", "password");
$info = imap_mailboxmsginfo($mailbox);
print("Driver: " . $info->Driver);
imap_close($mailbox);
?>
```

integer imap_msgno(integer stream, integer uid)

The `imap_msgno` function returns the message number based on a UID. To get the UID based on message number, use `imap_uid`.

Table 14.7   Properties for `imap_mailboxmsginfo`
Date
Driver
Mailbox
Nmsgs
Recent
Size
Unread

integer imap_num_msg(integer stream)

The `imap_num_msg` function returns the number of messages in the current mailbox.

```
<?
    $mailbox = imap_open("{mail.server.com}INBOX", "leon", "password");
    print("Number of Messages: " . imap_num_recent($mailbox));
    imap_close($mailbox);
?>
```

integer imap_num_recent(integer stream)

The `imap_num_recent` function returns the number of recent messages in the current mailbox.

```
<?
    $mailbox = imap_open("{mail.server.com}INBOX", "leon", "password");
    print("Number of Messages: " . imap_num_msg($mailbox));
    imap_close($mailbox);
?>
```

integer imap_open(string mailbox, string username, string password, integer flags)

Use `imap_open` to begin a connection to a mail server. The `mailbox` argument is usually formed by adding a hostname to the beginning of the mailbox. The hostname is enclosed in curly braces. Adding `/pop3` causes the `imap_open` function to connect to a POP server instead of an IMAP server. Adding `/nntp` allows you to connect to a usenet server. You may also specify a port number, using a colon to separate it from the hostname. A stream identifier is returned. Use this identifier with the IMAP functions that require a stream. The optional `flags` argument is a bitfield that uses the constants listed in Table 14.8.

Table 14.8 Constants Used by `imap_open`	
Constant	*Description*
CL_EXPUNGE	Expunge mailboxes automatically on close.
OP_ANONYMOUS	Don't use `.newsrc` file if connecting to an NNTP server.
OP_DEBUG	Debug protocol negotiations
OP_EXPUNGE	Expunge connections.
OP_HALFOPEN	Open connection, but not a mailbox.
OP_PROTOTYPE	Return driver prototype.
OP_READONLY	Open in read-only mode.
OP_SECURE	Don't do nonsecure authentication.
OP_SHORTCACHE	Use short caching.
OP_SILENT	Don't pass up events.

```
<?
    //connect to a normal IMAP server
    $mailbox = imap_open("{mail.server.com:143}INBOX", "leon", "password");

    //connect to a POP3 server
    $mailbox = imap_open("{mail.server.com/pop3:110}INBOX", "leon", "pass-
    word");

    //connect to a NNTP server
    $mailbox = imap_open("{mail.server.com/nntp:119}INBOX", "leon",
    "password");
?>
```

boolean imap_ping(integer stream)

The `imap_ping` function checks the stream to makes sure it is still alive. If new mail has arrived, it will be detected when this function is called.

```
<?
    $mailbox = imap_open("{mail.server.com}INBOX", "leon", "password");
    imap_ping($mailbox);
    imap_close($mailbox);
?>
```

integer imap_popen(string mailbox, string username, string password, integer flags)

The `imap_popen` function opens a persistent connection to an IMAP server. This connection is not closed until the calling process ends, so it may be reused by many page requests. At the time of this writing the code behind this function was unfinished.

string imap_qprint(string text)

The `imap_qprint` function converts a quote-printable string into an 8-bit string.

```
<?
    $converted = imap_qprint($qstring);
?>
```

imap_rename

You may use `imap_rename` as an alias for `imap_renamemailbox`.

boolean imap_renamemailbox(integer stream, string old_name, string new_name)

The `imap_renamemailbox` function changes the name of a mailbox.

```
<?
        $mailbox = imap_open("{mail.server.com}INBOX", "leon", "password");
        imap_renamemailbox($mailbox, "PHP", "PHP List");
        imap_close($mailbox);
?>
```

boolean imap_reopen(integer stream, string username, string password, integer flags)

Use `imap_reopen` to open a connection that has died. Operation is identical to `imap_open`.

```
<?
    $mailbox = imap_open("{mail.server.com}INBOX", "leon", "password");

    // if connection is dead, reopen
    if(!imap_ping($mailbox))
    {
        imap_reopen($mailbox, "leon", "password");
    }

    imap_close($mailbox);
?>
```

array imap_rfc822_parse_adrlist(string address, string host)

The `imap_rfc_parse_adrlist` function parses an email address given a default host and returns an array of objects. Each object has the following properties: `mailbox`, `host`, `personal`, `adl`. The `mailbox` property is the name before the @. The `host` property is the destination machine or domain. The `personal` property is the name of the recipient. The `adl` property is the source route, the chain of machines the mail will travel, if the address is specified in that style.

As the name of the function suggests, this function implements addresses according to RFC 822.

```
<?
    $address = "Leon Atkinson <leon@clearink.com>, vicky";
    $info = imap_rfc822_parse_adrlist($address, "clearink.com");
    while(list($adr_info) = each($info))
    {
        print("$adr_info->personal ");
        print("$adr_info->mailbox ");
        print("$adr_info->host ");
        print("$adr_info->adl<BR>\n");
    }
?>
```

string imap_rfc822_write_address(string mailbox, string host, string personal_info)

The `imap_rfc822_write_address` returns an email address. As its name suggests, this function implements addresses according to RFC 822.

```
<?
      print(imap_rfc822_write_address("leon", "clearink.com", "Leon
      Atkinson"));
?>
```

imap_scan

You may use `imap_scan` as an alias for `imap_scanmailbox`.

array imap_scanmailbox(integer stream, string fragment)

The `imap_scanmailbox` function returns an array of mailbox names that contain the given fragment.

```
<?
      $mailbox = imap_open("{news.server.com/nntp:119}",
          "leon", "password");
      $name = imap_scanmailbox($mailbox, "alt.");
      while(list($match) = each($name))
      {
          print("$match<BR>\n");
      }
      imap_close($mailbox);
?>
```

array imap_search(integer stream, string criteria, integer flags)

Use `imap_search` to get a list of message numbers based on search criteria. The `criteria` argument is a list of search codes separated by spaces. The codes are listed in Table 14.9. Some of them take an argument, which must always be surrounded by double quotes. The optional `flags` argument may be set to `SE_UID` to cause UIDs to be returned instead of message numbers.

Table 14.9   `imap_search` Criteria Codes
ALL
ANSWERED
BCC "string"
BEFORE "date"
BODY "string"
CC "string"
DELETED
FLAGGED
FROM "string"
KEYWORD "string"
NEW
OLD
ON "date"
RECENT
SEEN
SINCE "date"
SUBJECT "string"
TEXT "string"
TO "string"
UNANSWERED
UNDELETED
UNFLAGGED
UNKEYWORD "string"
UNSEEN

```
<?
    //get list of unread messages from Leon
    $mailbox = imap_open("{mail.server.com:143}INBOX",
        "leon", "password");
    $msgs = imap_search($mailbox, "UNSEEN FROM \"leon\"");
    imap_close($mailbox);
?>
```

string imap_setflag_full(integer stream, string sequence, string flag, string options)

The `imap_setflag_full` function sets a flag on a sequence of messages. The `options` argument, if supplied, may be set to `ST_UID`, which signals that the `sequence` argument contains UIDs instead of message numbers.

```
<?
    $mailbox = imap_open("{mail.server.com:143}INBOX",
        "leon", "password");
    imap_setflag_full($mailbox, "12-15", "U", ST_UID);
    imap_close($mailbox);
?>
```

array imap_sort(integer stream, integer criteria, integer reverse, integer options)

Use the `imap_sort` function to get a sorted list of message numbers based on sort criteria. The `criteria` argument must be one of the constants defined in Table 14.10. If the `reverse` argument is set to 1, the sort order will be reversed. The `options` argument is a bitfield that may be set with `SE_UID`, specifying that UIDs are used, or `SE_NOPREFETCH`, which will stop messages from being prefetched.

Table 14.10   Criteria Constants for `imap_sort`

Constant	Description
SORTARRIVAL	Arrival date
SORTDATE	Message date
SORTFROM	First mailbox in `from:` line
SORTSIZE	Size of message
SORTSUBJECT	Message subject
SORTCC	First mailbox in `cc:` line
SORTO	First mailbox in `to:` line

```
<?
    $mailbox = imap_open("{mail.server.com:143}",
        "leon", "password");
    $list = imap_sort($mailbox, SORTFROM, 0, SE_NOPREFETCH);
    while(list($msg_num) = each($list))
    {
        print("$msg_num ");
    }
    imap_close($mailbox);
?>
```

object imap_status(integer stream, string mailbox, integer options)

The imap_status function returns an object with properties describing the status of a mailbox. The only property guaranteed to exist is flags, which tells you which other properties exist. You choose the properties to generate with the options argument. Constants to use for options are listed in Table 14.11.

Table 14.11   imap_status Options

Constant	Description
SA_ALL	Turns on all properties
SA_MESSAGES	Number of messages in mailbox
SA_RECENT	Number of recent messages
SA_QUOTA	Disk space used by mailbox
SA_QUOTA_ALL	Disk space used by all mailboxes
SA_UIDNEXT	Next UID to be used
SA_UIDVALIDITY	Flag for the validity of UID data
SA_UNSEEN	Number of new messages

```
<?
  $mailbox = imap_open("{mail.server.com}INBOX",
      "leon", "password");
  $status = imap_status($mailbox, "INBOX",
      SA_UNSEEN | SA_MESSAGES);
  print("$status->unseen of $status->messages new messages");
  imap_close($mailbox);
?>
```

boolean imap_subscribe(integer stream, string mailbox)

Use `imap_subscribe` to subscribe to a mailbox.

```
<?
    $mailbox = imap_open("{mail.server.com}INBOX", "leon", "password");
    imap_subscribe($mailbox, "PHP");
    imap_close($mailbox);
?>
```

integer imap_uid(integer stream, integer message)

The `imap_uid` function returns the UID for the given message. To get the message number based on UID, use `imap_msgno`.

boolean imap_undelete(integer stream, integer message)

The `imap_undelete` function removes the deletion mark on a message.

```
<?
    // delete message number 3, then undelete
    $mailbox = imap_open("{mail.server.com}INBOX", "leon", "password");
    imap_delete($mailbox, 3);
    imap_undelete($mailbox, 3);
    imap_close($mailbox);
?>
```

boolean imap_unsubscribe(integer stream, string mailbox)

Use `imap_unsubscribe` to unsubscribe to a mailbox.

```
<?
    $mailbox = imap_open("{mail.server.com}INBOX", "leon", "password");
    imap_unsubscribe($mailbox, "PHP");
    imap_close($mailbox);
?>
```

string imap_utf7_decode(string data)

The `imap_utf7_decode` function takes UTF-7 encoded text and returns plain text.

string imap_utf7_encode(string data)

The `imap_utf7_encode` function returns UTF-7 encoded text.

Java

The coolest addition to PHP in 1999 was the code Sam Ruby added to allow PHP to use Java objects. Java is Sun's object-oriented language intended to be platform independent. Java is very popular, and you won't have any trouble finding books, Web sites, and free source code. Perhaps the best place to get information about Java used on Web servers is the Java Apache Project <http://java.apache.org/>.

The Java extension doesn't create any new functions, but it exposes a class called Java. You can use the new operator to instantiate any class in your class path. An object is returned that can be treated like any other PHP object. Its properties and methods match the Java class.

```
<?
    /*
    ** Adapted from Sam Ruby's example
    */

    //get version of Java
    $system = new Java("java.lang.System");
```

```
print("Java version: " .
      $system->getProperty("java.version") .
      "<BR>\n");

//print formatted date
$formatter = new Java("java.text.SimpleDateFormat",
      "EEEE, MMMM dd, yyyy 'at' h:mm:ss a zzzz");
print($formatter->format(new Java("java.util.Date")) . "<BR>\n");
?>
```

LDAP

LDAP is an acronym for Lightweight Directory Access Protocol. It is a universal method of storing directory information and is a partial implementation of the X.500 standard. LDAP was first described in RFC 1777 and RFC 1778.

Through TCP/IP, clients can access a centralized address book containing contact information, public encryption keys, and similar information. Many servers are live on the Internet. Dante, a nonprofit organization, maintains a list of LDAP servers organized by country at `<http://www.dante.net/np/pdi.html>`. A full discussion of LDAP is beyond the scope of this book, but abundant information can be found on the Web. A good starting point is the University of Michigan at `<http://www.umich.edu/~dirsvcs/ldap/index.html>`.

The functions in this section require either compiling LDAP support into the PHP module, or loading an extension module with `dl`. At the time of this writing, no extension existed for Windows. You can find a suitable LDAP library at the University of Michigan site stated above.

The LDAP module is the result of collaboration by Amitay Isaacs, Rasmus Lerdorf, Gerrit Thomson, and Eric Warnke.

boolean ldap_add(integer link, string dn, array entry)

The `ldap_add` function adds entries to the specified DN at the object level. The `entry` argument is an array of the attribute values. If an attribute can have multiple values, the array element should be an array itself. See the mail attribute in the example below. If you wish to add attributes at the attribute level, use `ldap_mod_add`.

```php
<?
        //connect to LDAP server
        if(!($ldap=ldap_connect("ldap.php.net")))
        {
                die("Could not connect to LDAP server!");
        }

        //set login DN
        $dn="cn=root, dc=php, dc=net";

        //attempt to bind to DN using password
        if(!ldap_bind($ldap, $dn, ""))
        {
                die("Unable to bind to '$dn'!");
        }

        // create entry
        $entry["cn"]="John";
        $entry["sn"]="Smith";
        $entry["mail"][0]="jsmith123@hotmail.com";
        $entry["mail"][1]="smith@bigfoot.com";
        $entry["objectclass"]="person";
        $entry["telephonenumber"] = "123-123-1234";
        $entry["mobile"] = "123-123-1235";
        $entry["pager"] = "123-123-1236";
        $entry["o"] = "ACME Web Design";
        $entry["title"] = "Vice President";
        $entry["department"] = "Technology";

        //create new entry's DN
        $dn = "cn=John Smith, dc=php, dc=net";

        //add entry
        if(ldap_add($ldap, $dn, $entry))
        {
                print("Entry Added!\n");
        }
        else
        {
                print("Add failed!");
        }
```

```
        //close connection
        ldap_close($ldap);
?>
```

boolean ldap_bind(integer link, string dn, string password)

Use ldap_bind to bind to a directory. Use the optional dn and password arguments to identify yourself. Servers typically require authentication for any commands that change the contents of the directory.

boolean ldap_close(integer link)

The ldap_close function closes the connection to the directory server.

integer ldap_connect(string host, integer port)

The ldap_connect function returns an LDAP connection identifier, or FALSE when there is an error. Both arguments are optional. With no arguments, ldap_connect returns the identifier of the current open connection. If the port argument is omitted, port 389 is assumed.

integer ldap_count_entries(integer link, integer result)

The ldap_count_entries function returns the number of entries in the specified result set. The result argument is a result identifier returned by ldap_read.

boolean ldap_delete(integer link, string dn)

The ldap_delete function removes an entry from the directory.

```
<?
        // connect to LDAP server
        if(!($ldap=ldap_connect("ldap.php.net")))
        {
                die("Unable to connect to LDAP server!");
        }
```

```
     //set login DN
     $dn="cn=root, dc=php, dc=net";

     //attempt to bind to DN using password
     if(!ldap_bind($ldap, $dn, "secret"))
     {
            die("Unable to bind to '$dn'!");
     }

     //delete entry from directory
     $dn="cn=John Smith, dc=clearink, dc=com";
     if(ldap_delete($ldap, $dn))
     {
            print("Entry Deleted!\n");
     }
     else
     {
            print("Delete failed!\n");
     }

     //close connection
     ldap_close($ldap);
?>
```

string ldap_dn2ufn(string dn)

The ldap_dn2ufn translates a DN into a more user-friendly form, with type specifiers stripped.

```
<?
     $dn = "cn=John Smith, dc=php, dc=net";
     print(ldap_dn2ufn($dn));
?>
```

integer ldap_errno(integer link)

The ldap_errno function returns the error number for the last error on a connection.

string ldap_error(integer link)

The ldap_error function returns a description of the last error on a connection.

string ldap_err2str(integer error)

Use `ldap_err2str` to convert an error number to a textual description.

array ldap_explode_dn(string dn, boolean attributes)

The `ldap_explode_dn` function splits a DN returned by `ldap_get_dn` into an array. Each element is a Relative Distinguished Name, or RDN. The array contains an element indexed by `count` that is the number of RDNs. The `attributes` argument specifies whether values are returned with their attribute codes.

```
<?
    //set test DN
    $dn = "cn=Leon Atkinson, o=Clear Ink, c=US";

    $rdn = ldap_explode_dn($dn, FALSE);

    for($index = 0; $index < $rdn["count"]; $index++)
    {
            print("$rdn[$index] <BR>\n");
    }
?>
```

string ldap_first_attribute(integer link, integer result, integer pointer)

The `ldap_first_attribute` function returns the first attribute for a given entry. The `pointer` argument must be passed as a reference. This variable stores a pointer in the list of attributes. The `ldap_get_attributes` function is probably more convenient.

integer ldap_first_entry(integer link, integer result)

The `ldap_first_entry` function returns an entry identifier for the first entry in the result set. This integer is used in the `ldap_next_entry` function. Use `ldap_get_entries` to retrieve all entries in an array.

boolean ldap_free_entry(integer entry)

The `ldap_free_entry` function frees memory associated with an entry. The entry identifier is obtained through either `ldap_first_entry` or `ldap_next_entry`.

boolean ldap_free_result(integer result)

Use `ldap_free_result` to clear any memory used for a result returned by `ldap_read` or `ldap_search`.

array ldap_get_attributes(integer link, integer result)

Use `ldap_get_attributes` to get a multidimensional array of all the attributes and their values for the specified result identifier. Attributes may be referenced by their names or by a number. The `count` element specifies the number of elements. Multivalue attributes have a `count` element as well, and each element is referenced by number. This function allows you to browse a directory, discovering attributes you may not have known existed.

string ldap_get_dn(integer ldap, integer result)

The `ldap_get_dn` function returns the DN for the specified result.

array ldap_get_entries(integer link, integer result)

The `ldap_get_entries` function returns a three-dimensional array containing every entry in the result set. An associative element, `count`, returns the number of entries in the array. Each entry is numbered from zero. Each entry has a `count` element and a `dn` element. The attributes for the entry may be referenced by name or by number. Each attribute has its own `count` element and a numbered set of values.

array ldap_get_values(integer link, integer entry, string attribute)

The `ldap_get_values` function returns an array of every value for a given attribute. The values will be treated as strings. Use `ldap_get_values_len` if you need to get binary data.

```
<?
    //connect to LDAP server
    if(!($ldap=ldap_connect("ldap.php.net")))
    {
        die("Could not connect to LDAP server!");
    }

    //set up search criteria
    $dn = "cn=John Smith, dc=php, dc=net";
    $filter = "sn=*";
    $attributes = array("givenname", "sn", "mail");

    //perform search
    if(!($result = ldap_read($ldap, $dn, $filter, $attributes)))
    {
        die("Nothing Found!");
    }

    $entry = ldap_first_entry($ldap, $result);
    $values = ldap_get_values($ldap, $entry, "mail");

    print($values["count"] . " Values:<OL>\n");

    for($index=0; $index < $values["count"]; $index++)
    {
        print("<LI>$values[$index]\n");
    }

    print("</OL>\n");

    ldap_free_result($result);
?>
```

integer ldap_get_values_len(integer link, integer entry, string attribute)

This function operates identically to `ldap_get_values`, except that it works with binary entries.

integer ldap_list(integer link, string dn, string filter, array attributes)

The `ldap_list` function returns all objects at the level of the given DN. The `attributes` argument is optional. If given, it limits results to objects containing the specified attributes.

```
<?

      /*
      ** ldap_list example
      ** This script explores the organizational units at
      ** the University of Michigan. Links are created
      ** to explore units within units.
      */

      if(!isset($dn))
```

Figure 14-3   `ldap_list`.

```
{
        $dn = "o=University of Michigan, c=US";
}

print("<B>Search DN:</B> $dn<BR>\n");

//connect to LDAP server
if(!($ldap=ldap_connect("ldap.itd.umich.edu")))
{
        die("Could not connect to LDAP server!");
}

$filter = "objectClass=*";
$attributes = array("ou", "cn");

//perform search
if(!($result = ldap_list($ldap, $dn, $filter, $attributes)))
{
        die("Nothing Found!");
}

$entries = ldap_get_entries($ldap, $result);

for($index = 0; $index < $entries["count"]; $index++)
{
        if($entries[$index]["ou"][0])
        {
                print("<A HREF=\"$PHP_SELF?dn=".$entries[$index]["dn"]."\">");
                print($entries[$index]["ou"][0]);
                print("</A>");
        }
        else
        {
                print($entries[$index]["cn"][0]);
        }

        print("<BR>\n");
}

ldap_free_result($result);

// close connection
ldap_close($ldap);
?>
```

Figure 14-3   Continued

boolean ldap_mod_add(integer link, string dn, array entry)

The `ldap_mod_add` function adds attributes to a DN at the attribute level. Compare this to `ldap_add`, which adds attributes at the object level.

boolean ldap_mod_del(integer link, string dn, array entry)

Use `ldap_mod_del` to remove attributes from a DN at the attribute level. Compare this to `ldap_delete`, which removes attributes at the object level.

boolean ldap_mod_replace(integer link, string dn, array entry)

The `ldap_mod_replace` function replaces entries for a DN at the attribute level. Compare this to `ldap_modify`, which replaces attributes at the object level.

boolean ldap_modify(integer link, string dn, array entry)

The `ldap_modify` function modifies an entry. Otherwise, it behaves identically to `ldap_add`.

string ldap_next_attribute(integer link, integer entry, integer pointer)

The `ldap_next_attribute` function is used to traverse the list of attributes for an entry. The `pointer` argument is passed by reference.

```
<?
    //connect to LDAP server
    if(!($ldap=ldap_connect("ldap.itd.umich.edu")))
    {
        die("Could not connect to LDAP server!");
    }

    // list organizations in the US
    $dn = "o=University of Michigan, c=US";
    $filter = "objectClass=*";

    //perform search
    if(!($result = ldap_list($ldap, $dn, $filter)))
    {
        die("Nothing Found!");
    }

    // get all attributes for first entry
    $entry = ldap_first_entry($ldap, $result);

    $attribute = ldap_first_attribute($ldap, $entry, &$pointer);
    while($attribute)
    {
        print("$attribute<BR>\n");
        $attribute = ldap_next_attribute($ldap,$entry, &$pointer);
    }

    ldap_free_result($result);
?>
```

integer ldap_next_entry(integer link, integer entry)

The ldap_next_entry function returns the next entry in a result set. Use ldap_first_entry to get the first entry in a result set.

```
<?
    //connect to LDAP server
    if(!($ldap=ldap_connect("ldap.itd.umich.edu")))
    {
        die("Could not connect to LDAP server!");
    }

    // list organizations in the US
```

```
$dn = "o=University of Michigan, c=US";
$filter = "objectClass=*";

//perform search
if(!($result = ldap_list($ldap, $dn, $filter)))
{
        die("Nothing Found!");
}

//get each entry
$entry = ldap_first_entry($ldap, $result);
do
{
        //dump all attributes for each entry
        $attribute = ldap_get_attributes($ldap, $entry);
        print("<PRE>");
        var_dump($attribute);
        print("</PRE>\n");
        print("<HR>\n");
}
while($entry = ldap_next_entry($ldap, $entry));

ldap_free_result($result);
?>
```

integer ldap_read(integer link, string dn, string filter, array attributes)

The `ldap_read` function functions similarly to `ldap_list` and `ldap_search`. Arguments are used in the same manner, but `ldap_read` searches only in the base DN.

integer ldap_search(integer link, string dn, string filter, array attributes)

The `ldap_search` function behaves similarly to `ldap_list` and `ldap_read`. The difference is that it finds matches from the current directory down into every subtree. The `attributes` argument is optional and specifies a set of attributes that all matched entries must contain.

```
<?
    /*
    ** Function: compareEntry
    ** This function compares two entries for
    ** the purpose of sorting.
    */
    function compareEntry($left, $right)
    {
            $ln = strcmp($left["last"], $right["last"]);
            if($ln == 0)
            {
                    return(strcmp($left["first"],
                            $right["first"]));
            }
            else
            {
                    return($ln);
            }
    }

    //connect to LDAP server
    if(!($ldap=ldap_connect("ldap.php.net")))
    {
            die("Could not connect to LDAP server!");
    }

    //set up search criteria
    $dn = "dc=php, dc=net";
    $filter = "sn=Atkinson";
    $attributes = array("givenname", "sn");

    //perform search
    if(!($result = ldap_search($ldap, $dn, $filter, $attributes)))
    {
            die("Nothing Found!");
    }

    //get all the entries
    $entry = ldap_get_entries($ldap, $result);

    print("There are " . $entry["count"] . " people.<br>\n");

    //pull names out into array so we can sort them
    for($i=0; $i < $entry["count"]; $i++)
    {
```

```
        //Note how we only use the first entry. This
        //code assumes people only have one first name,
        //and one last name.
        $person[$i]["first"] = $entry[$i]["givenname"][0];
        $person[$i]["last"] = $entry[$i]["sn"][0];
}

//sort by last name, then first name using
//compareEntry (defined above)
usort($person, "compareEntry");


//loop over each entry
for($i=0; $i < $entry["count"]; $i++)
{
        print($person[$i]["first"] . " " .
              $person[$i]["last"] . "<BR>\n");
}

//free memory used by search
ldap_free_result($result);
?>
```

boolean ldap_unbind(integer link)

The `ldap_unbind` function is an alias for `ldap_close`.

Semaphores

PHP offers an extension for using System V semaphores. If your operating system supports this feature, you may add this extension to your installation of PHP. At the time of this writing, only the Solaris, Linux, and AIX operating systems were known to support semaphores.

Semaphores are a way to control a resource so that it is used by a single entity at once, and they were inspired by the flags used to communicate between ships. The idea to use an integer counter to ensure single control of a resource was described first by Edsger Dijkstra in the early 1960s for use in operating systems.

A complete tutorial on semaphores is beyond the scope of this text. Semaphores are a standard topic for college computer science courses, and you will find adequate descriptions in books about operating systems. The Webopedia's page `<http://webopedia.internet.com/TERM/s/sema-`

`phore.html>` is unfortunately brief at the time of this writing. The whatis.com Web site `<http://www.whatis.com/>` references *Unix Network Programming* by W. Richard Stevens, which was published by Prentice Hall. The second edition was published in 1997 as two volumes. You can find out more about it on the Prentice Hall Professional Technical Reference Web   site   `<http://www.phptr.com/ptrbooks/ptr_013490012X.html>`.

Keep in mind that these PHP functions are wrappers for System V semaphore functions. Understanding them well may aid you in using the PHP functions. If you are interested in finding out exactly how PHP interacts with System V semaphores, I recommend reading the source code, particularly the `sysvsem.c` file. Tom May's comments are very clear.

boolean sem_acquire(integer identifier)

The `sem_acquire` function attempts to acquire a semaphore you've identified with the `sem_get` function. The function will block until the semaphore is acquired. Note that it is possible to wait forever while attempting to acquire a semaphore. One way is if a script acquires a semaphore to its limit and then tries to acquire it another time. In this case the semaphore can never decrement.

If you do not release a semaphore with `sem_release`, PHP will release it for you and display a warning.

```php
<?
        /*
        ** Semaphore example
        **
        ** To see this in action, try opening two or more
        ** browsers and load this script at the same time.
        ** You should see that each script will execute the
        ** fake procedure when it alone has acquired the
        ** semaphore. Pay attention to the output of the
        ** microtime function in each browser window.
        */

        //Define integer for this semaphore
        //This simply adds to readability
        define("SEM_COREPHP", 1970);

        //Get or create the semaphore
        //This semaphore can be acquired only once
        $sem = sem_get(SEM_COREPHP, 1);

        //acquire semaphore
```

```
if(sem_acquire($sem))
{
        //perform some atomic function
        print("Faking procedure... " . microtime());
        sleep(3);
        print("Finishing fake procedure... " . microtime());

        //release semaphore
        sem_release($sem);
}
else
{
        //we failed to acquire the semaphore
        print("Failed to acquire semaphore!<BR>\n");
}

?>
```

integer sem_get(integer key, integer maximum, integer permission)

Use `sem_get` to receive an identifier for a semaphore. If the semaphore does not exist, it will be created. The optional `maximum` and `permission` arguments are used only during creation. The `maximum` argument controls how many times a semaphore may be acquired. It defaults to 1. The `permission` argument controls read and write privileges to the semaphore in the same way file permissions do. It defaults to 0x666, which is read and write access for all users. The `key` argument is used to identify the semaphore among processes in the system. The integer returned by `sem_get` may be unique each time it is called, even when the same key is specified.

boolean sem_release(integer identifier)

Use `sem_release` to reverse the process of the `sem_acquire` function.

Shared Memory

PHP offers an extension for using System V shared memory. It follows the same restrictions as the System V semaphore functions, above. That is, your operating system must support this functionality. Solaris, Linux, and AIX are known to work with shared memory.

Shared memory is virtual memory shared by separate processes. It helps solve the problem of communication between processes running on the same machine. An obvious method might be to write information to a file, but access to permanent storage is relatively slow. Shared memory allows the creation of system memory that may be accessed by multiple processes, which is much faster. Since exclusive use of this memory is essential, you must use some sort of locking. This is usually done with semaphores. If you use the shared memory functions, make sure you include support for System V semaphores as well.

A full discussion of the use of shared-memory functions is beyond the scope of this text. I found a short description of shared memory at whatis.com `<http://www.whatis.com/>`. You may also pursue college courses about operating systems, or *Unix Network Programming* by W. Richard Stevens to learn more about shared memory.

The shared memory extension was added to PHP by Christian Cartus.

integer shm_attach(integer key, integer size, integer permissions)

The `shm_attach` function returns an identifier to shared memory. The `key` argument is an integer that specifies the shared memory. The shared memory will be created if necessary, in which case the optional `size` and `permissions` arguments will be used if present.

The size of the memory segment defaults to a value defined when PHP is compiled. Minimum and maximum values for the size are dependent on the operating system, but reasonable values to expect are a 1-byte minimum and a 128K maximum. There are also limits on the number of shared memory segments. Normal limits are 100 total segments and 6 segments per process.

The permissions for a memory segment default to 0x666, which is read and write permission to all users. This value operates like those used to set file permissions.

As with semaphores, calling `shm_attach` for the same key twice will return two different identifiers, yet they will both point to the same shared memory segment internally.

Keep in mind that shared memory does not expire automatically. You must free it using `shm_remove`.

```
<?
    /*
    ** Shared Memory example
    **
```

```
** This example builds on the semaphore example
** by using shared memory to communicate between
** multiple processes. This example creates shared
** memory but does not release it. Make sure you
** run the shm_remove example when you're done
** experimenting with this example.
*/

//Define integer for semaphore key
define("SEM_COREPHP", 1970);

//Define integer for shared memory key
define("SHM_COREPHP", 1970);

//Define integer for variable key
define("SHMVAR_MESSAGE", 1970);


//Get or create the semaphore
//This semaphore can only be acquired once
$sem = sem_get(SEM_COREPHP, 1);

//acquire semaphore
if(sem_acquire($sem))
{
     //attach to shared memory
     //make the memory 1K in size
     $mem = shm_attach(SHM_COREPHP, 1024);

     //attempt to get message variable, which
     //won't be there the first time
     if($old_message = shm_get_var($mem, SHMVAR_MESSAGE);
     {
     print("Previous value: $old_message<BR>\n");
     }

     //create new message
     $new_message = getmypid() . " here at " . microtime();

     //set new value
     shm_put_var($mem, SHMVAR_MESSAGE, $new_message);

     //detach from shared memory
     shm_detach($mem);
```

```
            //release semaphore
            sem_release($sem);
      }
      else
      {
            //we failed to acquire the semaphore
            print("Failed to acquire semaphore!<BR>\n");
      }

?>
```

boolean shm_detach(integer identifier)

Use `shm_detach` to free the memory associated with the identifier for a shared memory segment. This does not release the shared memory itself. Use `shm_remove` to do this.

value shm_get_var(integer identifier, integer key)

The `shm_get_var` function returns a value stored in a variable with `shm_put_var`.

boolean shm_put_var(integer identifier, integer key, value)

The `shm_put_var` function sets the value for a variable in a shared memory segment. If the variable does not exist, it will be created. The variable will last inside the shared memory until removed with `shm_remove_var`, or when the shared memory segment itself is destroyed with `shm_remove`. The `value` argument will be serialized with the same argument used for the `serialize` function. That means you may use any PHP value or variable—with one exception: at the time of this writing, objects lose their methods when serialized.

boolean shm_remove(integer identifier)

Use `shm_remove` to free a shared memory segment. All variables in the segment will be destroyed, so it is not strictly necessary to remove them. If you do not remove shared memory segments with this function, they may exist perpetually.

```
<?
    /*
    ** Shared Memory example 2
    **
    ** This example removes shared memory created
    ** by the previous shared memory example.
    */

    //Define integer for semaphore key
    define("SEM_COREPHP", 1970);

    //Define integer for shared memory key
    define("SHM_COREPHP", 1970);

    //Define integer for variable key
    define("SHMVAR_MESSAGE", 1970);


    //Get or create the semaphore
    //This semaphore can be acquired only once
    $sem = sem_get(SEM_COREPHP, 1);

    //acquire semaphore
    if(sem_acquire($sem))
    {
        //attach to shared memory
        //make the memory 1K in size
        $mem = shm_attach(SHM_COREPHP, 1024);

        //remove variable
        shm_remove_var($mem, SHMVAR_MESSAGE);

        //remove shared memory
        shm_remove($mem);

        //release semaphore
        sem_release($sem);
    }
    else
    {
        //we failed to acquire the semaphore
        print("Failed to acquire semaphore!<BR>\n");
    }

?>
```

boolean shm_remove_var(integer identifier, integer key)

The `shm_remove_var` function frees the memory associated with a variable within a shared memory segment.

SNMP

SNMP, the Simple Network Management Protocol, is a protocol for Internet network management. It was first described in RFC 1089. One place to start learning about SNMP is SNMP Research at `<http://www.snmp.com/>`. To use these functions under UNIX, you must have the UCD SNMP libraries. You can find them at `<http://ucd-snmp.ucdavis.edu/>`. Documentation at this site is more specific to the library PHP uses. I've attempted to follow their examples by translating them into equivalent PHP code.

At the time of this writing, no SNMP extension for Windows was available for PHP4. Presumably, the name would be `php_snmp.dll`. PHP3's library was called `php3_snmp.dll`. It did not use the UCD SNMP libraries and was available under Windows NT only. You can activate an extension with the `dl` function or with the `extension` directive in `php.ini`.

Mike Jackson, Rasmus Lerdorf, and Steven Lawrance have contributed to the SNMP extension.

boolean snmp_get_quick_print()

The `snmp_get_quick_print` function returns the status of the UCD SNMP library's `quick_print` setting. Consequently, this function is unavailable to Windows users. The `quick_print` setting controls how verbose object values are. By default, `quick_print` is FALSE, and values include types and other information. The UCD SNMP manual provides more information.

snmp_set_quick_print(boolean on)

The `snmp_set_quick_print` function sets the value of the UCD SNMP library's `quick_print` setting. Consequently, this function is unavailable to Windows users. See the description of `snmp_get_quick_print` for a brief description of the `quick_print` setting.

string snmpget(string host, string community, string object, integer timeout, integer retries)

The `snmpget` function returns the value of the specified object. The host may be numerical or named. You must also specify the community and the object. Optionally, you may supply a timeout in seconds and a number of times to retry a connection.

```
<?
        //find out how long the system has been up
        //should return something like
        //Timeticks: (586731977) 67 days, 21:48:39.77
        if($snmp = snmpget("ucd-snmp.ucdavis.edu",
                "demopublic", "system.sysUpTime.0"))
        {
                print($snmp);
        }
        else
        {
                print("snmpget failed!");
        }
?>
```

boolean snmpset(string host, string community, string object, string type, string value, integer timeout, integer retries)

The `snmpset` function sets the value of the specified object. The host may be numerical or named. You must also specify the community and the object. The `type` argument is a one-character string. Table 14.12 lists valid types. Optionally, you may supply a timeout in seconds and a number of times to retry a connection.

```
<?
        //show current value of the demo string
        $snmp = snmpget("ucd-snmp.ucdavis.edu",
                "demopublic", "ucdDemoPublicString.0");
        print("$snmp (original value)<BR>\n");

        //set it to something else
        snmpset("ucd-snmp.ucdavis.edu",
```

```
                "demopublic", "ucdDemoPublicString.0",
                "s", "Core PHP Programming");

        //see current value of the demo string
        $snmp = snmpget("ucd-snmp.ucdavis.edu",
                "demopublic", "ucdDemoPublicString.0");
        print("$snmp (new value)<BR>\n");
?>
```

snmprealwalk

This function is an alias to snmpwalk.

array snmpwalk(string host, string community, string object, integer timeout, integer retries)

The snmpwalk function returns an array of all objects in the tree that starts at the specified object. You can use an empty string for the object parameter to get all objects. Optionally, you may supply a timeout in seconds and a number of times to retry a connection.

Table 14.12   SNMP Types

Type	Description
a	IP Address
d	Decimal String
i	Integer
o	Object ID
s	String
t	Time Ticks
u	Unsigned Integer
x	Hex String
D	Double
F	Float
I	Signed 64-bit Integer
U	Unsigned 64-bit Integer

```
<?
        //get all the SNMP objects
        $snmp = snmpwalk("ucd-snmp.ucdavis.edu", "demopublic", "");

        reset($snmp);
        while(list($key, $value) = each($snmp))
        {
                print($value . "<BR>\n");
        }
?>
```

array snmpwalkoid(string host, string community, string object, integer timeout, integer retries)

The snmpwalkoid function is an alias to snmpwalk.

WDDX

The Web Distributed Data Exchange, or WDDX, is an XML language for describing data in a way that facilitates moving it from one programming environment to another. The intent is to relieve difficulty associated with sending data between applications that represent data differently. Traditionally this has been done by designing special interfaces for each case. For instance, you may decide that your PERL script will write out its three return data separated with tabs, using a regular expression to extract the text you later convert to integers. WDDX intends to unify the effort into a single interface. If you wish to learn more about WDDX, visit the home site at <http://www.wddx.org/>.

In order to use the functions in this section, you need only use --with-wddx when configuring PHP prior to compilation. At the time of this writing WDDX support wasn't compiled into the Windows binaries.

Andrei Zmievski added WDDX support to PHP.

wddx_add_vars(integer packet_identifier, string variable, ...)

The wddx_add_vars function is one of three functions for creating packets incrementally. After creating a packet with wddx_packet_start, you may add as many variables as you wish with wddx_add_vars. After the `packet_identifier` argument, you may pass strings with the names of variables in the local scope or arrays of strings. If necessary, PHP will explore multidimensional arrays for names of variables. The variables will be added to the packet until you use `wddx_packet_end` to create the actual packet as a string. See `wddx_packet_start`, below, for an example of use.

value wddx_deserialize(string packet)

The `wddx_deserialize` function returns a variable representing the data contained in a WDDX packet. If the packet contains a single value, it will be returned as an appropriate type. If the packet contains multiple values in a structure, an associative array will be returned.

```
<?
    //simulate WDDX packet
    $packet = "<wddxPacket version='0.9'>";
    $packet .= "<data>";
    $packet .= "<string>Core PHP Programming</string>";
    $packet .= "</data>";
    $packet .= "</wddxPacket>";

    //pull data out of packet
    $data = wddx_deserialize($packet);

    //test the type of the variable
    if(is_array($data))
    {
        //loop over each value
        foreach($data as $key=>$value)
        {
            print("$key: $value<BR>\n");
        }
    }
    else
    {
        //simply print the value
        print("$data<BR>\n");
    }
?>
```

string wddx_packet_end(integer packet_identifier)

The `wddx_packet_end` function returns a string for the packet created with `wddx_packet_start` and `wddx_add_vars`. See `wddx_packet_start`, below, for an example of use.

integer wddx_packet_start(string comment)

The wddx_packet_start function returns an identifier to a WDDX packet
you can build as you go. The optional comment argument will be placed in
the packet if supplied. Use the returned packet identifier with wddx_
add_vars and wddx_packet_end.

```
<?
    //create test data
    $Name = "Leon Atkinson";
    $Email = "corephp@leonatkinson.com";
    $Residence = "Martinez";

    $Info = array("Email", "Residence");

    //start packet
    $wddx = wddx_packet_start("Core PHP Programming");

    //add some variables to the packet
    wddx_add_vars($wddx, "Name", $Info);

    //create packet
    $packet = wddx_packet_end($wddx);

    //print packet for demonstration purposes
    print($packet);
?>
```

string wddx_serialize_value(value data, string comment)

The wddx_serialize_value function creates a WDDX packet containing a
single value. The data will be encoded with no name. The optional comment
field will be added to the packet as well.

```
<?
    print(wddx_serialize_value("Hello, World",
        "An example from Core PHP Programming"));
?>
```

string wddx_serialize_vars(string variable, …)

Use `wddx_serialize_vars` to create a packet containing many variables.
You may specify any number of variable names in the local scope. Each argument may be a string or an array. PHP will recursively explore multidimensional arrays for more names of variables if necessary. A WDDX packet is returned.

```
<?
        //create test data
        $Name = "Leon Atkinson";
        $Email = "corephp@leonatkinson.com";
        $Residence = "Martinez";

        $Info = array("Email", "Residence");

        //print packet
        print(wddx_serialize_vars("Name", $Info));
?>
```

XML

Although the functions in this section come last, they are among the most important functions available. The extensible markup language, XML, has steadily grown in popularity since being introduced in 1996. XML is a first cousin to HTML in that it, too, is derived from SGML, a generalized markup language that is nearly 20 years old. Like HTML, XML documents surround textual data with tags. Unlike HTML, XML can be used to communicate any type of data. The best place to start learning about XML is its home page at the W3C `<http://www.w3.org/XML/>`. Among the resources there, you will find book recommendations.

The functions in this section wrap the Expat library developed by James Clark `<http://www.jclark.com/xml/>`. This library is part of the PHP distribution, and its purpose is parsing XML documents. These functions work differently from other PHP extensions. A stream of data is fed to the parser. As complete parts of the data are recognized, events are triggered. These parts are the tags and the data they surround. You register the events with a handler, a function you write. You may specify FALSE for the name of any handler, and those events will be ignored.

In order to avoid repeating large blocks of code, I've written one example that uses most of the functions in this section. It's near the description of `xml_set_element_handler` and Figure 14.5. You will always need to create a parser. You will also want to create handlers for character data and starting and ending tags. Some of the other handlers may not be of use in most applications. You can leave them out, and that data will be ignored by the parser.

Stig Bakken added the XML extension to PHP.

string utf8_decode(string data)

The `utf8_decode` function takes UTF-8 text and returns ISO-8859-1 text.

string utf8_encode(string data)

The `utf8_encode` function returns the `data` argument as UTF-8 text.

string xml_error_string(integer error)

The `xml_error_string` function returns the description for the given error code.

integer xml_get_current_byte_ index(integer parser)

The `xml_get_current_byte_index` function returns the number of bytes parsed so far.

integer xml_get_current_column_ number(integer parser)

The `xml_get_current_column_number` function returns the column number in the source file where the parser last read data. This function is useful for reporting where an error occurred.

integer xml_get_current_line_number(integer parser)

The `xml_get_current_line_number` function returns the line number in the source file where the parser last read data. This function is useful for reporting where an error occurred.

integer xml_get_error_code(integer parser)

The `xml_get_error_code` function returns the last error code generated on the given parser. Constants are defined for all the errors. They are listed in Table 14.13. If no error has occurred, `XML_ERROR_NONE` is returned. If given an invalid parser identifier, `FALSE` is returned.

boolean xml_parse(int parser, string data, boolean final)

The `xml_parse` function scans over data and calls handlers you have registered. The size of the `data` argument is not limited. You could parse an entire file or a few bytes at a time. A typical use involves fetching data within a `while` loop.

The `final` argument is optional. It tells the parser that the data you are passing is the end of the file.

boolean xml_parse_into_struct(int parser, string data, array structure, array index)

The `xml_parse_info_struct` function parses an entire document and creates an array to describe it. You must pass the `structure` argument as a reference. Elements numbered from zero will be added to it. Each element will contain an associative array indexed by `tag`, `type`, `level`, and `value`. The `index` argument is optional. You must pass it by reference as well. It will contain elements indexed by distinct tags found in the XML file. The value of each element will be a list of integers. These integers are indices into the `structure` array. It allows you to index the elements of the `structure` array that match a given tag.

If you set any handlers, they will be called when you use `xml_parse_into_struct`.

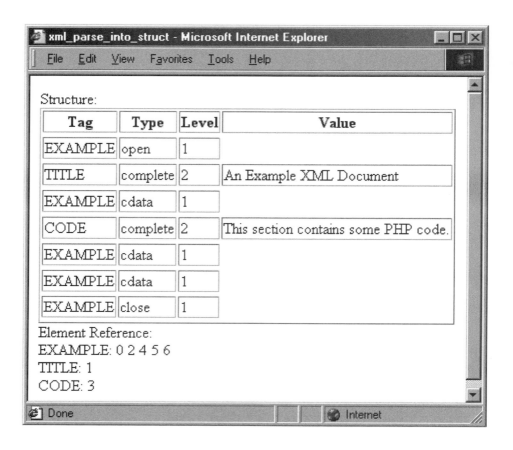

```
<?
    //create parser
    if(!($parser = xml_parser_create()))
    {
        print("Could not create parser!<BR>\n");
        exit();
    }

    //get entire file
    $data = implode(file("example.xml"), "");

    //parse file into array
    xml_parse_into_struct($parser, $data, &$structure, &$index);
```

Figure 14–4   `xml_parse_into_struct`.

```
        //destroy parser
        xml_parser_free($parser);

        print("Structure:<BR>\n");
        print("<TABLE BORDER=\"1\">\n");
        print("<TR>\n");
        print("<TH>Tag</TH>\n");
        print("<TH>Type</TH>\n");
        print("<TH>Level</TH>\n");
        print("<TH>Value</TH>\n");
        print("<TR>\n");

        foreach($structure as $s)
        {
                print("<TR>\n");

                print("<TD>{$s["tag"]}</TD>\n");
                print("<TD>{$s["type"]}</TD>\n");
                print("<TD>{$s["level"]}</TD>\n");
                print("<TD>{$s["value"]}</TD>\n");

                print("<TR>\n");
        }

        print("</TABLE>\n");

        print("Element Reference:<BR>\n");
        foreach($index as $key=>$value)
        {
                print("$key:");
                foreach($value as $i)
                {
                        print(" $i");
                }
                print("<BR>\n");
        }
?>
```

Figure 14–4 Continued

Table 14.13   XML Error Constants
XML_ERROR_ASYNC_ENTITY
XML_ERROR_ATTRIBUTE_EXTERNAL_ENTITY_REF
XML_ERROR_BAD_CHAR_REF
XML_ERROR_BINARY_ENTITY_REF
XML_ERROR_DUPLICATE_ATTRIBUTE
XML_ERROR_EXTERNAL_ENTITY_HANDLING
XML_ERROR_INCORRECT_ENCODING
XML_ERROR_INVALID_TOKEN
XML_ERROR_JUNK_AFTER_DOC_ELEMENT
XML_ERROR_MISPLACED_XML_PI
XML_ERROR_NONE
XML_ERROR_NO_ELEMENTS
XML_ERROR_NO_MEMORY
XML_ERROR_PARAM_ENTITY_REF
XML_ERROR_PARTIAL_CHAR
XML_ERROR_RECURSIVE_ENTITY_REF
XML_ERROR_SYNTAX
XML_ERROR_TAG_MISMATCH
XML_ERROR_UNCLOSED_CDATA_SECTION
XML_ERROR_UNCLOSED_TOKEN
XML_ERROR_UNDEFINED_ENTITY
XML_ERROR_UNKNOWN_ENCODING

integer xml_parser_create(string encoding)

Calling `xml_parser_create` is the first step in parsing an XML document. An identifier to be used with most of the other functions is returned. The optional `encoding` argument allows you to specify the character set used by the parser. The three character sets accepted are ISO-8859-1, US-ASCII, and UTF-8. The default is ISO-8859-1.

boolean xml_parser_free(integer parser)

The `xml_parser_free` function releases the memory being used by the parser.

xml_parser_get_option(integer parser, integer option)

The `xml_parser_get_option` function returns an option's current value. Table 14.14 lists the available options.

xml_set_object(integer parser, object container)

The `xml_set_object` function associates an object with a parser. You must pass the parser identifier and a reference to an object. This is best done within the object using the `this` variable. After using this function, PHP will call methods of the object instead of the functions in the global scope when you name handlers.

```
<?
    class myParser
    {
        var $parser;

        function parse($filename)
        {
            //create parser
            if(!($this->parser = xml_parser_create()))
            {
                print("Could not create parser!<BR>\n");
                exit();
            }

            //associate parser with this object
            xml_set_object($this->parser, &$this);

            //register handlers
            xml_set_character_data_handler($this->parser,
                "cdataHandler");
```

```
        xml_set_element_handler($this->parser,
            "startHandler", "endHandler");


        /*
        ** Parse file
        */
        if(!($fp = fopen($filename, "r")))
        {
            print("Couldn't open example.xml!<BR>\n");
            xml_parser_free($this->parser);
            return;
        }

        while($line = fread($fp, 1024))
        {
          xml_parse($this->parser, $line, feof($fp));
        }

        //destroy parser
        xml_parser_free($this->parser);
}


function cdataHandler($parser, $data)
{
        print($data);
}

function startHandler($parser, $name, $attributes)
{
        switch($name)
        {
            case 'EXAMPLE':
                print("<HR>\n");
                break;
            case 'TITLE':
                print("<B>");
                break;
            case 'CODE':
                print("<PRE>");
                break;
            default:
                //ignore other tags
        }
```

```
        }

        function endHandler($parser, $name)
        {
            switch($name)
            {
                case 'EXAMPLE':
                    print("<HR>\n");
                    break;
                case 'TITLE';
                    print("</B>");
                    break;
                case 'CODE':
                    print("</PRE>");
                    break;
                default:
                    //ignore other tags
            }
        }
    }

    $p = new myParser;
    $p->parse("example.xml");
?>
```

xml_parser_set_option(integer parser, integer option, value data)

Use `xml_parser_set_option` to change the value of an option. Table 14.14
lists the available options.

Table 14.14   XML Option Constants

```
XML_OPTION_CASE_FOLDING

XML_OPTION_SKIP_TAGSTART

XML_OPTION_SKIP_WHITE

XML_OPTION_TARGET_ENCODING
```

boolean xml_set_character_data_handler(integer parser, string function)

Character data is the text that appears between tags, and `xml_set_character_data_handler` sets the function executes when it is encountered. Character data may span many lines and may cause several events. PHP will not concatenate the data for you.

The function specified in the `function` argument must take two arguments. The first is the parser identifier, an integer. The second is a string containing the character data.

boolean xml_set_default_handler(integer parser, string function)

The `xml_set_default_handler` function captures any text not handled by the other handlers. This includes the DTD declaration and the XML tag.

The function specified in the `function` argument must take two arguments. The first is the parser identifier, an integer. The second is a string containing the data.

boolean xml_set_element_handler(integer parser, string start, string end)

Use `xml_set_element_handler` to assign the two functions that handle start tags and end tags.

The `start` argument must name a function you've created that takes three arguments. The first function is the parser identifier. The second is the name of the start tag found. The third is an array of the attributes for the start tag. The indices of this array are the attribute names. The elements are in the same order as they appeared in the XML.

The second function handles end tags. It takes two arguments, the first of which is the parser identifier. The other is the name of the tag.

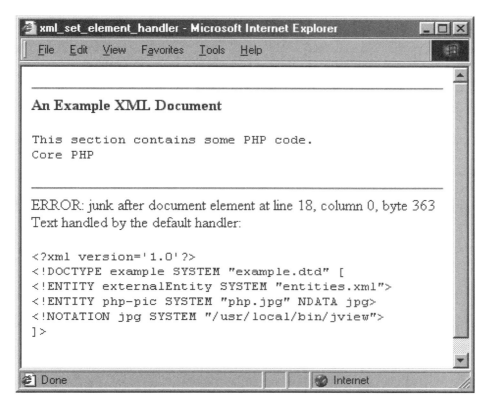

Figure 14–5 `xml_set_element_handler`.

```php
<?
    /*
    ** define functions
    */
    function cdataHandler($parser, $data)
    {
        print($data);
    }

    function startHandler($parser, $name, $attributes)
    {
        switch($name)
        {
            case 'EXAMPLE':
                print("<HR>\n");
```

```
                                break;
                    case 'TITLE':
                            print("<B>");
                            break;
                    case 'CODE':
                            print("<PRE>");
                            break;
                    default:
                            //ignore other tags
            }
}

function endHandler($parser, $name)
{
        switch($name)
        {
                case 'EXAMPLE':
                        print("<HR>\n");
                        break;
                case 'TITLE';
                        print("</B>");
                        break;
                case 'CODE':
                        print("</PRE>");
                        break;
                default:
                        //ignore other tags
        }
}

function piHandler($parser, $target, $data)
{
        if($target == "php")
        {
                eval($data);
        }
        else
        {
                print(htmlentities($data));
        }
}


function defaultHandler($parser, $data)
{
```

Figure 14–5   Continued

```
        global $defaultText;

        $defaultText .= $data;
}

function ndataHandler($parser, $name, $base, $systemID, $publi-
cID, $notation)
{
        print("<!—\n");
        print("NDATA\n");
        print("Entity: $name\n");
        print("Base: $base\n");
        print("System ID: $systemID\n");
        print("Public ID: $publicID\n");
        print("Notation: $notation\n");
        print("—>\n");
}

function notationHandler($parser, $name, $base, $systemID, $publicID)
{
        print("<!—\n");
        print("Notation: $name\n");
        print("Base: $base\n");
        print("System ID: $systemID\n");
        print("Public ID: $publicID\n");
        print("—>\n");
}

function externalHandler($parser, $name, $base, $systemID, $publicID)
{
        //here you could create another parser
        print("<!—Loading $systemID—>\n");

        return(TRUE);
}


/*
** Initialize
*/

//create parser
if(!($parser = xml_parser_create()))
{
        print("Could not create parser!<BR>\n");
        exit();
```

Figure 14–5 Continued

```
    }

    //register handlers
    xml_set_character_data_handler($parser, "cdataHandler");
    xml_set_element_handler($parser, "startHandler", "endHandler");
    xml_set_processing_instruction_handler($parser, "piHandler");
    xml_set_default_handler($parser, "defaultHandler");
    xml_set_unparsed_entity_decl_handler($parser, "ndataHandler");
    xml_set_notation_decl_handler($parser, "notationHandler");
    xml_set_external_entity_ref_handler($parser, "externalHandler");


    /*
    ** Parse file
    */
    if(!($fp = fopen("example.xml", "r")))
    {
        print("Couldn't open example.xml!<BR>\n");
        xml_parser_free($parser);
        exit();
    }

    while($line = fread($fp, 1024))
    {
      if(!xml_parse($parser, $line, feof($fp)))
      {
          //Error, so print full info
        print("ERROR: " .
          xml_error_string(xml_get_error_code($parser)) .
          " at line " .
          xml_get_current_line_number($parser) .
          ", column " .
          xml_get_current_column_number($parser) .
          ", byte " .
          xml_get_current_byte_index($parser) .
          "<BR>\n");
      }
    }

    //destroy parser
    xml_parser_free($parser);

    print("Text handled by the default handler:\n");
    print("<PRE>" . htmlentities($defaultText) . "</PRE>\n");
?>
```

Figure 14–5 Continued

boolean xml_set_external_entity_ref_handler (integer parser, string function)

XML entities follow the form of HTML entities. They start with an ampersand and end with a semicolon. Between these two characters is the name of the entity. An external entity is defined in another file. This takes the form `<!ENTITY externalEntity SYSTEM "entities.xml">` in your XML file. Each time the entity appears in the body of the XML file, the handler you specify in `xml_set_external_entity_ref_handler` is called.

The handler function must take five arguments. First is the parser identifier. Next is a string containing the names of the entities open for this parser. Then come the base, the system ID, and the public ID.

boolean xml_set_notation_decl_handler(integer parser, string function)

The handler registered with `xml_set_notation_decl_handler` receives notation declarations. This are formed like `<!NOTATION jpg SYSTEM "/usr/local/bin/jview">` and are meant to suggest a program for handling a data type.

The handler must take five arguments, the first of which is the parser identifier. The second is the name of the notation entity. The rest are base, system ID, and public ID, in that order.

boolean xml_set_processing_instruction_handler (integer parser, string function)

The `xml_set_processing_instruction_handler` function registers the function that handles tags of the following form: `<?target data?>`. This may be familiar; it's how PHP code is embedded in files. The `target` keyword identifies the type of data inside the tag. Everything else is data.

The `function` argument must specify a function that takes three arguments. The first is the parser identifier. The second is the target. The third is the data.

boolean xml_set_unparsed_entity_decl_handler (integer parser, string function)

This function specifies a handler for external entities that contain an `NDATA` element. These take the form of `<!ENTITY php-pic SYSTEM "php.jpg" NDATA jpg>`, and they specify an external file.

ALGORITHMS

An algorithm is a recipe for solving a problem. This section discusses broad problems in computer science and how to solve them, all in the context of PHP. These problems are inherent in any programming endeavor, but in most cases PHP makes handling them easier. However, the particular circumstances of the Web offer the seasoned programmer a new set of challenges. This section will bring theses issues to your attention.

Chapter 15 examines sorting and searching, along with a related topic, random numbers. Although PHP has built-in functions for sorting data, this chapter explores the theory behind sorting and develops sorting algorithms in PHP. This gives you the knowledge to code custom sorting functions when the need arises.

Chapter 16 discusses parsing and string evaluation. Much of this chapter is about regular expressions, a powerful way to describe patterns that are compared to strings. These are useful for validating user input.

Chapter 17 describes integrating PHP with a database. MySQL is used in the examples because it's Open Source. Databases allow you to manipulate data in powerful ways and are necessary for many Web applications.

Chapter 18 is about network issues, such as sending HTTP headers. Because PHP scripts execute as Web pages, network issues appear frequently.

Chapter 19 explores generating graphics with PHP. It develops examples that create buttons and graphs dynamically.

SORTING, SEARCHING, AND RANDOM NUMBERS

Topics in This Chapter

Chapter 15

Sorting and searching are two fundamental concepts of computer science. They are closely tied to almost every application: databases, compilers, even the World Wide Web. The more information you have online, the more important it becomes to know exactly where that information is.

Admittedly, sorting is not as serious a topic in the context of PHP as it is for C++. PHP offers some very powerful sorting functions, even one that allows you to define how to compare two elements. Since this chapter deals with some classic problems of computer science, you may be interested in learning about the concepts that become useful as you use more generalized languages like C or Ada. But further than that, these concepts will help you understand the internal workings of databases, Web servers, even PHP itself. You will be more capable of dealing with the inevitable problem unsolved by any built-in PHP function.

This chapter also discusses random numbers, which are useful for putting data out of order. The practical application of this usually takes the form of unique identifiers, for files or sessions.

Sorting

To sort means to put a set of like items into order. The rules of ordering can be simple, such as strings sorted by the order of the alphabet. They could be complex, such as sorting addresses first by country, then by state, then by city. The process of sorting can take several forms but always involves comparing two elements with a set of rules for ordering. The result of the comparison determines whether the two items are in order or out of order, therefore needing to be swapped.

There are three classes of sorts: exchange, insert, and select. In an exchange method, two elements are compared and possibly exchanged. This process continues until the list is in order. In an insert method, the elements are removed and placed in another list, one by one. Each time an element is moved, it is inserted into the correct position. When all elements are moved, the list is in order. Last, a selection sort involves building a second list by scanning the first and repeatedly selecting the lowest value. Insertion and selection sorts are two sides of a coin. The former scans the new list; the latter scans the old list.

As I said earlier, a sorting algorithm is essentially comparison and possible movement of elements in a list. On average, moving elements around takes the same amount of time, no matter what algorithm you use. Likewise, the comparison is independent of the actual sort. If we take these to be constants, then the most important question to ask about each algorithm is: How many times does the algorithm perform either of these costly actions?

Of course, the sort must be kept in context with the data. Some algorithms perform very well when the data are completely unordered but are slow when the data are already in order or in reverse order. Some sorts perform very poorly when there are many elements; others have such an overhead as to be inappropriate for smaller data sets. Like any technician, the programmer matches the tool to the job.

In the first part of this chapter I will describe the bubble sort and the quicksort. I will guide you through expressing the algorithms in PHP. I will then go on to describe the built-in sorting functions.

Bubble Sort

Bubble sort's one virtue is simplicity. The list is scanned repeatedly, once less than there are elements. Neighboring items are compared and swapped if out of order. Each time through the list you scan one less item because the lightest bubbles (to stick with the metaphor) have risen to the top.

The outermost `for` loop sets the limit for how far to allow bubbles to rise. The first time through, this is one, because the first element of the array is indexed by zero. After going through the inner loop once, we will be certain that the smallest number will be in the first position of the array. This is because the inner loop will compare the last element to the next to last element, swap them if they are out of order, and then move up a notch. Eventually the smallest element will be reached and swapped upward.

If n is the number of elements in the array, the bubble sort will always make $(n - 1)$ comparisons, then $(n - 2)$ and so on. In Listing 15.1, this means 7 elements require 21 comparisons $(6 + 5 + 4 + 3 + 2 + 1)$ in the first itera-

Listing 15.1   Bubble Sort

```
Listing 15.1 - Micro...  _ □ ×
 File   Edit   View   Fav »    

Unsorted

Array
(
    [0]  =>  6
    [1]  =>  13
    [2]  =>  99
    [3]  =>  2
    [4]  =>  33
    [5]  =>  19
    [6]  =>  84
)

Sorted

Array
(
    [0]  =>  2
    [1]  =>  6
    [2]  =>  13
    [3]  =>  19
    [4]  =>  33
    [5]  =>  84
    [6]  =>  99
)

     Internet
```

```php
<?
    /*
    ** BubbleSort
    ** sorts an array of numbers
    */
    function BubbleSort(&$input_array)
    {
        $limit = count($input_array);

        for($bubble = 1; $bubble < $limit; $bubble++)
        {
            for($position = $limit-1; $position >= $bubble; $po-
            sition—)
            {
                if($input_array[$position-1] >
                $input_array[$position])
                {
                    //exchange elements
                    $temp = $input_array[$position-1];
                    $input_array[$position-1] =
                    $input_array[$position];
                    $input_array[$position] = $temp;
                }
            }
        }
    }

    //define unsorted array
    $data = array(6, 13, 99, 2, 33, 19, 84);

    //print array
    print("<H3>Unsorted</H3>\n");
    print("<PRE>");
    print_r($data);
    print("</PRE>\n");

    //sort array
    BubbleSort(&$data);

    //print array again
    print("<H3>Sorted</H3>\n");
    print("<PRE>");
    print_r($data);
    print("</PRE>\n");
?>
```

tion, regardless of whether the array is in order or out of order. If the array is already in order, then no exchanges will be made. If it is in reverse order, an exchange will be made for every comparison.

It's easy to see that the bubble sort is very inefficient, but if you ran the example in Listing 15.1, you probably didn't get the impression it was slow. For tiny lists of fewer than a hundred elements, the bubble sort is fine. If you have to code your own sort, the bubble sort has the advantage of being easy to remember and simple enough to get right the first time.

Quicksort

Invented by Professor C.A.R. Hoare in 1961, quicksort has proven to be the best general-purpose sorting algorithm. Many computer languages offer a library version, and PHP uses it for its built-in sorting functions. It is based on the same idea of exchanging elements, but adds the concept of partitioning. In most implementations it relies on recursion, a topic discussed in Chapter 4.

The quicksort algorithm chooses a pivot element and then divides all elements by whether they are greater or lesser than the pivot. Each subsection is further divided similarly. When the granularity becomes small enough, elements are simply compared and possibly swapped, as in the bubble sort.

When we first call the `quicksort` function in Listing 15.2, we pass the first and last elements of the array as the left and right limits. This will cause the entire array to be sorted. The step taken inside the function is to pick a pivot. Considering performance, the median of all the numbers would be best. This would divide the array exactly in two. To find the median, however, takes work. Rather than add this overhead, I've chosen to simply pick the number in the middle.

Listing 15.2   Quicksort

```
<?
    /*
    ** Quicksort
    ** input_array is an array of integers
    ** left is the leftmost element to be considered
```

```
** right is the rightmost element to be considered
*/
function Quicksort(&$input_array, $left_limit, $right_limit)
{
      //start pointers
      $left = $left_limit;
      $right = $right_limit;

      //Choose the middle element for the pivot
      $pivot_point = intval(($left + $right)/2);
      $pivot = $input_array[$pivot_point];

      do
      {
            while(($input_array[$left] < $pivot) AND ($left <
            $right_limit))
            {
                  $left++;
            }

            while(($pivot < $input_array[$right]) AND ($right >
            $left_limit))
            {
                  $right--;
            }

            if($left <= $right)
            {
                  //swap elements
                  $temp = $input_array[$left];
                  $input_array[$left] = $input_array[$right];
                  $input_array[$right] = $temp;
                  $left++;
                  $right--;
            }

      }
      while($left <= $right);

      if($left_limit < $right)
      {
            Quicksort(&$input_array, $left_limit, $right);
      }

      if($left < $right_limit)
```

```
        {
                Quicksort(&$input_array, $left, $right_limit);
        }
    }

    $data = array(6, 13, 99, 2, 33, 19, 84);

    //print array
    print("<H3>Unsorted</H3>\n");
    print("<PRE>");
    print_r($data);
    print("</PRE>\n");

    //sort array
    Quicksort(&$data, 0, count($data)-1);

    //print array again
    print("<H3>Sorted</H3>\n");
    print("<PRE>");
    print_r($data);
    print("</PRE>\n");
?>
```

The next step is to divide the list into two halves. Starting from the outside, elements are checked for being greater than or less than the pivot. When two elements are found that are both on the wrong side, they are swapped. When the left and right pointers meet, each side is fed back to the quicksort function.

Built-In Sorting Functions

Usually it will not be necessary to write your own sort functions. PHP offers several functions for sorting arrays. The most basic is sort. This function is described, along with the other sorting functions, in Chapter 9, "Data Functions." It will be instructive to compare sort to rsort, asort, and ksort.

The sort function puts all the elements in the array in order from lowest to highest. If the array contains any strings, then this means ordering them by the ASCII codes of each character. If the array contains only numbers, then they are ordered by their values. The indices—the values used to reference the elements—are discarded and replaced with integers starting with zero. This is an important effect, which Listing 15.3 demonstrates. Notice that, although I use some numbers and a string to index the array, after I sort it, all the elements are numbered zero through four. Keep this in mind if you ever need to clean up the indices of an array.

Another point worth noting in Listing 15.3 is the order of the output: Apple, Blueberry, Watermelon, apple, pear. A dictionary might list apple just before or just after Apple, but the ASCII code for A is 65. The ASCII code for a is 97. Appendix B lists all the ASCII codes. Later in this chapter I'll explain how to code a case-insensitive sort.

The `rsort` function works exactly like `sort`, except that it orders elements in the reverse order. Try modifying the code in Listing 15.3 by changing `sort` to `rsort`.

Two other two sort functions, `asort` and `arsort`, work in a slightly different way. They preserve the relationship between the index and the element. This is most useful when you have an associative array. If the array is indexed by numbers, you probably do not want to preserve their indices. On the other hand, what if you did? Listing 15.4 illustrates a possible scenario.

Listing 15.3   `Using the sort Function`

```
Listing 15.3 - Microsoft I...  [_][□][X]
  File   Edit   View   Favorites  >>

Array
(
    [0]  =>  Apple
    [1]  =>  Blueberry
    [2]  =>  Watermelon
    [3]  =>  apple
    [4]  =>  pear
)

    Internet
```

```
<?
    /*
    ** Fill fruit array with random values
    */
```

```
        $fruit[1] = "Apple";
        $fruit[13] = "apple";
        $fruit[64] = "Blueberry";
        $fruit[3] = "pear";
        $fruit["last"] = "Watermelon";

        //sort the array
        sort($fruit);

        //dump array to show new order
        print("<PRE>");
        print_r($fruit);
        print("</PRE>\n");
?>
```

Here I've used `reset` to put the internal array pointer at the first element. I then get each following element with the `next` function. This is the order in which the elements exist in memory, but they retain their original indices, which are the numbers starting with zero that were used when the elements were added to the array.

If I had used `arsort`, the order would have been the exact opposite. Listing 15.5 is perhaps a more typical use of these functions. It is important to keep the elements in the array returned by `getdate` associated with their in-

---

Listing 15.4   Using the `asort` Function

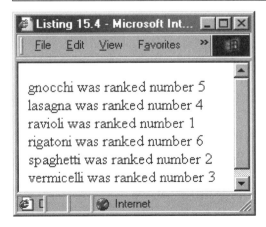

```
<?
    // Fill and array in order of preference
    $pasta = array(1=>"ravioli",
        "spaghetti",
        "vermicelli",
        "lasagna",
        "gnocchi",
        "rigatoni");

    // Sort the array, keeping indices
    asort($pasta);

    // Print array, now in alphabetical order
    foreach($pasta as $rank=>$name)
    {
        print("$name was ranked number $rank<BR>\n");
    }
?>
```

Listing 15.5   Using the **arsort** Function

```
Listing 15.5 - Microsoft I...  _ □ ✕
  File   Edit   View   Favorites  »

Array
(
    [0] => 957743038
    [year] => 2000
    [yday] => 127
    [seconds] => 58
    [minutes] => 43
    [hours] => 16
    [mday] => 7
    [mon] => 5
    [wday] => 0
    [weekday] => Sunday
    [month] => May
)

        Internet
```

```
<?

    //get an array from getdate
    $today = getdate();

    //Sort the array, keeping indices
    arsort($today);

    //Print array, now in descending order
    print("<PRE>");
    print_r($today);
    print("</PRE>\n");
?>
```

dices. Listing 15.5 sorts the array in reverse order by the elements. It may not be particularly useful but illustrates the use of this function.

The last sorting function I want to discuss in this section is `ksort`. This function sorts an array on the values of the indices. I've modified the code in Listing 15.6 to use `ksort` instead of `arsort`. Notice that now all the elements are in the order of their indices, or keys.

Listing 15.6   Using the `ksort` Function

```
Array
(
    [hours] => 16
    [mday] => 7
    [minutes] => 46
    [mon] => 5
    [month] => May
    [seconds] => 38
    [wday] => 0
    [weekday] => Sunday
    [yday] => 127
    [year] => 2000
    [0] => 957743198
)
```

```
<?
        /*
        ** printEmployees
        ** send entire list of employees to browser
        */
        function printEmployees($employee)
        {
                foreach($employee as $value)
                {
                        printf("%s (%s) %.2f/Hour <BR>\n",
                                $value[0],
                                $value[1],
                                $value[2]);
                }
        }

        // Create some employees (Name, Title, Wage)
        $employee = array(
                array("Smith, John", "Programmer", 20),
                array("Doe, Jane", "Programmer", 20),
                array("Mann, Joe", "Manager", 35),
                array("Smith, John", "CEO", 50),
                array("Leeds, Al", "President", 100));

        print("<B>Unsorted</B><BR>\n");
        printEmployees($employee);

        print("<B>Sorted by Name</B><BR>\n");
        usort($employee, "byName");
        printEmployees($employee);

        print("<B>Sorted by Title</B><BR>\n");
        usort($employee, "byTitle");
        printEmployees($employee);

        print("<B>Sorted by Salary</B><BR>\n");
        usort($employee, "bySalary");
        printEmployees($employee);
?>
```

The `ksort` function is perhaps most useful in situations where you have an associative array and you don't have complete control over the contents. In Listing 15.6 the script gets an array generated by the `getdate` function. If you run it with the `ksort` line commented out, you will see that the order is arbitrary. It's simply the order chosen when the function was coded. I could have typed a couple lines for each element based on the list of elements found in the description of the `getdate` function in Chapter 11, "Time, Date, and Configuration Functions." A more readable solution is to sort on the keys and to print each element in a loop. As you might have guessed, the `krsort` function sorts an array by its indices in reverse.

Sorting with a Comparison Function

The built-in sorting functions are appropriate in the overwhelming majority of situations. If your problem requires a sort that performs better than the one used in the built-in functions, you are faced with coding your own. If your problem is that you need to compare complex elements, such as objects or multidimensional arrays, the solution is to write a comparison function and plug it into the `usort` function.

The `usort` function allows you to sort an array using your own comparison function. Your comparison function must accept two values and return an integer. The two arguments are compared, and if a negative number is returned, then the values are considered to be in order. If zero is returned, they are considered to be equal. A positive number signifies that the numbers are out of order.

In Listing 15.7 I've created a multidimensional array with three elements: name, title, and wage. Sometimes I want to be able list employees by name, but other times I might want to list them by title or how much they make per hour. To solve this problem, I've written three comparison functions.

The `byName` function is a simple wrapper for `strcmp`. Names will be ordered by ASCII code. The `byTitle` function assigns an integer value to each title and then returns the comparison of these integers. The `bySalary` function compares the wage element, but if two employees make the same amount of money per hour, their names are compared.

Listing 15.7   Using the `usort` Function

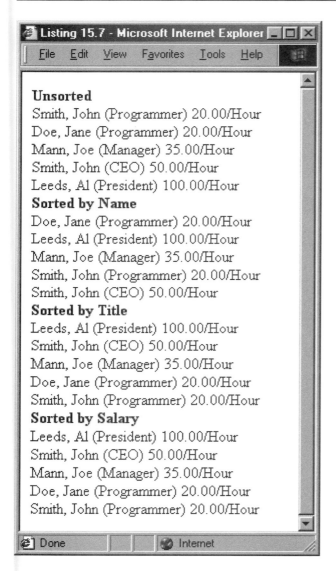

```
<?
        /*
        ** byName
        ** compare employees based on name
        */
```

```php
function byName($left, $right)
{
        return(strcmp($left[0], $right[0]));
}

/*
** byTitle
** compare employees based on title
*/
function byTitle($left, $right)
{
        if($left[1] == $right[1])
        {
                return(0);
        }
        else
        {
                $title = array(
                        "President"=>1,
                        "CEO"=>2,
                        "Manager"=>3,
                        "Programmer"=>4
                        );

                return($title[$left[1]] - $title[$right[1]]);
        }
}

/*
** bySalary
** compare employees based on salary, then name
*/
function bySalary($left, $right)
{
        if($left[2] == $right[2])
        {
                return(byName($left, $right));
        }
        else
        {
                return($right[2] - $left[2]);
        }
}

/*
```

```
 ** printEmployees
 ** send entire list of employees to browser
 */
function printEmployees($employee)
{
        foreach($employee as $value)
        {
                printf("%s (%s) %.2f/Hour <BR>\n",
                        $value[0],
                        $value[1],
                        $value[2]);
        }
}

// Create some employees (Name, Title, Wage)
$employee = array(
        array("Smith, John", "Programmer", 20),
        array("Doe, Jane", "Programmer", 20),
        array("Mann, Joe", "Manager", 35),
        array("Smith, John", "CEO", 50),
        array("Leeds, Al", "President", 100));

print("<B>Unsorted</B><BR>\n");
printEmployees($employee);

print("<B>Sorted by Name</B><BR>\n");
usort($employee, "byName");
printEmployees($employee);

print("<B>Sorted by Title</B><BR>\n");
usort($employee, "byTitle");
printEmployees($employee);

print("<B>Sorted by Salary</B><BR>\n");
usort($employee, "bySalary");
printEmployees($employee);
?>
```

The byName function is a simpler wrapper for strcmp. Names will be ordered by ASCII code. The byTitle function assigns an integer value to each title and then returns the comparison of these integers. The bySalary function compares the wage element, but if two employees make the same amount of money per hour, their names are compared.

Searching

Sorting organizes information into a form that aids in finding the exact piece being looked for. If you need to look up a phone number, it's easy to flip through the pages of a phone book until you find the approximate area where the number might be. With a bit of scanning you can find the number, because all the names are in order. For most of us, this process is automatic.

If you want to duplicate this process inside a PHP script, you have to think about each of the steps. The simplest way is to start at the beginning and look at every entry until you find the one you want. If you get to the end and haven't found it, it must not exist. I don't have to tell you this is probably the worst way to search, but sometimes this is all you have. If the data are unsorted, there is no better way.

You can dramatically improve your search time by doing a binary search. The requirement is that the data be sorted. Luckily, I've shown this to be relatively simple. The binary search involves repeatedly dividing the list into a half that won't contain the target value and a half that will.

To perform a binary search, start in the middle of the list. If the element in the middle precedes the element you are searching for, you can be sure it's in the half of the list that follows the middle element. You will now have half as many elements to search through. If you repeat these steps, you will zero in on your targeted value very quickly. To be precise, the worst case is that it will take $\log n$, or the base-two logarithm of the number of elements in the data. If you had 128 numbers, it would take at most 7 guesses. Listing 15.8 puts this idea into action.

Indexing

By sorting the data, you spend time up front, betting it will pay off when you need to search. But even this searching costs something. A binary search may take several steps. When you need to do hundreds of searches, you may look for further improvement in performance. One way is to perform every possible search beforehand, creating an index. A lot of work is done at first, which allows searches to be performed fast.

Let's explore how we can transform the binary search in Listing 15.8 into a single lookup. We want an array that, given a name, returns its position in the

Listing 15.8   A Binary Search

```
   [6] => Array
       (
            [0] => Porter, Carl
            [1] => Manager
            [2] => 35
       )

   [7] => Array
       (
            [0] => Tully, Joey
            [1] => Attorney
            [2] => 25
       )

   [8] => Array
       (
            [0] => Villarreal, John
            [1] => Attorney
            [2] => 25
       )

   [9] => Array
       (
            [0] => Welch, Eric
            [1] => Attorney
            [2] => 25
       )

)

Searching for Peterson, James
Position 5
Peterson, James CEO
```

```php
<?
    /*
    ** byName
```

```
** compare employees based on name
*/
function byName($left, $right)
{
      return(strcmp($left[0], $right[0]));
}

//Create some employees (Name, Title, Wage)
$employee = array(
      array("Foster, John", "Programmer", 20),
      array("DiBetta, Bob", "Programmer", 20),
      array("Tully, Joey", "Attorney", 25),
      array("Lipman, Jakob", "Attorney", 25),
      array("Villarreal, John", "Attorney", 25),
      array("Welch, Eric", "Attorney", 25),
      array("Porter, Carl", "Manager", 35),
      array("Marazzani, Rick", "Manager", 35),
      array("Peterson, James", "CEO", 50),
      array("Glidden, Jesse", "President", 100));

//Sort the list
usort($employee, "byName");

print("<PRE>");
print_r($employee);
print("</PRE>\n");

//Pick target
$Name = "Peterson, James";
print("Searching for $Name<BR>\n");

//Set range to search in
$lower_limit = 0;
$upper_limit = count($employee) - 1;

$TargetFound = FALSE;

while($lower_limit < $upper_limit)
{
      //Pick mid-point
      $index = intval(($lower_limit + $upper_limit)/2);

      if(strcmp($employee[$index][0], $Name) < 0)
      {
            //Target in upper half
            $lower_limit = $index + 1;
```

```
        }
        elseif(strcmp($employee[$index][0], $Name) > 0)
        {
                //Target in lower half
                $upper_limit = $index - 1;
        }
        else
        {
                //Target found
                $TargetFound = TRUE;
                $lower_limit = $index;
                $upper_limit = $index;
        }
}

// Print results
if($TargetFound)
{
        print("Position $index<BR>\n");
        print("{$employee[$index][0]} {$employee[$index][1]}<BR>\n");
}
else
{
        print("$Name not found!<BR>\n");
}
?>
```

original array. Our list of employees has two people with the same name, so we'll have to build a list of matches. Refer to the code in Listing 15.9. We won't bother sorting the list. It won't help, because we will be visiting every element of the array. As we visit each element, we create a new array. The index of this array is the name of the employee. Each element of the index will be an array of indices in the employee array. Once the index is created, finding an employee is a single statement. If the name is found in the array, we can retrieve the index values for the employee array.

This example is not very realistic because we're only making one search, and we're building the index with each request. The index needs to be built only once, as long as the employee array doesn't change. You could save the array to a file, perhaps using PHP serialization functionality, and then load it when needed. I wrote similar code for the FreeTrade project that indexes keywords that appear in pages of a Web site.

Listing 15.9   Indexing

```
Array
(
    [Smith, John] => Array
        (
            [0] => 0
            [1] => 3
        )

    [Doe, Jane] => Array
        (
            [0] => 1
        )

    [Mann, Joe] => Array
        (
            [0] => 2
        )

    [Leeds, Al] => Array
        (
            [0] => 4
        )

)

Found "Smith, John":
0: Smith, John Programmer 20
3: Smith, John CEO 50
```

```php
<?
    //Create some employees (Name, Title, Wage)
    $employee = array(
```

```php
        array("Smith, John", "Programmer", 20),
        array("Doe, Jane", "Programmer", 20),
        array("Mann, Joe", "Manager", 35),
        array("Smith, John", "CEO", 50),
        array("Leeds, Al", "President", 100));

//create index to names
foreach($employee as $key=>$value)
{
        $nameIndex[($value[0])][] = $key;
}

//peek at the index
print("<PRE>");
print_r($nameIndex);
print("</PRE>\n");

//use index to look for John Smith
$searchName = "Smith, John";
if(isset($nameIndex[$searchName]))
{
        print("Found \"$searchName\": <BR>\n");

        foreach($nameIndex["Smith, John"] as $value)
        {
                print("$value: ");
                print($employee[$value][0] . " ");
                print($employee[$value][1] . " ");
                print($employee[$value][2] . "<BR>\n");
        }
}
else
{
        print("Could not find \"$searchName\"<BR>\n");
}
?>
```

Of course, databases present a larger solution to managing data. In most cases, it's best to rely on a database to store large amounts of data, because databases have specialized code for searching and sorting. Databases are discussed in Chapter 17, "Database Interpretation."

Random Numbers

Closely tied to sorting and searching is the generation of random numbers. Often random numbers are used to put lists out of order. They offer the opportunity to create surprise. They allow you to squeeze more information onto a single page by choosing content randomly for each request. You see this every day on the Web in the form of quotes of the day, banner ads, and session identifiers.

There are two important qualities of truly random numbers: their distribution is uniform, and each successive value is independent of the previous value. To have a uniform distribution means that no value is generated more often than any other. The idea of independence is that, given a sequence of numbers returned by the generator, you should be unable to guess the next. Of course, we can't write an algorithm that really generates independent values. We have to have some formula, which by its nature is predictable. Yet, we can get pretty close using what is called a psuedorandom number generator. These use simple mathematical expressions that return seemingly random numbers. You provide a starting input called a seed. The first call to the function uses this seed for input, and subsequent calls use the previous value. Keep in mind that a seed will begin the same sequence of output values any time it's used. One way to keep things seeming different is to use the number of seconds on the clock to seed the generators.

The standard C library offers the `rand` function for generating random numbers, and PHP wraps it in a function of the same name. You pass upper and lower limits and integers are returned. You can seed the generator with the `srand` function, or just let the system seed it for you with the current time. Unfortunately, the standard generator on some operating systems can be inadequate. Previously, I suggested implementing your own random number generator if you needed better random numbers; however, Pedro Melo added a new set of functions to PHP that use the Mersenne Twister algorithm.

I won't attempt to describe the algorithm behind the Mersenne Twister algorithm because it's out of the scope of this text. You can visit the home page for more information <http://www.math.keio.ac.jp/~matumoto/emt.html>. You can read a careful description there to convince yourself of the validity of the algorithm if you wish.

Listing 15.10 is a very simple example that generates 100 random numbers between 1 and 100, using the `mt_rand` function. It then computes the average and the median. If the distribution of numbers is uniform, the average and median will be very close. The sample set is really small, though, so you will see lots of variance as you rerun the script.

Listing 15.10   Getting Random Numbers

```
<?
    // Seed the generator
    mt_srand(doubleval(microtime()) * 100000000);

    // Generate numbers
    print("<H3>Sample Set</H3>\n");
    $size = 100;
    for($i=0; $i < $size; $i++)
    {
        $n = mt_rand(1, $size);
        $sample[$i] = $n;
        $total += $n;
        print("$n<BR>\n");
    }

    print("Average: " . ($total/$size) . "<BR>\n");

    sort($sample);
    print("Median: " . ($sample[intval($size/2)]) . "<BR>\n");
?>
```

Random Identifiers

If you ever need to track users through a site, you will need to assign unique identifiers. In a database you can store all the information you know about the user and pass the identifier from page to page either through links or with cookies. You will have to generate these identifiers randomly, otherwise it is too easy for anyone to masquerade as a legitimate user. Fortunately, random identifiers are easy to generate.

Listing 15.11 illustrates how this works. A pool of characters to use in the session identifier is defined. Characters are picked randomly from the list to build a session identifier of the specified length. That identifier is used inside a link so that it is passed to the next page. This method works for any browser, even Lynx. Chapter 17 discusses the integration of this technique with a database.

It's very important to have random numbers here. Suppose you simply used the seconds on the clock. For an entire second, every session identifier would be the same. And it's very likely many people will be accessing a Web site during a single second. In Listing 15.11, I've used the time on the microsecond clock to seed the random generator, but even this allows the window of opportunity for getting a duplicate session identifier. One way to avoid this situation is to use a lockable resource that holds a seed—for example, a file. Once you lock the file, you can read the seed and write back a new one, at which point you are assured that two concurrent processes get the same seed.

Choosing Banner Ads

Another use for random numbers is choosing from banner ads. Suppose you've signed up three sponsors for your Web site. Each has a single banner you promise to display on an equal proportion of hits to your site. To accomplish this, generate a random number and match each number to a particular banner. In Listing 15.12, I've used a switch statement on a call to `mt_rand`. In a situation like this, you don't need to worry too much about using good seeds. You simply want a reasonable distribution of the three choices. Someone guessing which banner will display at midnight poses no security risk.

> **Listing 15.11   Generating a Session Identifier**

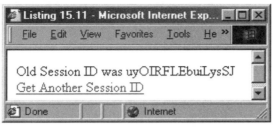

```php
<?
    /*
    ** SessionID
    ** generates a session id
    */
    function getSessionID($length=16)
    {
        // Set pool of possible characters
        $Pool = "ABCDEFGHIJKLMNOPQRSTUVWXYZ";
        $Pool .= "abcdefghijklmnopqrstuvwxyz";
        $lastChar = strlen($Pool) - 1;

        for($i = 0; $i < $length; $i++)
        {
            $sid .= $Pool[mt_rand(0, $lastChar)];
        }

        return($sid);
    }

    // Seed the generator
    mt_srand(100000000 * (double)microtime());

    if($sid != "")
    {
        print("Old Session ID was $sid<BR>\n");
    }

    $sid = getSessionID();

    print("<A HREF=\"$PHP_SELF?sid=$sid\">");
    print("Get Another Session ID");
    print("</A>\n");
?>
```

Listing 15.12   Random Banner Ad

```php
<?
    //Seed the generator
    mt_srand(doubleval(microtime()) * 100000000);

    //choose banner
    switch(mt_rand(1,3))
    {
        case 1:
                $bannerURL =
                "http://www.leonatkinson.com/random/";
                $bannerImage = "leon.jpg";
                break;
        case 2:
                $bannerURL = "http://www.php.net/";
                $bannerImage = "php_lang.jpg";
                break;
        default:
                $bannerURL = "http://www.phptr.com/";
                $bannerImage = "phptr.jpg";
    }
    //display banner
    print("<A HREF=\"$bannerURL\">");
    print("<IMG SRC=\"$bannerImage\" ");
    print("WIDTH=\"400\" HEIGHT=\"148\" BORDER=\"0\">");
    print("</A>");
?>
```

PARSING AND
STRING EVALUATION

Topics in This Chapter

- Tokenizing
- Regular Expressions
- Defining Regular Expressions
- Using Regular Expressions in PHP Scripts

P arsing is the act of breaking a whole into components, usually a sentence into words. PHP must parse the code you write as a first step in turning a script into an HTML document. There will come a time when you are faced with extracting or verifying data collected in a string. This could be as simple as a tab-delimited list. It could be as complicated as the string a browser uses to identify itself to a Web server. You may choose to tokenize the string, breaking it into pieces. Or you may choose to apply a regular expression. This chapter examines PHP's functions for parsing and string evaluation.

Tokenizing

PHP allows for a simple model for tokenizing a string. Certain characters, of your choice, are considered separators. Strings of characters between separators are considered tokens. You may change the set of separators with each token you pull from a string, which is handy for irregular strings—that is, ones that aren't simply comma-separated lists.

Listing 16.1 accepts a sentence and breaks it into words using the `strtok` function, described in Chapter 9, "Data Functions." As far as the script is concerned, a word is surrounded by a space, punctuation, or either end of the sentence. Single and double quotes are left as part of the word.

Listing 16.1   Tokenizing a String

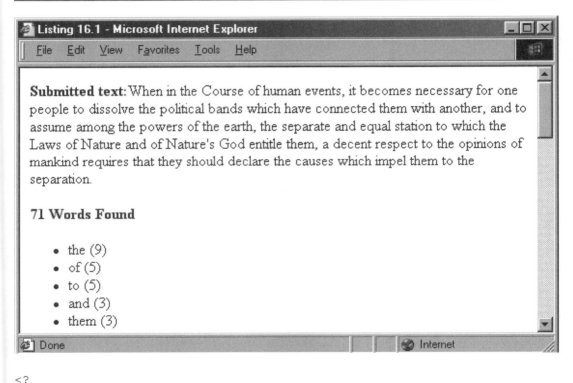

```
<?
    /*
    ** If submitted a sentence, parse it
    */
    if(isset($sentence))
    {
        print("<B>Submitted text:</B>");
        print("$sentence<BR><BR>\n");

        //add end marker
        $sentence .= " <END>";

        //set characters that separate tokens
```

```
$separators = " ,!.?";

//get each token
for($token = strtok($sentence, $separators);
        $token != "<END>";
        $token = strtok($separators))
{
        //skip empty tokens
        if($token != "")
        {
                // count each word
                $word_count[strtolower($token)]++;
                $total++;
        }
}

//first sort by word
ksort($word_count);

//next sort by frequency
arsort($word_count);

print("<B>$total Words Found</B>\n");
print("<UL>\n");
foreach($word_count as $key=>$value)
{
        print("<LI>$key ($value)\n");
}
print("</UL>\n");
}

print("<FORM ACTION=\"$PHP_SELF\" METHOD=\"post\">\n");
print("<INPUT NAME=\"sentence\" SIZE=\"40\">\n");
print("<INPUT TYPE=\"submit\" VALUE=\"Parse\">\n");
print("</FORM>\n");
?>
```

Notice the addition of <END> to the input variable. This special token allows the algorithm to detect the end of the input string. When strtok encounters the end of input, it returns FALSE, so your first inclination might be to test for FALSE in the for loop. Recall that an empty string is considered equivalent to FALSE. If two separators follow each other, strtok will return an empty string, as you'd expect. Since we don't want to stop tokenizing at the first repeated separator, we place a token at the end that we know won't appear in the input. If we're worried about people purposely putting <END> in the input string, we could strip it out first, but this isn't something that will be typed by accident. Since there's no security risk to the tokenizing ending too soon, I prefer to let hackers get invalid results.

The `strtok` function is useful only in the most simple and structured situations. An example might be reading a tab-delimited text file. The algorithm might be to read a line from a file, pulling each token from the line using the tab character, then continuing by getting the next line from the file.

Regular Expressions

Fortunately, PHP offers something more powerful than the `strtok` function: regular expressions. Written in a language of their own, regular expressions describe patterns that are compared to strings. The PHP source code includes an implementation of regular expressions that conform to the POSIX 1003.2 standard. This standard allows for expressions of an older style but encourages a modern style that I will describe. All the regular expression functions are described in Chapter 9.

In 1999, Andrei Zmievski added support for regular expressions that follow the style of Perl. They offer two advantages over PHP native regular expressions. They make it easier to copy an expression from a Perl script, and they take less time to execute.

It is beyond the scope of this text to examine regular expressions in depth. It is a subject worthy of a book itself. I will explain the basics, as well as demonstrate the various PHP functions that use regular expressions. An excellent resource for learning more about regular expressions is Chapter 2 of Ellie Quigley's *UNIX Shells by Example*. If you are interested in PERL-style regular expressions, first read the official documentation for Perl, compiled and edited by Tom Christiansen <http://www.perl.com/CPAN-local/doc/manual/html/pod/perlre.html>. You will then need to read the documentation at the PHP site itself that lists the differences between Perl and the PHP implementation <http://www.php.net/manual/pcre.pattern.syntax.php3>.

Defining Regular Expressions

At the highest level, a regular expression is one or more branches separated by the vertical bar character (|). This character is considered to have the properties of a logical-OR. Any of the branches could match with an evaluated string. Table 16–1 provides a few examples.

Each branch contains one or more atoms. These atoms may be followed by characters that modify the number of times the atom may be matched in succession. An asterisk (*) means the atom can match any number of times. A plus sign (+) means the atom must match at least once. A question mark (?) signifies that the atom may match once or not at all.

Alternatively, the atom may be bound, which means it is followed by curly braces, { and }, that contain integers. If the curly braces contain a single number, then the atom must be matched exactly that number of times. If the curly braces contain a number followed by a comma, the atom must be matched that number of times or more. If the curly braces contain two numbers separated by a comma, the atom must match at least the first number of times, but not more than the second number. See Table 16–2 for some examples of repetition.

An atom is a series of characters, some having special meaning, others simply standing for a character that must be matched. A period (.) matches any single character. A carat (^) matches the beginning of the string. A dollar sign ($) matches the end of the string. If you need to match one of the special characters (^ . [] $ () | * ? {} \), put a backslash in front of it. In fact, any character preceded by a backslash will be treated literally, even if it has no special meaning. Any character with no special meaning will be considered just a character to be matched, backslash or not. You may also group atoms with parentheses so that they are treated as an atom.

Table 16–1 Branches in a Regular Expression	
Sample	*Description*
apple	Matches the word apple.
apple|ball	Matches either apple or ball.
begin|end|break	Matches either begin, end, or break.

Table 16–2 Allowing Repetition of Patterns in Regular Expressions	
Sample	*Description*
a(b*)	Matches a, ab, abb, . . . — an a plus any number of b's.
a(b+)	Matches ab, abb, abbb, . . . — an a plus one or more b's.
a(b?)	Matches either a or ab — an a possibly followed by a b.
a(b{3})	Matches only abbb.
a(b{2,})	Matches abb, abbb, abbbb, . . . — an a followed by two or more b's.
a(b{2,4})	Matches abb, abbb, abbbb — an a followed by two to four b's.

Square brackets ([]) are used to specify a range of possible values. This may take the form of a list of legal characters. A range may be specified using the dash character (-). If the list or range is preceded by a carat (^), the meaning is taken to be any character not in the following list or range. Take note of this double meaning for the carat.

In addition to lists and ranges, square brackets may contain a character class. These class names are further surrounded by colons, so that to match any alphabetic character you write [:alpha:]. The classes are alnum, alpha, blank, cntrl, digit, graph, lower, print, punct, space, upper, and xdigit. You may wish to look at the man page for ctype to get a description of these classes.

Finally, two additional square bracket codes specify the beginning and ending of a word. They are [:<:] and [:>:], respectively. A word in this sense is defined as any sequence of alphanumeric characters and the underscore characters. Table 16–3 shows examples of using square brackets.

Using Regular Expressions in PHP Scripts

The basic function for executing regular expressions is ereg. This function evaluates a string against a regular expression, returning TRUE if the pattern described by the regular expression appears in the string. In this minimal

Table 16–3	Square Brackets in Regular Expressions

Sample	*Description*
a.c	Matches aac, abc, acc, . . . — Any three-character string beginning with an a and ending with a c.
^a.*	Matches any string starting with an a.
[a-c]*x$	Matches x, ax, bx, abax, abcx — Any string of letters from the first three letters of the alphabet followed by an x.
b[ao]y	Matches only bay or boy.
[^Zz]{5}	Matches any string, five characters long, that does not contain either an upper- or lowercase z.
[[:digit:]]	Matches any digit, equivalent to writing [0-9].
[[:<:]]a.*	Matches any word that starts with a.

form, you can check that a string conforms to a certain form. For example, you can ensure that a U.S. postal zip code is in the proper form of five digits followed by a dash and four more digits. Listing 16.2 demonstrates this idea.

Listing 16.2	Checking a ZIP Code

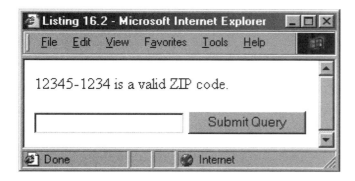

```
<?
     /*
     ** Check a ZIP code
```

```
** This script will test a zip code, which
** must be five digits, optionally followed by
** a dash and four digits.
*/

/*
** if zip submitted evaluate it
*/
if(isset($zip))
{
        if(ereg("^([0-9]{5})(-[0-9]{4})?$", $zip))
        {
                print("$zip is a valid ZIP code.<BR>\n");
        }
        else
        {
                print("$zip is <B>not</B> a valid ZIP code.<BR>\n");
        }
}

//start form
print("<FORM ACTION=\"$PHP_SELF\">\n");
print("<INPUT TYPE=\"text\" NAME=\"zip\">\n");
print("<INPUT TYPE=\"submit\">\n");
print("</FORM>\n");
?>
```

The script offers a form for inputting a zip code. It must have five digits and may be followed by a dash and four more digits. The functionality of the script hinges on the regular expression

```
^([0-9]{5})(-[0-9]{4})?$
```

which is compared to user input. It will be instructive to examine this expression in detail. It starts with a carat. This causes the expression to match only from the beginning of the evaluated string. If this were left out, the zip code could be preceded by any number of characters, such as abc12345-1234, and still be a valid match. Likewise, the dollar sign at the end of the expression matches the end of the string. This stops matching of strings like 12345-1234abc. The combination of using a carat and a dollar sign allows us to match only exact strings.

The first subexpression is `([0-9]{5})`. The square-bracketed range allows only characters from zero to nine. The curly braces specify that there must be exactly five of these characters.

The second subexpression is `(-[0-9]{4})?`. Like the first, it specifies exactly four digits. The dash is a literal character that must precede the digits. The question mark specifies that the entire subexpression may match once or not at all. This makes the four-digit extension optional.

You can easily expand this idea to check phone numbers or dates. Regular expressions provide a neat way of checking variables returned from forms. Consider the alternative of nesting if statements and searching strings with the `strpos` function.

You may also choose to have subexpression matches returned in an array. This is useful in situations where you need to break a string into components. The string a browser uses to identify itself is a good string for this method. Encoded in this string are the browser's name, version, and the type of computer it's running on. Pulling this information out into separate variables will allow you to customize your site based on the capabilities of the browser.

Listing 16.3 is a script for creating a set of variables that aid in cloaking a site for a particular browser. For the purpose of illustration, we will customize a link based on the browser being used. If the user visits the page with Netscape Navigator, we will provide a link to the download page for Microsoft Internet Explorer. Otherwise, we'll put a link to Netscape's download page. This is an example of customizing content, but the same method can be used to decide whether to use advanced features or not.

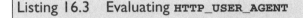

Listing 16.3   Evaluating `HTTP_USER_AGENT`

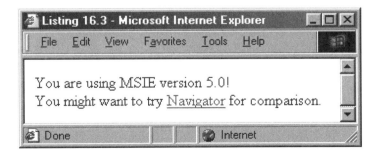

```
<?
    //evaluate user agent like
    //Mozilla/4.0 (compatible; MSIE 5.0; Windows 98; DigExt)
    ereg("^([[:alpha:]]+)/([[:digit:]\.]+)( .*)$",
        $HTTP_USER_AGENT, $match);

    $Browser_Name = $match[1];
    $Browser_Version = $match[2];
    $Browser_Description = $match[3];

    //look for clues that this is MSIE
    if(eregi("msie", $Browser_Description))
    {
        //looking for something like:
        //(compatible; MSIE 5.0; Windows 98; DigExt)
        eregi("MSIE ([[:digit:]\.]+);",
            $Browser_Description, $match);

        $Browser_Name = "MSIE";
        $Browser_Version = $match[1];
    }

    print("You are using $Browser_Name ");
    print("version $Browser_Version!<BR>\n");

    print("You might want to try ");

    if(eregi("mozilla", $Browser_Name))
    {
        print("<A
        HREF=\"http://www.microsoft.com/ie/download/default.asp\">");
        print("Internet Explorer");
        print("</A> ");
    }
    else
    {
        print("<A
        HREF=\"http://www.netscape.com/computing/download/index.html\">")
        ;
        print("Navigator");
        print("</A> ");
    }

    print("for comparison.\n");
?>
```

In this script the main `ereg` function is not used in an `if` statement. It assumes the browser will identify itself minimally as a name, a slash, and the version. The `match` array gets set with the parts of the evaluated string that match with the parts of the regular expression. There are three subexpressions for name, version, and any extra description. Most browsers follow this form, including Navigator and Internet Explorer. Since Internet Explorer always reports that it is a Mozilla (Netscape) browser, extra steps must be taken to determine if a browser is really a Netscape browser or an imposter. This is done with a call to `eregi`.

If you are wondering why element zero is ignored, that's because the zero element holds the substring that matches the entire regular expression. In this situation it is not interesting. Usually the zero element is useful when you are searching for a particular string in a larger context. For example, you may be scanning the body of a Web page for URLs. Listing 16.4 fetches the PHP home page and lists all the links on the page.

The main loop of this script gets lines of text from the file stream and looks for `HREF` properties. If one is found in a line, it will be placed in the zero element of the `match` array. The script prints it out and then removes it from the line using the `ereg_replace` function. This function replaces text matched with a regular expression with a string. In this case the script replaces the `HREF` property with an empty string. The reason for finding the link and then removing it is that it is possible for two links to be on one line of HTML. The `ereg` function will match the first substring only. The solution is to find and remove each link until none remain.

Notice that when removing the link a `replace` variable is prepared. Some links might contain a question mark, a valid character in a URL that separates a filename from form variables. Since this character has special meaning to regular expressions, the script places a backslash before it to let PHP know it's to be taken literally.

I frequently use `ereg_replace` to convert text for use in a new context. You can use `ereg_replace` for replacement of end-of-line characters with break tags. Listing 16.5 demonstrates this idea. You can also use it to collapse multiple spaces with a single space.

Listing 16.4   Scanning Text for URLs

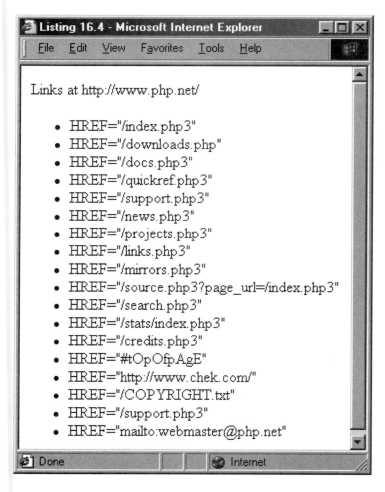

```php
<?
    //set URL to fetch
    $URL = "http://www.php.net/";

    //open file
    $page = fopen($URL, "r");

    print("Links at $URL<BR>\n");
    print("<UL>\n");
```

```php
while(!feof($page))
{
       //get a line
       $line = fgets($page, 1024);

       //loop while there are still URLs present
       while(ereg("HREF=\"[^\"]*\"", $line, $match))
       {
              //print out URL
              print("<LI>");
              print($match[0]);
              print("<BR>\n");

              //remove URL from line
              $replace = ereg_replace("\?", "\?", $match[0]);
              $line = ereg_replace($replace, "", $line);
       }
}

print("</UL>\n");

fclose($page);
?>
```

Listing 16.5   Replacing Linefeeds with HTML Line Breaks

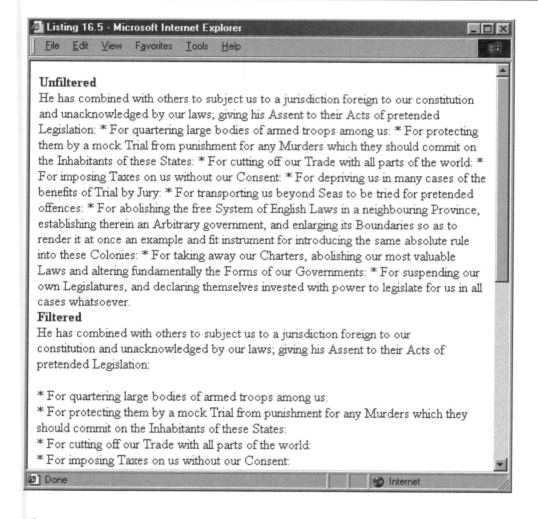

```
<?
    /*
    ** if text submitted show it
    */
    if(isset($text))
    {
        print("<B>Unfiltered</B><BR>\n");
        print($text);
```

```
        print("<BR>\n");

        //replace linefeed with <BR>
        //drop carriage returns
        $text = ereg_replace(10, "<BR>", $text);
        $text = ereg_replace(13, "", $text);

        print("<B>Filtered</B><BR>\n");
        print($text);
        print("<BR>\n");
    }

    //start form
    print("<FORM ACTION=\"$PHP_SELF\">\n");
    print("<TEXTAREA NAME=\"text\" COLS=\"40\" ROWS=\"10\">");
    print("</TEXTAREA><BR>\n");
    print("<INPUT TYPE=\"submit\">\n");
    print("</FORM>\n");
?>
```

By now you most likely understand regular expressions, but one new idea is worth noting. The call to `ereg_replace` in Listing 16.5 uses an integer to stand for a linefeed. This is because ASCII 10 is a linefeed character. You might think of using backslash-n here, but that would not give the results you want. Recall that the backslash character in regular expressions causes the character to be treated literally. The `ereg_replace` function allows you to specify a single character by ASCII value for its first argument.

DATABASE INTEGRATION

Topics in This Chapter

- Building HTML Tables from SQL Queries
- Tracking Visitors with Session Identifiers
- Storing Content in a Database
- Database Abstraction Layers

Chapter 17

PHP has strong support for many databases. If native support for your favorite database doesn't exist, there's always ODBC, which is a standard for external database drivers. Support for new databases seems to show up regularly. The universal remark in this regard from the PHP developers has been "give us a machine to test on and we'll add support."

MySQL is undoubtedly the most popular database used by PHP coders. Apart from being free, it suits Web development because of its blazing speed. In the examples for this chapter I'll assume you have a MySQL database. If you don't, you can either go to the MySQL Web site <http://www.mysql.com/> and investigate downloading and installing, or you can pursue changing the examples to work with another database.

Most relational databases use the Structured Query Language, or SQL. It is a fourth-generation language (4GL), which means it reads a bit more like English than PHP source code. A tutorial on SQL is beyond the scope of this book. If you're completely new to SQL, I recommend investigating the tutorials listed on the documentation page on the MySQL home page <http://www.mysql.com/doc.html>. An alternative would be to find a book such as *Hands-On SQL* by Robert Groth and David Gerber, published by Prentice Hall.

Building HTML Tables from SQL Queries

Perhaps the simplest task you can perform with a database and PHP is to extract data from a table and display it in an HTML table. The table could contain a catalog of items for sale, a list of projects, or a list of Internet name servers and their ping times. For illustration purposes, I'll use the first scenario. Imagine that a supermarket wants to list the items they have for sale on their Web site. As a proof of concept, you must create a page that lists some items from a database. We'll use the test database that's created when MySQL is installed. The PHP script for viewing the catalog of products will reside on the same machine as the database server.

The first step is to create the table. Listing 17.1 displays some SQL code for creating a simple, three-column table. The table is named catalog. It has a column called ID that is an integer with at most 11 digits. It cannot be null, and new rows will automatically be assigned consecutive values. The last line of the definition specifies ID as a primary key. This causes an index to be built on the column and disallows duplicate IDs. The other two columns are Name and Price.

Name is a variable-length character string that may be up to 32 characters long. Price is a floating-point number with six digits before the decimal point and two digits after. That's a perfect setup for money.

Next, we will need to put some items in the table. Since we're only creating a demo, we'll fill in some items we might expect in a supermarket along with some dummy prices. To do this we'll use the INSERT statement. Listing 17.2 is an example of this procedure.

Each SQL statement ends with a semicolon, much as in PHP. We're telling the MySQL server that we want to insert a row into the catalog table

---

Listing 17.1   Creating Catalog Table

```
CREATE TABLE catalog
(
    ID INT(11) NOT NULL AUTO_INCREMENT,
    Name VARCHAR(32),
    Price FLOAT(6,2),
    PRIMARY KEY (ID)
);
```

Listing 17.2   Inserting Data into Catalog Table

```
INSERT INTO catalog (Name, Price) VALUES ('Toothbrush', 1.79);
INSERT INTO catalog (Name, Price) VALUES ('Comb', 0.95);
INSERT INTO catalog (Name, Price) VALUES ('Toothpaste', 5.39);
INSERT INTO catalog (Name, Price) VALUES ('Dental Floss', 3.50);
INSERT INTO catalog (Name, Price) VALUES ('Shampoo', 2.50);
INSERT INTO catalog (Name, Price) VALUES ('Conditioner', 3.15);
INSERT INTO catalog (Name, Price) VALUES ('Deodorant', 1.50);
INSERT INTO catalog (Name, Price) VALUES ('Hair Gel', 6.25);
INSERT INTO catalog (Name, Price) VALUES ('Razor Blades', 2.99);
INSERT INTO catalog (Name, Price) VALUES ('Brush', 1.15);
```

---

and we'll be supplying only the name and price. Since we're leaving out ID, MySQL creates one. This is due to our defining the column as AUTO_INCRE-MENT. The VALUES keyword lets the server know we are about to send the values we promised earlier in the command. Notice the use of single quotes to surround text, as is standard in SQL.

Just to check that everything went well, Figure 17–1 shows the output you would get if you selected everything from the catalog table from within the MySQL client. I got this output by typing

```
SELECT * FROM catalog;
```

in the MySQL client.

```
ID      Name            Price
1       Toothbrush      1.79
2       Comb            0.95
3       Toothpaste      5.39
4       Dental Floss    3.50
5       Shampoo         2.50
6       Conditioner     3.15
7       Deodorant       1.50
8       Hair Gel        6.25
9       Razor Blades    2.99
10      Brush           1.15
10 rows in set (0.01 sec)
```

Figure 17–1   SELECT * FROM catalog

The last step is to write a PHP script that gets the contents of the table and dresses it up in an HTML table. Listing 17.3 lists PHP code for extracting the name and price values, displaying them in an HTML table. The first step in communicating with a database server is to connect to it. This is done with the `mysql_pconnect` function. It takes a hostname, a username, and a password. I usually create a user named `httpd` in my MySQL databases with no password. I also restrict this user to connections made from the local server. I name it after the UNIX user who will be executing the scripts—in other words, the Web server. If you are renting space from a hosting service, you may have a MySQL user and database assigned to you, in which case you'll need to modify the function arguments, of course.

Listing 17.3   Creating HTML Table from a Query

Item	Price
Toothbrush	1.79
Comb	0.95
Toothpaste	5.39
Dental Floss	3.50
Shampoo	2.50
Conditioner	3.15
Deodorant	1.50
Hair Gel	6.25
Razor Blades	2.99
Brush	1.15

```php
<?
    //connect to server, then test for failure
    if(!($dbLink = mysql_pconnect("localhost", "httpd", "")))
    {
        print("Failed to connect to database!<BR>\n");
        print("Aborting!<BR>\n");
        exit();
    }

    //select database, then test for failure
    if(!mysql_select_db("test", $dbLink))
    {
        print("Can't use the test database!<BR>\n");
        print("Aborting!<BR>\n");
        exit();
    }

    // get everything from catalog table
    $Query = "SELECT Name, Price ";
    $Query .= "FROM catalog ";
    if(!($dbResult = mysql_query($Query, $dbLink)))
    {
        print("Couldn't execute query!<BR>\n");
        print("MySQL reports: " . mysql_error() . "<BR>\n");
        print("Query was: $Query<BR>\n");
        exit();
    }

    //start table
    print("<TABLE BORDER=\"0\">\n");

    //create header row
    print("<TR>\n");
    print("<TD BGCOLOR=\"#CCCCCC\"><B>Item</B></TD>\n");
    print("<TD BGCOLOR=\"#CCCCCC\"><B>Price</B></TD>\n");
    print("</TR>\n");

    // get each row
    while($dbRow = mysql_fetch_object($dbResult))
    {
        print("<TR>\n");

        print("<TD>$dbRow->Name</TD>\n");
        print("<TD ALIGN=\"right\">$dbRow->Price</TD>\n");
```

```
        print("</TR>\n");
    }

    //end table
    print("</TABLE>\n");
?>
```

If the connection is successful, a MySQL link identifier will be returned. Notice that I'm testing for failure and performing the connection on one line. Link identifiers are always greater than zero, and zero is returned when the connection cannot be made. So, testing for a FALSE return value allows us to detect a failed connection. If that happens, we just abort the entire script.

The function used to connect to the database is mysql_pconnect. If you've flipped through the descriptions of the MySQL functions in Chapter 13, "Database Functions," you might remember another function called mysql_connect. These two functions operate identically inside a script, but mysql_pconnect returns persistent connections.

Most of the database functions that PHP offers incorporate the idea of a persistent connection—a connection that does not close when your script ends. If the same Web process runs another script later that connects to the same database server, the connection will be reused. This has the potential to save overhead. In practice, the savings are not dramatic, owing to the way Apache 1.3.x and earlier use child processes instead of threads. These processes serve a number of requests and then are replaced by new processes. When the process ends, it takes its persistent connection with it, of course.

Only under high loads will your script benefit from persistent connections, but that's exactly the time when it needs to benefit from them. Using mysql_pconnect costs nothing, so I use it by default. At the time of this writing, Apache 2.0 is nearing release. It promises a multithreaded approach that will certainly take full advantage of persistent connections.

The next step is to select a database. Here I've selected the database named store. Once we tell PHP which database to use, we get all rows from the catalog table. This is done with the mysql_query function. It executes a query on the given link and returns a result identifier. We will use this result identifier to fetch the results of the query.

Before we begin pulling data from the results, we must begin building an HTML table. This is done, as you might expect, by using an opening table tag. I've created a header row with a gray background and left the rest of the table behavior as default.

Now that the header row is printed, we can fetch each row from the result set. The fastest way to do this, executionwise, is to use `mysql_fetch_object`. This expresses each column in the result as the property of an object. The names of the columns are used for the names of the properties. You could also use `mysql_fetch_row` or `mysql_fetch_array`, which are equally efficient. Most of the time using an object seems more readable to me. You should avoid `mysql_result`, since this function does a costly lookup into a two-dimensional array.

When no more rows remain, FALSE will be returned. Capitalizing on this behavior, I put the fetch of the row inside a while loop. I create a row in the HTML table, printing object properties inside the table cells. When no rows remain, I close the table. I don't bother to close the connection to the database because PHP will do this automatically.

This is an extremely simply example, but it touches on all the major features of working with a database. Since each row is created in a loop, each is uniform. If the data change, there is no need to touch the code that turns it into HTML. You can just change the data in the database.

A good example of this technique in action is the Random Band Name Generator `<http://www.leonatkinson.com/random/>`, which creates random band names from a table of words, stored in a MySQL database to which anyone can add. Each refresh of the page fetches another ten names.

Tracking Visitors with Session Identifiers

As Web sites evolve into Web applications, the problem of maintaining state arises. The issue is that, from page to page, the application needs to remember who is visiting the page. The Web is stateless. Your browser makes a connection to a server, requests one or more files, and then closes the connection. Five minutes later when you click to a connecting page, the routine happens all over again. While a log is kept, the server doesn't re-member you. Any information you gave it about yourself three pages back may be saved somewhere, but it's not associated with you after that.

Imagine a wizardlike interface for ordering a pizza. The first screen asks you how many pizzas you want. Then you go through a page for each pizza, picking toppings and type of crust. Finally a page asks for your name and number so that your order can be emailed to the nearest pizza parlor. One way to handle this problem is to pass all the information gathered up to that point with each form submission. As you go from page to page, those data grow and grow. You're telling the server a partial version of your order many times. It works, but it's definitely wasteful of network bandwidth.

Using a database and a session identifier, you can store information as it becomes available. A single identifier is used as a key to the information. Once your script has the identifier, it can remember what has gone on before.

How the script gets the identifier is another issue. You have two choices. One is to pass the identifier as a variable inside every link or form. In a form this is simple to do with a hidden variable. In a link you have to insert a ques-tion mark and a variable definition. If your session ID is stored in a variable called `session`, then you might write something like

```
print("<A HREF=\"page2.php3?session=$session\">next</A>");
```

to send `session` to the next page. This technique works with all browsers, even Lynx.

An alternative is to use cookies. Like GET and POST form variables, cookies are turned into variables by PHP. So, you could create a cookie named `session`. The difference would be that, since cookies may only be set in headers, you'll have to send them to the browser before sending any HTML code. Check out the `setcookie` function in Chapter 8, "I/O Func-tions," if you wish to pursue this strategy. A more complex strategy attempts to use cookies, but falls back on GET variables if necessary.

Both methods are in wide use on the Internet. Check any e-commerce site. For the purpose of example, I'll present a strategy that uses GET vari-ables. The first step is to create a table to hold session identifiers. Listing 17.4 is SQL code for creating a simple session table in a MySQL database.

This table is keyed off an eight-character string. Each time the user moves to a new page, we will update the `LastAction` column. That way we can clear out any sessions that appear to be unused. Every visit to our page will trigger a clearing of all sessions without action for 30 minutes. Then we will

---

Listing 17.4　　Creating Session Table

```
CREATE TABLE session
(
  ID VARCHAR(8) NOT NULL,
  LastAction DATETIME,
  PRIMARY KEY (ID)
);
```

---

need to test each visitor for having a session identifier. If they don't have one, we will create one. If they do have one, we will need to check it to make sure it's valid.

The first time you load Listing 17.5, it will create a session for you. Each click of the "Refresh Page" link will cause the script to check the session. If the session identifier is not in the `session` table, then the session identifier will be rejected, and a new one will be created. You can try submitting a bad session identifier by erasing a character in the location box of your browser.

Listing 17.5　　Checking Session ID

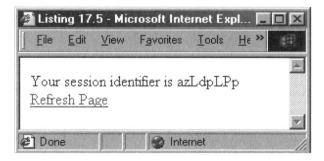

```
<?
        /*
        ** Demonstration of using session identifiers
        */

        function SessionID($length=8)
        {
```

```
        // Set pool of possible characters
        $Pool = "ABCDEFGHIJKLMNOPQRSTUVWXYZ";
        $Pool .= "abcdefghijklmnopqrstuvwxyz";
        $lastChar = strlen($Pool) - 1;

        for($i = 0; $i < $length; $i++)
        {
                $sid .= $Pool[mt_rand(0, $lastChar)];
        }

        return($sid);
}


//Seed the generator
mt_srand(time());

//connect to server, then test for failure
if(!($dbLink = mysql_pconnect("localhost", "httpd", "")))
{
        print("Failed to connect to database!<BR>\n");
        print("Aborting!<BR>\n");
        exit();
}

//select database, then test for failure
if(!mysql_select_db("test", $dbLink))
{
        print("Can't use the test database!<BR>\n");
        print("Aborting!<BR>\n");
        exit();
}

//clear out any old sessions
$Query = "DELETE FROM session ";
$Query .= "WHERE LastAction < '";
$Query .= date("Y-m-d H:i:s", (time()-10800));
$Query .= "'";
if(!($dbResult = mysql_query($Query, $dbLink)))
{
        //can't execute query
        print("Couldn't remove old sessions!<BR>\n");
        print("MySQL Reports: " . mysql_error() . "<BR>\n");
```

```
        exit();
}

//check session
if(isset($session))
{
        //we have a session, so check it
        $Query = "SELECT * ";
        $Query .= "FROM session ";
        $Query .= "WHERE ID='" . addslashes($session) . "' ";

        if(!($dbResult = mysql_query($Query, $dbLink)))
        {
                //can't execute query
                print("Couldn't query session table!<BR>\n");
                print("MySQL Reports: " . mysql_error() . "<BR>\n");
                exit();
        }

        //if we have a row, then the match succeeded
        if(mysql_numrows($dbResult))
        {
                //session exists, update last action
                $Query = "UPDATE session ";
                $Query .= "SET LastAction = now() ";
                $Query .= "WHERE ID='$session' ";
                if(!($dbResult = mysql_query($Query, $dbLink)))
                {
                        //can't execute query
                        print("Couldn't update session table!<BR>\n");
                        print("MySQL Reports: " . mysql_error() . "<BR>\n");
                        exit();
                }
        }
        else
        {
                //session is bad
                print("Bad Session ID ($session)!<BR>\n");
                $session = "";
        }
}
```

```
//if session is empty, we need to create it
if($session == "")
{
        //no session, so create one
        $session = SessionID(8);

        //insert session to database
        $Query = "INSERT INTO session ";
        $Query .= VALUES ('$session', now()) ";
        if(!($dbResult = mysql_query($Query, $dbLink)))
        {
                //can't execute query
                print("Couldn't insert into session table!<BR>\n");
                print("MySQL Reports: " . mysql_error() . "<BR>\n");
                exit();
        }
}

print("Your session identifier is $session<BR>\n");
print("<A HREF=\"$PHP_SELF?session=$session\">");
print("Refresh Page");
print("</A><BR>\n");
?>
```

The next logical step is to add another table for storing the information you need to know about the person browsing your site. One of the columns should be for storing the session identifier from the session table. I'll leave this as an exercise for you.

Storing Content in a Database

Information stored in a database is not limited to short strings, like the 32-character item name from Listing 17.3. You can create 64K blobs, which are enough to store a good-sized Web page. The advantage here is that pages exist in a very structured environment. They can be identified by a number, and relationships can be drawn between them using only these numbers. The disadvantage is that, since the information is now in a database, you can't just load the file into your favorite editor. You have to balance the costs and benefits; most Web sites don't need every piece of content stored in a database.

A situation where it makes a lot of sense to put the content in a database is a Bulletin Board System, or BBS. The system stores messages, which are more than just Web pages. Each message has its own title, creation time, and author. This structure can be conveniently wrapped up into a database table. Furthermore, since each message can be given a unique identifier, we can associate messages in a parent-child tree. A user can create a new thread of discussion that spawns many other messages. Messages can be displayed in this hierarchical structure to facilitate browsing.

As with all database-related systems, the first step is to create a table. Listing 17.6 creates a table for storing messages. Each message has a title, the name of the person who posted the message, when the message was posted, a parent message, and the body of text. The parent ID might be zero, in which case we understand the message to be the beginning of a thread. The body doesn't have to be plain text. It can contain HTML. In this way it allows users to create their own Web pages using their browsers.

The script in Listing 17.7 has two modes: listings message titles and viewing a single message. If the `messageID` variable is empty, then a list of every message in the system is shown organized by thread. This is accomplished by the `showMessages` function. You might want to turn back to Chapter 4, "Functions," specifically the section on recursion. The `showMessages` func-

---

Listing 17.6   Create Message Table

```
CREATE TABLE Message
(
  ID INT NOT NULL AUTO_INCREMENT,
  Title VARCHAR(64),
  Poster VARCHAR(64),
  Created DATETIME,
  Parent INT,
  Body BLOB,
  PRIMARY KEY(ID)
);
```

Listing 17.7   A Simple BBS

```
<?
    print("<H1>Leon's BBS</H1>\n");

    //connect to server, then test for failure
    if(!($dbLink = mysql_pconnect("localhost", "httpd", "")))
    {
        print("Failed to connect to database!<BR>\n");
        print("Aborting!<BR>\n");
        exit();
    }

    //select database, then test for failure
    if(!mysql_select_db("test", $dbLink))
    {
        print("Can't use the test database!<BR>\n");
```

```
        print("Aborting!<BR>\n");
        exit();
}

/*
** recursive function that spits out all
** descendent messages
*/
function showMessages($parentID)
{
        global $dbLink;

        $dateToUse = Date("U");

        print("<UL>\n");

        $Query = "SELECT ID, Title, Created ";
        $Query .= "FROM bbsMessage ";
        $Query .= "WHERE Parent=$parentID ";
        $Query .= "ORDER BY Created ";

        if(!($dbResult = mysql_query($Query, $dbLink)))
        {
                //can't execute query
                print("Couldn't query bbsMessage table!<BR>\n");
                print("MySQL Reports: " . mysql_error() . "<BR>\n");
                exit();
        }

        while($row = mysql_fetch_object($dbResult))
        {
                //show message title as a link to view the body
                print("<LI>($row->Created) <A HREF=\"");
                print("$PHP_SELF?messageID=$row->ID\">");
                print("$row->Title</A><BR>\n");

                //show children of this message
                showMessages($row->ID);
        }

        print("</UL>\n");
}
```

```
/*
** print out a form for adding a message with
** parent id given
*/
function postForm($parentID, $useTitle)
{
      print("<FORM ACTION=\"$PHP_SELF\" METHOD=\"post\">\n");

      print("<INPUT TYPE=\"hidden\" NAME=\"inputParent\" ");
      print("VALUE=\"$parentID\">\n");

      print("<INPUT TYPE=\"hidden\" NAME=\"ACTION\" ");
      print("VALUE=\"POST\">\n");

      print("<TABLE BORDER=\"1\" CELLSPACING=\"0\" ");
      print("CELLPADDING=\"5\" WIDTH=\"400\">\n");

      print("<TR>\n");

      print("<TD WIDTH=\"100\"><B>Title</B></TD>\n");

      print("<TD WIDTH=\"300\">");
      print("<INPUT TYPE=\"text\" NAME=\"inputTitle\" ");
      print("SIZE=\"35\" MAXLENGTH=\"64\" VALUE=\"$useTitle\">");
      print("</TD>\n");

      print("</TR>\n");

      print("<TR>\n");

      print("<TD WIDTH=\"100\"><B>Poster</B></TD>\n");

      print("<TD WIDTH=\"300\">");
      print("<INPUT TYPE=\"text\" NAME=\"inputPoster\" ");
      print("SIZE=\"35\" MAXLENGTH=\"64\">");
      print("</TD>\n");

      print("</TR>\n");

      print("<TR>\n");

      print("<TD COLSPAN=\"2\" WIDTH=\"400\">");
      print("<TEXTAREA NAME=\"inputBody\" ");
      print("COLS=\"45\" ROWS=\"5\"></TEXTAREA>");
```

```
        print("</TD>\n");
        print("</TR>\n");

        print("<TR>\n");

        print("<TD COLSPAN=\"2\" WIDTH=\"400\" ALIGN=\"middle\">");
        print("<INPUT TYPE=\"submit\" VALUE=\"Post\">");
        print("</TD>\n");

        print("</TR>\n");

        print("</TABLE>\n");
        print("</FORM>\n");
}

/*
** perform actions
*/
if($ACTION != "")
{
        if($ACTION == "POST")
        {
                $Query = "INSERT INTO bbsMessage ";
                $Query .= "VALUES(0,";
                $Query .= "'" . addslashes($inputTitle) . "', ";
                $Query .= "'" . addslashes($inputPoster) . "', ";
                $Query .= "now(), $inputParent, ";
                $Query .= "'" . addslashes($inputBody) . "')";

                if(!($dbResult = mysql_query($Query, $dbLink)))
                {
                        //can't execute query
                        print("Couldn't insert into bbsMessage table!<BR>\n");
                        print("MySQL Reports: " . mysql_error() . "<BR>\n");
                        exit();
                }
        }

}

/*
** Show Message or show list of messages
*/
```

```
if($messageID > 0)
{
        $Query = "SELECT ID, Title, Poster, Created, Parent, Body ";
        $Query .= "FROM bbsMessage ";
        $Query .= "WHERE ID=$messageID ";

        if(!($dbResult = mysql_query($Query, $dbLink)))
        {
                //can't execute query
                print("Couldn't query bbsMessage table!<BR>\n");
                print("MySQL Reports: " . mysql_error() . "<BR>\n");
                exit();
        }

        if($row = mysql_fetch_object($dbResult))
        {
                print("<TABLE BORDER=\"1\" CELLSPACING=\"0\" ");
                print("CELLPADDING=\"5\" WIDTH=\"400\">\n");

                print("<TR>");
                print("<TD WIDTH=\"100\"><B>Title</B></TD>");
                print("<TD WIDTH=\"300\">$row->Title</TD>");
                print("</TR>\n");

                print("<TR>");
                print("<TD WIDTH=\"100\"><B>Poster</B></TD>");
                print("<TD WIDTH=\"300\">$row->Poster</TD>");
                print("</TR>\n");

                print("<TR>");
                print("<TD WIDTH=\"100\"><B>Posted</B></TD>");
                print("<TD WIDTH=\"300\">$row->Created</TD>");
                print("</TR>\n");

                print("<TR>");
                print("<TD COLSPAN=\"2\" WIDTH=\"400\">");
                print("$row->Body");
                print("</TD>");
                print("</TR>\n");

                print("</TABLE>\n");

                postForm($row->ID, "RE: $row->Title");
```

```
        }

        print("<A HREF=\"$PHP_SELF\">List of Messages</A><BR>\n");

    }
    else
    {
        print("<H2>List of Messages</H2>\n");

        // get entire list
        showMessages(0);

        postForm(0, "");

    }
?>
```

tion uses recursion to travel to every branch of the tree of messages. It starts by getting a list of all the messages that have no parent. These are the root-level messages, or beginnings of threads. After showing each root-level message, showMessages is called for the thread. This process continues until a message is found with no children. UL tags are used to display the message titles. The indention aids the user in understanding the hierarchy.

For the efficiency-minded, this use of recursion is not optimal. Each thread will cause another call to showMessages, which causes another query to the database. There is a way to query the database once and traverse the tree of messages in memory, but I'll leave that as exercise for you.

If a message title is clicked on, the page is reloaded with messageID set. This causes the script to switch over into the mode where a message is displayed. The fields of the message are displayed in a table. If the message contains any HTML, it will be rendered by the browser, because no attempt is made to filter it out. This restriction is best applied as part of the code that adds a new message.

Regardless of the two modes, a form is shown for adding a message. If a message is added while the list of messages is shown, the message will be added to the root level. If a message is added while the user is viewing a message, then it will be considered a reply. The new message will be made a child of the viewed message.

This BBS is simple, but the core functionality exists. A more sophisticated solution might involve allowing only authenticated users to add messages, or keeping messages private until approved by a moderator. You can use this same structure to build any application that manages user-submitted data, such as a guest book. If you are searching for a sophisticated BBS solution, I suggest checking out Brian Moon's Phorum project `<http://www.phorum.org/>`.

Database Abstraction Layers

Imagine creating a Web application that uses MySQL and later being asked to make it work with Oracle. All the PHP functions are different, so you'd have to change every one. In addition, as MySQL and Oracle each use slightly different SQL, you will probably have to change most of your queries. One solution to this problem is adding an abstraction layer. This separates your business logic—the rules of your application—from the code that interfaces with the database. A single function calls the right function based on the type of database you need to query.

Perhaps the most popular database abstraction layer is part of the PHP Base Library `<http://phplib.netuse.de/>`. This library also contains code for session management. Another abstraction layer is Metabase, available at the PHP Classes Repository `<http://phpclasses.upperdesign.com/>`.

Despite abstraction layers, incompatibilities between databases continue to offer challenges. MySQL uses a special qualifier for column definitions called AUTO_INCREMENT. It causes a column to be populated automatically with integers in ascending order. In Oracle this functionality can be approximated using a sequence and a trigger. The differences are difficult to reconcile systematically. In 1999, Scott Ambler proposed a solution in his white paper "The Design of a Robust Persistence Layer for Relational Databases" `<http://www.ambysoft.com/persistenceLayer.html>`. A careful analysis of the problems is explored as well as a detailed design, neither of which I can do justice to in the context of this chapter.

An abstraction layer trades some performance in favor of robustness. Certain unique, high-performance features of each database must be abandoned. The abstraction layer will provide the common set of functionality. But what you gain is independence from any particular database.

NETWORK

Topics in This Chapter

- HTTP Authentication
- Controlling Browser Cache
- Setting Document Type
- Email with Attachments
- Verifying an Email Address

18

M ost anything you write in PHP will be in the context of a network. It's a language intended primarily to produce HTML documents via the HTTP protocol. PHP allows you to code without worrying about the underlying protocols, but it also allows you to address the protocols directly when necessary. This chapter deals intimately with two important protocols, HTTP and SMTP. These are the protocols for transferring Web documents and mail. I've attempted to describe some common problems and provide solutions. This chapter may address a particular problem you face, such as protecting a Web page with basic HTTP authentication, but it also illustrates generally how to use HTTP headers and communicate with remote servers.

HTTP Authentication

If you have any experience with the Web, you're familiar with basic HTTP authentication. You request a page, and a small dialog window appears asking for username and password. As described in Chapter 8, "I/O Functions," PHP allows you to open URLs with the `fopen` function. You can even specify a username and password in the URL in the same way you do in Navigator's location box. Authentication is implemented using HTTP headers, and you can protect your PHP pages using the `header` function.

To protect a page with basic HTTP authentication, you must send two headers. The `WWW-Authenticate` header tells the browser that a username and password are required. It also specifies a realm that groups pages. A username and password are good for an entire realm, so users don't need to authenticate themselves with each page request. The other header is the status, which should be `HTTP/1.0 401 Unauthorized`. Compare this to the usual header, `HTTP/1.0 200 OK`.

Listing 18.1 is an example of protecting a single page. The HTML to make a page is put into functions because it needs to be printed whether the authentication succeeds or fails. The `PHP_AUTH_USER` and `PHP_AUTH_PW` variables are created automatically by PHP if a username and password are passed by the browser. The example requires my name, leon, for the username and *secret* for the password. A more complex scheme might match username and password against a list stored in a file or a database.

Listing 18.1   Requiring Authentication

```php
<?
    /*
    ** Define a couple of functions for
    ** starting and ending an HTML document
    */
    function startPage()
    {
        print("<HTML>\n");
        print("<HEAD>\n");
        print("<TITLE>Listing 18.1</TITLE>\n");
        print("</HEAD>\n");
        print("<BODY>\n");
    }

    function endPage()
    {
        print("</BODY>\n");
        print("</HTML>\n");
    }
```

```
/*
** test for username/password
*/
if(($PHP_AUTH_USER == "leon") AND ($PHP_AUTH_PW == "secret"))
{
        startPage();

        print("You have logged in successfully!<BR>\n");

        endPage();
}
else
{
        //send headers to cause a browser to request
        //username and password from user
        header("WWW-Authenticate: Basic realm=\"Leon's Protected Area\"");
        header("HTTP/1.0 401 Unauthorized");

        //show failure text
        print("This page is protected by HTTP Authentication.<br>\n");
        print("Use <B>leon</B> for the username, and <B>secret</B> ");
        print("for the password.<br>\n");
}
?>
```

Now that you know how to protect a page, it may be instructive to work the other direction, requesting a protected page. As I said earlier, the `fopen` function allows you to specify username and password as part of a URL, but you may have a more complicated situation where you need to use `fsockopen`. An `Authentication` request header is necessary. The value of this header is a username and password separated by a colon. This string is base64 encoded, in compliance with the HTTP specification.

Listing 18.2 requests the script in Listing 18.1. You may need to modify the URI to make it work on your Web server. The script assumes you have installed all the examples on your Web server in `/corephp/listings`. If you are wondering about the `\r\n` at the end of each line, recall that all lines sent to HTTP servers must end in a carriage return and a linefeed.

Listing 18.2   Requesting a Protected Document

```
<?
    //open socket
    if(!($fp = fsockopen("localhost", 80)))
    {
        print("Couldn't open socket!<BR>\n");
        exit;
    }

    //make request for document
    fputs($fp, "HEAD /corephp/listings/18-1.php HTTP/1.0\r\n");

    //send username and password
    fputs($fp, "Authorization: Basic " .
        base64_encode("leon:secret") .
        "\r\n");

    //end request
    fputs($fp, "\r\n");

    //dump response from server
    fpassthru($fp);
?>
```

Controlling Browser Cache

One hassle of writing dynamic Web pages is the behavior of caches. Browsers maintain their own cache, and by default they will check for a newer version of the page only once per session. Some ISPs provide their own cache as well. The intention is to avoid wasteful retransmission of pages. However, if the content on your page potentially changes with each request, it can be annoying if an old version appears. If you are developing an e-commerce site, it can be critical that each page is processed anew.

On the other hand, your page may be dynamically building a page that contains information that doesn't change very often. My experience has been that caches are smart enough to store URLs that appear to be ordinary HTML files, but not URLs that contains variables following a question mark. Your PHP may use variables in the URL, though. If the information on these pages changes infrequently, you want to let the cache know.

RFC 2616 describes the HTTP 1.1 protocol, which offers several headers for controlling the cache. Listing 18.3 shows the headers to send to prevent a page from being cached. The `Last-Modified` header reports the last time a document was changed, and setting it to the current time tells the browser this version of the page is fresh. The `Expires` header tells the browser when this version of the document will become stale and should be requested again. Again we use the current time, hopefully causing the browser to keep the document out the cache. Perhaps the most important header, `Cache-Control` tells the browser how to cache the page. In this situation, we are requesting the page not be cached. The fourth header is for the benefit of older browsers that understand only HTTP 1.0. Try reloading the script in Listing 18.3 rapidly. You should see the date update each time.

Listing 18.4 causes a page to be cached for 24 hours. Like Listing 18.3, the `Last-Modified`, `Expires` and `Cache-Control` headers are used to control

---

Listing 18.3   Sending Headers to Prevent Caching

```
<?
        header("Last-Modified: " . gmdate("D, d M Y H:i:s") . " GMT");
        header("Expires: " . gmdate("D, d M Y H:i:s") . " GMT");
        header("Cache-Control: no-cache, must-revalidate");
        header("Pragma: no-cache");
?>
<HTML>
<HEAD>
<TITLE>Listing 18.3</TITLE>
</HEAD>
<BODY>
The time is <? print(date("D, d M Y H:i:s")); ?><BR>
</BODY>
</HTML>
```

cache behavior. The last modification time is sent as the actual modification of the file. The expiration time is sent as 24 hours from now. And the cache is instructed to let the document age for 86,400 seconds, the number of seconds in a day. To prove to yourself that the file is being returned by the cache, try reloading the page quickly. The dates on the page should remain the same.

Notice that all the dates in these two examples use GMT, or Greenwich Mean Time. This is specified by the HTTP protocol. Forgetting to convert from your local time zone to GMT can be an annoying source of bugs.

Listing 18.4   Sending Headers to Encourage Caching

```
<?

    //report actual modification time of script
    $LastModified = filemtime(__FILE__) + date("Z");
    header("Last-Modified: " .
        gmdate("D, d M Y H:i:s", $LastModified) . " GMT");

    //set expiration time 24 hours (86400 seconds) from now
    $Expires = time() + 86400;
    header("Expires: " .
        gmdate("D, d M Y H:i:s", $Expires) . " GMT");

    //tell cache to let page age for 24 hours (86400 seconds)
    header("Cache-Control: max-age=86400");
?>
<HTML>
<HEAD>
<TITLE>Listing 18.4</TITLE>
</HEAD>
<BODY>
The time is <? print(gmdate("D, d M Y H:i:s")); ?> GMT<BR>
<BR>
This document was last modified
<? print(gmdate("D, d M Y H:i:s", $LastModified)); ?> GMT<BR>
It expires
<? print(gmdate("D, d M Y H:i:s", $Expires)); ?> GMT<BR>
</BODY>
</HTML>
```

Setting Document Type

By default, PHP sends an HTTP header specifying the document as being HTML. The `Content-Type` header specifies the MIME type `text/html`, and the browser interprets the code as HTML. Sometimes you will wish to create other types of documents with PHP. You will learn in Chapter 19, "Generating Graphics," about creating images, which may require an `image/png` content type. MIME types are administered by IANA, the Internet Assigned Numbers Authority. You can find a list of official media types at `<http://www.isi.edu/in-notes/iana/assignments/media-types/>`.

At times, you may wish to take advantage of how browsers react to different types of content. For example, `text/plain` displays in a fixed-width font with no interpretation of HTML. If you use `*/*` for the content type, the browser displays a dialog window for saving the file. Perhaps the most interesting use is for launching a helper application.

Listing 18.5 creates a tab-delimited text file that may launch Microsoft Excel. Take note that the computer must meet a few qualifications, however. First, it probably needs to be running Windows, and it must have Microsoft Excel installed. Newer versions of Excel associate the `application/vnd.ms-excel` content type with `.xls` files. My experience has been that these headers will cause an Excel OLE container inside either MSIE or Netscape Navigator on a Windows machine, but your mileage may vary. Other browsers will likely ask the user if the file should be saved.

Notice the second header in Listing 18.5, `Content-Disposition`. This is not part of the HTTP 1.1 standard but is widely implemented. It allows you to suggest a file name. If you add `attachment;` to the header, the browser may choose to open Excel in a separate window.

Using `Content-Type` this way is almost black magic, since browsers don't follow a standard when encountering different MIME types. This technique has proven to be most successful for me when writing intranet applications where I had the luxury of serving a narrow set of browsers.

Email with Attachments

Sending plain email with PHP is easy. The `mail` function handles all the messy protocol details behind the scenes. But if you want to send attachments, you will need to dig into an RFC, specifically RFC 1341. This RFC

Listing 18.5   Sending a Tab-Delimited Excel File

```
<?

    //set the document type
    header("Content-Type: application/vnd.ms-excel");
    header("Content-Disposition: filename=\"listing18-5.txt\"");

    //send some tab-delimited data
    print("Listing 18.5\r\n");

    for($i=1; $i < 100; $i++)
    {
        print("$i\t");
        print(($i * $i) . "\t");
        print(($i * $i * $i) . "\r\n");
    }
?>
```

describes MIME, Multipurpose Internet Mail Extensions. You can read it at the faqs.org site <http://www.faqs.org/rfcs/rfc1341.html>, but I'll show you a somewhat naïve implementation.

There are several example implementations to be found on the Web. Check out David Sklar's networking section <http://px.sklar.com/section.html?section_id=10>. Most of these put functionality into a class and attempt to incorporate every aspect of the standard. Listing 18.6 contains code that sends email with multiple attachments using two simple functions. Use this example as a basis for learning the process, and expand its functionality if necessary.

Listing 18.6   Sending Attachments

```php
<?
    /*
    ** Function: makeAttachment
    ** Input: ARRAY attachment
    ** Output: STRING
    ** Description: Returns headers and data for one
    ** attachment. It expects an array with elements
    ** type, name, and content. Attachments are naively
    ** base64 encoded, even when unnecessary.
    */
    function makeAttachment($attachment)
    {
        //send content type
        $headers = "Content-Type: " . $attachment["type"];

        if($attachment["name"] != "")
        {
            $headers .= "; name=\"{$attachment["name"]}\"";
        }

        $headers .= "\r\n";

        $headers .= "Content-Transfer-Encoding: base64\r\n";

        $headers .= "\r\n";

        $headers .= chunk_split(base64_encode($attachment["content"]));
        $headers .= "\r\n";
```

```
      return($headers);
}


/*
** Function: mailAttachment
** Input: STRING to, STRING from, STRING subject, ARRAY attachment
** Output: none
** Description: Sends attachments via email. The attachment
** array is a 2D array. Each element is an associative array
** containing elements type, name and content.
*/
function mailAttachment($to, $from, $subject, $attachment)
{
      //add from header
      $headers = "From: $from\r\n";

      //specify MIME version 1.0
      $headers .= "MIME-Version: 1.0\r\n";

      //multiple parts require special treatment
      if(count($attachment) > 1)
      {
            //multiple attachments require special handling
            $boundary = uniqid("COREPHP");

            $headers .= "Content-Type: multipart/mixed";
            $headers .= "; boundary = $boundary\r\n\r\n";
            $headers .= "This is a MIME encoded message.\r\n\r\n";
            $headers .= "--$boundary";

            foreach($attachment as $a)
            {
                  $headers .= "\r\n";
                  $headers .= makeAttachment($a);
                  $headers .= "--$boundary";
            }

            $headers .= "--\r\n";
      }
      else
      {
            $headers .= makeAttachment($attachment[0]);
      }
```

```
        //send message
        mail($to, $subject, "", $headers);
    }

    //add text explaining message
    $attach[] = array("content"=>"This is Listing 18.6",
        "type"=>"text/plain");

    //add script to list of attachments
    $fp = fopen(__FILE__, "r");
    $attach[] = array("name"=>basename(__FILE__),
        "content"=>fread($fp, filesize(__FILE__)),
        "type"=>"application/octet-stream");
    fclose($fp);

    //send mail to root
    mailAttachment("root@localhost",
        "httpd@localhost",
        "Listing 18.6",
        $attach);

    print("Mail sent!<BR>\n");
?>
```

The `mailAttachment` function assembles the parts that make up a MIME message. These parts are sent in the fourth argument of the `mail` function, which is generally used for headers. In the case of a MIME message, this area is used for both headers and attachments. After sending the customary `From` headers, a `MIME-Version` header is sent. Unless there's only one attachment, a boundary string must be created. This is used to divide attachments from one another. We want to avoid using a boundary value that might appear in the message itself, so we use the `uniqid` function.

Each attachment is surrounded by the boundaries that always start with two dashes. The attachment itself is prepared by the `makeAttachment` function. Each attachment requires `Content-Type` and `Content-Transfer-Encoding` headers. The type of content depends on the attachment itself. If an image file is being sent, it might be `image/jpg`. These are the same codes discussed above with regard to the HTTP protocol. For the sake of simplicity, this function always encodes attachments using base64, which can turn binary files into 7-bit ASCII. This prevents them from being corrupted as they travel through the network. As you might imagine, text files don't require encoding, and complete implementations encode attachments based on content type.

It may be instructive to see the assembled message in full. Try sending yourself a message. On a UNIX operating system, you should be able to peek at the file itself inside `/var/spool/mail` before reading it, or perhaps inside `~/Mail/received` afterward.

Verifying an Email Address

It doesn't take much experience with email to discover what happens when it is misaddressed. The email is returned to you. This is called bounced email. Consider for a moment a Web site that allows users to fill out a form that includes an email address and sends a thank-you message. Certainly many people will either mistakenly mistype their addresses or purposely give a bad address. You can check the form of the address, of course, but a well-formed address can fail to match to a real mail box. When this happens, the mail bounces back to the user who sent the mail. Unfortunately, this is probably the Web server itself.

Reading through the bounced email can be interesting. Those running an e-commerce site may be concerned about order confirmations that go undelivered. Yet, the volume of mail can be very large. Add to this that delivery failure is not immediate. To the process that sends the mail, it appears to be successful. It may be worthwhile to verify an email address before sending mail.

RFC 821 describes the SMTP protocol, which is used for exchanging email. You can read it at the faqs.org Web site <http://www.faqs.org/rfcs/rfc821.html>. It lives up to its name, simple mail transfer protocol, in that it's simple enough to use interactively from a telnet session. In order to verify an address, you can connect to the appropriate SMTP server and begin sending a message. If you specify a valid recipient, the server will return a 250 response code, at which point you can abort the process.

It sounds easy, but there's a catch. The domain name portion of an address, the part after the @, is not necessarily the same machine that receives email. Domains are associated with one or more mail exchangers—machines that accept STMP connections for delivery of local mail. The `getmxrr` function returns all DNS records for a given domain.

Now consider Listing 18.7. The `verifyEmail` function is based on a similar function written by Jon Stevens. As you can see, the function attempts to fetch a list of mail exchangers. If a domain doesn't have mail exchangers, the script guesses that the domain name itself accepts mail.

Listing 18.7   Verifying an Email Address

```php
<?
        /*
        ** Function: verifyEmail
        ** Input: STRING address, REFERENCE error
        ** Output: BOOLEAN
        ** Description: Attempts to verify an email address by
        ** contacting a mail exchanger. Registered mail
        ** exchangers are requested from the domain controller first,
        ** then the exact domain itself. The error argument will
        ** contain relevant text if the address could not be
        ** verified.
        */

        function verifyEmail($address, &$error)
        {
                global $SERVER_NAME;

                list($user, $domain) = split("@", $address, 2);

                //make sure the domain has a mail exchanger
                if(checkdnsrr($domain, "MX"))
                {
                        //get mail exchanger records
                        if(!getmxrr($domain, $mxhost, $mxweight))
                        {
                                $error =
                                "Could not retrieve mail exchangers!<BR>\n";
                                return(FALSE);
                        }
                }
                else
                {
```

```php
            //if no mail exchanger, maybe the host itself
            //will accept mail
            $mxhost[] = $domain;
            $mxweight[] = 1;
    }

    //create sorted array of hosts
    for($i = 0; $i < count($mxhost); $i++)
    {
            $weighted_host[($mxweight[$i])] = $mxhost[$i];
    }
    ksort($weighted_host);

    //loop over each host
    foreach($weighted_host as $host)
    {
            //connect to host on SMTP port
            if(!($fp = fsockopen($host, 25)))
            {
                    //couldn't connect to this host, but
                    //the next might work
                    continue;
            }


            /*
            ** skip over 220 messages
            ** give up if no response for 10 seconds
            */
            set_socket_blocking($fp, FALSE);

            $stopTime = time() + 10;
            $gotResponse = FALSE;

            while(TRUE)
            {
                    //try to get a line from mail server
                    $line = fgets($fp, 1024);

                    if(substr($line, 0, 3) == "220")
                    {
                            //reset timer
                            $stopTime = time() + 10;
                            $gotResponse = TRUE;
```

```
        }
        elseif(($line == "") AND ($gotResponse))
        {
               break;
        }
        elseif(time() > $stopTime)
        {
               break;
        }
}

if(!$gotResponse)
{
      //this host was unresponsive, but
      //maybe the next will be better
      continue;
}

set_socket_blocking ($fp, TRUE);

//sign in
fputs($fp, "HELO $SERVER_NAME\r\n");
fgets($fp, 1024);

//set from
fputs($fp, "MAIL FROM: <info@$domain>\r\n");
fgets($fp, 1024);

//try address
fputs($fp, "RCPT TO: <$address>\r\n");
$line = fgets($fp, 1024);

//close connection
fputs($fp, "QUIT\r\n");
fclose($fp);

if(substr($line, 0, 3) != "250")
{
      //mail server doesn't recognize
      //this address, so it must be bad
      $error = $line;
    return(FALSE);
}
else
```

```
            {
                    //address recognized
                    return(TRUE);
            }
        }

        $error = "Unable to reach a mail exchanger!";
        return(FALSE);
}


if(verifyEmail("leon@clearink.com", &$error))
{
        print("Verified!<BR>\n");
}
else
{
        print("Could not verify!<BR>\n");
        print("Error: $error<BR>\n");
}
?>
```

SMTP servers precede each message with a numerical code, such as the 250 code mentioned above. When first connecting with a server, any number of 220 messages are sent. These contain comments, such as the AOL servers' reminders not to use them for spam. No special code marks the end of the comments; the server simply stops sending lines. Recall that by default the `fgets` function returns after encountering the maximum number of characters specified or an end-of-line marker. This will not work in the case of an indeterminate number of lines. The script will wait forever after the last comment. Socket blocking must be turned off to handle this situation.

When `set_socket_blocking` turns off blocking, `fgets` returns immediately with whatever data is available in the buffer. The strategy is to loop continually, checking the buffer each time through the loop. There will likely be some lag time between establishing a connection and receiving the first message from the server. Then, as `220` messages appear, the script must begin watching for the data to stop flowing, which means the server is likely waiting for a command. To avoid the situation where a server is very unresponsive, a further check must be made against a clock. If ten seconds pass, the server will be considered unavailable.

GENERATING GRAPHICS

Topics in This Chapter

Chapter 19

This chapter explores generating graphics using the GD extension functions described in Chapter 12. "Image Functions." It is important to be aware of the issues involved with the creation of graphics on the fly. The first is that it is relatively costly in terms of CPU time. In most cases the flexibility of dynamic graphics is not worth what you pay in the load imposed on the server. Another issue is that making nice-looking graphics from PHP functions is not easy. Common techniques like drop shadows are next to impossible. As you will see in the examples that follow, a lot of work goes into creating simple, flat charts. Last, while there is adequate support for text, functions you'd expect in a word processor do not exist. Text does not wrap at line ends. There is no concept of leading, spacing, or descenders. Regardless, generating graphics makes sense in some situations. This chapter contains some real examples that you can start using with very little modification.

In the first edition of this text, the examples in this chapter created GIF images. Since then, the GD library has dropped support for GIFs because a key component of the GIF standard relies on a patented process for compressing data. Instead, the GD library now produces PNG and JPEG images. Turn back to Chapter 12 for more information on this issue.

Dynamic Buttons

Images wrapped in anchor tags are a common navigational device. Instead of plain text, this method allows you to create buttons similar to those created in the operating system, or even fanciful icons. In most cases it is best to leave these as graphics created in your favorite graphics editor, because the time between changes is relatively long. On the other hand, if you have a button that changes often, it may make sense to create it dynamically with PHP. The content of the button, the label, needs to be available as a string in PHP. It could be a statement setting the value of a variable. It could also be a value retrieved from a file or a database.

An illustration will make this idea clear. Many corporate Web sites have a section for press releases. Instead of just a list of text links, your client wants a graphic of a flaming newspaper for each press release, all under the title "Hot off the Press." Each burning newspaper has text over the top with the headline from the press release. With a small company that issues only one press release a month, you are better off creating these graphics by hand. With a company that issues a press release each week, it starts to make sense to automate the process. You can put the press releases into a database and generate a graphic on the fly as surfers view the list of press releases. One advantage of this approach is that if the CEO finds out you're putting flaming newspapers on the site, you can make a minor modification and the graphics become the company logo with the press-release title over it.

Seriously, you must consider the tradeoffs associated with dynamically created graphics. You don't want to save yourself 15 minutes a month if it makes every page download 30 seconds longer. If you've been working with the Web for any time at all, you know to reuse graphics throughout the site because the browser caches them. The first page may take longer to load, but each successive page is faster because the graphics are already loaded in the browser. Dynamic graphics can be cached, of course, but the browser uses the URL to cache files. The GET-method form variables are part of the URL, so `http://www.site.com/button.php3?label=home&from=1` and `http://www.site.com/button.php3?label=home&from=2` may create two identical graphics but are different as far as the browser cache is concerned.

These are only some of the issues involved with dynamic buttons. To demonstrate the process, I'll provide an example and describe the steps. Listing 19.1 is a script that creates a JPEG of a button with a text label. The button is rectangular and has some highlighting and shadowing. The label has a drop-shadow effect applied to it and is centered both vertically and horizontally.

Listing 19.1   JPEG Button

```php
<?
    /*
    ** JPEG button
    ** Creates a graphical button based
    ** on form variables.
    */

    //set parameters if not given
    if(!isset($ButtonWidth))
    {
        $ButtonWidth = 100;
    }

    if(!isset($ButtonHeight))
    {
        $ButtonHeight = 30;
    }

    if(!isset($ButtonLabel))
    {
        $ButtonLabel = "CLICK";
    }

    if(!isset($ButtonFont))
    {
        $ButtonFont = 5;
    }

    //create image and colors
    $image = imagecreate($ButtonWidth, $ButtonHeight);
    $colorBody = imagecolorallocate($image, 0x99, 0x99, 0x99);
    $colorShadow = imagecolorallocate($image, 0x33, 0x33, 0x33);
    $colorHighlight = imagecolorallocate($image, 0xCC, 0xCC, 0xCC);

    //create body of button
    imagefilledrectangle($image,
        1, 1, $ButtonWidth-2, $ButtonHeight-2,
        $colorBody);
```

```
//draw bottom shadow
imageline($image,
      0, $ButtonHeight-1,
      $ButtonWidth-1, $ButtonHeight-1,
      $colorShadow);

//draw right shadow
imageline($image,
      $ButtonWidth-1, 1,
      $ButtonWidth-1, $ButtonHeight-1,
      $colorShadow);


//draw top highlight
imageline($image,
      0, 0,
      $ButtonWidth-1, 0,
      $colorHighlight);

//draw left highlight
imageline($image,
      0, 0,
      0, $ButtonHeight-2,
      $colorHighlight);


//determine label size
$ButtonLabelHeight = imagefontheight($ButtonFont);
$ButtonLabelWidth = imagefontwidth($ButtonFont) *
      strlen($ButtonLabel);

//determine label upper left corner
$ButtonLabelX = ($ButtonWidth - $ButtonLabelWidth)/2;
$ButtonLabelY = ($ButtonHeight - $ButtonLabelHeight)/2;


//draw label shadow
imagestring($image,
      $ButtonFont,
      $ButtonLabelX+1,
      $ButtonLabelY+1,
      $ButtonLabel,
      $colorShadow);

//draw label
```

```
imagestring($image,
      $ButtonFont,
      $ButtonLabelX,
      $ButtonLabelY,
      $ButtonLabel,
      $colorHighlight);

//output image
header("Content-type: image/jpeg");
imagejpeg($image);
?>
```

The first step the script takes is to make sure it has valid information for all the parameters. These include the size of the button and the text with which to label the button. I've chosen to use the built-in fonts, which are numbered one through five. Chapter 12 has descriptions of functions for loading different fonts, and I encourage you to modify my script to incorporate them.

The next step is to create an image. There are two ways to do this. You can create an image of a specific size which is blank, or you can load an existing JPEG. I've chosen the former because it allows the script to make buttons of any size. You can make much more stylish buttons using the latter method. This is another good exercise.

The button will be drawn with three colors: a body color, a highlight color, and a shadow color. I've chosen to go with three shades of gray. These colors must be allocated with the `imagecolorallocate` function. Using the body color, the script makes a rectangle that is one pixel smaller than the entire image. The border around this rectangle is created with four lines. The lines on the bottom and right sides are drawn in the shadow color, and the top and left sides are drawn with the highlight color. This creates an illusion of the button being three-dimensional.

To finish the button, the script draws the label. First the text is drawn slightly off center in the shadow color. Then the text is drawn in the highlight color over it and exactly centered, making the text look as though it is floating over the button.

At this point the script has created the image and needs to send it to the browser. It is very important that the header be sent to let the browser know that this file is a JPEG. Without it, you get a garbled bunch of strange characters.

This wraps up the script that creates a button, but to really make use of it, we have to use it in the context of a Web page. Listing 19.2 demonstrates the

Listing 19.2　Creating Button Dynamically

```php
<?

    //define button labels
    $label = array("HOME",
        "ABOUT US",
        "OUR PRODUCTS",
        "CONTACT US");

    //display all buttons
    foreach($label as $text)
    {
        //link back to this page
        print("<A HREF=\"$PHP_SELF\">");

        //create dynamic image tag
        print("<IMG SRC=\"19-1.php");
        print("?ButtonLabel=" . htmlentities($text));
        print("&amp;ButtonWidth=145");
        print("&amp;ButtonHeight=25");
        print("\" BORDER=\"0\"");
        print("WIDTH=\"145\" HEIGHT=\"25\">");

        print("</A><BR>\n");
    }
?>
```

minimal steps. I've created an array of four button labels I want to create. I then loop through the array, each time creating an image tag. The source of the image is the previous script. I pass the script some parameters to set the size of the button and the label. I leave the font as the default, but I could have set that as well.

Generating Graphs on the Fly

Perhaps a more likely use of dynamic graphics is in generating graphs. Since graphs rely on data, they lend themselves to very formula-driven creation. If the data change often, using PHP to generate the graphs is a good idea. In the following examples, I've written the data into the script, but pulling data from a database is not difficult. Sending the data from a form is probably not a practical idea for large amounts of data. The GET method imposes a relatively small limit on the total size of a URL that varies between Web servers. You could use the POST method, however. The two examples I'll show are a bar graph and a pie chart. Each uses the same set of data, which is a fictitious survey of favorite meat.

Bar Graphs

Bar graphs are a good way to compare values to each other. Creating them is a relatively simple task because each data point is a rectangle. The height of the rectangle represents the value of the data point. To make the transition, a scaling factor is used. In Listing 19.3 the graph is 200 pixels tall and the scaling factor is two. This means that a data point with the value 75 will be 150 pixels tall.

The business of creating the graph is similar to the process described above where a button is created. A blank image is created, several colors are allocated, and functions are called for drawing shapes into the image. The script allows the width of the bars to adapt to the width of the graph. The width of the graph is divided by the number of bars drawn. A ten-pixel gutter is drawn between the bars. In the center of the bar the data point's label is written along with its value.

Listing 19.3   Creating a Bar Graph

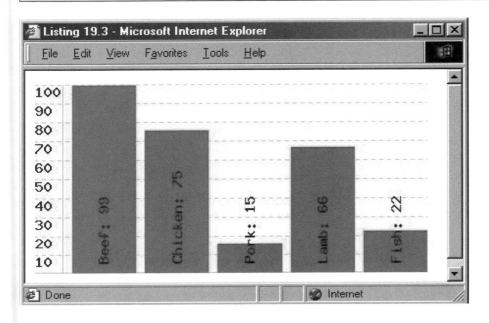

```
<?
        /*
        ** JPEG Bar graph
        */

        //fill in graph parameters
        $GraphWidth = 400;
        $GraphHeight = 200;
        $GraphScale = 2;
        $GraphFont = 5;
        $GraphData = array("99", "75", "15", "66", "22");
        $GraphLabel = array("Beef", "Chicken", "Pork", "Lamb", "Fish");

        //create image
        $image = imagecreate($GraphWidth, $GraphHeight);

        //allocate colors
        $colorBody = imagecolorallocate($image, 0xFF, 0xFF, 0xFF);
        $colorGrid = imagecolorallocate($image, 0xCC, 0xCC, 0xCC);
        $colorBar = imagecolorallocate($image, 0xFF, 0x00, 0x00);
        $colorText = imagecolorallocate($image, 0x00, 0x00, 0x00);
```

```
//fill background
imagefill($image, 0, 0, $colorBody);

//draw vertical grid line
$GridLabelWidth = imagefontwidth($GraphFont)*3 + 1;
imageline($image,
     $GridLabelWidth, 0,
     $GridLabelWidth, $GraphHeight-1,
     $colorGrid);

//draw horizontal grid lines
for($index = 0; $index < $GraphHeight; $index += $GraphHeight/10)
{
     imagedashedline($image,
          0, $index,
          $GraphWidth-1, $index,
          $colorGrid);

     //draw label
     imagestring($image,
          $GraphFont,
          0,
          $index,
          round(($GraphHeight - $index)/$GraphScale),
          $colorText);
}

//add bottom line
imageline($image,
     0, $GraphHeight-1,
     $GraphWidth-1, $GraphHeight-1,
     $colorGrid);

//draw each bar
$BarWidth = (($GraphWidth-$GridLabelWidth)/count($GraphData)) - 10;
for($index = 0; $index < count($GraphData); $index++)
{
     //draw bar
     $BarTopX = $GridLabelWidth + (($index+1) * 10) + ($index *
          $BarWidth);
     $BarBottomX = $BarTopX + $BarWidth;
     $BarBottomY = $GraphHeight-1;
     $BarTopY = $BarBottomY - ($GraphData[$index] * $GraphScale);

     imagefilledrectangle($image,
```

```
                    $BarTopX, $BarTopY,
                    $BarBottomX, $BarBottomY,
                    $colorBar);

            //draw label
            $LabelX = $BarTopX +
                    (($BarBottomX - $BarTopX)/2) -
                    (imagefontheight($GraphFont)/2);
            $LabelY = $BarBottomY-10;

            imagestringup($image,
                    $GraphFont,
                    $LabelX,
                    $LabelY,
                    "$GraphLabel[$index]: $GraphData[$index]",
                    $colorText);

    }

//output image
header("Content-type: image/jpeg");
imagejpeg($image);
?>
```

Pie Charts

Pie charts are a good way to see how a value represents a percentage of a whole. Each data point is a slice of a pie with a unique color. A legend associates the colors with each data point's label and value.

Since the pie chart is round, it represents a much more complex problem. PHP's image functions allow you to draw an arc or a triangle, but not a pie slice. The solution is to draw the arc at the end of the slice, then two lines that connect the center of the circle to the ends of the arc. These elements are drawn in the color of the slice and the imagefilltoborder function is used to fill the shape.

The arc itself is easy to draw, since the imagearc function will draw an arc based on starting and stopping degrees. To find the coordinates of the ends of the arc requires some trigonometry. I've added a function to the script for finding the coordinates of a point on a circle of a certain degree and diameter. The return values are for a circle centered on (0, 0), so an offset must be added to them to get the coordinates in the graph.

When each of the slices is drawn, a black border is added to the circle and a small box is drawn for each color used. The data point's label and value are drawn next to the colored box.

As with the bar graph above, the data used in the chart come from an array hard-coded into the script in Listing 19.4. It is possible to keep the chart up to date by editing every time the data change, but it may be better to link it with a database.

Listing 19.4   Creating a Pie Chart

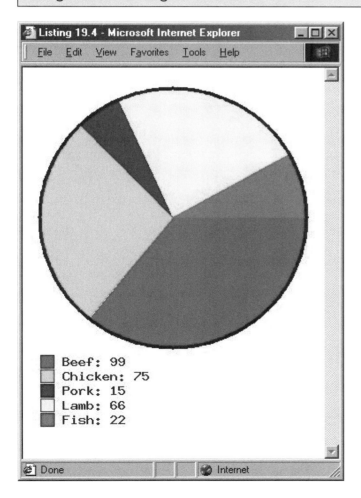

```
<?

    /*
    ** JPEG Pie Chart
    */

    /*
    ** get x,y pair on circle,
    ** assuming center is 0,0
    */
    function circle_point($degrees, $diameter)
    {
            $x = cos(deg2rad($degrees)) * ($diameter/2);
            $y = sin(deg2rad($degrees)) * ($diameter/2);

    return (array($x, $y));
    }


    //fill in chart parameters
    $ChartDiameter = 300;
    $ChartFont = 5;
    $ChartFontHeight = imagefontheight($ChartFont);
    $ChartData = array("99", "75", "15", "66", "22");
    $ChartLabel = array("Beef", "Chicken", "Pork", "Lamb", "Fish");

    //determine graphic size
    $ChartWidth = $ChartDiameter + 20;
    $ChartHeight = $ChartDiameter + 20 +
            (($ChartFontHeight + 2) * count($ChartData));

    //determine total of all values
    for($index = 0; $index < count($ChartData); $index++)
    {
            $ChartTotal += $ChartData[$index];
    }

    $ChartCenterX = $ChartDiameter/2 + 10;
    $ChartCenterY = $ChartDiameter/2 + 10;


    //create image
    $image = imagecreate($ChartWidth, $ChartHeight);

    //allocate colors
    $colorBody = imagecolorallocate($image, 0xFF, 0xFF, 0xFF);
    $colorBorder = imagecolorallocate($image, 0x00, 0x00, 0x00);
```

```
$colorText = imagecolorallocate($image, 0x00, 0x00, 0x00);

$colorSlice[] = imagecolorallocate($image, 0xFF, 0x00, 0x00);
$colorSlice[] = imagecolorallocate($image, 0x00, 0xFF, 0x00);
$colorSlice[] = imagecolorallocate($image, 0x00, 0x00, 0xFF);
$colorSlice[] = imagecolorallocate($image, 0xFF, 0xFF, 0x00);
$colorSlice[] = imagecolorallocate($image, 0xFF, 0x00, 0xFF);
$colorSlice[] = imagecolorallocate($image, 0x00, 0xFF, 0xFF);
$colorSlice[] = imagecolorallocate($image, 0x99, 0x00, 0x00);
$colorSlice[] = imagecolorallocate($image, 0x00, 0x99, 0x00);
$colorSlice[] = imagecolorallocate($image, 0x00, 0x00, 0x99);
$colorSlice[] = imagecolorallocate($image, 0x99, 0x99, 0x00);
$colorSlice[] = imagecolorallocate($image, 0x99, 0x00, 0x99);
$colorSlice[] = imagecolorallocate($image, 0x00, 0x99, 0x99);

//fill background
imagefill($image, 0, 0, $colorBody);


/*
** draw each slice
*/
$Degrees = 0;
for($index = 0; $index < count($ChartData); $index++)
{
      $StartDegrees = round($Degrees);
      $Degrees += (($ChartData[$index]/$ChartTotal)*360);
      $EndDegrees = round($Degrees);

      $CurrentColor = $colorSlice[$index%(count($colorSlice))];

      //draw arc
      imagearc($image,
            $ChartCenterX,
            $ChartCenterY,
            $ChartDiameter,
            $ChartDiameter,
            $StartDegrees,
            $EndDegrees,
            $CurrentColor);

      //draw start line from center
      list($ArcX, $ArcY) = circle_point($StartDegrees, $ChartDiameter);
      imageline($image,
      $ChartCenterX,
      $ChartCenterY,
```

```
        floor($ChartCenterX + $ArcX),
        floor($ChartCenterY + $ArcY),
        $CurrentColor);


    //draw end line from center
    list($ArcX, $ArcY) = circle_point($EndDegrees, $ChartDiameter);
    imageline($image,
    $ChartCenterX,
    $ChartCenterY,
        ceil($ChartCenterX + $ArcX),
        ceil($ChartCenterY + $ArcY),
        $CurrentColor);

    //fill slice
    $MidPoint = round((($EndDegrees - $StartDegrees)/2) +
    $StartDegrees);
    list($ArcX, $ArcY) = circle_point($MidPoint, $ChartDiameter/2);
    imagefilltoborder($image,
        floor($ChartCenterX + $ArcX),
        floor($ChartCenterY + $ArcY),
        $CurrentColor,
        $CurrentColor);

}


//draw border
imagearc($image,
    $ChartCenterX,
    $ChartCenterY,
    $ChartDiameter,
    $ChartDiameter,
    0,
    180,
    $colorBorder);

imagearc($image,
    $ChartCenterX,
    $ChartCenterY,
    $ChartDiameter,
    $ChartDiameter,
    180,
    360,
    $colorBorder);
```

```
imagearc($image,
       $ChartCenterX,
       $ChartCenterY,
       $ChartDiameter+7,
       $ChartDiameter+7,
       0,
       180,
       $colorBorder);

imagearc($image,
       $ChartCenterX,
       $ChartCenterY,
       $ChartDiameter+7,
       $ChartDiameter+7,
       180,
       360,
       $colorBorder);


imagefilltoborder($image,
       floor($ChartCenterX + ($ChartDiameter/2) + 2),
       $ChartCenterY,
       $colorBorder,
       $colorBorder);


//draw legend
for($index = 0; $index < count($ChartData); $index++)
{
       $CurrentColor = $colorSlice[$index%(count($colorSlice))];
       $LineY = $ChartDiameter + 20 + ($index*($ChartFontHeight+2));

       //draw color box
       imagerectangle($image,
              10,
              $LineY,
              10 + $ChartFontHeight,
              $LineY+$ChartFontHeight,
              $colorBorder);

       imagefilltoborder($image,
              12,
              $LineY + 2,
              $colorBorder,
              $CurrentColor);
```

```
        //draw label
        imagestring($image,
              $ChartFont,
              20 + $ChartFontHeight,
              $LineY,
              "$ChartLabel[$index]: $ChartData[$index]",
              $colorText);
    }


    //output image
    header("Content-type: image/jpeg");
    imagejpeg($image);
?>
```

Stretching Single-Pixel Images

The following technique takes advantage of the behavior of most browsers with the width and height properties of the image tag. It does not require the GD extension, because it doesn't actually manipulate an image. It relies on the browser to stretch an image to match the width and height specified in the IMG tag. This allows you to stretch a single-pixel image into a large bar.

Refer to Listing 19.5. An HTML table is used to line up graph labels with bars. The largest data element will fill 100 percent of the graph width, which is specified by the graphWidthMax variable. Each element is pulled from the data array and used to scale graphWidthMax. This produces a horizontally oriented bar graph, but the same method can make a vertical graph, too.

Listing 19.5   Bar Graph Using Stretched Images

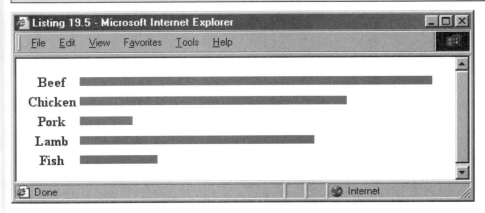

```php
<?
    //fill in graph parameters
    $graphWidthMax = 400;
    $graphData = array(
            "Beef"=>"99",
            "Chicken"=>"75",
            "Pork"=>"15",
            "Lamb"=>"66",
            "Fish"=>"22");
    $barHeight = 10;
    $barMax = max($graphData);

    print("<TABLE BORDER=\"0\">\n");

    foreach($graphData as $label=>$rating)
    {
            //calculate width
            $barWidth = intval($graphWidthMax * $rating/$barMax);

            print("<TR>\n");

            //label
            print("<TH>$label</TH>\n");

            //data
            print("<TD>");
            print("<IMG SRC=\"reddot.jpg\" ");
            print("WIDTH=\"$barWidth\" HEIGHT=\"$barHeight\" ");
            print("BORDER=\"0\">");
            print("</TD>\n");

            print("</TR>\n");
    }

    print("</TABLE>\n");
?>
```

Part 4

SOFTWARE ENGINEERING

Software engineering is more than just programming. Like a civil engineer carefully designing and building a skyscraper, a software engineer carefully designs and implements software systems. Even small PHP scripts may benefit from software engineering concepts. This section explores the issues involved in using PHP in a Web site.

Chapter 20 is about integrating PHP and HTML. You can use PHP just in key places or in generating every page of a site. This chapter helps you decide.

Chapter 21 discusses system specification and design. It develops an approach for designing a system with PHP, including a phase of careful requirements analysis. A survey is made of existing methods for designing with PHP.

Chapter 22 touches on issues of efficiency and debugging. It provides information to help measure performance, and it describes remote debugging.

INTEGRATION
WITH HTML

Chapter 20

By this time, you have learned the basics of PHP. You have a reference for the functions. And you've been introduced to some fundamental problems of programming. But all the examples I've shown have been pieces, snippets for the sake of illustration. This chapter will discuss how to integrate PHP into a Web site. It will help you decide whether to build a site completely with PHP, to sprinkle PHP throughout the site, or to simply create a few key PHP-driven pages. I'll also discuss issues involved in using PHP to generate HTML.

Sprinkling PHP within an HTML Document

The first and most obvious approach to using PHP is to build HTML files as you have always done, inserting PHP tags as if they were HTML tags. This could take the form of repeating HTML that you replace with a call to a PHP function. It could take the form of a large block of PHP code that generates database output. Or it could be a script that processes a form submission. These are all situations where the impact of PHP on the site is slight.

This is a good first step for those new to programming. You are able to insert the smallest amount of PHP code as a test. As your experience and confidence grow, so will your reliance on PHP.

Let's examine creating a PHP function to replace repeating HTML. One great aspect of cascading style sheets is that they allow you to redefine how tags behave. Unfortunately, this technology is available only in the newest versions of Navigator and Internet Explorer. You can provide similar functionality on the server side with PHP. Suppose we would like all of our headers to be in uppercase letters, bold, size 7, and blue. The solution is to write a function that takes a string and prints it in the proper format.

In Listing 20.1 I've created a function called `PrintTitle`. This function wraps a given string in HTML tags. In some ways the code is more readable than if I had simply written it as static HTML, because each time there is a title, we see the call to the `PrintTitle` function. This may have more meaning than the collection of tags for which it stands. This is one of the benefits of functions in general: they wrap up functionality into a single name.

Another benefit is that I can be sure each title will be rendered in exactly the same way. Less text to type for each title means less chance of leaving out part of the formula. This is nice to the programmer, who undoubtedly is eager to find a shortcut to typing long segments of identical HTML. A higher degree of quality is ensured. If a call to the function is mistyped, PHP will display an error. If no errors are displayed, the titles are most likely displayed identically and in the correct format. If the title turns out to need changing, the code must be altered in only one place. This is a good antidote to the painful phrase, "I changed my mind. . . ."

Another similar use of PHP is to dress up what is essentially CGI output: a large block of PHP surrounded by HTML so that the output of the code simply appears in a larger page. This is a similar approach offered by SSI (Server-Side Includes). An SSI tag may call a CGI and insert the output in its place.

The approach is appropriate in situations where your site is mostly static, but certain key areas must be dynamic. The advantage is very low impact on the Web server. PHP is used only when absolutely needed. In Listing 20.2 the code generates information that doesn't change, but it's easy to imagine code that pulls stock quotes from a database. It eliminates the need to edit the HTML page each time the information changes, but parts that don't change often, like the layout of the page, are left as static HTML.

While Listing 20.2 is an example of dynamic output, you are often faced with the opposite situation. Your site may be completely static, but you need to accept catalog requests. PHP is a good solution for accepting form

Listing 20.1   Formatting Function

```
<?
      function PrintTitle($title)
      {
            print("<CENTER>");
            print("<FONT COLOR=\"#0000FF\" SIZE=\"5\">");
            print("<B>");
            print(strtoupper($title));
            print("</B>");
            print("</FONT>");
            print("</CENTER>\n");
      }
?>
<HTML>
<HEAD>
<TITLE>Listing 20.1</TITLE>
</HEAD>

<BODY>
<? PrintTitle("Listing 20.1"); ?>
This is an example of using a function to repeat
a commonly-used piece of HTML code.<BR>
<BR>
<? PrintTitle("how it works"); ?>
Any time a title needs to be created, the <CODE>PrintTitle</CODE>
function is called with the text of the title.<BR>
<BR>
<? PrintTitle("advantages"); ?>
The code is more readable<BR>
Less text to type for each title<BR>
Easy to change every title<BR>
</BODY>
</HTML>
```

submissions. The first step is to create an HTML page that asks for name and address. Listing 20.3 demonstrates.

The page in Listing 20.3 is a very simple submission form. Each of the input tags will be turned into a PHP variable when the submit button is clicked. This calls the script listed in Listing 20.4. A file named req.txt will be opened for appending, and each of the form fields will be written into the file. Each field is separated by tab characters, which allows you to import the file into a spreadsheet easily.

Listing 20.2   Dressing Up CGI Output

```
<HTML>
<HEAD>
<TITLE>Listing 20.2</TITLE>
</HEAD>
<BODY>
<H1>Color Chart</H1>
<P>The following chart displays the colors
safe for displaying in all browsers. These
colors should not dither on any computer
with a color palette of at least 256
colors.</P>
<P>This chart will only display on browsers
that support table cell background colors.</P>
<?
        $color = array("00", "33", "66", "99", "CC", "FF");

        for($Red = 0; $Red < count($color); $Red++)
        {
            print("<TABLE>\n");

            for($Green = 0; $Green < count($color); $Green++)
            {
                print("<TR>\n");

                for($Blue = 0; $Blue < count($color); $Blue++)
                {
                    $CellColor = $color[$Red] .
                        $color[$Green] . $color[$Blue];

                    print("<TD BGCOLOR=\"#$CellColor\">");
                    print("<TT>$CellColor</TT>");
                    print("</TD>\n");
                }

                print("</TR>\n");
            }

            print("</TABLE>\n");
        }
?>
</BODY>
</HTML>
```

Listing 20.3   Catalog Request Form

```
<HTML>
<HEAD>
<TITLE>Listing 20.3</TITLE>
</HEAD>
<BODY>
Please enter name and address to receive a free catalog.
<FORM ACTION="20-4.php">
<TABLE>
<TR>
        <TD>Name</TD>
        <TD><INPUT TYPE="text" NAME="InputName"></TD>
</TR>
<TR>
        <TD>Address</TD>
        <TD><INPUT TYPE="text" NAME="InputAddress"></TD>
</TR>
<TR>
        <TD>City</TD>
        <TD><INPUT TYPE="text" NAME="InputCity"></TD>
</TR>
<TR>
        <TD>State</TD>
        <TD><INPUT TYPE="text" NAME="InputState"></TD>
</TR>
<TR>
        <TD>ZIP</TD>
        <TD><INPUT TYPE="text" NAME="InputZIP"></TD>
</TR>
<TR>
        <TD><INPUT TYPE="reset"></TD>
        <TD><INPUT TYPE="submit"></TD>
</TR>
</TABLE>
</FORM>
</BODY>
</HTML>
```

Listing 20.4   Form Submission

```
<HTML>
<HEAD>
<TITLE>Listing 20.4</TITLE>
</HEAD>
<BODY>
<?
      /*
      ** process form input, append it to file
      */
      $CatalogRequests = fopen("req.txt", "a");
      if($CatalogRequests)
      {
            fputs($CatalogRequests, "$InputName\t");
            fputs($CatalogRequests, "$InputAddress\t");
            fputs($CatalogRequests, "$InputCity\t");
            fputs($CatalogRequests, "$InputState\t");
            fputs($CatalogRequests, "$InputZIP\n");
            fclose($CatalogRequests);
      }
?>
Thank you for your catalog request!<BR>
<BR>
<A HREF="20-3.html">Return to Site</A><BR>
</BODY>
</HTML>
```

Using PHP to Output All HTML

Any of the examples in the previous section is an excellent first step toward introducing PHP into a Web site. Their impact in terms of server load is relatively low. I like to think of sites using similar approaches as being PHP-enabled, as if they had a small injection of PHP that makes them extraordinary. The step beyond this is what I think of as PHP-powered: a site made completely of PHP. In this approach every byte of output comes from PHP. The print (or echo or printf) function is used to send HTML tags. Every page is a script inside a single pair of PHP tags.

You might have noticed that most of the examples in the book take this approach. I have found that while this requires extra time up front, the code is much more maintainable. Once information is put in the context of a PHP variable, it's easy to add something dynamic to it later. It also has the advantage of ultimately being more readable as the page becomes more complex. As a simple example, compare Listing 20.5 to Listing 20.6. The idea is to change the background color of the page depending on the time of day.

My experience has been that having all the HTML inside the PHP script allows very quick changes. I don't have to search for the opening and closing tags buried inside the HTML as in Listing 20.5. It also allows me to break code up into separate lines in the source code that appear as a single line in the output. An example is the header text. I can enhance the readability but not sacrifice the presentation. This has become very handy when dealing with tables. Leaving any whitespace between a TD tag and an image causes an extra pixel to appear. In an HTML file, the solution is to run the whole thing together on one line. Inside a PHP script I can have many print calls and send an endline only in the last. The result is a single line in the output, but very readable source code.

The usefulness of these techniques, like that of many others, increases with the size of the project. I've created 50-page Web applications using both approaches and can attest to the value of putting everything inside the PHP code.

Listing 20.5   Mixing PHP and HTML

```
<HTML>
<HEAD>
<TITLE>Listing 20.5</TITLE>
</HEAD>
<?
      $Hour = date("H");
      $Intensity = round(($Hour/24.0)*(0xFF));
      $PageColor = dechex($Intensity) .
            dechex($Intensity) .
            dechex($Intensity);
?>
<BODY BGCOLOR="#<? print($PageColor); ?>">
<H1>Listing 20.5</H1>
</BODY>
</HTML>
```

Listing 20.6   Converting Script to Be Completely PHP

```
<?
        print("<HTML>\n");
        print("<HEAD>\n");
        print("<TITLE>Listing 20.6</TITLE>\n");
        print("</HEAD>\n");

        $Hour = date("H");
        $Intensity = round(($Hour/24.0)*(0xFF));
        $PageColor = dechex($Intensity) .
                dechex($Intensity) .
                dechex($Intensity);

        print("<BODY BGCOLOR=\"#$PageColor\">\n");
        print("<H1>Listing 20.6</H1>\n");
        print("</BODY>\n");
        print("</HTML>\n");
?>
```

Separating HTML from PHP

The last approach I want to discuss involves using the include and require functions. As you may recall from Chapter 8, "I/O Functions," these functions include a file in the PHP code. The file is considered to be a PHP file, regardless of the extension on the name. If PHP code appears in the included file, it is surrounded in <? and ?> tags. You may want to turn back to the functional reference to refresh yourself on the differences between include and require, but they aren't particularly important to this discussion.

Certain chunks of HTML must appear on every well-formed page. Additionally you may develop repeating elements such as a company logo. Rather than write them into every page, you may choose to put them into a file and dynamically include them. Listing 20.7 contains HTML you might include at the top of every page on a site. In Listing 20.8 are two lines to close a page. Listing 20.10 wraps the content in Listing 20.9 with the opening and closing code to form a complete page.

Listing 20.7   Start of HTML Page

```
<HTML>
<HEAD>
<TITLE>PHP</TITLE>
</HEAD>
<BODY>
```

Listing 20.8   End of HTML Page

```
</BODY>
</HTML>
```

Listing 20.9   Page Content

```
This is the body of the page.<BR>
It's just a bit of HTML.<BR>
```

Listing 20.10   Page-Building Script

```
<?
      /*
      ** include code to open HTML page
      */
      require("20-7.html");

      /*
      ** include content
      */
      require("20-9.html");

      /*
      ** include code to close HTML page
      */
      require("20-8.html");
?>
```

In this way, HTML and PHP are separated into modules. In this example I have hard-coded the inclusion of a two-line HTML file, but I could just as easily have included the color tables from Listing 20.2. The HTML in Listing 20.7 can be reused from page to page, and if I need to add something to every page on the site, I need to edit only that one file. I might want to add the PHP function from Listing 20.1. It will then be available for use inside the code from Listing 20.9.

It may occur to you that this approach is exhibiting another pattern. Every page on the site will simply become three calls to `require`. The first and last calls will always be the same. In fact every page on the site will vary simply by the name of the file included in the second `require` statement. This takes us beyond the issue of integrating HTML and PHP and into the structural design of a site. It is possible to create a site that has exactly one PHP script. This idea is developed in Chapter 21, "Design."

Creating `<SELECT>` Fields

An HTML `SELECT` tag allows you to list several options that appear as a pull-down menu. I am often in the situation of creating the contents of the list on the fly. Sometimes the contents are pulled from a database, such as for choosing from among users in a Web application. Other times the contents are generated, such as choosing month, day, and year. There are two aspects to this problem. First, there is the fairly simple problem of creating all the values for the `OPTION` tags. This is best accomplished in a loop. The second issue deals with preselecting one of the options.

Regardless of the source of the contents, database or otherwise, the technique is similar. To illustrate, I'll develop a function for generating three `SELECT` fields for getting a date from the user: month, day, and year. To generate a list of the months, it is best to draw from an array to display their names. Days and years are numbers, so their values and displayed names are the same. Listing 20.11 demonstrates.

The options for each selector are generated in a `for` loop. Months range from 1 to 12, days from 1 to 31. For years, I've chosen to present an 11-year range around the current year. Notice that if you submit a date, it refreshes the page and sets the form with the date you chose. The key is the addition of the `if` statement. Each time through the loop the current value is tested against the one to be selected.

Listing 20.11   Date Selector

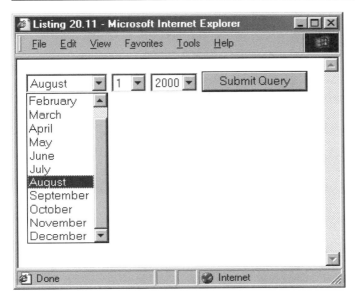

```
<?
    /*
    ** create three selectors for date
    */
    function DateSelector($name, $date=FALSE)
    {
        static $MonthName;

        //create MonthName first time
        if(!isset($MonthName))
        {
            $MonthName = array(1=>"January", "February", "March",
                "April", "May", "June", "July", "August",
                "September", "October", "November", "December");
        }

        //if no date, use current time
        if(!$date)
        {
            $date = time();
        }

        /*
```

```
** Month
*/
print("<SELECT NAME=\"{$name}Month\">\n");

//loop over months 1 to 12
for($m=1; $m <= 12; $m++)
{
        print("<OPTION VALUE=\"$m\"");
        if(date("m", $date) == $m)
        {
                print(" SELECTED");
        }
        print(">{$MonthName[$m]}\n");
}
print("</SELECT>\n");

/*
** Day
*/
print("<SELECT NAME=\"{$name}Day\">\n");

//loop over days 1 to 31
for($d=1; $d <= 31; $d++)
{
        print("<OPTION VALUE=\"$d\"");
        if(date("d", $date) == $d)
        {
                print(" SELECTED");
        }
        print(">$d\n");
}
print("</SELECT>\n");

/*
** Year
*/
print("<SELECT NAME=\"{$name}Year\">\n");

//loop over 10 year range
for($y = (date("Y", $date) - 5);
    $y <= (date("Y", $date) + 5); $y++)
{
        print("<OPTION VALUE=\"$y\"");
        if(date("Y", $date) == $y)
        {
                print(" SELECTED");
        }
```

```
                print(">$y\n");
        }
        print("</SELECT>\n");
}

print("<HTML>\n");
print("<HEAD>\n");
print("<TITLE>Listing 20.11</TITLE>\n");
print("</HEAD>\n");

print("<BODY>\n");

/*
** choose default date
*/
if(isset($SampleMonth))
{
        //construct time
        $UseDate = mktime(0, 0, 0,
                $SampleMonth,
                $SampleDay,
                $SampleYear);
}
else
{
        //use now
        $UseDate = time();
}

print("<FORM ACTION=\"$PHP_SELF\">\n");

DateSelector("Sample", $UseDate);

print("<INPUT TYPE=\"submit\">\n");
print("</FORM>\n");

print("</BODY>\n");
print("</HTML>\n");
?>
```

Passing Arrays in Forms

Though it may not be apparent, it is possible to pass arrays from a form. To understand how, you must recall how form fields are turned into PHP variables. Each field is read in order by PHP and turned into an assignment statement. A URL like `http://www.somesite.com/script.php3?name =leon` creates an assignment like `$name = "leon"`, which means that before the script begins executing, the `name` variable is set.

The name of the form field is treated as the left side of an assignment statement. This means that if other special characters appear as part of the name of the field, they will interpreted accordingly. You can include square brackets to force the variable to be an array. An empty pair of square brackets will add a value to an array using consecutive integers. So, if you name multiple fields in a form with the same name that ends in a pair of empty brackets, an array will be constructed for you when the form is submitted. Listing 20.12 illustrates this method.

There are limitations to this technique. Only single-dimension arrays are passed correctly. You also need to be aware of buggy browsers. You should always place double quotes around field names anyway, but I've run into browsers that don't pass fields properly when fields ending in square brackets aren't quoted.

Listing 20.12   Passing an Array via a Form

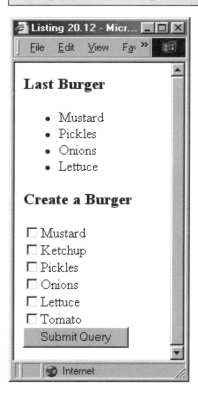

```
<?
    print("<HTML>\n");
    print("<HEAD>\n");
    print("<TITLE>Listing 20.12</TITLE>\n");
    print("</HEAD>\n");

    print("<BODY>\n");

    if(isset($part))
    {
        print("<H3>Last Burger</H3>\n");
        print("<UL>\n");

        foreach($part as $name)
        {
            print("<LI>$name\n");
        }

        print("</UL>\n");
    }

    $Option = array("Mustard", "Ketchup",
        "Pickles", "Onions", "Lettuce", "Tomato");

    print("<H3>Create a Burger</H3>\n");
    print("<FORM ACTION=\"$PHP_SELF\">\n");

    foreach($Option as $name)
    {
        print("<INPUT TYPE=\"checkbox\" ");
        print("NAME=\"part[]\" VALUE=\"$name\">");
        print("$name<BR>\ n");
    }

    print("<INPUT TYPE=\"submit\">\n");
    print("</FORM>\n");

    print("</BODY>\n");
    print("</HTML>\n");
?>
```

DESIGN

Topics in This Chapter

- Writing Requirements Specifications
- Writing Design Documents
- Using CVS
- Modularization Using `include`
- FreeEnergy
- FastTemplate
- Midgard
- Ariadne
- Preserving State and Providing Security
- Cloaking
- URLs Friendly to Search Engines
- Running a Script Regularly

Chapter 21

uilding a Web site with PHP is not the same as building a static Web site. If you choose simply to sprinkle PHP code occasionally throughout the site, the effect may be minimal, of course. If you choose to use PHP to generate every page, you will find many opportunities for transforming patterns into functions. As I wrote in Chapter 20, "Integration with HTML," elements such as opening and closing body tags can be put into a function or an included file. The consequence of this situation is that you no longer have a Web *site*. You have a Web *application*.

When this happens, it becomes more important to draw upon formal development techniques. Certainly, structured design is useful when building static Web sites. The case is made plainly in *Web Site Engineering* by Thomas Powell. The addition of PHP makes careful design critical. I can't cover every topic of software engineering as it applies to Web applications in the context of a chapter. I recommend reading Powell's book as an excellent starting point.

After introducing the basics of software requirements and design, I will explore some specific design issues and solutions.

Writing Requirements Specifications

Before you can design a system, it is important to understand what it's supposed to do. Too often this comes in the form of a verbal request such as, "We need a home page with a guest book and a visitor counter," which is never further defined. This usually leads to the building of a prototype that is 25 percent of what the client wants. Changes are made to the prototype, and the site is now 50 percent of what the client wants now. During the time the changes were made, the client has moved the target.

The solution to this problem is to set a target and stick with it. This should start with a statement of the goals for the project. In my experience the most important question left unasked is about motivation. When a client asks for a large animated scene to appear on their index page, often the motivation is a desire to seem familiar with leading-edge technology. Instead of blindly fulfilling the client's request, it is better to look for the best solution for the "Why?". A slick graphical design can say more about the client's attention to advances in technology.

Once you have asked "Why?" enough times, you should have a list of several goals for the project. These goals should suggest a set of requirements. If one of the system's goals is to generate more business, one requirement may be to raise visitor awareness of items in the client's catalog. This may evolve into a requirement that products appear throughout the site on a rotational basis. This could be implemented as banners or kickers strategically placed within the site. Don't, however, tie yourself down with design issues. This earliest stage of site development should concentrate solely on the goals of the system.

From a solid base of goals, you can begin to describe the system requirements. This usually takes the form of a requirements specification document, a formal description of the black-box behavior expected from the site. The goals will suggest a collection of functional requirements and constraints on the design. As I've said, having a goal of increasing sales suggests, among other things, that the site should raise customer awareness of catalog items. Another requirement could be that the site provide some free service to attract visitors. An example is a loan company offering a mortgage calculator. It is a good idea to informally explore possible solutions to requirements, but it's still important to keep design decisions out at this time.

The requirements specification is formal and structured, but it should be understandable by nonexperts in the implementation technology. The description of the system's behavior serves partially as a contract between the client and developer. Clear statements will eliminate misunderstandings that have a high cost later in development. That is not to say that the document shouldn't be precise. When possible, state requirements in measurable terms. Constraining page size to 30K is an objective standard and easily tested. Requiring the site to inspire confidence in the client company is not easily measurable, but sometimes it's all you have.

Table 21–1 lists six things toward which a requirements specification should aspire. It should only specify external behavior. Every requirement should be expressed as the answer to a "What?" question. It should specify constraints. These are best expressed as quantities: How many hits per day? Maximum page size? Maximum page depth? The requirements specification should allow you to change it later. While you should use natural language, don't write a long narrative. Number sections of the document and use diagrams where necessary. It should be a document that helps a future programmer learn about the system. Don't be surprised if that programmer is you six months later.

The requirements should pay attention to the entire life of the system. If the system needs to be able to recover from a catastrophic failure within an hour, write it into the specification. And the follow-up to this idea is that you should describe how the system deals with adversity—not just disaster, but also illegal user input. Some systems ignore user input that is not understood. How many times have you seen a "404 Document Not Found" error? It's nice when that page includes a link to the index page of the site.

Keeping these guidelines in mind, refer to Table 21–2, which outlines the structure of a requirements specification. The overview should be a page or less that reviews the goals of the site. If the goals were detailed in another

---

Table 21–1   Properties of Requirements Specifications

- Only specifies external system behavior
- Specifies constraints on the implementation
- Allows easy modification
- Serves as a reference tool for system maintainers
- Records forethought about the life cycle of the system
- Characterizes acceptable responses to undesired events

Table 21–2   Requirements Specification Document Structure

- Overview of System Goals
- Operating and Development Environments
- External Interfaces and Data Flow
- Functional Requirements
- Performance Requirements
- Exception Handling
- Implementation Priorities
- Foreseeable Modifications
- Design Suggestions

document, make this document available. It is important to preserve the thought that went into the project at each phase. The requirements build on the goals, and in turn the design will build on the requirements. But being able to refer to the original goals of the system will be helpful to the designer and even the implementer.

The operating and development environments are sometimes overlooked in requirements specifications. This includes both the browser and the Web server. If you are developing an intranet application, you may be fortunate enough to optimize for a particular browser version. I've found that while a large company may impose a standard browser for the organization for which you've developed an application, another standard may apply to the users in another organization a thousand miles away. My wish for you is that you never build a system for Netscape Navigator version 3.01, only to be asked to make the system work for Microsoft Internet Explorer version 3.02.

The Web server is perhaps more under your control and certainly less finicky about differences in source code. If you are using PHP, most likely you will be using Apache. It's a good idea to use identical versions of both Apache and PHP for your development and live environments.

For the most part, your list of external interfaces will include the Internet connection between the browser and the Web server, the local file system, and possibly a database connection. I find it helpful to create a diagram that shows the relationship between data elements, the simplest of which might be a box labeled *Browser* connected to a box labeled *Server*. The line would have arrows at each end to show that information travels in both directions.

This diagram is a description of the context, not a design of the data structure. Whether you will be using a database may be obvious, but which database may not. If the system will be storing data *somehow,* just show data flowing into a box that could be database or flat file. The goal is to describe how data moves around in the system.

The functional requirements will certainly be the largest part of the document. If you have drawn a data flow diagram, you may have a very good idea of how the system breaks up into modules. The more you can partition the functionality into distinct pieces, the easier it will be to group the functional requirements. I've written many requirements documents for Web applications that are essentially data warehouses. My approach has been to dedicate a section to each of the major data entities. A project management application might have a collection of project descriptions, a collection of users, and a collection of comments. Each of these would have a section in the functional requirements that lists first all the information they store and then the ways the information can be manipulated.

The performance requirements are constraints on the functionality. You may wish to outline a minimum browser configuration for use of the site. Maximum page weights are a good idea. If the client is dictating that a certain technology be used, it should be noted in this section. It's good to know in advance that while you will be allowed to use PHP, you have to deal with Oracle and Internet Information Server on Windows NT.

The exception-handling section describes how the system deals with adversity. The two parts of this are disaster and invalid input. Discuss what should happen if the Web server suddenly bursts into flame. Decide whether backups will be made hourly, daily, or weekly. Also decide how the system handles users entering garbage. For example, define whether filling out a form with a missing city asks the user to hit the back button or automatically redisplays the form with everything filled out and the missing field marked with a red asterisk.

If the client has a preference for the order of implementation, outline it. My experience has been that, faced with a dire deadline before the project begins, the client will bargain for which functionality will appear in the first round. Other requirements may not be critical to the system, and the client is willing to wait. If there is a preference in this area, it is very important for the designer and implementers to know in advance.

Farther in the future are the foreseeable modifications. The client may not be ready to create a million-dollar e-commerce site just yet, but they may expect to ask you to plug this functionality into the site a year from now. It may not make sense to use an expensive database to implement a 50-item catalog, but building a strong foundation for later expansion will likely be worthwhile.

The last part of the requirements specification is a collection of design hints. This represents the requirements writer's forethought about pitfalls for the designer. You might summarize a similar project. You might suggest a design approach.

Writing Design Documents

Once you have created a requirements specification document, you will have to decide whether to write a design document. Often it is not necessary, especially when a few people are working on a small project. You may wish to choose key elements of a complete design document and develop them to the point of usefulness.

The first part of design is concerned with the architecture of the system. The system should be broken into sections that encompass broad groups of functionality. A Web application for project management might break down into a module that handles project information, a module that handles users, and a module that handles timesheet entries. An informational Web site can be broken down by the secondary pages—that is, the pages one click away from the home page. The "About Us" section serves to inform visitors about the company itself, while a catalog area is a resource for learning about the items the company sells.

Depending on the type of site, you should choose some sort of diagram that shows the subsystems and how they relate to each other. These are called entity relationship diagrams. I almost always create a page-flow diagram. Each node in the graph is a page as experienced by the user. Lines representing links connect the page to other pages on the site. Another useful diagram is one that shows the relationship between database tables. Nodes represent tables, and you may wish to list the fields inside boxes that stand for the tables. Lines connect tables and show how fields match. It's also helpful to indicate whether the relationship between the tables is one to one or one to many.

The next phase of design is interface specification. This defines how subsystems communicate. It can be as simple as listing the URLs for each page. If the site has forms, all the fields should be enumerated. If you are tracking user sessions, you will want to specify how you will be doing this, with cookies or form variables. Define acceptable values for the session identifier. If the site will be communicating with files or a database, this phase will define names of files or login information for databases.

The largest part of a design document is a detailed description of how each module works. At this point it's acceptable to specify exactly the method for implementing the module. For example, you may specify that a list of catalog items be presented using the UL tag. On the other hand, if it doesn't matter, I suggest leaving it out. The person writing the actual code will probably have the best idea for solving the problem.

I suggest pursuing a style guide, which may be part of the design document or may stand alone. This document specifies the style of the code in the project. You'll find an example in Appendix G, but don't bother flipping there now. The style guide deals with issues like how to name variables, or where to place curly braces. Many of these issues are arbitrary. What's important is that a decision is made and followed. A large body of code formatted according to a standard is easier to read.

For the rest of this chapter I'd like to present some design ideas you may choose to adopt. PHP's dynamic nature allows for structural designs that can't be achieved in plain HTML. It is a shame to waste this functionality by using PHP as a faster alternative to CGI. I encourage you to consider using PHP as the engine that powers a completely dynamic Web site.

Using CVS

CVS, Concurrent Versions System, is an open-source system that allows developers to track all changes to a project. A central repository stores the files that make up the project. Developers check out copies, modify them, and check them back in. The system records all changes, which allows team members to check out any previous version of any given file. The system also is able to merge differences if two developers make independent changes to the same file.

In the context of project management, I have come to believe CVS is essential. It allows developers to collaborate efficiently, even when they are in separate locations. Popular Net projects such as Apache, Linux, and PHP use CVS and probably wouldn't be as successful if they didn't.

Even a brief tutorial is out of the scope of this text, so I will direct you to Karl Fogel's book, *Open Source Development with CVS* <http://cvsbook.red-bean.com/>. The chapters that deal with CVS specifically are free to download, but I recommend buying the book if you decide to use CVS. Beyond the mechanics of CVS itself, it documents how CVS fits into the development process.

Modularization Using include

Despite its name, the include function is not equivalent to C's preprocessor command of the same name. In many ways it is like a function call. Given the name of a file, PHP attempts to parse the file as if it appeared in place of the call to include. The difference from a function is that the code will be parsed only if the include statement is executed. You can take advantage of this by wrapping calls to include in if statements. The require function, on the other hand, will always include the specified file, even if it is inside an if block that is never executed. It has been discussed several times on the PHP mailing list that require is faster than include because PHP is able to inject the specified file into the script during an early pass across the code. However, this applies only to files specified by a static path. If the call to require contains a variable, it can't be executed until the runtime. It may be helpful to adopt a rule of using require only when outside a compound statement and when specifying a static path.

Almost anything I write in PHP uses include extensively. The first reason is that it makes the code more readable. But the other reason is that it breaks the site into modules. This allows multiple people to work on the site at once. It forces you to write code that is more easily reused, within the existing site and on your next project. Most Web sites have to rely on repeating elements. Consistent navigation aids the user, but it is also a major problem when building and maintaining the site. Each page has to have a duplicate code block pasted into it. Making this a module and including it allows you to debug the code once, making changes quickly.

You can adopt a strategy that consists of placing functions into include modules. As each script requires a particular function, you can simply add an include. If your library of functions is small enough, you might place them all into one file. However, you likely will have pieces of code that are needed on just a handful of pages. In this case, you'll want this module to stand alone.

As your library of functions grows, you may discover some interdependencies. Imagine a module for establishing a connection to a database, plus a couple of other modules that rely on the database connection. Each of these two scripts will include the database connection module. But what happens when both are themselves included in a script? The database module is included twice. This may cause a second connection to be made to the database, and if any functions are defined, PHP will report the error of a duplicate function.

In C, programmers avoid this situation by defining constants inside the included files, and you can adopt a similar strategy. You can define a constant inside your module. If this constant is already defined when the module is executed, control is immediately returned to the calling process. A function named `printBold` is defined in Listing 21.1. This function is needed in the script shown in Listing 21.2. I've purposely placed a bug in the form of a second include. The second time the module is included, it will return before redeclaring the function.

Listing 21.1   Preventing a Double Include

```
<?

    /*
    ** Avoid double includes
    */
    $included_flag = 'INCLUDE_' . basename(__FILE__);
    if(defined($included_flag))
    {
        return(TRUE);
    }
    define($included_flag, TRUE);

    function printBold($text)
    {
        print("<B>$text</B>");
    }
?>
```

Listing 21.2   Attempting to Include a Module Twice

```
<?

    //load printBold function
    include("21-1.php");

    //try loading printBold function again
    include("21-1.php");

    printBold("Successfully avoided a second include");
?>
```

FreeEnergy

I used the technique of including modules on several Web applications, and it led me to consider all the discrete elements of a Web page. Headers and footers are obvious, and so are other repeating navigational elements. Sometimes you can divide pages up into the content unique to the page, the stuff that comes before it, and the stuff that comes after it. This could be hard to maintain, however. Some of the HTML is in one file, some in another. If nothing else you'll need to flip between two editor windows.

Consider for a moment a Web page as an object—that is, in an object-oriented way. On the surface, a Web page is a pair of HTML tags containing HEAD tags and BODY tags. Regardless of the design or content of the page, these tags must exist, and inside them will be placed further tags. Inside the BODY tags a table can be placed for controlling the layout of the page. Inside the cells of the table are either links to other pages on the site or some content unique to the page.

FreeEnergy is a system that attempts to encapsulate major pieces of each page into files to be included on demand. Before I proceed, I want to state my motivations clearly. My first concern when developing a Web site is that it be correct and of the highest quality. Second is that it may be developed and maintained in minimal time. After these needs are addressed, I consider performance. Performance is considered last because of the relatively cheap cost of faster hardware. Moore's law suggests that eighteen months from now, CPU speed and memory capacity will have doubled for the same price. This doubling costs nothing but time. Also, experience has shown that a small minority of code contributes to a majority of the time spent processing. These small sections can be optimized later, leaving the rest of the code to be written as clearly as possible.

The FreeEnergy system uses more calls to `include` than you'd find where you are simply making a few includes at the top of your pages. Hits to the file system do take longer than function calls, of course. You could place everything you might need in one large file and include it on every page, but you will face digging through that large file when you need to change anything. A trade has been made between the performance of the application and the time it takes to develop and maintain it.

I called this system FreeEnergy because it seems to draw power from the environment that PHP provides. The `include` function in PHP is quite unique and central to FreeEnergy, especially the allowance for naming a script with a variable. The content unique to a page is called a screen. The screen name is passed to a single PHP script, which references the screen name in a large array that matches the screen to corresponding layout and navigation modules.

The FreeEnergy system breaks Web pages into five modules: action, layout, navigation, screen, and utility. Action modules perform some sort of write function to a database, a file, or possibly to the network. Only one action module executes during a request, and they are executed before the screen module. An action module may override the screen module named in the request. This is helpful in cases where an action module is attempting to process a form and the submitted data are incomplete or otherwise unsatisfactory. Action modules never send data directly to the screen. Instead, they add messages to a stack to be popped later by the layout module. It is possible that an action module will send header information, so it's important that no output be produced.

Layout modules contain just enough code to arrange the output of screen and navigation modules. They typically contain `table` tags, as is the custom for controlling the layout of a Web page. Inside the table cells, calls to `include` are placed. They may be invoking navigation modules, or screen modules.

Navigation modules contain links and repeating elements. In the vernacular used by engineers I work with, these are "top nav," "bottom nav," and "side nav." Consider the popular site, Yahoo. Their pages generally consist of the same navigation across the top and some at the bottom. Their top nav includes their logo and links to important areas of their site. If the Yahoo site were coded in FreeEnergy, there would probably be a dynamic navigation module for generating the path to the current section, such as

Home > Computers and Internet > Software > Internet > World
Wide Web > Servers > Server Side Scripting > PHP.

Screen modules contain the content unique to the particular page being displayed. They may be plain HTML, or they may be primarily PHP code, depending on context. A press release is static. It can be prepared by someone unfamiliar with PHP. They only need to know that the screen module is an HTML fragment.

Any module may rely on a utility module in much the same way utility files are used in other contexts. Some utility modules are called each page load. Others are collections of functions or objects related to a particular database table.

All modules are collected in a `modules` directory that further contains a subdirectory for each module type. To enhance security, it is placed outside of the Web server's document root. Within the document root is a single PHP script, `index.php`. This script begins the process of calling successive modules and structuring their output with the standard HTML tags.

Because I've been using this system for some time, you have the opportunity to example several working models. One example is FreeTrade, an open-source framework for building e-commerce sites <http://www.working-dogs.com/freetrade/>.

FastTemplate

One interesting thing I've learned in my years in the Web development business is that no two shops build Web applications the same way. Some have a mix of people who may be talented in certain areas, but all can do the same type of work. Others enforce a strict separation between those who do HTML and those who write scripts. Others draw the line between a graphic design group and an engineering group that does HTML and scripting. It can become inefficient for an HTML group to be requesting changes from a scripting group.

FastTemplate addresses this problem by separating HTML from PHP. Templates are written in HTML and may contain special codes surrounded by curly braces. A PHP script loads the templates, defines values for the special codes and replaces them. The codes may be replaced with other templates or with data created by PHP.

The implication is that people unable to work with PHP code will be comfortable working with template files that better resemble plain HTML. Small changes to the HTML can be made without interaction with the engineers, who might be grumpy about making changes. In addition, the engineers won't have to worry about novices introducing errors into their scripts.

If you face these issues, I encourage you to visit the FastTemplate home page `<http://www.thewebmasters.net/php/>`. You can download the class itself along with documentation and examples. You may also like to read an article written by Sascha Schumann that appeared on the PHPBuilder site `<http://www.phpbuilder.com/>`.

Midgard

Another approach to Web site design with PHP is the Midgard project `<http://www.midgard-project.org/>`. The maintainers are Jukka Zitting and Henri Bergius. Rather than code a solution in PHP alone, they have pursued integrating PHP into their own application server. Midgard is capable of organizing more than 800,000 pages of content using a Web-based interface. For this reason it is ideal for operating Magazine sites.

Midgard is an open source project, of course. You can download an official release, or grab a snapshot through CVS. In order to install it, you must modify PHP slightly, but instructions are available at the Midgard site. Because it requires compilation, running Midgard on Windows is probably not worth the effort.

Ariadne

Still in beta at time of writing, Ariadne is a Web application framework from Muze, a development agency in the Netherlands. It's available under the GNU Public License. Auke van Slooten leads the project. The source code can be downloaded from the Muze site `<http://www.muze.nl/software/ariadne/>`.

Ariadne stores PHP source code as objects in a MySQL database. These objects interact with each other using a virtual file system. A rich user interface is presented to the user through Web pages, but advanced users may dig deeper, as well. Another major component controls access rights for users or groups.

Preserving State and Providing Security

Chapter 15, "Sorting, Searching, and Random Numbers," outlines session identifiers, but it may not have been immediately obvious why you would want to implement them. You may wish to secure your Web application by requiring visitors to identify themselves with a login and password. Requiring this page after page, though, would be very annoying. You may even want to track users through the site without actually identifying them. The process should be invisible and should not intrude on the experience.

One solution is to generate a random session identifier. This identifier must not be easy to guess and must be unique to each user. The session could be stored in a database or a file and passed in every link or form. The site simply checks that the session is valid each time a page is requested. If the session is invalid, you may display an error message, send the user back to the login page, or just generate a new session identifier, depending on context.

In a site that requires users to log in, the session identifier will be associated with a user identifier, which would be the key to a table of user information. You may also keep track of the last time the session requested a page and have all those with no activity in a given period, perhaps 15 minutes, expire. This protects users who walk away from their computers without explicitly logging out.

You may also choose to associate arbitrary variables with each session. This is relatively easy to implement with a relational database. Create a table where each row is uniquely identified by session identifier and variable name. Creating a variable is as easy as inserting a row into the table. You can fetch each variable with each request, or fetch them only as needed. Another approach would be serializing an array of values and storing it in a single table column.

Chapter 7, "I/O and Disk Access," describes the session-handling system built into PHP 4, and Chapter 8, "I/O Functions," offers a list of the functions available. These functions present a system that handles the chores of moving data between variables and permanent storage. Although the default handler stores variables on the local file system, it is possible to write your own handler that stores them in a database.

Cloaking

When creating a plain HTML site, you confront two paths: create a site that works great in only one browser, or create a mediocre site that works in all browsers. PHP allows you to create a site that works great in any browser. The HTTP_USER_AGENT variable contains the string most browsers send to the Web server to identify themselves. This variable may be used to choose between versions of content. This cloaks the inner workings of the site from the browser. A seamless experience is provided to visitors, despite differences in browser capabilities.

Chapter 16, "Parsing and String Evaluation," contains an example of using regular expressions to parse HTTP_USER_AGENT into understandable elements. In most cases browser name and version are sufficient, though operating system is also helpful. My experience is that there are subtle differences between identical versions of browsers running on Windows or the Macintosh. One design element I have cloaked in the past is a JavaScript rollover, a graphic button that changes when the mouse is passed over it. For example, the label on the button may glow. This is accomplished in JavaScript by replacing the image. Unfortunately, this is not possible in older browsers. The code to accomplish this may be included only for browsers capable of executing it.

Another cloak I've used in the past involved graphic hard rules. An HTML trick is to create a single-pixel image and stretch it by setting the height and width attributes to values larger than one. This effect can be used to stretch the pixel into a line that becomes a hard rule. And unlike the HR tag, the rule can be any color. For older browsers that don't allow stretching of images, I send an HR tag instead to approximate the effect. Alternatively, I could have pointed to a graphic of the appropriate size.

Consider combining the strategy of cloaking with FreeEnergy. You can choose different layout modules for different browsers. The text-only Lynx browser doesn't allow you to arrange elements using HTML tables, as is customary, and may jumble your content. Because the content is separated from the layout code, you could create a Lynx-friendly version of an entire site by creating a single layout module.

URLs Friendly to Search Engines

Search engines such as Google `<http://www.google.com/>` and Alta Vista `<http://www.altavista.com/>` attempt to explore the entire Web. They have become an essential resource for Internet users, and anyone who maintains a public site benefits from being listed. Search engines use robots, or spiders, to explore pages in a Web site, and they index PHP scripts the same way they index HTML files. When links appear in a page, they are followed. Consequently, the entire site becomes searchable.

Unfortunately, robots will not follow links that appear to contain form variables. Links containing question marks may lead a robot into an endless loop, so they are programmed to avoid them. This presents a problem for sites that use form variables in links. Passing form variables in anchor tags is a natural way for PHP to communicate, but it can keep your pages out of the search engines. To overcome this problem, data must be passed in a format that resembles URLs.

First, consider how a Web server accepts a URI and matches it to a file. The URI is a virtual path, the part of the URL that comes after the host name. It begins with a slash and may be followed by a directory, another slash, and so forth. One by one, the Web server matches directories in the URI to directories in the filesystem. A script is executed when it matches part of the URI, even when more path information follows. Ordinarily this extra path information is thrown away, but you can capture it.

Look at Listing 21.3. This script works with Apache compiled for UNIX but may not work with other Web servers. It relies on the `PATH_INFO` environment variable, which may not be present in a different context. Each Web server creates a unique set of environment variables, although there is overlap.

You may be accessing the code in Listing 21.3 from the URL `http://localhost/corephp/figures/21-5.php/1234.html`. In this case, you are connecting to a local server that contains a directory named `corephp/`

Listing 21.3   Using Path Info

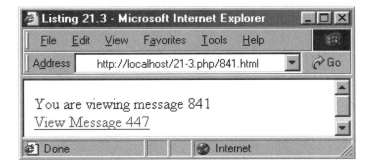

```
<?
        /*
        ** Pull message ID from $PATH_INFO
        */
        if($PATH_INFO != "")
        {
                ereg("^/([[:digit:]]+)(.*)$", $PATH_INFO, $match);
                $ID = $match[1];
        }
        else
        {
                $ID = 0;
        }

        print("You are viewing message $ID<BR>\n");

        //pick a random ID
        $nextID = rand(1, 1000);
        print("<A HREF=\"$SCRIPT_NAME/$nextID.html\">View Message
                $nextID</A><BR>\n");
?>
```

figures in its document root. A default installation of Apache might place this in /usr/local/apcache/htdocs. The name of the script is 21-5.php, and everything after the script name is then placed in the PATH_INFO variable. No file named 1234.html exists, but to the Web browser it appears to be an ordinary HTML document. It appears that way to a spider as well.

The code in Listing 21.3 doesn't really do much. It uses a regular expression to extract the numbers between the last slash and the `.html` extension. The script pretends this is an identifier. It could be referencing a record in a relational database. I've added some code to use a random number to create a link to another imaginary record. Remember the BBS from Chapter 17, "Database Integration?" This method could be applied, and each message would appear to be a single HTML file.

I've introduced only the essential principles of this method. There are a few pitfalls, and a few enhancements to be pursued. Keep in mind that Web browsers do their best to fill in relative URLs, and using path information this way may foil their attempts to request images that appear in your scripts. Therefore, you must use absolute paths. You might also wish to name your PHP script so that it doesn't contain an extension. This is possible with Apache by setting the default document type, using the `DefaultType` configuration directive. You can also use Apache's `mod_rewrite`. I encourage you to read about these parts of Apache at its home site <http://www.apache.org/docs/>.

Running a Script Regularly

Both UNIX and Windows NT have facilities for running programs according to a schedule. In UNIX you can edit your crontab file, and in Windows you use the scheduling service. These are useful when you wish to perform some maintenance function as part of your PHP-powered site. You may write a script to download the list of files at the Slashdot site <http://www.slashdot.org/>. Another script might rebuild the index for a local search engine. Both crontab and the scheduling service take a command line and execute it at a given time. If you're not familiar with the details, either read the main page for crontab, or type `at /?` in a Windows command shell.

You have two choices for invoking a PHP script from the command line. If you have PHP as a stand-alone executable, you can call it and use the path to the script for the only argument. This is probably the way to go on a Windows machine, because the installation provides `php.exe`. A UNIX installation likely will be compiled as an Apache module, and no stand-alone executable will be available. In this case, you can use another program to make an HTTP connection. The text-only browser, Lynx <http://lynx.browser.org/> is well suited for this purpose.

Remember, the Web server executes PHP scripts. Executing scripts from the root user's crontab will allow them greater ability to do damage. It's probably best to execute the script from the Web server's crontab. Using Lynx to run the script avoids this issue but raises another. Unless you put the script in a protected directory, anyone will be able to run it. Simply protect the script with a username and password. Lynx will allow you to specify these on the command line.

EFFICIENCY AND DEBUGGING

Chapter 22

In this final chapter, I will touch upon some issues of efficiency and debugging, which are more art than science. Efficiency should not be your first concern when writing code. You must first write code that works, and hopefully your second concern is keeping the code maintainable. As I write this, the Zend optimizer has become available. An optimizer can reduce memory use and execution time for you behind the scenes, but it can't address all issues of efficiency.

You will pick up some tactical design issues as you gain more experience in programming. These begin to gel as idioms—repeated structures applied to similar problems. Individuals and organizations tend to develop their own idioms, and you will notice them in code found in magazine articles and code repositories. Once you accept an idiom as your own, you can consider it a solved problem. This consistency saves time when writing code and when reading it later.

In most projects, a tiny minority of code is responsible for most of the execution time. Consequently, it pays to measure first and optimize the slowest section. If performance increases to acceptable levels, stop optimizing.

When a bug appears in your script, the time you spent writing meaningful comments and indenting will pay off. Sometimes just reading over troublesome code will reveal its flaws. Most of the time you will print incremental values of variables to understand the problem.

Among the many books on the subject, I can recommend two. The first is *Writing Solid Code* by Steve Maguire. It's oriented toward writing applications in C, but many of the concepts apply to writing PHP scripts. The other is *The Practice of Programming* by Brian Kernighan and Rob Pike; Chapter 7 will be of particular interest.

Measuring Performance

Three factors affect the time it takes to go from clicking on a link to seeing a completed Web page. First is the network. Your request must travel from the browser to the server, and the Web page must travel back to your browser. This will vary with location and the speed of connection. Second is the time it takes for a browser to display a Web page, once it has the HTML. Neither of these things is a function of PHP itself. Furthermore, they are largely outside of our control. We can try to keep the size of the HTML document small, and we can avoid complex HTML like nested tables, but we can't upgrade everyone's 28.8 modem. What we can control is the time it takes to assemble an HTML document with a PHP script.

The best way to measure how long a script runs is to print the time in important points in your script. Because most scripts take less than a second to run, you must use the `microtime` function. If you place the output in HTML comments, the display of the page will not be disturbed. Of course, the print statement itself will take some time. You can minimize this by simply printing the output of `microtime` instead of trying to convert its output into an integer. You can do the math later by hand or in a spreadsheet.

Listing 22.1 is a contrived example of a script that performs complex math, then writes to a file. Figure 22–1 shows the output. The first HTML comment contains the time on the clock when the script begins. That's followed by time when the 10,000 cosine calculations have finished. Finally we see the time when the 10,000 lines are written to a file.

The `microtime` function returns two numbers. The first is a fraction of a second, the other the number of seconds since January 1, 1970. Notice that from the first comment to the next, the number of seconds changed from 950996931 to 950996932. The fraction changed from 0.95462500 to 0.38373500. In total 0.42911 seconds elapsed. Doing the math for the second part shows it took 0.080332 seconds. If the performance of this script were not satisfactory, I'd first look into improving the first half. It takes five times longer to execute than the rest.

Listing 22.1	Measuring Script Performance

```
<?
      print("\n<!-- " . microtime() . " -->\n");

      //fake some long calculation
      for($index = 0; $index < 10000; $index++)
      {
            $value += (cos(time()%360));
      }

      print("\n<!-- " . microtime() . " -->\n");

      //write to file
      $fp = fopen("data.txt", "w");
      for($index = 0; $index < 10000; $index++)
      {
            fputs($fp, "Testing performance\n");
      }
      fclose($fp);

      print("\n<!-- " . microtime() . " -->\n");
?>
```

Fetching Database Query Results

For most of the databases supported by PHP, you can get columns in two
ways. You can specify a value by row number and column name, or you can
fetch rows one at a time in an array. For MySQL this involves `mysql_result`
and `mysql_fetch_row`, respectively.

Using `mysql_result` is much slower than the fetch functions. PHP has to
work harder to find the exact piece of data you need. First, the specified row

```
<!-- 0.95462500 950996931 -->

<!-- 0.38373500 950996932 -->

<!-- 0.46406700 950996932 -->
```

Figure 22-1 Output of `microtime`

must be referenced. Then the data in that row must be searched for a column with a matching name. You can imagine that executing `mysql_result` several times inside a loop can add up to a very slow script. Each call has to start at the beginning and find the appropriate data element.

Alternatively, you may fetch an entire row into an object, as I have done in most of the examples so far. This allows you to reference the exact element without searching through the entire data set. The challenge is to match up the results of the query with the array elements. If you have created a query such as

```
SELECT *
FROM user u, employer e
WHERE u.Employer = e.ID
```

you may have a hard time. You will have to examine the structure of each table to see the order of the columns. A better approach is to specify the columns you need, leaving out any you won't use. This would transform the query into something like

```
SELECT u.ID, u.Name, e.Name
FROM user u, employer e
WHERE u.Employer = e.ID
```

which specifies only three columns. You can be sure, regardless of the order of the columns in the table, that the user ID will be column zero.

Another advantage is that, since the resulting data have been narrowed to three columns, each fetch will be much smaller. The savings go all the way back to the database, because it will return only three pieces of data times the number of rows. None of the unused rows from the first version of the query will be sent through the network from the database server to PHP. In turn, PHP doesn't need to put them into the array.

When to Store Content in a Database

When I speak of content, I mean static text, perhaps containing HTML. There is no rule saying that content should never be placed in a database, or that it should always be put in a database. In the case of a bulletin board, it makes sense to put each message in a database. Messages are likely to be added continually. It is convenient to treat them as units, manipulating them by their creation dates or authors. At the other extreme, a copyright message that appears at the bottom of every page of a site is more suited to a text file that is retrieved with the `require` function.

Somewhere between these two extremes is a break-even point. The reason is that databases provide a tradeoff. They allow you to handle data in complex ways. They allow you to associate several pieces of information around a common identifier. However, you trade away some performance, as retrieving data is slower than if you opened a file and read the contents.

Many Web sites are nothing more than a handful of pages dressed up in a common graphic theme. A hundred files in a directory are easy to manage. You can name each one to describe their contents and refer to them in a URL such as `http://www.mysite.com/index.php?screen=about_us` and still get the benefit of systematically generating the layout and navigation. Your PHP script can use the value of the `screen` variable as the name of a local file, perhaps in a directory named `screens`. Developers can work on the page contents as they are accustomed, because they know the code is stored in a file named `about_us` in a directory named `screens`.

When the content grows to a thousand pages, keeping each in a separate file starts to become unmanageable. A relational database will help you better organize the content. With a site so large it's likely that there will be many versions of the navigation. In a database it is easy to build a table that associates page content with navigation. You can also automate hyperlinks by creating one-way associations between pages. This would cause a link to automatically appear on a page.

The biggest problem with this approach is the lack of good tools for editing the site. Developers are used to fetching files into an editor via FTP. Asking these same people to start using a database shell is most likely out of the question. The cost of teaching SQL to anyone who might work on the site may eliminate any benefit gained when the content is put into the database. So, you are faced with creating your own tools to edit the content. The logical path is to create Web-based tools, since coding a desktop application is a major project in itself, especially if both Windows and Macintosh users are to be accommodated. As you might guess, Web-based site editors are less than ideal. However, with very large sites they become bearable, because the alternative of managing such a large static site is a greater evil, so to speak.

In-Line Debugging

There are times when code produces unexpected results. Examining the code reveals nothing. In this case the best thing to do is some in-line debugging. PHP scripts generate HTML to be interpreted by a browser, and HTML has a comment tag. Therefore, it is a simple matter to write PHP code that reports diagnostic information inside HTML comments.

Often I create database queries dynamically, based on user input. A stray character or invalid user input can cause the query to return an error. Sometimes I will print the query itself. I also print the results of the error functions, such as `mysql_error`. The same applies to code unrelated to databases. Printing diagnostic information, even if it is as simple as saying "got here," can help.

Remote Debugging

You may enable remote debugging for all scripts by editing the configuration file `php.ini`, or you may use the `debugger_on` function, described in Chapter 8, "I/O Functions." Once enabled, PHP will attempt to connect to a remote host and port each time a script is run.

You will need a port listening program to get the debugging information. There are numerous free port listeners for Windows. I've found Port Listener by Hauke X to work well. Similar programs exist for UNIX as well.

All debugging messages are sent to the listening host, regardless of the error reporting level set in `php.ini`. Messages are sent in a special format

```
date time host(pid) type:message-data
```

followed by a linefeed.

The date is in the format `YYYY-MM-DD`. Time is in the format `HH:MM:UUU-UUU`. The last six digits of time are the seconds and microseconds. The `host` is the name of the server and `pid` is the process identifier. The type is a special code described in Table 22–1. The rest of the line is a message terminated with a linefeed.

Using the remote debugger is as simple as executing a PHP script and watching the debug information appear in the port listener output.

Table 22–1	Debugging Types

Type	Description
end	The end of an error message.
frames	The number of frames in the call stack.
function	The name of the function where the error occurred.
location	The filename and line number that generated the error message.
message	A PHP error message.
start	This type signifies the beginning of a debugging message. The data-message for this line will be the type of error.

Simulating HTTP Connections

When writing PHP scripts, it is not necessary to understand every detail of the HTTP protocol. I would be straying to include a treatise here, but you ought to have enough understanding so that you could simulate a connect by using telnet. You may know that Web servers listen on port 80 by default. HTTP is a text-based protocol, so it's not hard to telnet directly to a Web server and type a simple request. HTTP has several commands that should be familiar; GET and POST are used most often. HEAD is a command that returns just the headers for a request. Browsers use this command to test whether they really want to get an entire document.

It is especially helpful to simulate an HTTP connection when your script sends custom headers. Figure 22–2 is an example showing a request I made to the PHP home page. The text in bold is what I typed. The remote server returned everything else.

```
[1] leon [/export/home/leon] ?> telnet www.php.net 80
Trying 208.247.106.167...
Connected to www.php.net.
Escape character is '^]'.
HEAD / HTTP/1.0

HTTP/1.1 200 OK
Date: Sun, 20 Feb 2000 00:53:51 GMT
Server: Apache/1.3.10-dev (Unix) DAV/0.9.15-dev PHP/4.0b4-dev
X-Powered-By: PHP/4.0b4-dev
Last-Modified: Mon, 31 Jan 2000 04:33:04 GMT
Vary: User-Agent
Connection: close
Content-Type: text/html; charset=iso-8859-1

Connection closed by foreign host.
[2] leon [/export/home/leon] ?>
```

Figure 22–2   Simulating an HTTP Connection

Appendix A

BACKSLASH CODES

The following codes may be included in strings and have special meaning when printed to the browser or to a file. It is important to note that they do not have special meaning when passed to other functions, such as ones communicating with a database or evaluating a regular expression.

Code	Description
\"	Double Quotes
\\	Backslash Character
\n	New Line
\r	Carriage Return
\t	Horizontal Tab
\x00 - \xFF	Hex Characters

Appendix B

ASCII CODES

The following table lists the first 128 characters of the ASCII code. PHP allows for ASCII codes in the range of 0 to 255, but above code 127 the representation differs across operating systems.

Decimal	Hex	Character	Description
0	00		Null
1	01		Start of Heading
2	02		Start of Text
3	03		End of Text
4	04		End of Transmission
5	05		Enquiry
6	06		Acknowledge
7	07		Bell
8	08		Backspace
9	09		Character Tabulation
10	0A		Line Feed

Decimal	Hex	Character	Description
11	0B		Line Tabulation
12	0C		Form Feed
13	0D		Carriage Return
14	0E		Shift Out
15	0F		Shift In
16	10		Datalink Escape
17	11		Device Control One
18	12		Device Control Two
19	13		Device Control Three
20	14		Device Control Four
21	15		Negative Acknowledge
22	16		Synchronous Idle
23	17		End of Transmission Block
24	18		Cancel
25	19		End of Medium
26	1A		Substitute
27	1B		Escape
28	1C		File Separator
29	1D		Group Separator
30	1E		Record Separator
31	1F		Unit Separator
32	20		Space
33	21	!	Exclamation Mark
34	22	"	Quotation Mark
35	23	#	Number Sign
36	24	$	Dollar Sign
37	25	%	Percent Sign
38	26	&	Ampersand
39	27	'	Apostrophe
40	28	(	Left Parenthesis
41	29	)	Right Parenthesis

Decimal	*Hex*	*Character*	*Description*
42	2A	*	Asterisk
43	2B	+	Plus Sign
44	2C	,	Comma
45	2D	–	Hyphen-Minus
46	2E	.	Period
47	2F	/	Forward Slash
48	30	0	Zero
49	31	1	One
50	32	2	Two
51	33	3	Three
52	34	4	Four
53	35	5	Five
54	36	6	Six
55	37	7	Seven
56	38	8	Eight
57	39	9	Nine
58	3A	:	Colon
59	3B	;	Semicolon
60	3C	<	Less-Than Sign
61	3D	=	Equals Sign
62	3E	>	Greater-Than Sign
63	3F	?	Question Mark
64	40	@	At Symbol
65	41	A	Uppercase A
66	42	B	Uppercase B
67	43	C	Uppercase C
68	44	D	Uppercase D
69	45	E	Uppercase E
70	46	F	Uppercase F
71	47	G	Uppercase G
72	48	H	Uppercase H

Decimal	Hex	Character	Description
73	49	I	Uppercase I
74	4A	J	Uppercase J
75	4B	K	Uppercase K
76	4C	L	Uppercase L
77	4D	M	Uppercase M
78	4E	N	Uppercase N
79	4F	O	Uppercase O
80	50	P	Uppercase P
81	51	Q	Uppercase Q
82	52	R	Uppercase R
83	53	S	Uppercase S
84	54	T	Uppercase T
85	55	U	Uppercase U
86	56	V	Uppercase V
87	57	W	Uppercase W
88	58	X	Uppercase X
89	59	Y	Uppercase Y
90	5A	Z	Uppercase Z
91	5B	[	Left Square Bracket
92	5C	\	Backslash
93	5D	]	Right Square Bracket
94	5E	^	Carat
95	5F	_	Underscore
96	60	'	Accent
97	61	a	Lowercase A
98	62	b	Lowercase B
99	63	c	Lowercase C
100	64	d	Lowercase D
101	65	e	Lowercase E
102	66	f	Lowercase F
103	67	g	Lowercase G

Decimal	Hex	Character	Description
104	68	h	Lowercase H
105	69	i	Lowercase I
106	6A	j	Lowercase J
107	6B	k	Lowercase K
108	6C	l	Lowercase L
109	6D	m	Lowercase M
110	6E	n	Lowercase N
111	6F	o	Lowercase O
112	70	p	Lowercase P
113	71	q	Lowercase Q
114	72	r	Lowercase R
115	73	s	Lowercase S
116	74	t	Lowercase T
117	75	u	Lowercase U
118	76	v	Lowercase V
119	77	w	Lowercase W
120	78	x	Lowercase X
121	79	y	Lowercase Y
122	7A	z	Lowercase Z
123	7B	{	Left Curly Bracket
124	7C	|	Vertical Line
125	7D	}	Right Curly Bracket
126	7E	~	Tilde
127	7F		Delete

If you are interested in how characters are rendered in a particular browser, the following script will print each character in a table.

```
<HTML>
<HEAD>
<TITLE>ASCII Characters</TITLE>
</HEAD>
<BODY>
```

```
<TABLE BORDER="1" CELLSPACING="0" CELLPADDING="5">
<?
  for($index=0; $index <= 255; $index++)
  {
        print("<TR>");
        print("<TD>$index</TD>");
        print("<TD>".chr($index)."</TD>");
        print("</TR>\n");
  }
?>
</TABLE>
</BODY>
</HTML>
```

Appendix C

OPERATORS

Operator	Operation It Performs
+	Addition
–	Subtraction
*	Multiplication
/	Division
%	Modulo Division
++	Increment
–	Decrement
<	Is Less Than
>	Is Greater Than
<=	Is Less Than or Equal To
>=	Is Greater Than or Equal To
==	Is Equal To
!=	Is Not Equal To
AND &&	And
OR ||	Or
XOR	Exclusive Or

Operator	*Operation It Performs*
!	Not
&	And
|	Or
^	Exclusive Or
~	One's Complement or NOT
>>	Shift all bits to the right
<<	Shift all bits to the left
.	Concatenate
$	Reference a Variable
&	Reference Variable Storage
->	Reference a Class Method or Property
=>	Set argument default or assign array element index
@	Suppress Function Errors
?	Tertiary Conditional Expression
=	Assign right side to left side
+=	Add right side to left side
-=	Subtract right side from left side
*=	Multiply left side by right side
/=	Divide left side by right side
%=	Set left side to left side module right side
&=	Set left side to bitwise AND of left side and right side
|=	Set left side to bitwise OR of left side and right side
^=	Set left side to bitwise XOR of left side and right side
.=	Set left side to concatenation of left side and right side

Appendix D

PHP TAGS

There are several ways to mark an area of PHP script in a Web page, displayed below. The results of the script, if any, will take the place in the final output. If a line break follows the closing tag, it will be removed. This helps you write more readable code.

```
<?
?>
```

This is the classic method for marking PHP code. Many of the examples found on the Internet use this method, probably because it's the method that's been available the longest. PHP version 2 used this method except that the second question mark was omitted.

This method is called "short tags" and support for it may be turned on or off. One way is to use the `short_tags` function described in Chapter 11, "Time, Date, and Configuration Functions." A directive in the `php.ini` file controls enabling short tags for all scripts. You can also configure PHP to enable short tags before you compile it.

```
<?php
?>
```

This method was added to make PHP scripts compatible with XML, which get confused by the short tags described above.

```
<SCRIPT LANGUAGE="php">
</SCRIPT>
```

Some text editors, Microsoft's Frontpage in particular, do not understand tags that start with `<?` , so support for this longer tagging method was added.

```
<%
%>
```

This method emulates ASP-style tags.

```
<%=
%>
```

Unlike other methods, these tags are shorthand for a call to the `echo` function. This is probably best illustrated with an example.

```
<% $name="Leon"; %>
Hi, my name is <%= $name %>.<BR>
```

This method is controlled by compile-time and run-time directives and will only be available if enabled.

Finally, you can run a script from the command line like :

```
#! /usr/local/bin/php -q
<? print "hello\n"; ?>
```

You must compile PHP as a stand-alone executable, of course. The `-q` tells PHP to be quiet, to refrain from printing HTTP headers.

Appendix E

PHP COMPILE-TIME CONFIGURATION

The following are commands accepted by the `configure` script. There's more information about what each does if you type `./configure —help` in your shell.

```
--disable-debug
--disable-libtool-lock
--disable-pear
--disable-posix
--disable-rpath
--disable-short-tags
--disable-url-fopen-wrapper
--enable-bcmath
--enable-discard-path
--enable-dmalloc
--enable-fast-install[=PKGS]
--enable-force-cgi-redirect
--enable-freetype-4bit-antialias-hack
--enable-inline-optimization
```

```
--enable-magic-quotes
--enable-maintainer-mode
--enable-memory-limit
--enable-roxen-zts
--enable-safe-mode
--enable-shared[=PKGS]
--enable-static[=PKGS]
--enable-sysvsem
--enable-sysvshm
--enable-track-vars
--enable-trans-sid
--enable-ucd-snmp-hack
--enable-versioning
--enable-xml
--with-adabas[=DIR]
--with-aolserver=DIR"
--with-apache[=DIR]
--with-apxs[=FILE]
--with-aspell[=DIR]
--with-cdb[=DIR]
--with-config-file-path=PATH
--with-cpdflib[=DIR]
--with-custom-odbc[=DIR]
--with-cybercash[=DIR]
--with-db2[=DIR]
--with-db3[=DIR]
--with-dbase
--with-dbm[=DIR]
--with-dbmaker[=DIR]
--with-dom[=DIR]
--with-empress[=DIR]
--with-esoob[=DIR]
--with-exec-dir[=DIR]
```

```
--with-fdftk[=DIR]

--with-fhttpd[=DIR]

--with-filepro

--with-ftp

--with-gd[=DIR]

--with-gdbm[=DIR]

--with-gettext[=DIR]

--with-gnu-ld

--with-hyperwave

--with-ibm-db2[=DIR]

--with-icap[=DIR]

--with-imap[=DIR]

--with-informix[=DIR]

--with-interbase[=DIR]

--with-iodbc[=DIR]

--with-java[=DIR]

--with-jpeg-dir[=DIR]

--with-ldap[=DIR]

--with-mcal[=DIR]

--with-mcrypt[=DIR]

--with-mhash[=DIR]

--with-mm[=DIR]

--with-mod-dav=DIR

--with-mod_charset

--with-msql[=DIR]

--with-mysql[=DIR]

--with-ndbm[=DIR]

--with-oci8[=DIR]

--with-openlink[=DIR]

--with-oracle[=DIR]

--with-pdflib[=DIR]

--with-pgsql[=DIR]

--with-phttpd=DIR"
```

```
--with-png-dir[=DIR]
--with-readline[=DIR]
--with-regex=TYPE
--with-roxen=DIR
--with-servlet[=DIR]
--with-snmp[=DIR]
--with-solid[=DIR]
--with-sybase-ct[=DIR]
--with-sybase[=DIR]
--with-thttpd=SRCDIR
--with-tiff-dir[=DIR]
--with-tsrm-pth[=pth-config]
--with-tsrm-pthreads
--with-ttf[=DIR]
--with-unixODBC[=DIR]
--with-velocis[=DIR]
--with-wddx
--with-yp
--with-zeus=DIR
--with-zlib-dir[=DIR]
--with-zlib[=DIR]
--without-gd
--without-pcre-regex
```

Appendix F

INTERNET RESOURCES

The first place to look for information about PHP on the Internet is PHP's home site `<http://www.php.net/>`. Many of the sites listed in this appendix appear on pages of that site. You can download the latest source code an executables there. You can read the latest news. And you will find information about the various mailing lists, which can be a great source of support. To subscribe to the general mailing list, send mail to `php-general@lists.php.net`. You will get an email to confirm your subscription. Be prepared to get hundreds of messages a day. I suggest sending the messages into their own folder using a filter. If you'd prefer to just browse the messages, try the archives at the AIMS group mailing list archives `<http://marc.theaimsgroup.com/?l=php3-general>`.

Another great resource is Nathan Wallace's FAQTS.com site `<http://www.faqts.com/>`. His site is a collection of frequently-asked questions, including a large section about PHP.

The links below are just a sample of what's available. The PHP home site and the portals below list many more.

Portals

`<http://www.zend.com/>` Zend

`<http://www.phpbuilder.com/>` PHP Builder

`<http://www.weberdev.com/>` WeberDev

`<http://devshed.com/Server_Side/PHP/>` DevShed's PHP Resources

`<http://www.phpwizard.net/>` PHP Wizard

`<http://www.php-center.de/>` PHP Center (in German)

`<http://www.phpindex.com/>` PHP Index (in French)

`<http://www.phpx.com/>` Chinese PHP Developer's Union (in Chinese)

Software

`<http://px.sklar.com/>` PX: PHP Code Exchange

`<http://phplib.netuse.de/>` PHP Base Library

`<http://phpclasses.upperdesign.com/>` PHP Classes Repository

`<http://www.hotscripts.com/PHP/Scripts_and_Programs/>` HotScripts' PHP Section

`<http://www.samoun.com/alain/ultraedit/>` -UltraEdit wordfiles for PHP

`<http://dcl.sourceforge.net/>` Double Choco Latte, a bug tracking system

`<http://www.phorum.org/>` Phorum, threaded discussions

`<http://horde.org/imp/>` Web to mail interface

`<http://www.htmlwizard.net/phpMyAdmin/>` MySQL Web interface

`<http://kidsister.tjw.org/>` KidSister, software for tracking tasks

`<http://www.midgard-project.org/>` Midgard

Jobs and Services

`<http://hosts.php.net/>` Searchable database of hosting services that offer PHP

`<http://www.phpbuilder.com/jobs/>` Jobs listing at PHP Builder

`<http://www.schaffner.net/emp/>` Brian Schaffner's Jobs listing

Appendix G

PHP STYLE GUIDE

This is a sample style guide based on the one used by the FreeTrade project `<http://www.working-dogs.com/freetrade/>`.

Comments

Every file should start with a comment block describing its purpose, version, author, and a copyright message. The comment block should be a block comment in the style below.

```
/*
** File: test
** Description:  This is a test program
** Version: 1.0
** Created: 1/1/2000
** Author: Leon Atkinson
** Email: leon@clearink.com
**
** Copyright (c) 2000 Your Group.  All rights reserved.
*/
```

Every function should have a block comment specifying name, input/output, and what the function does.

```
/*
** Function: doAdd
** Input:   INTEGER a, INTEGER b
** Output: INTEGER
** Description:  Adds two integers
*/
function doAdd($a, $b)
{
        return(a+b);
}
```

Ideally, every while, if, for or similar block of code should be preceded by a comment explaining what happens in the block. Sometimes this is unnecessary.

```
// get input from user char by char
while(getInput($inputChar))
{
        storeChar($inputChar);
}
```

Explain sections of code that aren't obvious.

```
//TAB is ASCII 9
define(TAB, 9);

// change tabs to spaces in userName
while($index=0; $index < count($userName); $index++)
{
      $userName[$index] = ereg_replace(TAB, " ", $userName[$index]);
}
```

Function Declarations

As previously stated, functions should have a comment block explaining what they do and their input/output. The function block should align starting at one tab from the left margin unless the function is part of a class definition. Opening and closing braces should also be one tab from the left margin. The body of the function should be indented two tabs.

```php
<?php
    /*
    ** doAdd
    ** Adds two integers
    ** Input:  $a, $b
    ** Output: sum of $a and $b
    */
    function doAdd($a, $b)
    {
        return(a+b);
    }
?>
```

Compound Statements

Flow control primitives should be compound statements, even if they only contain one instruction. Like functions, compound statements should have opening braces that start at column zero relative to scope.

Code within the braces forms a new scope and should be indented.

```php
// tell the user if a is equal to ten
if($a==10)
{
    printf("a is ten.\n");
}
else
{
    printf("a is not ten.\n");
}
```

Naming

The names of variables, constants, and functions are to begin with a lower-case letter. In names that consist of more than one word, the words are written together and each word starts with an uppercase letter. Use short names for variables used in a small scope, such as just inside a `for` loop. Use longer names for variables used in larger scopes.

Function names should begin with a lowercase letter and use capitals for subsequent words.

```
/*
** Function getAddressFromEnvironment
** Input: $Prefix - prefix used to generate address form
** Return: array suitable for addressFields
*/
function getAddressFromEnvironment($Prefix)
{
      global $AddressInfo;

      //get list of all address fields
      //from the AddressInfo array
      reset($AddressInfo);
      while(list($field, $info) = each($AddressInfo))
      {
             $ReturnValue[$field] = trim($GLOBALS[($Prefix .
             $info[ADDR_VAR])]);
      }

      return($ReturnValue);
}
```

Function names should suggest an action or verb. Use names like `updateAddress` or `makeStateSelector`. Variable names should suggest a property or noun, such as `userName,` or `Width`. Use pronounceable names, such as `User`, not `usr`. Use descriptive names for variables used globally, use short names for variables used locally.

Be consistent and use parallelism. If you are abbreviating number as `num`, always use that abbreviation. Don't switch to using `no` or `nmbr`.

Values that are treated as constants, that is, not changed by the program, should be declared in the beginning of the scope in which they are used. In PHP this is done with the `define` function. Each of these constants should be paired with a comment that explains use. They should be named exclusively with uppercase letters, with underscores to separate words. You should use constants in place of any arbitrary values to improve readability.

```
// maximum length of a name to accept
define("MAX_NAME_LENGTH",  32);
print("Maximum name length is " . MAX_NAME_LENGTH);
```

Constants that belong to a specific module should use a consistent prefix.

```
//text with which to label the field
define("ADDR_LABEL", 0);

//name of the form field (sans prefix of course)
define("ADDR_VAR", 1);

//error message to display for missing fields
define("ADDR_ERROR", 2);
```

Variables are to be declared with the smallest possible scope. This means using function parameters when it's appropriate.

Lines should not exceed 78 characters. Break long lines at common separators and align the fragments in an indented block.

```
if(($size  max_size) OR
      (isSizeInvalid($size)))
{
      print("Invalid size");
}
```

Expressions

Write conditional expressions so that they read naturally aloud. Sometimes eliminating a not operator (!) will make an expression more understandable. Use parentheses liberally to resolve ambiguity. Using parentheses can force an order of evaluation. This saves the time a reader may spend remembering precedence of operators.

Keep each line simple. The trinary operator (x ? 1 : 2) usually indicates too much code on one line. if..elseif..else is usually more readable. Don't sacrifice clarity for cleverness.

Index

G

T

LICENSE AGREEMENT AND LIMITED WARRANTY

READ THE FOLLOWING TERMS AND CONDITIONS CAREFULLY BEFORE OPENING THIS SOFTWARE PACKAGE. THIS LEGAL DOCUMENT IS AN AGREEMENT BETWEEN YOU AND PRENTICE-HALL, INC. (THE "COMPANY"). BY OPENING THIS SEALED SOFTWARE PACKAGE, YOU ARE AGREEING TO BE BOUND BY THESE TERMS AND CONDITIONS. IF YOU DO NOT AGREE WITH THESE TERMS AND CONDITIONS, DO NOT OPEN THE SOFTWARE PACKAGE. PROMPTLY RETURN THE UNOPENED SOFTWARE PACKAGE AND ALL ACCOMPANYING ITEMS TO THE PLACE YOU OBTAINED THEM FOR A FULL REFUND OF ANY SUMS YOU HAVE PAID.

1.   **GRANT OF LICENSE:** In consideration of your payment of the license fee, which is part of the price you paid for this product, and your agreement to abide by the terms and conditions of this Agreement, the Company grants to you a nonexclusive right to use and display the copy of the enclosed software program (hereinafter the "software") on a single computer (i.e., with a single CPU) at a single location so long as you comply with the terms of this Agreement. The Company reserves all rights not expressly granted to you under this Agreement.

2.   **OWNERSHIP OF SOFTWARE:** You own only the magnetic or physical media (the enclosed software) on which the software is recorded or fixed, but the Company retains all the rights, title, and ownership to the software recorded on the original software copy(ies) and all subsequent copies of the software, regardless of the form or media on which the original or other copies may exist. This license is not a sale of the original software or any copy to you.

3.   **COPY RESTRICTIONS:** This software and the accompanying printed materials and user manual (the "Documentation") are the subject of copyright. You may not copy the Documentation or the software, except that you may make a single copy of the software for backup or archival purposes only. You may be held legally responsible for any copying or copyright infringement which is caused or encouraged by your failure to abide by the terms of this restriction.

4.   **USE RESTRICTIONS:** You may not network the software or otherwise use it on more than one computer or computer terminal at the same time. You may physically transfer the software from one computer to another provided that the software is used on only one computer at a time. You may not distribute copies of the software or Documentation to others. You may not reverse engineer, disassemble, decompile, modify, adapt, translate, or create derivative works based on the software or the Documentation without the prior written consent of the Company.

5.   **TRANSFER RESTRICTIONS:** The enclosed software is licensed only to you and may not be transferred to any one else without the prior written consent of the Company. Any unauthorized transfer of the software shall result in the immediate termination of this Agreement.

6.   **TERMINATION:** This license is effective until terminated. This license will terminate automatically without notice from the Company and become null and void if you fail to comply with any provisions or limitations of this license. Upon termination, you shall destroy the Documentation and all copies of the software. All provisions of this Agreement as to warranties, limitation of liability, remedies or damages, and our ownership rights shall survive termination.

7.   **MISCELLANEOUS:** This Agreement shall be construed in accordance with the laws of the United States of America and the State of New York and shall benefit the Company, its affiliates, and assignees.

8.   **LIMITED WARRANTY AND DISCLAIMER OF WARRANTY:** The Company warrants that the software, when properly used in accordance with the Documentation, will operate in substantial conformity with the description of the software set forth in the Documentation. The Company does not warrant that the software will meet your requirements or that the operation of the software will be uninterrupted or error-free. The Company warrants that the media on which the software is delivered shall be free from defects in materials and workmanship under normal use

for a period of thirty (30) days from the date of your purchase. Your only remedy and the Company's only obligation under these limited warranties is, at the Company's option, return of the warranted item for a refund of any amounts paid by you or replacement of the item. Any replacement of software or media under the warranties shall not extend the original warranty period. The limited warranty set forth above shall not apply to any software which the Company determines in good faith has been subject to misuse, neglect, improper installation, repair, alteration, or damage by you. EXCEPT FOR THE EXPRESSED WARRANTIES SET FORTH ABOVE, THE COMPANY DISCLAIMS ALL WARRANTIES, EXPRESS OR IMPLIED, INCLUDING WITHOUT LIMITATION, THE IMPLIED WARRANTIES OF MERCHANTABILITY AND FITNESS FOR A PARTICULAR PURPOSE. EXCEPT FOR THE EXPRESS WARRANTY SET FORTH ABOVE, THE COMPANY DOES NOT WARRANT, GUARANTEE, OR MAKE ANY REPRESENTATION REGARDING THE USE OR THE RESULTS OF THE USE OF THE SOFTWARE IN TERMS OF ITS CORRECTNESS, ACCURACY, RELIABILITY, CURRENTNESS, OR OTHERWISE.

IN NO EVENT, SHALL THE COMPANY OR ITS EMPLOYEES, AGENTS, SUPPLIERS, OR CONTRACTORS BE LIABLE FOR ANY INCIDENTAL, INDIRECT, SPECIAL, OR CONSEQUENTIAL DAMAGES ARISING OUT OF OR IN CONNECTION WITH THE LICENSE GRANTED UNDER THIS AGREEMENT, OR FOR LOSS OF USE, LOSS OF DATA, LOSS OF INCOME OR PROFIT, OR OTHER LOSSES, SUSTAINED AS A RESULT OF INJURY TO ANY PERSON, OR LOSS OF OR DAMAGE TO PROPERTY, OR CLAIMS OF THIRD PARTIES, EVEN IF THE COMPANY OR AN AUTHORIZED REPRESENTATIVE OF THE COMPANY HAS BEEN ADVISED OF THE POSSIBILITY OF SUCH DAMAGES. IN NO EVENT SHALL LIABILITY OF THE COMPANY FOR DAMAGES WITH RESPECT TO THE SOFTWARE EXCEED THE AMOUNTS ACTUALLY PAID BY YOU, IF ANY, FOR THE SOFTWARE.

SOME JURISDICTIONS DO NOT ALLOW THE LIMITATION OF IMPLIED WARRANTIES OR LIABILITY FOR INCIDENTAL, INDIRECT, SPECIAL, OR CONSEQUENTIAL DAMAGES, SO THE ABOVE LIMITATIONS MAY NOT ALWAYS APPLY. THE WARRANTIES IN THIS AGREEMENT GIVE YOU SPECIFIC LEGAL RIGHTS AND YOU MAY ALSO HAVE OTHER RIGHTS WHICH VARY IN ACCORDANCE WITH LOCAL LAW.

ACKNOWLEDGMENT

YOU ACKNOWLEDGE THAT YOU HAVE READ THIS AGREEMENT, UNDERSTAND IT, AND AGREE TO BE BOUND BY ITS TERMS AND CONDITIONS. YOU ALSO AGREE THAT THIS AGREEMENT IS THE COMPLETE AND EXCLUSIVE STATEMENT OF THE AGREEMENT BETWEEN YOU AND THE COMPANY AND SUPERSEDES ALL PROPOSALS OR PRIOR AGREEMENTS, ORAL, OR WRITTEN, AND ANY OTHER COMMUNICATIONS BETWEEN YOU AND THE COMPANY OR ANY REPRESENTATIVE OF THE COMPANY RELATING TO THE SUBJECT MATTER OF THIS AGREEMENT.

Should you have any questions concerning this Agreement or if you wish to contact the Company for any reason, please contact in writing at the address below.

Robin Short
Prentice Hall PTR
One Lake Street
Upper Saddle River, New Jersey 07458

ABOUT THE CD

What's Included

The CDROM attached to this book contains:
- examples.zip and examples.tar.gz

These archives contain all the example code from Chapters 8–14. Files are named after the function they demonstrate.
- listings.zip and listings.tar.gz

These archives contain the numbered listings from Chapters 1–7 and 15–22. Files are named after chapter in which they appear.
- php-4.0.0.tar.gz

This file is an archive of the source code for the final release of PHP 4, the newest version at time of production. Use it to install PHP on a Unix system.
- php-4.0.0-Win32.zip

This file is an archive of a binary distribution of the final release of PHP 4 for Windows operating systems.
- apache_1.3.12.tar.gz

This file is an archive of the files necessary to compile the Apache Web server.
- apache_1_3_12_win32.exe

This file is a program for installing the Apache Web server on a Windows operating system.

Licensing

- Use of the Core PHP Programming CDROM is subject to the terms of the License Agreement following the index in this book.
- This product includes software developed by the Apache Group for use in the Apache HTTP server project (http://www.apache.org/).
- This product includes PHP, freely available from http://www.php.net/

Technical Support

Prentice Hall does not offer technical support for any of the programs on the CDROM. However, if there is a problem with the CD, you may obtain a replacement copy by sending an email describing the problem to disc_exchange@phptr.com.